R. L. Gamble

THE EARLY PREHISTORY
OF SCOTLAND

THE EARLY PREHISTORY
OF SCOTLAND

EDITED BY
TONY POLLARD
AND
ALEX MORRISON

EDINBURGH UNIVERSITY PRESS
FOR
THE UNIVERSITY OF GLASGOW

Dalrymple Monograph no. 3

© Edinburgh University Press 1996

Edinburgh University Press
22 George Square, Edinburgh

Typeset in Ehrhardt by
Nene Phototypesetters, Northampton
and printed and bound in Great Britain by
Redwood Books, Trowbridge, Wiltshire

CIP Data for this book is available
from the British Library

ISBN 0 7486 0677 7

CONTENTS

PART 5: SOCIAL CHANGE

PREFACE

This book represents the first overview of current research into the early pre-history of northern Britain, and most particularly Scotland, since the publication of Lacaille's seminal *Stone Age in Scotland* in 1954. Indeed, many of the contributions included here had their origins as papers presented at a conference marking the fortieth anniversary of Lacaille's publication, held at Glasgow University in October 1994. The importance of Lacaille's contribution is acknowledged here in the first paper, by Alex Morrison, presenting a review of his archaeological achievements.

The aim of the conference was not only to commemorate Lacaille's work but more importantly to assess the advances made in the field of early prehistoric archaeology in Scotland over the past forty years. In order to do this it was essential to bring together as many of those scholars working in the field as possible. The fruits of this gathering are in these pages, with contributions by archaeologists already established in the field and also a number by younger writers, for some of whom this book represents the first venture into publication. The editors believe that this mixture has produced a work of considerable breadth, bringing together papers based on fieldwork and those demonstrating a more theoretical approach, the majority of the latter written by the younger contributors. Many of the ideas contained here are seeing the light of day, at least in published form, for the first time. Some are based on doctoral research, both on-going and recently completed. Studies from outside Scotland are included but, at the same time, they maintain a northern focus. It should need no re-iteration here that Scotland is a recently created political entity and, as such, bears little relevance to our understanding of the early prehistoric settlement of northern Britain, other than in the context of the historical development of the subject. The problems of working on the north-western periphery of Europe are placed in their historical perspective by Peter Woodman, who considers the role of Lacaille and others, particularly those in Ireland, in creating a concept of early prehistory 'on the edge'.

Lacaille recognised that 'something has already been achieved to suggest the methods of further investigations is due to the collaboration of the archaeologist with the geologist, the botanist and the zoologist' (1954: 316). The accuracy of this forecast can be gauged here from a number of specialist papers by palaeobotanists, all of whom have contributed to a review of current trends in the study of the early prehistoric environment. The issue of environmental change, as evidenced through the charcoal record, is given full consideration by Richard Tipping and Kevin Edwards, with the former providing an overview of the evidence for northern Scotland, and the latter reporting on recent analyses carried out in the Outer Hebrides. This discussion is complemented by Jenny Moore's paper, which fuels the debate on the causes of woodland fires and seriously considers the practical issues which lie behind the burning of woodlands. These chapters prepare the ground for Paul Mayewski et al. who report on the preliminary results of the pioneering Greenland Ice Core Project, making special reference to their relevance to northern Britain.

A great many sites have been discovered over the past forty years, though unfortunately many of them have suffered from inadequate investigation and recording. However, a number of well-planned programmes of fieldwork have been initiated. These include major excavations such as Morton Farm (Coles 1971), the Oronsay shell mounds (Mellars 1987) and Kinloch Fields, Rhum (Wickham-Jones 1990). A number of projects have also tackled larger units of analysis, subjecting large tracts of the landscape to survey and excavation in order to locate and assess the pattern of prehistoric settlement and subsistence in these regions. Two notable examples of this latter type of project are discussed here. The editors are especially pleased to see the inclusion of Kevin Edwards' tribute to the late Tom Affleck, which also includes a review of Tom's work in the southwest of Scotland. Tom was a student of Alex Morrison, a source of inspiration to Tony Pollard and a sorely missed friend of both. Perhaps the most important large-scale project of recent years is the Southern Hebrides Research Project which, though still on-going, has already vastly increased our knowledge of the extent of early prehistoric activity on the islands of Colonsay and Islay. A preliminary report and overview of this work is included here in a contribution by Steve Mithen and Mark Lake. The application of computer-based Geographical Information Systems is still a relatively new approach to the study of prehistoric landscapes, but an idea of its potential is provided by Penny Spikins, who summarises her model of Mesolithic social territories in northern England.

In this work, the term early prehistory is not confined to the Palaeolithic – for which convincing evidence has yet to be located in Scotland – nor indeed the Mesolithic, though it is fair to say that the majority of chapters here are concerned with what traditionally would be termed the Mesolithic. It has become increasingly apparent over the last ten years or so that the traditional divide between the Mesolithic and the Neolithic is not generally applicable to the prehistory of Scotland. Despite the acknowledgement of this problem, the terms Mesolithic and Neolithic have been maintained here; they are after all only terms invented by archaeologists to help make sense of an otherwise abstract past and as such cannot help but be value laden, as would be any replacement terms. The so-called Mesolithic–Neolithic transition is considered by Ian Armit and Bill Finlayson, who provide a background to an issue before reviewing the Scottish evidence. The concept of social change is also addressed by Andrew Jones, who considers the preparation and consumption of food in early prehistoric Orkney, and in doing so presents a thought-provoking introduction to his on-going programme of doctoral research.

It is also to Orkney that Alan Saville turns in his valuable reconsideration of the microliths reported from various locations within the archipelago by Lacaille (1935). Lacaille's prodigious output (see Morrison for a full bibliography) also included a discussion of stone axe polishers from various sites in southern England and France (1962). This interest is also reflected in the present volume, where Kevin Taylor, making special reference to Scottish examples, takes a fresh look at these artefacts, utilising metaphor to provide a refreshing insight into the role of these artefacts in the negotiation of social relations. So much of our understanding of early prehistoric activity is dependent on the recovery and analysis of lithic assemblages, which in many cases represent the sum total of our knowledge in large areas of Scotland. An important contribution to this aspect of our work has been provided by Bill Finlayson, Nyree Finlay and Steven Mithen in their summary of the techniques developed during the processing and analysis of the extensive lithic assemblages recovered during the Southern Hebrides Project. This paper will serve as a valuable template to anyone wishing to tackle the daunting task of analysing large stone tool assemblages, especially when used in conjunction with works such as Wickham-Jones's report on the Rhum excavations (1990). The fact that our understanding of early prehistoric material culture need not be limited to stone tools is demonstrated by Biddy Simpson, who reviews the nature and role of shell beads which have been recovered from a number of Scottish coastal sites.

Though it has become increasingly apparent that the Mesolithic in Scotland can no longer be regarded as a purely coastal phenomenon, it cannot be doubted that the marine environment played an important role in the hunter-gatherer food quest, just as it continued to do in later 'mixed' economies which included agriculture. The importance of the marine resource base and the rich character of coastal evidence is reflected in several papers. Clive Bonsall discusses the problem of the 'Obanian', presenting the case against accepting west coast shell midden sites as a specific cultural phenomenon. This issue is further considered by Tony Pollard, John Atkinson and Iain Banks, who – in their presentation of preliminary results from the re-excavation of an 'Obanian' shell midden on the island of Risga – suggest that a number of factors may explain the presence of large numbers of flint tools here and their absence on more typical 'Obanian' sites. The nature of the coastal environment and its influence on the lives of those people living in its vicinity is further considered by Tony Pollard, who emphasises the importance of shell middens as a focus for various types of social activity.

Much water has passed under the bridge since the first appearance of Lacaille's book. A good many more sites have been discovered and excavated over the past forty years. Scientific techniques such as radiocarbon dating have been introduced and refined, and our understanding of prehistoric environmental conditions has advanced considerably. However, as Peter Woodman demonstrated in his review of the Mesolithic in Scotland (1989), there is no room for complacency, with much work still to be done both in making sense of the material already at our disposal and in the identification and investigation of further sites. Even as this preface is being written, a recently discovered Mesolithic site is undergoing excavation in south-west Scotland, its discovery brought about by just one of the large-scale rural developments – in this case a gas pipeline – which in today's economic climate play a key role in dictating research strategies. It would therefore be foolish to claim that this book represents any form of final statement; instead, it is hoped that the present volume will take its place beside Lacaille's and from there allow us to take another step on the road to more fully understanding our distant past. Lacaille closed his book with an epilogue in which he stated: 'This study is but the prelude to this field of inquiry which affords unlimited scope for future researches' (1954: 316). It is hoped that something of this unlimited scope is reflected in the present volume, with the wide variety of papers going some way towards giving shape and form to those who have for too long been the invisible people of Scottish prehistory.

The publication of this book has been made possible by generous grants from several sources. The conference which provided the impetus for this volume was supported by the Wellcome Trust, who sponsored Lacaille's landmark publication, and Glasgow Archaeological Society. A generous publication grant was provided by the Curators of the Dalrymple Fund, the volume representing the third in a growing series of Dalrymple Monographs.

TONY POLLARD AND ALEX MORRISON

REFERENCES

Coles, J. M. 1971. The early settlement of Scotland: excavations at Morton, Fife. *Proceedings of the Prehistoric Society* 37, 284–366.

Lacaille, A. D. 1935. The small flint knives of Orkney. *Proceedings of the Society of Antiquaries of Scotland* 69, 251–64.

Lacaille, A. D. 1954. *The Stone Age in Scotland*. Oxford University Press.

Lacaille, A. D. 1962. Three grinding stones. *Antiquaries Journal* 43, 190–6.

Mellars, P. A. 1987. *Excavations on Oronsay, Prehistoric Human Ecology on a small Island*. Edinburgh.

Wickham-Jones, C. R. 1990. *Rhum: Mesolithic and Later Sites at Kinloch, Excavations 1984–1986*. Edinburgh: Society of Antiquaries Monograph Series 7. Edinburgh.

Woodman, P. C. 1989. A review of the Scottish Mesolithic: a plea for normality! *Proceedings of the Society of Antiquaries of Scotland* 119, 1–32.

I

'THE NORTHWARD MARCH OF PALAEOLITHIC MAN IN BRITAIN'

AN APPRECIATION OF ARMAND DONALD LACAILLE

ALEX MORRISON

The conference 'The Stone Age in Scotland: Forty Years On' was held in October 1994 to commemorate the 40th anniversary of the publication of *The Stone Age in Scotland*, and the year also marked the centenary of the birth of its author, Armand Donald Lacaille, in August 1894. He was born in Paris but was brought up mainly in Glasgow, where the family was important in Scottish educational circles. His grandfather was French, but in the 1860s he came to St Leonards-on-Sea and later settled in Glasgow, where he was a pioneer in women's education: an example of this is a printed copy of the first of a series of lectures (in French) on French literature of the seventeenth century which he gave in November 1877, in the University of Glasgow, for the Glasgow Association for the Higher Education of Women.

Donald Lacaille's interest in history and prehistory began at an early age, and his knowledge of the archaeology of the west of Scotland grew from a period when he would undertake long cycle trips, particularly in the Loch Lomond area. He could speak and write equally well in English and French, and some of his later papers were written in French for publication in French journals.

At the age of 20 he volunteered for service with the Scottish Rifles at the outbreak of the First World War in 1914. He was invalided out of the front line in 1915 and after convalescence was transferred to Scottish Command in Edinburgh. He found this rather dull and eventually applied for a posting to the Intelligence Corps at Abbeville in France, where his bilingualism was an asset, and there he spent the rest of the war. During this period in northern France he undoubtedly expanded his knowledge and experience of French Lower Palaeolithic stratigraphy and material culture along the river terraces of the region.

After war service and until 1923, Lacaille worked as Foreign Correspondent and Foreign Sales Manager for Ioco Rubber and Waterproofing Co., Glasgow and Birmingham. In his spare time he carried on with his archaeological fieldwork and research, and in 1922 he was elected a Fellow of the Society of Antiquaries of Scotland. His early papers were mainly on Early Christian and Medieval topics, reflecting his fieldwork around Loch Lomond and adjoining regions (Lacaille 1924, 1925, 1927, 1928, 1929, 1930, 1932, 1934, 1935). From 1923 until 1928 he had various teaching posts, the most important of which was a period at Alloa Academy, where he was a senior French teacher. It was during this period at Alloa that he met Lucy Drysdale, who also taught at the Academy; they were married in 1929. At some point during this five-year period he went as a private tutor to Jamaica where he had the opportunity to gain experience of fieldwork and excavation in Jamaica and Central America.

In 1928 the Wellcome Historical Medical Museum, then based at 54 Wigmore Street, London was recruiting young graduates for its scientific staff and an advert had appeared in *Nature* announcing a vacancy in a London museum for 'a University Graduate qualified and experienced in archaeology, anthropology or natural science'. Lacaille applied for the position and it is interesting to note how he described his experience and knowledge in his application. 'Although not a university graduate, I yet venture to apply for the position in view of my qualifications and high standing in the archaeological world ...'; 'knowledge of geology, ... prehistoric field research, early Christian and medieval ecclesiology'; 'lectured widely on archaeological topics'; 'presented numerous antiquities of own finding to different museums (prehistoric, Roman, early Christian, mediaeval and ethnological)'; 'Skilled in surveying, planning and drawing of ancient sites and monuments'. He mentioned work in Scotland, France, Jamaica, Central America, and added 'I am a man of University training, but on account of the War and personal affairs I was not able to continue my studies'. He may not have been a graduate, but his knowledge and experience were far ahead of what could have been expected from any recent normal graduate and one could almost imagine that he was over-qualified.

The names given for referees were impressive: J. G. Callander, Director of the National Museum of Antiquities, Edinburgh; Professor Thomas Bryce, Professor of Anatomy at the University of Glasgow, President of the Glasgow Archaeological Society and Vice-President of the Society of Antiquaries of Scotland, well known for his excavations of chambered cairns in the west of Scotland; Ludovic Mann, one of the best-known antiquaries in Scotland at the time and a friend of the Lacaille family; and Sir Ian Colquhoun, Lord Lieutenant of Dunbartonshire, a county in which much of Lacaille's early fieldwork had been carried out.

Callander mentioned the work of Lacaille over the previous seven years, noting that he had done 'a large amount of original research and has made many important discoveries', 'undertaken with full appreciation of the absolute necessity of scientific accuracy in recording discoveries'. Bryce stated that Lacaille's 'work in the field has made him familiar with the Scottish antiquities of the Stone and Bronze Ages and he has made a special study of the early Christian crosses'. Mann said that Lacaille belonged 'to the new school of archaeologists who insist upon the most absolute precision in the surveys of sites, their dimensions and orientation, and the recording of the facts observed with extraordinary accuracy'. Other names given by Lacaille for reference were: Dr W. Douglas Simpson, Librarian, Aberdeen University; James S. Richardson, Inspector of Ancient Monuments, H. M. Office of Works, Edinburgh; and Dr Ernest Bolton, Director of the Bristol Corporation Art Galleries and Museum.

Following an interview with (Sir) Henry Wellcome under cloak-and-dagger conditions at the Welbeck Palace Hotel, Lacaille was appointed to the scientific staff from November 1928, at a salary of £300 per annum. The terms of his employment were fairly strict, and he had to agree not to write about any discoveries made, or original work done, in the course of his duties without the consent of his employers. This consent, in Lacaille's case, seems never to have been witheld, possibly because he had already acquired a position of respect in the archaeological field with his previous work, and he produced many more publications than any other employee during his years with the Wellcome Museum. There is a note of September 1929, from Lacaille to L. W. G. Malcolm, an anthropologist who was museum conservator from 1925 to 1934, asking for permission to use the sentence: 'I have seen a series of Australian stone surgical instruments in the Wellcome Historical Medical Museum', in a paper he was writing.

His main work was the cataloguing, classification, comparison and preparation for exhibition of the prehistoric, particularly Stone Age material, which had been and was being acquired by the Museum, much of it purchased by Sir Henry Wellcome himself. It was estimated that at one point there were about 150 000 artefacts in the prehistoric collection from 'eoliths' to Neolithic material. In 1929 there is a note from Lacaille asking the Museum to acquire copies of Déchelette's *Manuel d'Archéologie* (4 vols) and de Mortillet's *Musée Préhistorique* as 'working references'. Much of his work is recorded in the monthly and quarterly reports he produced for the Museum. His main place of work was at the Museum's store in the disused Burndept Wireless Ltd factory at Hythe Road, Willesden, rather than at the Wigmore Street headquarters.

He was also involved with the ethnological collections, and a fair amount of his time was taken up with travelling around Britain and France, discovering and buying archaeological, historical and ethnological material for the Museum. In late 1930 he was in Ireland buying up collections and supervising their packing and despatching to the Museum in London. Among the items listed were brass figures, weapons and wooden figures from Borneo, Malaya, Sarawak, Siam, China, etc., and 'religious trinkets' from sites in Ireland.

In May 1931, Lacaille was buying a 'collection' in Paris; in June he was buying objects in Cornwall; in July he was back in France taking photographs of French colonial material in Bordeaux. In August of that year, possibly while on holiday, a letter to the Museum states that he was 'studying ancient remains on Loch Lomondside' (the results of this fieldwork were to be published in 1934 and 1935) and also trying to get a Scottish mortsafe for the Museum.

Lacaille's knowledge of the earlier Stone Age in Scotland was already widely appreciated at this time, and there is a request from him to the conservator, L. W. G. Malcolm, dated 20 May 1932, asking for permission to have some slides made and to attend the Prehistoric Congress 'as I have been cornered into giving a brief survey of the Scottish Mesolithic'.

Some excerpts from his 1932 reports show how often he was able to pursue his own interests while on Museum business.

Sunday, 11 September 1932. 'Afternoon; visited Stewarton [Shewalton] Moor near Irvine in a windstorm. Identified Bronze Age working floor. Collected various small flint pieces, one arrowhead and hammerstones, pounders and whetstones. Site revealed by the wind lifting the sand.'

Monday, 12 September 1932. 'In Ayr. Later in Glasgow. Purchased Hebridean spinning-wheel, bone Celtic engraved ladle, eighteenth-century fire-blower, powder-horn and an old Western Scottish fishing-reel ...'

Tuesday, 13 September 1932. Still in Glasgow. 'Obtained information regarding *Azilian* site available for excavation in Argyllshire. The suggestion is that the site be excavated under an archaeologist's supervision taking ten weeks to do at the rate of only £5 per week at most, that is £50 in all. Half of the relics would go to Glasgow and half to the WHMM. This proposition is worthy of consideration as the work would be under the strictest secrecy and would cover an epoch practically unstudied not only in Scotland, but in the British Isles.'

14 to 26 September: in Glasgow, Maybole, Minishant, Girvan, Ayr, Paisley, Luss (meeting with Sir Ian Colquhoun, Lord Lieutenant of Dunbartonshire), Perth, Edinburgh, Dundee.

Monday, 26 September 1932. Searching Edinburgh for 'shops selling curios'.

Saturday, 1 October 1932. In Dundee. Purchased 'an old Scottish medical and veterinary mallet, a very fine and primitive cruisie with hooks, too good to miss, and a Dundee whale harpoon of a type not used since 1820. This is considered a rare piece. All these objects for 12/6d.'

16 October to 5 November 1932: in Orkney and Shetland, buying mainly folk material.

There is a letter (dated 1 November 1932) to Lacaille at the Pentland Hotel, Thurso, from A. L. Dean, the Secretary of the Wellcome Historical Medical Museum, asking him to complete the tour as soon as possible, because 'large quantities of ethnographical material' had to be moved from Willesden to 'the new building'. This was a reference to the newly completed premises at 183–193 Euston Road, the present-day site of the Wellcome Trust and Wellcome Institute.

In the spring of 1934 Lacaille was again in Scotland, and there is a note in his report 'on Inchlonaig, Loch Lomond, visited quartz-working site and examined *c*.4 cwt of material, including humanly fractured pieces'. The note is accompanied by a sketch and location details. In September of the same year he attended the XIième Congrès Préhistorique de France at Périgueux (Fig. 1.1) and in October he was visiting and photographing sites in the Dordogne and

Fig. 1.1. The XIIème Congrès Préhistorique de France at Périgueux, September 1934. Lacaille is at the extreme left of the second row from the front.

working on river terraces. A photo from the Wellcome Institute Library (Fig. 1.2) shows him about this period.

There was continuous support from Sir Henry Wellcome for Lacaille's work and he was encouraged to look for new sites. In 1935 Lacaille was able to 'take advantage of the opportunity to complete my interrupted tour of 1932 by visiting localities in the Hebrides and Scottish western areas with a view to getting prehistoric, neo-archaic, primitive and other material for WHMM'. This also gave Lacaille the opportunity to carry out any relevant fieldwork connected with his Stone Age studies. A letter from Banchory in May 1935 reports on his work on the Mesolithic flint sites along the terraces of the River Dee, where he co-operated with H. M. L. Paterson.

His work in the Museum was seen and appreciated by a wide range of visitors. There is an article by F. Regnault in the *Bulletin de la Société Préhistorique Française* (May 1937), praising Lacaille's exhibits. Sir Henry's eclectic tastes and the wide-ranging mixture of ethnographical and archaeological material was, in effect, producing a pre-war 'museum of mankind'. By 1938 Lacaille's 'Gallery of Prehistoric Medicine and Surgery' was in the planning stage; a letter from the Secretary to Lacaille mentions the find of the red-deer-antler barbed point from the River Irvine at Shewalton (published by Lacaille the following year); his salary was £425 per annum.

Sir Henry Wellcome died in 1936. He had been keenly interested in archaeology for many years; he instigated and personally supervised a four-year (1910–14) season of excavations at Jebel Moya in the southern Sudan, with results eventually published in 1949–51, for which Lacaille wrote up the flaked stone industries (Addison 1949, Addison and Crawford 1951, Symons 1993) and towards the end of his life he supported excavations at Lachish in Palestine; he had been actively engaged in finding and acquiring for the Museum a wide range of archaeological and ethnographical material, initially to demonstrate human achievements in the field of medicine through the ages, but eventually, and inevitably, to cover much of early man's economic and social development as well. After his death, buying and collecting virtually ceased and a programme for the elimination of material regarded as irrelevant was initiated. A letter from P. Johnston-Saint, conservator, to Lacaille in June 1939 mentioned that the Trustees had decided 'to dispose of all the archaeological material outside that which is directly connected with the history of medicine'. The Museum certainly reduced the scope of its collections, but the prehistoric material was retained mostly intact until after the war.

Compared with the previous twelve years, activity in the Museum in the early war years was much reduced. Lacaille's monthly report for August 1940 mentions the Burchell collection of Mesolithic material from Ireland as part of the Museum's collections. In 1941 he was awarded a Leverhulme Research Grant of £50 for work on 'the Mesolithic cultures of Scotland'. A letter from A. L. Dean, the secretary, refers to Lacaille's 'Introduction' to 'his forthcoming work

Fig. 1.2. Donald Lacaille in 1935 (photograph courtesy of Wellcome Institute Library).

on the colonization of Scotland'. This could be one of the papers produced
during the war years or perhaps the beginning of his major study. He was diag-
nosed as having a duodenal ulcer in March 1941.

In January 1942, Lacaille, with Professor A. E. Cave, lectured to the Society of
Antiquaries of London on the Châtelperronian, and in November to the same
Society on two prehistoric mortars. In 1943 he received permission to assist in the
arrangement of an archaeological exhibition in Glasgow, requested by the President
of the Glasgow Archaeological Society, Mr J. M. Davidson. At a meeting of the
Council of the Society of Antiquaries of London in May 1943, Lacaille was
appointed member of the General Council of the Council for British Archaeology
to consider '*inter alia*: the contribution of archaeology to the post-war world; the
future conduct of archaeological research; the preservation of ancient monuments; the training of archaeologists; archaeology and education in schools and
universities; museums and the public; and the State and archaeology'. He also
served on the Natural Sciences Panel of the Council for British Archaeology. It is
an indication of his standing in British, or perhaps more importantly Scottish,
archaeology, that he was one of three names considered for the position of Keeper
of the National Museum of Antiquities of Scotland in 1944.

An exhibition of French Late-Middle and Upper Palaeolithic and Mesolithic
material was prepared by Lacaille in 1946 for students of London University
Institute of Archaeology qualifying for the Diploma in Archaeology. The
students and the Director of the Institute, Professor V. Gordon Childe, attended
a lecture by Lacaille, and Childe commented 'on the unknown riches of the
Wellcome Historical Medical Museum'. Again, in 1947, he was requested by
Kathleen Kenyon to lecture and give demonstrations of *Prehistoric Lithic Technology* for students of the Institute of Archaeology's Diploma in Archaeology.
He represented the Museum at the British Association's meeting at Dundee and
was serving on the Council of the Prehistoric Society. In 1948 he had a fort-
night's leave in south-western France to take 'the opportunity of refreshing my
memory of classic sites'. The following year he was listed as preparing the script
for the Wellcome Film Unit's film *Stone Age Tools*.

This was Lacaille's most productive period, in the years between the end of
the war and his retirement. Apart from individual papers on various aspects of
the English and Scottish Stone Age, he was undoubtedly developing his research
towards the publication of his book. This can be traced in the titles of some of
his publications at the time: 'The northward march of Palaeolithic man in
Britain'; 'The Stone Age background of Scotland'; 'The deglaciation of Scotland
and the forming of man's environment'; and 'The chronology of the deglaciation
of Scotland'.

A letter in March 1949 refers to the typing of a chapter on 'The Age and
Affinities of the Obanian Culture'. In July/August 1951, he noted that the
typescript for *The Stone Age in Scotland* was 'finally checked over', and in
September/October the galley proofs were received.

During the post-war years, space and funding for the Museum were drastic-
ally restricted and for several years it was exiled to 28 Portman Square with space
only for temporary thematic exhibitions. Lacaille was responsible for organising
the 1951 exhibition in the Museum on 'Prehistoric Man in Health and Sickness'.
This dealt with the evolution of human beings and their appearance (illustrated
by casts of skulls and figurines), their culture, environment and health, including
early attempts at surgery and trepanning. Most of the examples of material
culture were taken from the Wellcome collection and the exhibition was regarded
as a great success.

In view of the trustees' decision to disperse the 'non-medical' material of the
collections in 1939, it is worth quoting in full from a memo from the Director
of the Museum, Dr E. A. Underwood as late as 1961:

> The prehistoric collection of the Wellcome Museum is made up largely of
> stone-age material, both Palaeolithic and Neolithic. At a rough estimate
> there are about 150 000 artefacts in the collection. These illustrate all the
> Stone Age cultures from the Eolithic to the Neolithic. The artefacts come
> from most parts of the world in which the remains of prehistoric man have
> been found, and the collections from England, Scotland, Ireland and
> France are especially rich. As in many similar collections, there are arte-
> facts of other materials, but these are relatively few as compared with the
> numbers of the more durable stone artefacts.
>
> The importance and breadth of the collection may be illustrated by
> reference to the exhibition on 'Prehistoric Man in Health and Sickness'
> which was held by the Museum in 1951. This exhibition was divided into
> the following sections: (1) Prehistoric times; (2) Anatomy of prehistoric
> man; (3) Animals in prehistoric art; (4) Tools of successive cultures;
> (5) Domestic arts and crafts; (6) Domestic conditions; (7) Toilet and
> personal ornament; (8) Disposal of the dead; (9) Palaeopathology, animal
> and plant; (10) Human palaeopathology; (11) Evolution of the surgical
> knife; (12) Prehistoric medicine and surgery. The Catalogue of this exhi-
> bition is long out of print. I do not think that any other museum in the
> world could put up a similar exhibition.
>
> No justification is needed for the existence of this collection in the
> museum which has the word 'Medical' in its title, but which is universally
> known as a great cultural collection. Neither am I at all influenced by re-
> marks and suggestions made from time to time regarding the disposition
> of the collection by persons who invariably have no medical knowledge
> whatever, and who moreover are not disinterested parties. I hold the view
> very strongly that before the Middle Ages human activities in the days
> before the specialization of crafts and implements influenced one another
> in ways which are difficult to define. The further one goes back in time
> the more difficult it is to define these inter-relations. In such matters I feel

that the views of those who have worked with the collections for many years are of more lasting value than scholastic arguments.

This viewpoint must be close to that of Sir Henry Wellcome himself, and in no small way the final sentence is a tribute to the work of Donald Lacaille.

In December of 1951 Lacaille was elected Fellow of the British Museums Association. In the following spring, work was begun, with W. F. Grimes, Director of the London Museum, on excavations on Caldey Island. In the summer, Lacaille continued with fieldwork at weekends in the Middle Thames area, studying the brickearths and their archaeological content. In the autumn he represented the Museum at the Pan-African Congress on Prehistory; he left London three weeks before the Congress, visiting archaeological sites in Spain and North Africa before arriving at Algiers, the Congress venue. On the return journey he travelled through France, visiting sites and museums. In the summer of 1953 the page proofs of *The Stone Age in Scotland* were still 'being gone over', and in the autumn of that year he was working on the proofs of a paper on the first Lower Palaeolithic hand-axe to be discovered in South Wales.

The book was published in 1954 and, sadly, Lacaille's mother died in the same year. In December, his report notes that he took a party of students from Cambridge, accompanied by Charles McBurney, to see the gravel pits in the Taplow area of Buckinghamshire.

Despite the apparently strict conditions of employment in the Museum, Lacaille had a great deal of freedom. No restrictions were placed on his research and publication and he was able to travel around quite a bit. His journeys were nearly always used to increase his knowledge of the sources and environment of the material he worked with, and a lot of this work was undertaken in his holiday periods. In 1956 he attended the fifteenth Congress on French Prehistory at Poitiers/Angoulême and the following year he was on leave visiting museums and sites in Italy and Belgium. His notes for December 1958 showed that he visited 'the distinguished octogenarian', the Abbé Breuil, in Paris.

Lacaille retired from the Wellcome Historical Medical Museum in 1959, after 31 years' service. Tribute was paid to him by Dr E. A. Underwood, the Director of the Museum, who said that he 'had illuminated the palaeolithic as no one else had ever done' and that his book on the Stone Age in Scotland would remain a classic. He had been a Fellow of the Societies of Antiquaries of Scotland and London for many years, and in 1960 he was elected Honorary Fellow of the Society of Antiquaries of Scotland.

In a sense he did not really retire. In 1961 he undertook archaeological work for the Nature Conservancy on sites at Fyfield Down, Marlborough, and at Kingley Down, Chichester. From October 1963 to May 1964, he was employed as a consultant on the collections in the City Museum in Gibraltar. Fig. 1.3 is a photograph from about this period.

In October 1962 he was awarded a Wellcome Research Fellowship at £1 000

Fig. 1.3. Lacaille in retirement.

per annum for five years, subject to annual review. His remit was to sort out the material contained in the Wellcome Stone Age collection (from Britain, France, Africa and Asia, some of it collected by Lacaille himself), with a view to preparing a catalogue. He had a full-time secretary, a labourer every morning, and expenses (for fares etc.). He started work in June 1963 and had to supply a quarterly report of his work. His grant was renewed in 1964 and 1965. Although the Museum's financial position had now improved, further rationalisation of the collections became inevitable, and this time the prehistoric material could not escape. There was ongoing discussion of the eventual transfer of the Wellcome Prehistoric Collection to the British Museum, which Lacaille thought would be the best place for it. He was obviously upset at the idea of the material finally leaving the Wellcome Museum, but he was grateful to have the opportunity to continue with his research and complete the cataloguing. In a letter of April 1965, he mentions his friends and colleagues at the British Museum – R. L. S. Bruce-Mitford, J. W. Brailsford and G. de G. Sieveking. In February

1966, Lacaille had a heart attack and developed an acute form of arthritis which deprived him for a time of the use of both his hands. A letter from his secretary to Dr P. O. Williams, Director of the Wellcome Trust, in May 1966, referred to Lacaille as being 'very depressed, for his … condition has deprived him of the use of both his hands which are splinted from elbow to finger-tip'. In that month he renounced the Fellowship, hoping to ask for renewal in September. In the meantime the collections had been transferred to the British Museum. The grant was to be renewed for a fourth year from December 1966, if Lacaille was sufficiently fit, and he returned to work, this time in the British Museum. His health was not good and his letters mention 'the vagaries of the heating and lighting systems in the British Museum', and that 'conditions here are not good for work or study'. The grant was renewed for a fifth and final year in September 1967 and the Fellowship ended in November 1968. Lacaille had always been keenly involved with local archaeology societies and about this time he was President of the Watford and South Herts Archaeological Society, to which he gave his presidential address in 1967.

His later work was mainly on the Palaeolithic in the south of England, and he published 'Some Wiltshire palaeoliths' in 1971, when he was 77. One of the greatest achievements of his later life was to gain the degree of Master of Philosophy of the University of Southampton in March 1973, at the age of 78. The degree was awarded for a thesis on 'The Mesolithic facies in Greater London and their Pleistocene background'. At the graduation, the Vice-Chancellor, Professor L. Gower, said that Lacaille had worked on his thesis at a time of life when most people rested on their laurels, and that they were deeply honoured that Mr Lacaille had chosen to study under the supervision of the university's department of archaeology.

A. D. Lacaille died in January 1975, aged 80.

His book, *The Stone Age in Scotland*, has so far been the only attempt at a detailed synthesis of the pre-farming stone age in Scotland. His study combined archaeological and environmental evidence in an overview which is still useful to the worker in this period. The picture of the early stone age presented in 1954 showed a limited distribution of Mesolithic culture based on 70–80 sites, although many of them marked areas where further discoveries have been made in more recent times. A number of locations recorded simply 'stone industries', some of which can now be seen to have no real evidence for Mesolithic classification; others were obviously sites which included material from later periods. Fewer than twenty of these sites had been excavated.

Lacaille rejected the idea of Late-glacial occupation of Scotland, seeing the recolonisation of northern Europe following deglaciation as a 'rolling frontier' slowly advancing northwards – his 'northward march of Palaeolithic man' (Lacaille 1946). This frontier reached Scotland late in the Postglacial period, initially involving 'Larnian' colonists from Ireland at the time of the maximum marine transgression, followed later by people with a microlithic ('Tardenoisian')

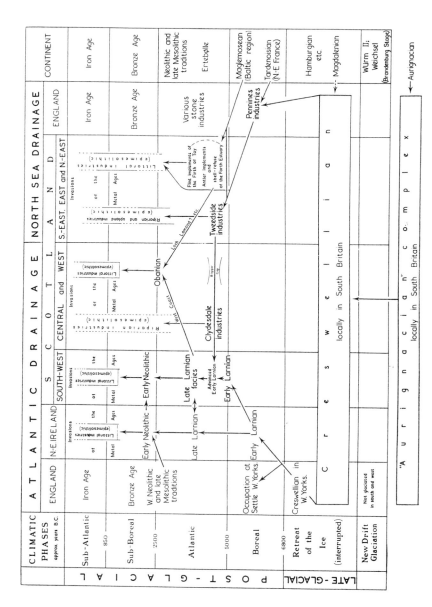

Table 1.1. Lacaille's 'tentative chronology of the Stone Age cultures of Scotland', from *The Stone Age in Scotland* (1954).

tradition and also influences of ultimate 'Baltic origin' (Table 1.1). He was also convinced of 'epimesolithic' survival in certain environments.

There were weaknesses in his survey which had lasting effects. He was greatly influenced by the work in Ireland and based many of his ideas on Hallam Movius's *Irish Stone Age* (1942), importing the Larnian label and continuing Movius's use of the designation Obanian for the sites of coastal Argyll and the Inner Hebrides. His approach to chronology (Table 1.1) was old-fashioned and unfortunately did not benefit from the new radiocarbon–dating technique which was just beginning to have an impact on the chronology of the Mesolithic in other parts of Europe. Despite this his ideas on chronology exercised a strong influence on subsequent thinking about the Scottish Mesolithic. The concept of an initial colonisation in the mid–Holocene and a settlement pattern tied almost exclusively to the exploitation of coastal resources has been entrenched in the literature until modified by the discoveries made and range of radiocarbon dates secured in more recent times.

There were some complaints in the reviews that nearly half of the book had to be read before the Stone Age in Scotland was mentioned, but these were ably answered by Sonia Cole, who wrote in *Antiquity* (1954: 233–4) that 'most workers will be grateful for the detailed treatment of the period of deglaciation and its chronology which makes an indispensable background to the story of man in Scotland'.

The *Times Literary Supplement* described it as 'a book which, while never straying from the scientific study of the material involved, is always admirably easy to read ... an outstanding addition to archaeological literature'.

Although he had no formal training as an archaeologist, and there were few who had at the time, Lacaille had become a recognised authority in his chosen area of study by the time he started working for the Wellcome Historical Medical Museum in 1928. As previously mentioned, what Sir Henry Wellcome had assembled was, in fact, a 'museum of mankind' and Lacaille, in the fields of archaeological and ethnographical research, was making good use of that material and bringing it to the notice of the wider academic and archaeologically interested public, while at the same time continuing with his own original research and fieldwork.

Despite his record of close to one hundred publications (about 10 per cent in French), it has been said that he regarded himself very much as an amateur; this is hardly a realistic assessment of his position and acceptance in the world of British archaeology. However, if he wanted to regard himself as such, then perhaps we should remember that the basic core of our knowledge of the Stone Ages was produced by the so-called 'amateurs' of the nineteenth and twentieth centuries. The question of status matters little, since there can be no doubt that Donald Lacaille's book and his many papers form a major contribution to the study of the Palaeolithic and Mesolithic in Britain.

ACKNOWLEDGEMENTS

I would like to thank Mr Charles Lacaille for talking to me about his father and his career and for allowing me to use personal papers and photographs. I also thank the Wellcome Trust and the Wellcome Institute for the History of Medicine for permission to read Donald Lacaille's reports and other papers and to quote from them. I thank the Contemporary Medical Archives Centre staff who located and delivered some of the material. In particular I am grateful to Mr H. J. M. Symons, Curator of Early Printed Books in the Institute, for his help in finding papers, for answering my many questions and for providing many useful comments on, and corrections of, the first draft of this paper.

PUBLICATIONS BY A. D. LACAILLE

Mesolithic Bibliography for Scotland

1930. Mesolithic implements from Ayrshire. *Proc. Soc. Antiq. Scot.* 64, 34–47.

1931. Silex tardenoisiens de Shewalton. *Bull. Soc. Préhist. Franç.* 28, 301–12.

1932. A survey of the Scottish Tardenoisian industries. *Proc. 1st International Prehistoric Congress, London, 1932,* 100.

1933. Small implements of quartz from Ward Hill, Dunrossness, Shetland. *Proc. Soc. Antiq. Scot.* 67, 327–35.

1935. The Tardenoisian micro-burin in Scotland. *Proc. Soc. Antiq. Scot.* 69, 443–5.

1936. (with H. M. L. Paterson) Banchory microliths. *Proc. Soc. Antiq. Scot.* 70, 419–34.

1937. A stone industry, potsherds, and a bronze pin from Valtos, Uig, Lewis. *Proc. Soc. Antiq. Scot.* 71, 279–96.

1939. A barbed point of deer-antler from Shewalton, Ayrshire. *Proc. Soc. Antiq. Scot.* 73, 48–50.

1940a. Some Scottish core-tools and ground-flaked implements of stone. *Proc. Soc. Antiq. Scot.* 74, 6–13.

1940b. The microlithic industries of Scotland. *Trans. Glasgow Archaeol. Soc.* 9, 56–74. (Paper read to Glasgow Archaeological Society on Thursday, 18 April 1935.)

1941. (with W. J. McCallien) The Campbeltown raised beach and its contained stone industry. *Proc. Soc. Antiq. Scot.* 75, 55.

1942. Scottish micro-burins. *Proc. Soc. Antiq. Scot.* 76, 103.

1944. Unrecorded microliths from Tentsmuir, Deeside and Culbin. *Proc. Soc. Antiq. Scot.* 78, 5–16.

1945. The stone industries associated with the raised beach at Ballantrae. *Proc. Soc. Antiq. Scot.* 79, 81–106.

1946. The northward march of Palaeolithic man in Britain. *Proc. Geol. Assoc.* 57, pt 2, 57–81. (Paper read to the Geological Association on 7 October 1944.)

1947. The scraper in prehistoric culture. (Its evolution; its penetration into Scotland; its survivals.) *Trans. Glasgow Archaeol. Soc.* 11, 38–93. (Paper read to Glasgow Archaeological Society on 19 April 1941.)

1948a. The Stone Age background of Scotland. *Trans. Dumfriesshire Galloway Natur. Hist. Antiq. Soc.* 26, 9–40.

1948b. The deglaciation of Scotland and the forming of man's environment. *Proc. Geol. Assoc.* 59, 151–71.

1949. (with J. M. Davidson and J. Phemister). A Stone Age site at Woodend Loch, near Coatbridge. *Proc. Soc. Antiq. Scot.* 83, 77–98.

1950. The chronology of the deglaciation of Scotland. *Proc. Geol. Assoc.* 61, 121–44.

1951. A stone industry from Morar, Inverness-shire; its Obanian (Mesolithic) and later affinities. *Archaeologia* 94, 103–39. (Paper read to Society of Antiquaries of London on 20 January 1949.)

1954a. Stone Age tools. *Trans. Glasgow Archaeol. Soc.* 13, 17–32.

1954b. *The Stone Age in Scotland.* London: Oxford University Press.

Other Papers on Scottish Archaeology

1924. Some antiquities in Strathfillan; cupped boulder near Helensburgh, and a cross-slab in Glen Fruin, Dunbartonshire. *Proc. Soc. Antiq. Scot.* 58, 124.

1925. Some ancient crosses in Dunbartonshire and adjoining counties. *Proc. Soc. Antiq. Scot.* 59, 143.

1927. The Capelrig crosses, Mearns, Renfrewshire; St Blane's Chapel, Lochearnhead, Perthshire; and a sculptured slab at Kilmaronock, Dunbartonshire. *Proc. Soc. Antiq. Scot.* 61, 122.

1928. Ecclesiastical remains in the neighbourhood of Luss, with notes on some unrecorded crosses and hog-backed stones. *Proc. Soc. Antiq. Scot.* 62, 85.

1929. Ardlui megaliths and their associations; crosses at Luib and Alloway, and a short cist at Ednam, Roxburghshire. *Proc. Soc. Antiq. Scot.* 63, 325–52.

1930. The bull in Scottish folklore, place-names, and archaeology. *Folklore* 41, 221.

1931. A Bronze Age cemetery near Cowdenbeath, Fife. *Proc. Soc. Antiq. Scot.* 65, 261.

1932. The site of St Blane's Chapel in Rannoch. *Proc. Soc. Antiq. Scot.* 66, 128.

1934. Loch Lomondside fonts and effigy. *Proc. Soc. Antiq. Scot.* 68, 100.

1935a. The small flint knives of Orkney. *Proc. Soc. Antiq. Scot.* 69, 251.

1935b. Sculptured rock; holy-water stoup; and sarcophagus at Luss. *Proc. Soc. Antiq. Scot.* 69, 416.

1937a. A stone industry, potsherds, and a bronze pin from Valtos, Uig, Lewis. *Proc. Soc. Antiq. Scot.* 71, 279.

1937b. Report on the flints found at Hower, a prehistoric structure on Papa Westray, Orkney. *Proc. Soc. Antiq. Scot.* 71, 316.

1938. Scottish gravers of flint and other stones. *Proc. Soc. Antiq. Scot.* 72, 180.

1940. Aspects of intentional fracture (being notes on the flaking of rocks other than flint as exemplified by some Scottish artefacts). *Trans. Glasgow Archaeol. Soc.* 9, 313–41.

1943 (in paper by A. Young). A report on split quartzes from a Late Bronze Age burial near Fowlis Wester. *Proc. Soc. Antiq. Scot.* 77, 179.

1953. Stone basins (some examples from the West of Scotland as guides to typology). *Trans. Glasgow Archaeol. Soc.* 12, 43.

1963. A perforated stone implement from Glen Fruin, Dunbartonshire, and cup-markings in North Drymen, Stirlingshire. *Proc. Soc. Antiq. Scot.* 96, 348–52.

1965. Notes on a Loch Lomondside parish. *The Innes Review* 16, 147.

British Palaeolithic Bibliography

1936a. The Palaeolithic sequence at Iver, Bucks. *Antiq. Journ.* 16, 420–43.

1936b. (with K. P. Oakley) The Palaeolithic sequence at Iver, Bucks. *Antiq. Journ.* 16, 420–43.

1936c. Quartzites taillés de la région Londonienne. *Compte Rendu de la Douzième Session du Congrès Préhistorique de France*, 609–29.

1938. A Levallois side-scraper from the brickearth at Yiewsley, Middlesex. *Antiq. Journ.* 18, 55–7.

1939. The Palaeolithic contents of the gravels at East Burnham, Bucks. *Antiq. Journ.* 19, 166–81.

1940. The palaeoliths from the gravels of the Lower Boyn Hill Terrace around Maidenhead. *Antiq. Journ.* 20, 245–71.

1942. Lower Palaeolithic tools with retouched edges. *Antiq. Journ.* 22, 56–9.

1944. Palaeolithic implements manufactured in naturally holed flints, from Rossington, Yorks and Dartford, Kent. *Antiq. Journ.* 24, 144–6.

1946. Some flint implements of special interest from Lincolnshire, Hampshire and Middlesex. *Antiq. Journ.* 26, 180–5.

1954a. Palaeoliths from the lower reaches of the Bristol Avon. *Antiq. Journ.* 34, 1–27.

1954b. A hand-axe from Pen-y-Lan, Cardiff. *Antiq. Journ.* 34, 64–7.

1959. Palaeoliths from brickearth in south-east Buckinghamshire. *Records of Buckinghamshire* 16, 274–88.

1960a. Remarkable stone implements from Piccadilly and Swanscombe, Kent. *Antiq. Journ.* 40, 65–6.

1960b. Massive Acheulian implements from Thames and Solent gravels. *Man*, 143.

1960c. On Palaeolithic choppers and cleavers (notes suggested by some Buckinghamshire examples). *Records of Buckinghamshire* 16, 330–44.

1960d. The Muswell Hill axe. *Trans. London Middlesex Archaeol. Soc.* 20, 80.

1961. The palaeoliths of Boyn Hill, Maidenhead. *Antiq. Journ.* 41, 154–85.

1966. Two contrasting palaeoliths from Buckinghamshire. *Antiq. Journ.* 46.

1969. Palaeoliths of special interest. *Univ. London Inst. Archaeol. Bull.* 8–9, 101–8.

1971. Some Wiltshire palaeoliths. In G. de G. Sieveking (ed.) *Prehistoric and Roman Studies*, 69–87.

Other Papers on English and Welsh Archaeology

1933. Mediaeval sepulchral monuments at Linton, Herefordshire. *Woolhope Nat. Field Club*, 1.

1936a. Outil façonné dans un fragment de hache polie du Comté de Sussex. *Bull. Soc. Préhist. Franç.* 23, 3.

1936b. Quartzites taillés de la région londonienne. *Congrès Préhistorique. Compte rendu de la deuxième session, Toulouse-Foix, 1936*, 609–29.

1937a. An enigmatic pebble. *Antiq. Journ.* 17, 193.

1937b. Prehistoric pottery found at Iver, Bucks. *Records of Buckinghamshire* 13, 316.

1939. Iron Age pottery from Burnham, Bucks. *Antiq. Journ.* 19, 166.

1942. Flaked quartz implements from Cornwall. *Antiq. Journ.* 22, 215.

1943a. Two prehistoric mortars. *Antiq. Journ.* 23, 56. (Paper read to the Society of Antiquaries of London, on 26 November 1942.)

1943b. (with P. Corder) A Belgic clay pot-stand. *Antiq. Journ.* 23, 58.

1943c. (with P. Corder) Belgic pottery from Poyle Brickworks. *Records of Buckinghamshire* 14, 175.

1946. Some flint implements of special interest from Lincolnshire, Hampshire and Middlesex. *Antiq. Journ.* 26, 180.

1955a. (with W. F. Grimes) The prehistory of Caldey (Part I). *Archaeologia Cambrensis* 104, 85–165.

1955b. Artefacts of Graig Lwyd rock from Nailsworth, Glos. *Trans. Bristol and Glos. Archaeol. Soc.* 74, 5.

1959. Prehistory at Iver Sub. *Southern Beam* (the magazine of the Southern Division of the Central Electricity Generating Board, Portsmouth) 10, no. 7, 18–21; and also in no. 8, 10–14.

1961a. (with W. F. Grimes) The prehistory of Caldey (Part II). *Archaeologia Cambrensis* 110, 30.

1961b. Mesolithic facies in Middlesex and London. *Trans. London Middlesex Archaeol. Soc.* 20, 101. (Also published in the *Archaeological News Letter* 7 (Jan.–Feb. 1965), 243–8.)

1962. A cup-marked sarsen near Marlborough, Wiltshire. *Arch. News Letter* 7, 123–5.

1963. Three grinding stones. *Antiq. Journ.* 43, 190.

1964. Mesolithic industries beside Colne waters in Iver and Denham, Buckinghamshire. *Records of Buckinghamshire* 17, 148–64.

1966. Mesolithic facies in the Transpontine fringes. *Surrey Archaeol. Coll.* 63, 1–43.

Miscellaneous Papers

1928. La croix aux temps préhistoriques et la cupule pendant le Christianisme primitif. *Bull. Soc. Préhist. Franç.* 25, 453.

1932. Contribution à l'étude du Paléolithique Supérieur du Gâtinais. *Bull. Soc. Préhist. Franç.* 29, 272.

1935. Contribution à l'étude du Paléolithique Inférieur du Périgord. *Bull. Soc. Préhist. Franç.* 32, 278.

1943. A Jamaican communal mortar and rock-carving. *Man*, 66.

1946. A mediaeval rock-dwelling at Les Eyzies-de-Tayac (Dordogne). *Antiq. Journ.* 26, 72.

1947. Chatelperron: a new survey of its industry (with notes on a human skull by Professor A. J. E. Cave). *Archaeologia* 92, 95.

1949. Flaked stone industries. Chapter 7 of *The Wellcome Excavations in the Sudan*, by Frank Addison, published for the Trustees of the late Sir Henry Wellcome, Oxford.

1950. Infant feeding-bottles in prehistoric times. *Proc. Roy. Soc. Med.* 43, 7. (Also published in the *Archaeological News Letter* 4 (Mar.–Apr. 1952), 104–6.)

1951a. Pointe pédonculée et pointe néolithique de Combe-Capelle. *Bull. Soc. Préhist. Franç.* 48, 482.

1951b. The stone industries of Singa – Abu Hugar. In *Fossil Mammals of Africa*, no. 2, *The Pleistocene Fauna of Two Blue Nile Sites*, British Museum (Natural History).

1953. The evolution of the knife in the Old Stone Age. In E. Ashworth Underwood (ed.) *Science, Medicine and History* (Essays on the evolution of scientific thought and medical practice written in honour of Charles Singer).

1954. The Magdalenian tectiform of La Mouthe and its modern counterpart. *Man*, 161.

BOOKS AND ARTICLES ON THE WELLCOME INSTITUTE

Addison, F. 1949. *The Wellcome Excavations in the Sudan*, vols I–II. London: Oxford University Press.

Addison, F. and Crawford, O. G. S. 1951. *The Wellcome Excavations in the Sudan*, vol. III. London: Oxford University Press.

Hall, A. R. and Bembridge, B. A. 1986. *Physic and Philanthropy: A History of the Wellcome Trust 1936–1986*. Cambridge University Press.

Russell, G. M. 1986. The Wellcome Historical Medical Museum's dispersal of non-medical material, 1936–1983. *Museums Journ.* 86 (Suppl.), S1–S36.

Skinner, G. M. 1986. Sir Henry Wellcome's museum for the science of history. *Med. Hist.* 30, 383–419.

Symons, J. 1993. *Wellcome Institute for the History of Medicine: A Short History*. London: Wellcome Trust.

Part 1
The Environmental Background

2

A MESOLITHIC OF THE WESTERN AND NORTHERN ISLES OF SCOTLAND?

EVIDENCE FROM POLLEN AND CHARCOAL

KEVIN J. EDWARDS

INTRODUCTION

Armand Lacaille's (1954) *The Stone Age in Scotland* and Caroline Wickham-Jones's (1994) *Scotland's First Settlers* may be separated by forty years, but they have one thing in common as far as Mesolithic settlement is concerned: neither volume is able to point to an archaeological presence in either the Western Isles or in the Northern Isles Shetland group (Fig. 2.1). The more recent book is able to denote progress, however, for it hints at the author's recent work with lithics which shows an Orkney Mesolithic and it alludes to the palynological data from Callanish, Lewis, by Sjoerd Bohncke (1988) where birch pollen suffers early declines. From the known Mesolithic archaeological viewpoint both the Outer Hebrides and the Northern Isles are practically barren. The word barren, in the minds of many, also applies to both the past as well as the present landscapes of the insular fringe of Scotland. This misconception would have us believe that the outlying islands were unwooded and hence represented inhospitable deterrents to early prehistoric peoples. Notwithstanding statements from some palaeoecologists (Birks 1991, Lowe 1993), pollen-analytical and related research tells a different story. It demonstrates that the resource base of these areas was far from being one in which trees could play no part in Mesolithic times. Some published, and even more unpublished, palynological research (Figs 2.2 and 2.3) provides strong evidence for early and mid-postglacial vegetational changes which can be plausibly hypothesised to reflect anthropogenic impacts. This chapter aims to bring some of this evidence before an archaeological audience which, although environmentally aware, cannot be expected necessarily to be familiar with the specialist palynological literature.

THE WOODLAND CONTEXT

Past Research

In their map of potential woodland distribution prior to the onset of large-scale forest clearance, McVean and Ratcliffe (1962, and cf. Bennett 1989) depict the

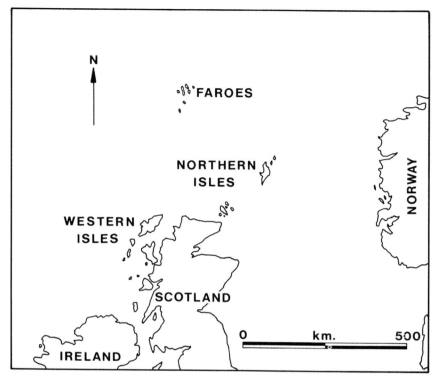

Fig. 2.1. Location of the Western and Northern Isles.

Western (and by implication the Northern Isles [McVean 1964]) as being largely unwooded other than for some patches of birch.

The method of presentation of old pollen diagrams from the southern part of the Long Island (Blackburn 1946, Harrison and Blackburn 1946), where taxa are expressed as percentages of total tree pollen (TLP), tended to accentuate the contribution of herbaceous taxa, but this is somewhat illusory, for at the South Uist site of Stoney Bridge (Harrison and Blackburn 1946) for instance, tree and shrub pollen approach 80 per cent TLP in the basal sample.

A perception of the status of woodland in the Western Isles is provided by the study at Little Loch Roag, Lewis (Birks and Madsen 1979) (Fig. 2.4). For the whole of the Postglacial, this shows a very sparse arboreal pollen content (generally around 10 per cent, but never reaching more than 30 per cent of TLP) and the pollen diagram is dominated by grasses (Poaceae [Gramineae]), sedges (Cyperaceae) and heather (*Calluna vulgaris*) together with indications of tall-herb and fern communities. The low representation for woodland taxa (especially birch [*Betula*], hazel [cf. *Corylus/Myrica*], alder [*Alnus glutinosa*] and willow [*Salix*]) are taken to represent local areas of scrub in the midst of otherwise

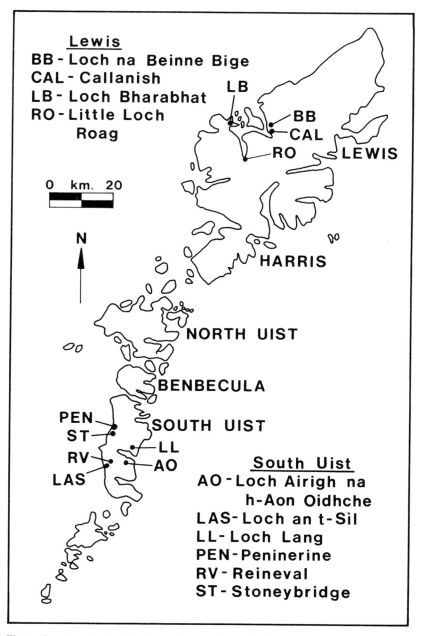

Fig. 2.2. Location of pollen sites in the Western Isles mentioned in the text.

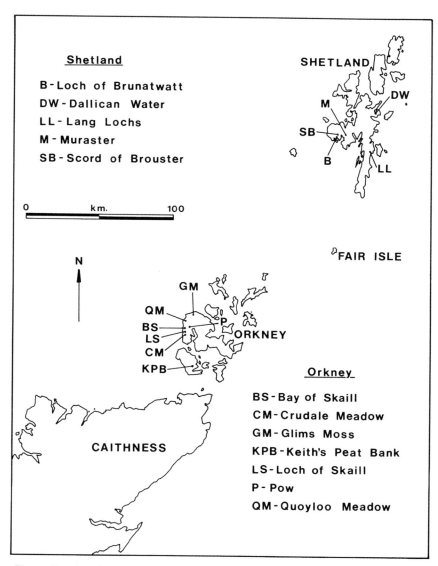

Fig. 2.3. Location of pollen sites in the Northern Isles mentioned in the text.

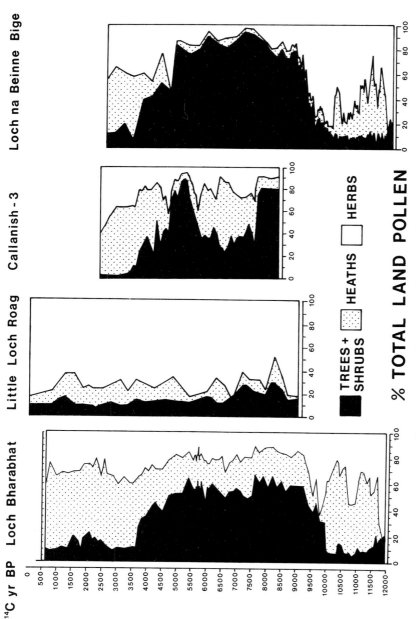

Fig. 2.4. Summary pollen diagrams from northwest Lewis.

treeless regional vegetation (Birks 1991). Birks holds to his belief that the Little Loch Roag site demonstrates only small areas of scrub in Lewis, even though wood remains of pine, birch, willow and other species are found in peats close to the pollen site as well as elsewhere in Lewis (Wilkins 1984). The apparent disparity 'is simply that pollen primarily provides an integrated record of *regional* vegetation over a large area, whereas macrofossils reflect strictly *local* patterns' (Birks 1991: 35).

In Shetland, the pollen diagram from Murraster, west Mainland (Jóhansen 1975) shows that birch and hazel were frequent in the early postglacial, but that the pollen catchment area did not possess a complete woodland cover. This pattern is also evident in pollen diagrams from Orkney (e.g. Glims Moss and Loch of Skaill, [Keatinge and Dickson 1979]). Some sites, however, have produced high percentages of arboreal pollen (e.g. Bay of Skaill inter-tidal peat and Pow [Keatinge and Dickson 1979]).

Thus, evidence available until 1979 was predominantly reflecting early postglacial landscapes which were relatively open, but there were strong contraindications from both the southern Outer Hebrides and from Orkney. In terms of the woodland resource, the existence of only sparse birch and hazel scrub might not be seen as a particularly attractive proposition for Mesolithic communities, nor for animals which might have formed a resource for hunters. On the other hand, Palaeolithic communities survived tundra conditions; but why choose relative famine in outlying areas when a woodland feast was available in the Inner Hebrides or on the mainland?

More Recent Studies

The widespread existence of *in situ* wood macrofossils dated to between 9 140 ± 65 and 3 910 ± 70 (Wilkins 1984) obviously indicates that trees grew during Mesolithic times in certain locations of currently treeless areas of the Outer Hebrides; and small fragmented stands of woodland can be found at the present day (cf. Bennett and Fossitt 1988). The species found fossil are necessarily those restricted to sedimentary environments and they usually represent a narrow range, such as *Betula*, *Salix* and *Pinus*; furthermore, without the advantage of many published radiocarbon dates, it is not possible to say which were growing during the Mesolithic in specific locations. Since the 1980s, further pollen data have become available which radically alter the notion of a general treelessness in these areas, and hence our perception of them as a zone of potential low attraction for people and animals.

Bohncke's (1988) Callanish-3 profile (Fig. 2.4) shows substantial amounts of *Betula* (around 70 per cent TLP) with another 10 per cent shrub pollen from *c*. 8 400 BP. He makes the point that the birch may have occupied sheltered valleys presently submerged. Nearby Loch na Beinne Bige has up to 90 per cent arboreal pollen for an estimated first 5 000 years of the Postglacial, while Loch Bharabhat, to the northwest of Little Loch Roag, has up to 65 per cent AP for the same period

– in both cases birch and hazel pollen make up the greater proportion (Edwards et al. 1994) (Fig. 2.4), although elm, oak and alder are well in evidence.

In a consideration of the pollen data from Loch Lang, South Uist (Bennett et al. 1990), the authors argued that woodland in the area around the loch covered perhaps half the landscape during the early Postglacial. Although dominated by birch and hazel, the pollen spectra also have good representation for oak, elm and alder. Similarly at Loch an t-Sil on South Uist, *Betula*, *Corylus* and other AP taxa rise to over 74 per cent TLP at an estimated 7 650 BP.

In the Northern Isles also, pollen analyses are revealing sites with considerable amounts of tree and shrub pollen. At the Mainland (Shetland) site of Loch of Brunatwatt, in undated but clearly early postglacial deposits, the profile is characterised by the highest percentages of *Betula* pollen (up to 55.2 per cent TLP) yet reported from Shetland (Edwards and Moss 1993) (Fig. 2.5). Total tree and shrub percentages achieve 88.5 per cent. Given the high percentages for *Betula*, Coryloid (cf. *Corylus avellana*, up to 27.6 per cent) and *Salix* (up to 12.2 per cent), there is little doubt that all three taxa were locally present and all three are found in Shetland today. The consistent presence of *Alnus* (up to 7.3 per cent) and *Quercus* (up to 8.0 per cent) may also suggest their local presence. At the neighbouring site of Scord of Brouster, *Betula-Corylus* dominated woodland (AP + Shrub pollen values up to around 80 per cent TLP), with *Salix* and *Sorbus aucuparia*, existed prior to Neolithic clearance (Keith-Lucas 1986). Woodland pollen attains levels of 70 per cent (with *Corylus* at 55 per cent) shortly before 8 000 BP at Lang Lochs Mire (Hulme and Shirriffs 1994), while at Dallican Water, Bennett et al. (1992) concluded that the representation of birch, hazel, oak, alder is such that all four genera were present in Shetland (and elm and ash less certainly) in the early to mid-Postglacial.

The Orkney site of Keith's Peat Bank on Hoy, has tree and shrub pollen percentages of about 60 per cent (birch, hazel, willow) at *c.* 6 500 BP (Fig. 2.6). Even greater values were found at Crudale Meadow and Quoyloo Meadow where arboreal pollen maxima of 80 per cent of a TLP + spores sum were found prior to inferred elm decline times, 'suggesting that dense-canopied woodland once occupied much of the landscape around the basins' (Bunting 1994: 779).

WOODLAND REDUCTION AND THE FIRE RECORD

The existence of far more extensive woodland than previously realised in the distal island groups provides a potential resource – whether it be food, timber and firewood for humans or food and shelter for animals. Can we move beyond the potential and see signs of human impact in the pollen diagrams? The recent analyses, often with their close sampling which improves temporal resolution, and the counting of microscopic charcoal which may be used as a fossil indicator of fire (Patterson et al. 1987), have been enlightening in these respects.

The Callanish-3 profile (Bohncke 1988) has a sharp reduction in *Betula*, with increases in *Salix*, *Calluna*, Poaceae, *Potentilla*-type and charcoal. This is

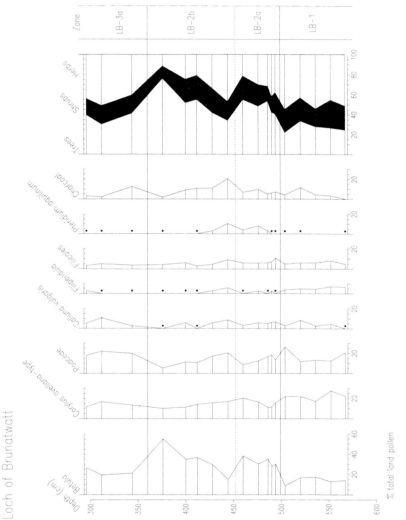

Fig. 2.5. Selected pollen taxa from Loch of Brunatwatt, Mainland, Shetland (after Edwards and Moss 1993).

suggestive of woodland clearance in which willow was not affected, and with the spread of grass and heath in cleared areas. Bohncke (ibid. 451) considered that forest burning may have been taking place and that heather moor and grassland may have attracted deer and other mammals.

On South Uist, Bennett et al. 1990 propose that Mesolithic age microscopic charcoal could derive from human activity, but they do not associate them with any particular changes in the pollen record from Loch Lang. At Loch an t-Sìl, 8 km to the southwest, however, contiguous 1 cm thick pollen samples (each covering an estimated ~11 ^{14}C years of accumulation) reveal two phases of woodland removal (mainly birch and hazel) at *c.* 8 040 and 7 870 BP, lasting 130 and 70 radiocarbon years respectively (Fig. 2.7). These are associated with expansions in Poaceae, *Calluna* and charcoal and reductions in undifferentiated ferns (Pteropsida monolete indet. ≡ Filicales) and royal fern (*Osmunda regalis*). The removal of birch and hazel may be anthropogenic in origin and the expansions in grass and heather could indicate their spread into cleared areas. Whether the extension of browse in order to attract animals was the intention or a useful by-product of cropping woodland, remains unknown. The sustained charcoal peaks do not have to indicate woodland removal by fire, but simply the burning of felled wood for heating or cooking purposes (cf. Edwards 1990). The process of heather burning may also have been occurring and this is discussed below.

Of interest is the reduction of ferns at the times of the opening in the woodland at Loch an t-Sìl. A similar feature is observed in the Shetland sites of Dallican Water (Bennett et al. 1990) and Loch of Brunatwatt (Edwards and Moss 1993). At Dallican Water, a decrease in ferns and tall-herbs during Mesolithic times is taken to indicate possible grazing, with the red deer as the favoured candidate. Its ability to swim between islands (though distances between Orkney, Fair Isle and Shetland would be 43 and 38 km) and its frequent association with Mesolithic sites, may favour its presence – it may even have been transported to Shetland by hunter-gatherers intent on introducing a valuable resource. At Loch of Brunatwatt, the temporary reduction in birch values in subzone LB-2b is striking and coincides with a decline in *Pteridium aquilinum* (bracken) and temporary increases in Poaceae, *Calluna* and charcoal (Fig. 2.5). From *c.* 6 400 ^{14}C years BP in the profile from Keith's Peat Bank, Hoy, the *Betula* and *Polypodium* curves decline abruptly, Poaceae, *Calluna* and charcoal rise and undifferentiated fern spore values are depressed (Fig. 2.6). Once again, clearance of woodland would appear to be involved, there is a high fire incidence, and fern representation is lowered.

HEATHLAND MANAGEMENT

The creation and/or maintenance of heaths as a grazing resource during and since the Mesolithic has had a long palynological history, especially in England (e.g. Dimbleby 1962, Simmons 1969, Moore 1993, Caseldine and Hatton 1993).

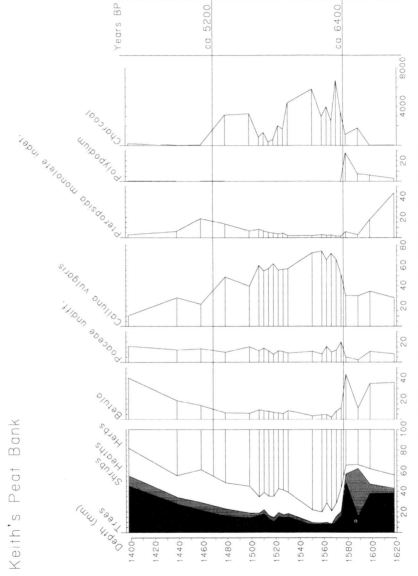

Fig. 2.6. Selected pollen and spore taxa from Keith's Peat Bank, Hoy, Orkney.

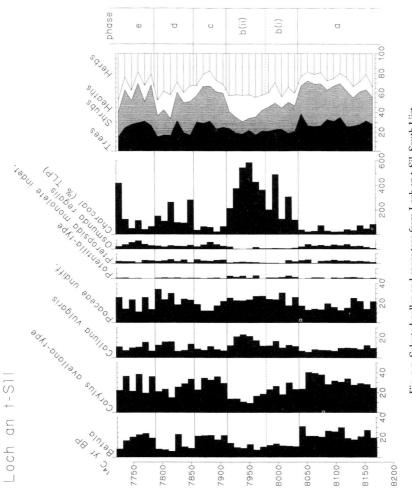

Fig. 2.7. Selected pollen and spore taxa from Loch an t-Sil, South Uist.

There has been less discussion of this in a Scottish context although the expansion in heathland plants and charcoal at Callanish have been discussed above. A transect of sites across South Uist, however, provides indications that *Calluna* heaths can be linked circumstantially with fire (Edwards et al. 1995) at various times, including the Mesolithic. Thus, at Peninerine, charcoal and *Calluna* pollen peak and remain at fairly high levels from *c.* 7 800 BP, and at Loch an t-Sìl, a rise in *Calluna* and charcoal occurs at around 8 300 BP (Fig. 2.7).

CLIMATE AND FIRE INCIDENCE

The possibility that fire incidence is related to climatic dryness can be addressed only briefly here. In the transect of sites across South Uist, charcoal peaks or sustained high levels of charcoal occur metachronously (Fig. 2.8) (Edwards et al. 1995). This would seem to provide few grounds for assuming that periods of dryness are of over-riding influence in creating the sedimentary charcoal record. In a wider survey, however, Tipping (this volume) favours a climatic explanation for the increased incidence of charcoal during Mesolithic times. More charcoal records with more reliable quantification of the evidence are needed to test the competing hypotheses.

CONCLUSIONS

Archaeological and environmental evidence suggests that the Inner Hebrides were colonised in the early Postglacial. Rhum has archaeological evidence for occupation at *c.* 8 500 BP (Hirons and Edwards 1990, Wickham-Jones 1990) and Oronsay was occupied from about 6 200 BP (Mellars 1987). Islay may even have been occupied in the immediate postglacial period, i.e. before 9 000 BP (Edwards and Mithen 1995). The palynological evidence from the Western and Northern Isles is sufficiently similar to that from the Inner Hebrides to justify the notion of a human presence in Mesolithic times. It can be said with some certainty that the woodland resource was there, that woodland was clearly being reduced and that combustible materials were being burned (for whatever reason). In addition, heathland spread may have been facilitated by human activity and the management of heath was also a possibility. The conjectures concerning grazing and the repression of fern and tall-herb communities are an interesting addition to the palynologically-derived patterns for the Mesolithic economy. For the moment, there is insufficient evidence from the sites examined here, to justify acceptance of a hypothesis of a climatically-related cause for burning.

Natural circumstances make it difficult to find sites in these areas: there is obscuring blanket peat; acid soils in which bones do not survive; in the Western Isles especially, there was the mid-postglacial marine transgression with its higher sea levels which may have led to coastal inundation, the submergence of signs of coastal occupation including camp sites and shell middens, and promotion of the landward movement of machair sands which themselves have encroached upon likely Mesolithic settlement areas. The changes in the palaeoecological

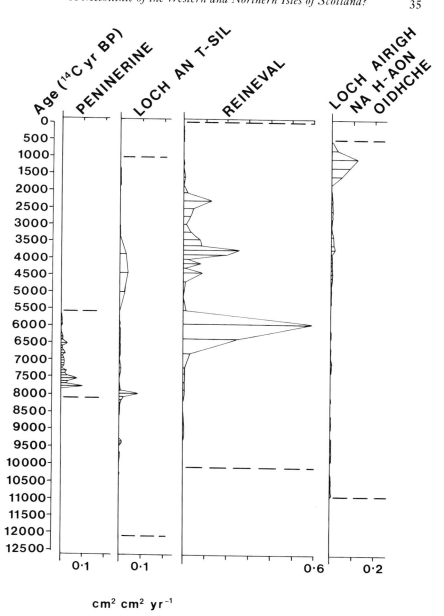

Fig. 2.8. Microscopic charcoal accumulation rate curves from South Uist (after Edwards et al. 1995).

record must mean something. A plausible working hypothesis is that they reflect early human impacts. As such they provide a challenge to the archaeologist to find these sites. Inland southwestern Scotland (Edwards et al. 1984), Caithness and Orkney (Wickham-Jones 1994), were once seen as Mesolithic-free zones. The present writer has every confidence that a Mesolithic presence is waiting to be found in all areas of the Western and Northern Isles.

ACKNOWLEDGEMENTS

The Leverhulme Trust is thanked for financial support concerning research in the Western and Northern Isles.

REFERENCES

Bennett, K. D. 1989. A provisional map of forest types for the British Isles 5 000 years ago. *Journal of Quaternary Science* 4, 141–4.

Bennett, K. D., Boreham, S., Sharp, M. J. and Switsur, V. R. 1992. Holocene history of environment, vegetation and human settlement on Catta Ness, Lunnasting, Shetland. *Journal of Ecology* 80, 241–73.

Bennett, K. D. and Fossitt, J. 1988. A stand of birch by Loch Eynort, South Uist, Outer Hebrides. *Transactions of the Botanical Society of Edinburgh* 45, 245–52.

Bennett, K. D., Fossitt, J. A., Sharp, M. J. and Switsur, V. R. 1990. Holocene vegetational and environmental history at Loch Lang, South Uist, Scotland. *New Phytologist* 114, 281–98.

Birks, H. J. B. 1991. Floristic and vegetational history of the Outer Hebrides. In Pankhurst, R. J. and Mullin, J. M. (eds), *Flora of the Outer Hebrides*. London: Natural History Museum Publications, 32–7.

Birks, H. J. B. and Madsen, B. J. 1979. Flandrian vegetational history of Little Loch Roag, Isle of Lewis, Scotland. *Journal of Ecology* 67, 825–42.

Blackburn, K. B. 1946. On a peat from the island of Barra, Outer Hebrides. Data for the study of post-glacial history. X. *New Phytologist* 45, 44–9.

Bohncke, S. J. P. 1988. Vegetation and habitation history of the Callanish area. In Birks, H. H., Birks, H. J. B., Kaland, P. E. and Moe, D. (eds), *The Cultural Landscape – Past, Present and Future*. Cambridge: Cambridge University, 445–61.

Bunting, M. J. 1994. Vegetation history of Orkney, Scotland: pollen records from two small basins in west Mainland. *New Phytologist* 128, 771–92.

Caseldine, C. and Hatton, J. 1993. The development of high moorland on Dartmoor: fire and the influence of Mesolithic activity on vegetation change. In Chambers, F. M. (ed.), *Climate Change and Human Impact on the Landscape*. London: Chapman & Hall, 119–31.

Dimbleby, G. W. 1962. *The Development of British Heathlands and Their Soils*. Oxford: Oxford Forestry Memoir 23.

Edwards, K. J. 1990. Fire and the Scottish Mesolithic: evidence from microscopic charcoal. In Vermeersch, P. M. and Van Peer, P. (eds), *Contributions to the Mesolithic in Europe*. Leuven: Leuven University Press, 71–9.

Edwards, K. J., Ansell, M. and Carter, B. A. 1984. New Mesolithic sites in south-west Scotland and their significance as indicators of inland penetration. *Transactions of the Dumfriesshire and Galloway Natural History and Antiquarian Society* 58, 9–15.

Edwards, K. J. and Mithen, S. 1995. The colonisation of the Hebridean islands of western Scotland: evidence from the palynological and archaeological records. *World Archaeology* 26, 348–65.

Edwards, K. J. and Moss, A. G. 1993. Pollen data from the Loch of Brunatwatt, west Mainland. In Birnie, J. F., Gordon, J. E., Bennett, K. D. and Hall, A. M. (eds), *The Quaternary of Shetland: Field Guide.* Cambridge: Quaternary Research Association, 126–9.

Edwards, K. J., Whittington, G., Coles, G. M. and Lomax, T. 1994. *Environmental Change in the Callanish Area of Lewis, Scotland.* Unpublished report submitted to Scottish Natural Heritage and Comhairle nan Eilean, 1–27.

Edwards, K. J., Whittington, G. and Hirons, K. R. 1995. The relationship between fire and long-term wet heath development in South Uist, Outer Hebrides, Scotland. In Thompson, D. B. A., Hestor, A. J. and Usher, M. B. (eds), *Heaths and Moorland: Cultural Landscapes.* Edinburgh: HMSO, 240–8.

Harrison, J. W. H. and Blackburn, K. B. 1946. The occurrence of a nut of *Trapa natans* L. in the Outer Hebrides, with some account of the peat bogs adjoining the loch in which the discovery was made. *New Phytologist* 45, 124–31.

Hirons, K. R. and Edwards, K. J. 1990. Pollen and related studies at Kinloch, Isle of Rhum, Scotland, with particular reference to possible early human impacts on vegetation. *New Phytologist* 116, 715–27.

Hulme, P. D. and Shirriffs, J. 1994. The Late-glacial and Holocene vegetation of the Lang Lochs Mire area, Gulberwick, Shetland: a pollen and macrofossil investigation. *New Phytologist* 128, 793–806.

Jøhansen, J. 1975. Pollen diagrams from the Shetland and Faroe Islands. *New Phytologist* 75, 369–87.

Keatinge, T. H. and Dickson, J. H. 1979. Mid-Flandrian changes in vegetation on Mainland, Orkney. *New Phytologist* 82, 585–612.

Keith-Lucas, M. 1986. Vegetation development and human impact. In Whittle, A., Keith-Lucas, M., Milles, A., et al., *Scord of Brouster: An Early Agricultural Settlement on Shetland. Excavations 1977–1979.* Oxford: Oxford University Committee for Archaeology, Monograph 9, 92–118.

Lacaille, A. M. D. 1954. *The Stone Age in Scotland.* London: Oxford University Press.

Lowe, J. J. 1993. Isolating the climatic factors in early- and mid-Holocene palaeo-botanical records from Scotland. In Chambers, F. M. (ed.), *Climate Change and Human Impact on the Landscape.* London: Chapman & Hall, 67–82.

McVean, D. N. 1964. Regional pattern of the vegetation. In Burnett, J. H. (ed.), *The Vegetation of Scotland.* Edinburgh: Oliver & Boyd, 568–78.

McVean, D. N. and Ratcliffe, D. A. 1962. *Plant Communities of the Scottish Highlands.* London: HMSO.

Mellars, P. A. 1987. *Excavations on Oronsay: Prehistoric Human Ecology on a Small Island.* Edinburgh: Edinburgh University Press.

Moore, P. D. 1993. The origin of blanket mire, revisited. In Chambers, F. M. (ed.), *Climate Change and Human Impact on the Landscape.* London: Chapman & Hall, 217–24.

Patterson, W. A. III, Edwards, K. J. and Maguire, D. J. 1987. Microscopic charcoal as a fossil indicator of fire. *Quaternary Science Reviews* 6, 3–23.

Simmons, I. G. 1969. Evidence for vegetation changes associated with Mesolithic man in Britain. In Ucko, P. J. and Dimbleby, G. W. (eds), *The Domestication and Exploitation of Plants and Animals.* Duckworth: London, 111–19.

Wickham-Jones, C. R. 1990. *Rhum: Mesolithic and Later Sites at Kinloch, Excavations 1984–1986*. Edinburgh: Society of Antiquaries of Scotland, Monograph Series no. 7.

Wickham-Jones, C. R. 1994. *Scotland's First Settlers*. London: Batsford.

Wilkins, D. A. 1984. The Flandrian woods of Lewis (Scotland). *Journal of Ecology* 72, 251–8.

3

MICROSCOPIC CHARCOAL RECORDS, INFERRED HUMAN ACTIVITY AND CLIMATE CHANGE IN THE MESOLITHIC OF NORTHERNMOST SCOTLAND

RICHARD TIPPING

INTRODUCTION

The recording of microscopic charcoal particles from lake sediments, peats and soils has in the last decade or two become a widely adopted aspect of Holocene (last 10 000 ^{14}C years) pollen analysis (Tolonen 1986; Patterson, Edwards and Maguire 1987). The value of these data are readily apparent in numerous studies, which have embraced such topics as changes in climatically-induced fire frequency in natural ecosystems (Swain 1973, 1978; Cwynar 1978; Singh, Kershaw and Clark 1981; Green 1981, 1982; Clark, J. S. 1988a) and the role of human interference in changing the structure and composition of woodlands (Iversen 1941; Tolonen 1978; Simmons and Innes 1981, 1987; Edwards 1988, 1989; Clark, J. S., Merkt and Muller 1989; Bennett, Simonson and Peglar 1989; Caseldine and Hatton 1993; Morrison 1994).

A number of serious methodological and interpretative problems still exist. There are differences in obtaining the data, from chemical assay (Robinson 1984, Winkler 1985) to visual estimation, and results from different techniques are not comparable. The visual estimation/counting of particles has become most widely established (Tolomen 1986), but there can be uncertainties in the correct identification of charcoal (Patterson et al. 1987; Renberg & Wik 1985; Wiltshire, Edwards and Bond 1992) and there are widely divergent methods of recording and data presentation (Waddington 1969; Mehringer, Arno and Petersen 1977; Clark, R. L. 1982; Clark, J. S. 1988b; Patterson et al. 1987; Horn, Horn and Byrne 1992) which hamper comparisons. We have few empirical data concerning the sources of microscopic charcoal (Clark, J. S. 1988c), the effects on charcoal representation of differences in site and sediment characteristics (Tolonen 1986), of possible contrasts in charcoal production of different plant communities (woodland vs. heathland vs. grassland, for example), and only a limited understanding of the nature, intensity and other characteristics of fires in generating charcoal (Hobbs and Gimingham 1987, Johnson 1992).

One of the most critical interpretative issues remains the cause of fires which generated the microscopic charcoal in our palaeoenvironmental records. Change through time in the representation of charcoal is a record of changing fire frequency and/or intensity; there are no causal implications in the charcoal record. Thus the distinction made above between 'natural' and 'anthropogenic' fire ecology is not necessarily one that can be supported from these data alone – they are inferred. The inferences are generally strengthened by the association (or absence) of vegetation and/or sedimentological changes that are ascribed to human impact on the landscape. These 'anthropogenic' signals are, however, themselves frequently ambiguous in origin and difficult to assign to a specific cause. The problem of causal attribution is inevitably made harder in the mesolithic period, when human impact on plant communities, though perhaps measurable, is acknowledged to have been insubstantial (Simmons, Dimbleby and Grigson 1981; Edwards and Ralston 1984), and where clear evidence of agriculture, such as cereal remains, is absent.

Yet it is this period between $c.$ 10 000 and 5 000 ^{14}C BP, that has attracted the attention of many workers interested in the relations between human activity and anthropogenic woodland manipulation by fire. The theoretical basis for this was established in the 1970s (Simmons 1975; Jacobi, Tallis and Mellars 1976; Mellars 1976; Coles 1976), based on ethnographic and historical data, principally on native North American indians (Stewart 1956, Cronon 1983). However, establishing a clear theoretical model for hunter-gatherer woodland 'management' is not the same as demonstrating its existence in the past. Despite the clear need for caution in assigning cause to charcoal records (Edwards 1988, above), there appears increasingly to be a desire to associate increases in fire frequency/intensity with human activities in the mesolithic period. The extension of this argument is then to use charcoal records to infer, by proxy, the presence of hunter-gatherer groups in regions where the archaeological record would not support this. By itself this is not necessarily a problem, for if carefully argued and painstakingly researched, palaeoenvironmental data can be shown to provide a reasonable substitute for archaeological data, as in north Yorkshire (Simmons 1993; Turner, Innes and Simmons 1993; Day 1993) or south Wales (Smith and Cloutman 1988). Investigations into very fine spatial and temporal vegetation disturbances as detailed as these are, however, all too few, time consuming and costly.

The concern here is with analyses of high quality, but where interpretations of human-induced fire ecology are based on less securely established data. The contribution to the debate presented here takes as its starting point interpretations of charcoal data from several sites in northernmost Scotland where peaks in charcoal representation firmly dated to the mesolithic period are ascribed, with differing degrees of confidence, to anthropogenic activity. But in many instances this is done with no evidence of other possible indications of human presence, archaeological or palynological. These analyses are here re-examined, and regional patterns elucidated. Finally, an assessment of the temporal patterning in charcoal records is compared with data on early–mid Holocene climate change in north west Europe, a causal mechanism rarely considered in these latitudes (Rackham 1980). All dates referred to in this discussion are presented as ^{14}C (uncalibrated) years Before Present (BP).

NORTHERNMOST SCOTLAND IN THE EARLY–MID HOLOCENE (MESOLITHIC)

Northernmost Scotland is defined in this paper as the mainland region including most of Caithness and all of northern Sutherland. It includes the outer isles, the Outer Hebrides, the Orkney and the Shetland Islands. This is not a well-defined geographic province, but has reasonable ecological coherence. Fig. 3.1 is a representation of the major woodland types in Scotland at *c*.5 000 BP, derived in part from earlier syntheses (McVean and Ratcliffe 1962; Birks, Deacon and Peglar 1975; Birks 1977, 1988; Moore 1977; Bennett 1989; Fossitt 1990) but incorporating new data (Tipping in press): in turn these reconstructions are based on numerous radiocarbon dated (mostly) pollen sequences. Northernmost Scotland is thus defined as the region typified at the end of the mesolithic period by an 'open birch-hazel' (*Betula-Corylus*) woodland.

In the first few thousand years of the Holocene northernmost Scotland, as with the rest of the British Isles, experienced dramatic changes in the appearance of the landscape and the plant communities that clothed it. It is most probable that no trees survived the climatic extremes at the end of the Loch Lomond Stadial (*c*.11 000–10 000 BP, Tipping 1991). Trees migrated from refugia in southern Britain and the continent (Huntley and Birks 1983) in response to ameliorating climatic and soil conditions. Tree colonisation was complex, and took several thousand years, although current models suggest that climatic warming sufficient to accommodate most tree species was rapid, probably less than 100 years (Kutzbach and Guetter 1986; Atkinson, Briffa and Coope 1987). But a time-lag existed between the climatic and edaphic conditions amenable to tree growth and the arrival of the trees themselves, induced by different modes of seed dispersal, distance from refugia and chance events (Huntley and Birks 1983, Birks 1989).

The pattern of colonisation of the major tree taxa is readily established by radiocarbon dated pollen diagrams (e.g. Birks 1989). The sequence of migration is remarkably similar across the country, though the timing differs through geographical and edaphic constraints, competitive interactions with already colonised trees (Bennett 1986) and stresses imposed through taxa approaching their latitudinal range-limits, important in northern Scotland. Birch (*Betula*) is consistently the first tree to colonise, at *c*.10 000–9 600 BP, and its near-synchronous appearance across the mainland indicates a virtual absence of stresses, climatic, edaphic or competitive. Hazel (*Corylus*) is the next migrant, at around 9 500–9 000 BP. Elm (*Ulmus*) and oak (*Quercus*) arrived in Scotland between 8 500 and 8 000 BP. The rate of migration for each was dramatically slowed as the Grampian Mountains were approached, and climatic constraints might have existed such that neither tree became established as a dominant in

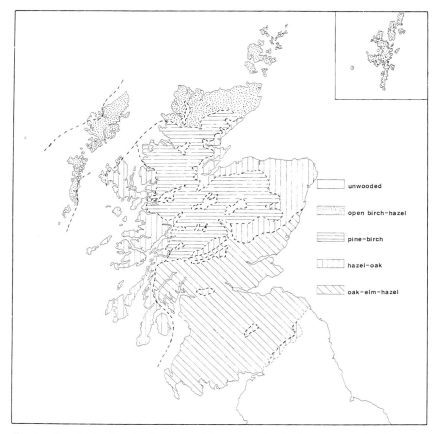

Fig. 3.1. The distribution of major woodland types across Scotland at *c.*5 000 BP. Northernmost Scotland is defined as that province typified by open birch-hazel woodland; this woodland type was established by 9 000 BP, and changed little in the next 4 000 years.

northernmost Scotland. At this time, however, numbers of pine trees were expanding sufficiently in the north west of the country to be identified in the regional pollen record, though they did not colonise the northernmost mainland until much later (*c.* 4 400 BP) and under special edaphic and climatic conditions (Gear and Huntley 1991). The colonisation and establishment of alder (*Alnus*) was clearly not synchronous everywhere (Chambers and Elliott 1989, Bennett and Birks 1990, Tallantire 1992), and it is likely that small populations of alder colonised many areas considerably earlier (Chambers and Price 1985) and later (O'Sullivan 1975, Tipping 1995a) than they are detected in regional pollen records, but could not fully consolidate their position until some environmental disturbance, including the possibility of mesolithic woodland interference (Smith 1984).

It is probably wrong to assume that extensive areas of closed canopy wood-land covered either the northernmost mainland, or the Northern and Western Isles. An open scrub woodland is more likely to have existed. Tree and shrub types present within the woods were probably more varied than implied by Fig. 3.1 (Bennett et al. 1990, 1992, 1993; Fossitt 1990; Bunting 1993, 1994), but the importance of woodland in the landscape should not be overestimated. Trees would probably have varied greatly in density dependent on their location, altitude and degree of exposure to wind and sea spray. Trees may have been absent on the north western edge of Lewis (Birks and Madsen 1979), as on St Kilda (Walker 1984), and even on the eastern side of the region. Peglar (1979) and Robinson (1987) argued for essentially treeless landscapes due to exposure. Beneath this always poor canopy cover a species-rich under-storey of tall herbs, grasses and ferns was probably an important component, seen in many pollen diagrams (e.g. Peglar 1979, Bennett et al. 1992). Fossitt (1990) has argued that woodland, though extensive, was discontinuous on the Outer Hebrides, and experienced disturbance and decline, at one site severe, at around 7 900 BP, which she regarded as climatic in origin, comparable in age to a similar change on Colonsay, sustained until *c*. 6 200 BP (Andrews et al. 1987), and similarly not seen to be anthropogenic.

Until very recently mesolithic artefacts were not known from the region, but new find-spots reported from the mainland and Orkney (Wickham-Jones 1990, 1994; Wickham-Jones and Firth 1990) tend to suggest that lack of fieldwork is at least partly responsible for the pattern, together with the loss of localities due to postglacial sea-level rise (Ritchie 1966, Bohncke 1988), peat and machair development (Edwards, Whittington and Hirons 1995). There is probably no requirement to assume mesolithic human populations to have been absent from the northernmost mainland. Bennett et al's (1992) argument for mesolithic settlement of the Shetlands remains open to interpretation, however (Tipping in press). The suggestion of Lateglacial human occupation to account for the reindeer antler concentrations at Creag nan Uamh, Assynt (Lawson and Bonsall 1986, Morrison and Bonsall 1989) has been re-evaluated following further radio-carbon dating (Murray et al. 1993), and the suggestion of Lateglacial human presence in the Inner Hebrides (Edwards and Mithen 1995) is no more than speculative.

CHARCOAL RECORDS FROM NORTHERNMOST SCOTLAND

The geographical spread of charcoal diagrams for northernmost Scotland is depicted in Fig. 3.2. All the sites used are radiocarbon dated, and the chron-ologies seem secure. South Uist has an exceptional concentration of sites, the products of investigations by Bennett et al. (1990), Fossitt (1990) and Edwards et al. (1995). To the east sites are very much fewer. The mainland is repre-sented by only three pollen diagrams for which charcoal counts are available or known to the author, and no charcoal analyses with secure dating controls

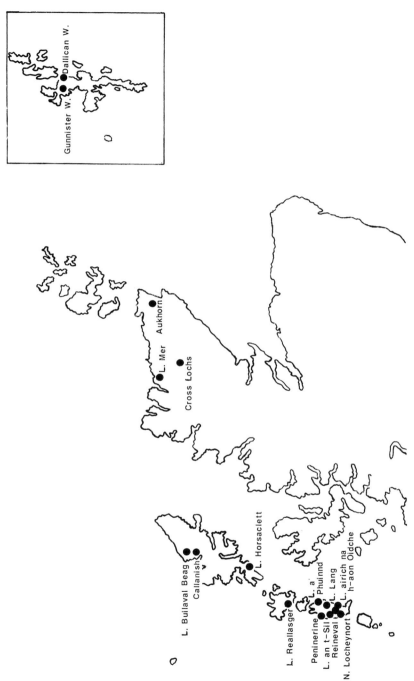

Fig. 3.2. The distribution of stratigraphic and radiocarbon dated charcoal records across northernmost Scotland used in this analysis (see also Fig. 3.3). The inner Hebrides and the bulk of the Scottish mainland are excluded from the analysis (see Fig. 3.1). See text for sources.

pertaining to the mesolithic are available for Orkney (Keatinge and Dickson 1979; Bunting 1993, 1994). The number of sites from the Shetlands may soon rival the Uists in published analyses (Birnie et al. 1993) but only those from Dallican Water (Bennett et al. 1992) and Gunnister (Bennett et al. 1993) are currently available.

Some sites are lakes, others peat accumulations: no allowance can be made here for possible differences in the ways charcoal is recruited to these sites. With the exception of data from Cross Lochs (Charman 1990, 1992, 1994a) and Loch Mer (Gear 1989) all the sites have counts of microscopic charcoal produced during the routine counting of pollen. Nevertheless, no direct comparison between, for instance, numbers of particles can be attempted because of differences in the measurement or representation of charcoal (above). Charman (1992) and Gear (1989) quantified macroscopic (visible to the eye) charcoal particles, Gear producing a continuous curve, Charman reporting charcoal only when abundant in the peat stratigraphy.

Fig. 3.3 presents a series of summary curves for charcoal representation at these sites, arranged from west (South Uist) to east (Shetlands). The interpretation is deliberately simplistic, in recognition of the differences in data presentation between sites. Charcoal counts are here expressed in four subjective categories: absence, low, moderate and high abundance on the relative significance of total charcoal patterns. The data are plotted against ^{14}C years BP using the radiocarbon chronologies from the sites. The ages of basal sediments at sites which do not extend to 10 000 BP are indicated by double lines. From these data there seem to be particular sites which produce more interesting records: compare the complex fluctuations at Loch Reallasger with Loch Horsaclett, both from the Outer Hebrides and analysed using the same methods by the one worker (Fossitt 1990). Such differences might reflect site-specific factors affecting the recruitment of charcoal (compare also the major differences in representation between the adjacent Shetland sites of Dallican Water (Bennett et al. 1992) and Gunnister Water (Bennett et al. 1993)).

At the majority of sites where an interpretation of the charcoal stratigraphy has been made by the analyst/s an anthropogenic explanation has been preferred. Only Gear (1989) has seen the patterns at Loch Mer (Fig. 3.3) as climatic in origin, controlled by the frequency of anti-cyclonic conditions. Bennett et al. (1990) (also 1992) considered that 'small, local fires, ... anthropogenic in origin' (1990: 295) were the likeliest sources for microscopic charcoal at Loch Lang, South Uist and on Shetland. They dismissed woodland fires (anthropogenic or natural), seeming to assume that if present, these would have been sufficiently large to occur in other records from the islands; they note an apparent lack of regional correlation in temporal charcoal trends. Bohncke (1988) at Callanish more confidently linked increased charcoal counts at $c.7 900$ BP (from low to moderate in Fig. 3.3) to human woodland disturbance. Similarly, Edwards et al. (1995) prefer to see increased charcoal representation at Peninerine,

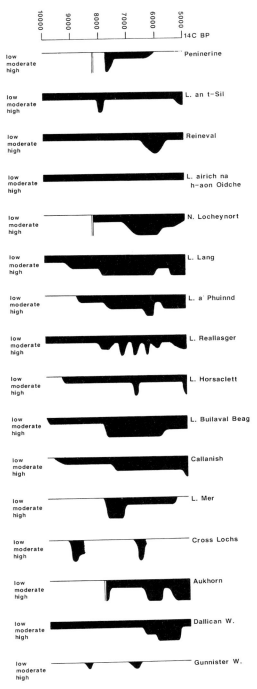

Fig. 3.3. The depiction of relative changes in charcoal abundance at stratigraphic sequences in northernmost Scotland between 10 000 and 5 000 BP, plotted against ^{14}C years BP. See text for explanation.

Loch an-t Sìl and Reineval (Fig. 3.3) as due to anthropogenic management of coastal and upland heaths as a grazing resource.

Both Robinson (1987) and Charman (1992, 1994a) invoked mesolithic human activity to explain peaks in charcoal at the bases of two peat deposits (Figs 3.2, 3.3); 'This charcoal almost certainly arose from man-made fires', argued Robinson (1987: 195), adding that lightning strikes would generally fail to ignite plant matter (following Rackham 1980 – see later). Both workers place great emphasis on charcoal patterns as anthropogenic indicators given the difficulties of recognising apparent human woodland disturbance in vegetation already largely open and herb-rich, but both concede that no palynological anthropogenic indicator herbs (Behre 1981) are encouraged by these burning events, as might be expected from broadly comparable studies (e.g. Simmons and Innes 1987).

REGIONAL TEMPORAL PATTERNS IN THE CHARCOAL RECORDS

The variability of charcoal records between sites would seem to make synthesis across the region difficult. As with the interpretations of individual records (above) a simple and certainly simplistic approach is thought to suit the data best. Fig. 3.4a is a cumulative summary of the charcoal records depicted in Fig. 3.3. For each record the representation of charcoal is scored thus: absence 0, low 1, moderate 3, high 4. The 5 000 years are divided into 250 year time-slices. If all sites (Fig. 3.3) were to record high charcoal representation for one 250 year interval this would equal a percentage frequency of 100 per cent. Clearly there is no period in which fire was so important (Fig. 3.4a). Prior to 8 000 BP charcoal abundance is subdued. The earliest Holocene (pre-9 250 BP) has an almost insignificant fire incidence, only marginally increasing in the next *c*.1 250 years. But a strong shift to increasing charcoal abundance, a doubling of the fire incidence, is seen throughout the region at *c*.8 000 BP. This is then sustained until 5 000 BP.

In part this dramatic change at 8 000 BP has been reported before, at Callanish (Bohncke 1988), at one of Fossitt's (1990) sites, and by Robinson (1987) at Aukhorn. Indeed, the pattern exhibited in Fig. 3.3 at many sites in the Western Isles (Peninerine – Callanish inc.) might suggest Bennett et al's (1990) dismissal of regional correlations (above) to be incorrect. If so it certainly allows the possibility that what is being recorded is a regional increase in the burning of 'natural' plant communities, and not the product simply of local domestic fires. But could human agency have contributed to such a dramatic increase in fires over such an area?

NORTH–WEST EUROPEAN EARLY–MID HOLOCENE CLIMATE CHANGE

In interpretations of Holocene landscape evolution it is a frequent but mistaken opposition to see climate change and human impact as mutually exclusive causal factors. There is no reason in most instances to see them as hostile alternatives. Given that, however, two common discriminatory tests as to probable cause, anthropogenic or climatic, can usefully be applied to problems such as the one under discussion here. The first test is to explore the degree of synchroneity in an event across a large enough region, on the supposition that a regionally synchronous event is unlikely, this early in the Holocene, to have an anthropogenic cause. A good example of this type of reasoning is discussion of the elm (*Ulmus*) decline (e.g. Smith and Pilcher 1973, Smith 1981). Limitations exist in the precision of the dating techniques applied, and this is a problem here, as in some instances the sampling resolution of analyses is poor, the temporal precision of dates weak, there being possible difficulties in comparing radiocarbon dates obtained on lake muds with those on peats, and the likelihood of radiocarbon 'plateaux' affecting the earliest Holocene (Lowe 1991). Nevertheless, within the limits of the radiocarbon technique and the 250 year sampling resolution applied to the individual analyses here, the shift to increasing charcoal abundance at *c.*8 000 BP appears valid, although caution as to precise synchroneity needs to be made because of an apparent short-lived 'flat-spot' in the calibration curve at 7 900 BP (Pearson, Becker and Qua 1993), persisting for a few centuries.

A second test is to compare the timing of this apparently synchronous event with our understanding of the chronology of climate change. A number of palaeoclimatic reconstructions have been produced from specific sites throughout north west Europe, a region sufficiently small to expect climate shifts to be (i) more-or-less synchronous and (ii) in the same direction (but see below), and sufficiently large to allow the incorporation of a sufficient number of authoritative records. Attention is paid to one particular aspect of climate change, change in precipitation, since this is more likely to determine the combustibility of organic matter (Johnson 1992). Fluctuations in the levels of closed-basin lakes, in fluvial discharge of large rivers and changes in physical and biological properties of peat deposits provide this information. Other commonly used palaeoclimate indicators (e.g. glacier fluctuations, ice-sheet records, coleopteran data) are more likely to record temperature fluctuations, and are not used. Reconstructions more correctly record fluctuations in the 'dryness' and 'wetness' of the regional or local water-table, since in many reconstructions it is not possible to distinguish between the effects of, for instance, increasing temperature on evapotranspiration and decreases in precipitation. The data evaluated below are thought to be reliable descriptors of precipitation change, but this is not to say that the different approaches are directly comparable. Although not yet established, it may be that lake-level fluctuations and changes in mean discharge of major rivers reflect only major shifts, whereas although peat stratigraphies seem capable of generating extraordinarily detailed series of fluctuations (van Geel, Bohncke and Dee 1981; Tipping 1995b, in prep.) there is as yet little way of estimating significant from small-scale oscillations.

Our understanding of palaeoclimates has changed dramatically over the last few years. It is no longer correct to view the first 3 500–4 000 years of the Holocene as a gradual amelioration from the last glaciation. The onset of the present inter-glacial is seen to be exceptionally rapid (Atkinson et al. 1987, Taylor et al. 1993), with the 'climatic optimum' occurring within the first 1 000 years (Kutzbach and Guetter 1986). The 'Boreal-Atlantic' transition as a time of increasing precipi-tation has been revised (Chambers and Elliott 1989, Bennett and Birks 1990). Climatic variability in the Holocene may be every bit as abrupt, though not as extreme, as in the earlier Devensian Lateglacial (Beget 1983). It is clear, how-ever, that no clear synthesis of regional climatic shifts has emerged for the early Holocene, and the data are themselves inconsistent and not easily interpreted.

Studies of lake-level fluctuations throughout north west Europe all show strong correlations in support of a 'dry' phase in the early Holocene, culminating at around 9 000–8 800 BP (Gaillard 1985, Digerfeldt 1988, Magny 1992, Harrison and Digerfeldt 1993, Peglar 1979, Ince 1983, Lowe 1993, Tipping (1993, un-published). After *c*.9 000 BP there is some disagreement between 'sub'-regions. Lakes in southern Sweden (Digerfeldt 1988, Harrison and Digerfeldt 1993) are comparatively high, while those in the Jura Mountains of France (Magny 1992) show significant reductions in level. Data are few for British lakes, but O'Sullivan's (1975) work in the Cairngorm Mountains suggests closer com-parison with the Jura than with Sweden, showing a pronounced 'dry' shift at *c*.8 000 BP. Mclean (1992) reported lowered lake levels in the English Lake District between *c*.7 300 and 5 300 BP, and in the same region Oldfield (1965) argued for a drop in lake-levels at *c*.7 200 BP. This 'dry' shift at or just after *c*.7 000 BP is seen at sites in southern Scotland (Mannion 1982, Tight 1987), in south Swedish lakes (Gaillard 1985, Digerfeldt 1988) and in south west Germany (Clark et al. 1989). The end of this 'dry' phase is poorly defined, although Pennington et al. (1972) identified palynological and chemical changes from lakes in north west Scotland suggestive of increased groundwater tables after *c*.6 200 BP. Starkel's (1984) analyses of fluvial palaeo–discharges are less comprehensive than his 1991 review, but together they suggest a pre-9 000 BP phase of reduced discharge across Europe, taken to represent reduced levels of precipitation, with a second such phase defined between 8 000 and 7 000 BP, and again after 6 000 BP.

A number of peat stratigraphies suggest a phase of lowered groundwater tables before and at *c*.9 000 BP (van Geel et al. 1981; Huntley 1994; Tipping 1995a,b in prep.). A series of fluctuations in the next *c*.1 000 years (van Geel et al. 1981, Tipping 1995b) is ended by a shift to 'drier' conditions at or just before 8 000 BP, though seemingly short-lived at De Borchert (van Geel et al. 1981) and of uncertain duration at Burnfoothill Moss (Tipping 1995b). On Lewis, Wilkins (1984) noted the survival of tree stumps in peat between 9 200 and 7 800 BP, but their absence thereafter until *c*.5 000 BP, a pattern confirmed by Fossitt (1990). On Shetland radiocarbon dated tree and shrub remains broadly accord with this pattern (Bennett and Sharp 1993) save for two dated *Salix* (willow) specimens at around 7 000 BP. The preservation of wood remains prior to 7 800 BP might have been through elevated groundwater tables and increased precipitation

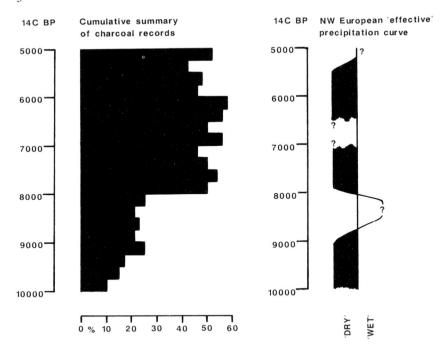

Fig. 3.4. (a) cumulative summary of the charcoal records for the sites in Fig. 3.3 plotted against ¹⁴C
years BP (see text for explanation). (b) synthesis of changes in 'effective' precipitation relevant to
northernmost Scotland from north west European palaeoclimatic reconstructions plotted against
¹⁴C years BP (see text for explanation).

(cf. Bridge, Haggart and Lowe 1990), and their absence after this due to lowered
peat growth rates in a period of reduced rainfall. Dixon (1993) produced
humification data from a radiocarbon dated peat near Lairg, south of the 'flow'
country (using colorimetry, a measure of the aerobic breakdown of peat and so
of groundwater tables; Blackford & Chambers 1991), which suggested a 'dry'
shift to have occurred at $c.8\,300$ BP. Contrary to these lines of evidence, Charman
(1994b) suggested that a drier peat surface was established at Cross Lochs earlier,
after $c.8\,800$ BP, and in central Scotland Tipping (1995a) has associated phases
of soil inwashing across peat with increased precipitation and the series of
'pluvial' episodes identified by Dubois and Ferguson (1985) from deuterium/
hydrogen ratios within subfossil pines from the Cairngorms, the first at around
7 300 BP, a second between 6 200 and 5 800 BP. However, one intriguing product
of this review is that Dubois and Ferguson's 'wet' shifts are not in accord with
most other data-sets.

Fig. 3.4b is a suggested reconstruction of 'dry'-'wet' shifts for the period
10 000–5 000 BP. Question-marks indicate uncertainties in either direction of
shift or timing, and reflect the provisional nature of the reconstruction. A dry

phase seems to characterise the north west European climate for the first 1 000 ¹⁴C years of the Holocene, detected in many analyses (above). Shortly after 9 000 BP a number of studies suggest a shift to a wetter climate, though of uncertain significance or intensity, after which a shift to increased dryness at *c*.8 000 BP is argued for. The evidence is not unanimous (above) but the majority of indicators suggest this likelihood. The course of climatic change after 8 000 BP is quite poorly defined. There is no attempt in Fig. 3.4b to indicate the intensity of climatic shifts, but Harrison and Digerfeldt (1993) stress how strongly arid was the 'dry' phase at *c*.9 000 BP.

CORRELATION OF EARLY–MID HOLOCENE CHARCOAL AND CLIMATIC RECORDS

Fig. 3.4 compares the syntheses of charcoal and 'effective' precipitation records. There is a clear danger in presenting summaries such as these, in the divorcing of these sequences from the data used in constructing them, and in the way in which these 'black-&-white' syntheses can appear too authoritative. Each of these summary curves has errors (above), and it is stressed that our knowledge both of the meaning of charcoal counts and of early Holocene climate change is far from complete. However, my interpretation of these patterns is straightforward. The intensely arid phase before *c*.9 000 BP is not accompanied by any evidence for regionally significant burning events. However, the return of drier conditions at *c*.8 000 BP does coincide with an increase in burning that is regionally significant and broadly synchronous (above).

DISCUSSION

The period 9 200–9 000 BP saw the colonisation of *Corylus* (hazel) in northern Scotland, as elsewhere in the British Isles (Birks 1989). Smith (1970) invoked human agency as a possible cause in its establishment, through deliberate fire-setting, an idea partly endorsed recently by Huntley (1993), though he considered natural fires at this time of greater aridity to have been the main agent. However, from the data in Figs 3.3 and 3.4a, and from other reviews (Clark et al. 1989, Edwards 1990, Bennett et al. 1990, Simmons 1993) there is no evidence for a generally elevated fire incidence at this time, although individual records show burning events, e.g. Cross Lochs (Charman 1992) (Fig. 3.3).

Why there should be no response in the charcoal records to this intensely dry phase (Harrison and Digerfeldt 1993) is unclear. The co-dominance of birch and hazel in the woodlands remained essentially unchanged between 9 000 and 8 000 BP; the canopy cover may indeed have been more open at 9 000 BP (Peglar 1979, Tipping in press). However, one significant floristic change between 9 000 and 8 000 BP is the establishment or expansion of areas of *Calluna* (ling) heath, on blanket peat or more likely as dry acid heath. Peat at Aukhorn began to form at *c*.8 000 BP (Robinson 1987), and was colonised by a *Calluna* heath. Peglar (1979) saw areas of acid heath spreading around the Loch of Winless in north east Caithness from c.8 400 BP. On Lewis, at Callanish, heath expanded after c.8 400 BP, around Loch Builaval Beag widespread blanket peat, colonised by *Calluna* developed at c.7 900 BP (Fossitt 1990), and heath pollen types increased at c.7 700 BP around Little Loch Roag (Birks and Madsen 1979, Birks 1991). *Calluna* heath developed at c.8 100 BP at Peninerine, at c.8 800–8 300 BP at Loch an t-Sìl, and expanded at c.8 500–8 000 BP at Loch Airigh na h-Aon Oidche, on South Uist (Edwards et al. in press) (Fig. 3.2). Elsewhere on the Western Isles and the northern mainland blanket peat spread and a strong rise in *Calluna* pollen appears to be a later phenomenon (Pennington et al. 1972; Keatinge and Dickson 1979; Bennett et al. 1990; Fossitt 1990; Mills, C. pers. comm.).

This may have had an edaphic cause. Soil acidification in the early Holocene was suggested for north west Scotland by Pennington et al. (1972), perhaps before 9 000 BP, and these increasingly acid substrates would readily have supported heathland. By c.8 000 BP there may have been many areas of heath in northernmost Scotland representing a generally greater proportion of potentially flammable organic matter. With the ensuing centuries the proportions of dry heath and blanket peat were increased rather than reduced, and this might explain the continuing importance of fire in the northern landscape (Fig. 3.4b). Climatically induced vegetation burning in this country has generally been dismissed in the past, principally because of Rackham's (1980, 1986) conviction that 'native woods (except pine-woods) will not burn' (1986: 69) by other than deliberate means. This influential argument relies on two basic tenets. The first of these is related to the natural resistance of most woodland communities. The single exception above is an important one, since the ecology of coniferous forests, even those that existed in north west Scotland, are thought to be determined by natural fire (Durno and McVean 1959). However, Rackham's views have also been challenged from analyses of early–mid Holocene woodlands in south west Germany, where Clark et al. (1989) suggested that increased natural burning events brought on by either decreased precipitation or increased temperatures may have been central in the establishment of mixed-oak forests; perhaps significantly this is dated to around 7 500 BP. But more important in the present discussion is, firstly, the recognition that the woodland communities of northernmost Scotland were totally different in composition and structure to those in eastern England which Rackham has most intensively studied, and secondly, that at or around 8 000 BP these woodlands were over quite large areas being replaced, permanently or temporarily, by *Calluna* heath which was far more readily combustible (Radley 1965).

Rackham's argument also makes no allowance for the significance of climate change in the postglacial. Major shifts in relative aridity (above) would be expected to make currently non-flammable plant communities far more susceptible to chance events such as lightning strikes. Johnson (1992) summarises much data on fire susceptibility of Canadian boreal coniferous forests, and shows that even today, with its marked human impact, lightning is the most significant cause of fires. The occurrence of individual fires is controlled by the presence of dry fuels, an ignition source and wind, but fire susceptibility is governed by the position of warm airstreams, and so is synoptically and seasonally constrained. General circulation models (GCM) of early Holocene climate change suggest that northern hemisphere summers were warmer than today (Kutzbach and Guetter 1986). High-pressure atmospheric circulation cells moved northwards following the dramatic amelioration at the start of the Holocene, and may have determined the spatial distribution of precipitation (Harrison and Digerfeldt 1993) and prevalence of weather situations capable of inducing fire.

A final aspect of current interpretations of mesolithic age burning events in northernmost Scotland, and elsewhere, concerns the necessity of anthropogenic woodland manipulation. The reconstructions of woodland density discussed earlier all stress the openness and poor canopy cover of these plant communities. Models of hunter-gatherer woodland interference (Simmons 1975, Mellars 1976) hinge on the requirement that woodlands are deliberately opened up by fire to promote the grass-herb ground layer, and so to attract grazing animals to specific points in the landscape. It is perhaps very unlikely that such modifications to woodland structure would be needed in northernmost Scotland. Some workers have argued that domestic fires were sources of charcoal (Bennett et al. 1990), but others (Robinson 1987, Charman 1992) purposefully invoked models of fire-generated woodland clearance that were developed for woodlands far to the south (e.g. Simmons and Innes 1987), of very different composition and structure. This is not to argue that anthropogenic tree clearance did not take place, but it does imply that human agency is perhaps unnecessary to explain the decline of wood-land. Climatic stresses and increased fire incidence might themselves have led to the replacement of woodland by heath, and once initiated, this would result in a 'positive feedback' of accelerating heath cover at the expense of trees.

It is interesting to speculate whether the climate-induced model of fire inci-dence developed here can be applied to more southerly locations. Of critical importance is the availability of a readily combustible fuel (Johnson 1992), and in regions where dry heath or grassland are not significant components of early and mid-Holocene landscapes, probably over most of north west Europe (Huntley and Birks 1983), there need be no recognisable climatic signal in charcoal records. One consequence of the model presented here is that the cause of burning events is made even more ambiguous (cf. Edwards 1988). Discrimi-nation between anthropogenic and climatically-induced burning events might be possible, however, if analyses are undertaken with sufficient concern for temporal and spatial precision. It might be plausible, for instance, to re-interpret Caseldine and Hatton's (1993) argument for human interference in the tran-sition from woodland to moorland on Dartmoor when it is noted that increased and sustained burning is recorded as commencing at $c.7\,700$ BP, and was appar-ently sustained until $c.6\,300$ BP. But where temporally precise analyses have been made from the comparatively dense mesolithic woods of the North York Moors burning events appear to be shortlived (Simmons, Turner and Innes 1989), and these brief events seem not to be of the same character as those in the extreme north or the far south west. We urgently need high-resolution pollen and charcoal analyses from our northern peat and lake sequences.

CONCLUSIONS

Given our current limited understanding of the sources and origins of microscopic charcoal to typical pollen sites (Clark 1988c), and the lack of synthesis for climate change in the early–mid Holocene, it is currently difficult to present the arguments outlined above as more than an hypothesis that deserves further attention. Nevertheless, there is thought to be sufficient to demand a revision of existing models of mesolithic anthropogenic impacts, given the apparent regional synchroneity at $c.8$ 000 BP of increased burning in the northernmost Scottish landscape, its occurrence at a time when increasing proportions of combustible dry heath were becoming available, and when a climatic shift to increased relative aridity would have rendered the vegetation more readily flammable.

ACKNOWLEDGEMENTS

I would like to thank Tony Pollard for inviting me to contribute to this publication; Kevin Edwards, Graeme Whittington and Ken Hirons for graciously providing much unpublished data from South Uist; and Kevin Edwards, Julie Fossitt, Jim Innes and Coralie Mills for review and discussion of this contribution.

REFERENCES

Andrews, M. V., Beck, R. B., Birks, H. J. B. and Gilberston, D. D. 1987. The past and present vegetation of Oronsay and Colonsay. In Mellars, P. (ed.), *Excavations on Oronsay – Prehistoric Human Ecology on a Small Island*. Edinburgh: Edinburgh University Press, 52–77.

Atkinson, T. C., Briffa, K. R. and Coope, G. R. 1987. Seasonal temperatures in Britain during the past 22 000 years, reconstructed using beetle remains. *Nature* 325, 587–93.

Beget, J. E. 1983. Radiocarbon-dated evidence of worldwide early Holocene climate change. *Geology* 11, 389–93.

Behre, K.-E. 1981. The interpretation of anthropogenic indicators in pollen diagrams. *Pollen et Spores* 23, 225–45.

Bennett, K. D. 1986. Competitive interactions among forest tree populations in Norfolk, England, during the last 10 000 years. *New Phytologist* 103, 603–20.

Bennett, K. D. 1989. A provisional map of forest types for the British Isles 5 000 years ago. *Journal of Quaternary Science* 4, 141–4.

Bennett, K. D. and Birks, H. J. B. 1990. Postglacial history of alder (*Alnus glutinosa* (L.) Gaertn.) in the British Isles. *Journal of Quaternary Science* 5, 123–34.

Bennett, K. D., Boreham, S., Hill, K., et al. 1993. Holocene environmental history at Gunnister, north Mainland, Shetland. In Birnie, J., Gordon, J., Bennett, K. and Hall, A. (eds), *The Quaternary of Shetland: Field Guide*. Cambridge: Quaternary Research Association, 83–98.

Bennett, K. D., Boreham, S., Sharp, M. J. and Switsur, V. R. 1992. Holocene history of environment, vegetation, and human settlement in Catta Ness, Lunnasting, Shetland. *Journal of Ecology* 80, 241–73.

Bennett, K. D., Fossitt, J. A., Sharp, M. J. and Switsur, V. R. 1990. Holocene vegetational and environmental history at Loch Lang, South Uist, Western Isles, Scotland. *New Phytologist* 114, 281–98.

Bennett, K. D. and Sharp, M. J. 1993. Holocene vegetation and environment. In Birnie, J., Gordon, J., Bennett, K. and Hall, A. (eds), *The Quaternary of Shetland: Field Guide*. Cambridge: Quaternary Research Association, 77–82.

Bennett, K. D., Simonson, W. D. and Peglar, S. M. 1990. Fire and man in post-glacial woodlands of eastern England. *Journal of Archaeological Science* 17, 635–42.

Birks, H. J. B. 1977. The Flandrian forest history of Scotland: a preliminary synthesis. In Shotton, F. W. (ed.), *British Quaternary Studies – Recent Advances*. Oxford: Clarendon Press, 119–36.

Birks, H. J. B. 1988. Long-term ecological change in the British uplands. In Usher, M. B. and Thompson, D. B. A. (eds), *Ecological Change in the Uplands*. Oxford: Oxford University Press, 37–56.

Birks, H. J. B. 1989. Holocene isochrone maps and patterns of tree-spreading in the British Isles. *Journal of Biogeography* 16, 503–40.

Birks, H. J. B. 1991. Floristic and vegetational history of the Outer Hebrides. In Pankhurst, R. J. and Mullin, J. M. (eds), *Flora of the Outer Hebrides*. London, 32–7.

Birks, H. J. B., Deacon, J. and Peglar, S. M. 1975. Pollen maps for the British Isles 5 000 years ago. *Proceedings of the Royal Society of London* B189, 87–105.

Birks, H. J. B. and Madsen, B. J. 1979. Flandrian vegetational history at Little Loch Roag, Isle of Lewis, Scotland. *Journal of Ecology* 67, 825–42.

Birnie, J., Gordon, J., Bennett, K. and Hall, A. (1993). *The Quaternary of Shetland: Field Guide*. Cambridge: Quaternary Research Association.

Blackford, J. J. and Chambers, F. M. 1991. Proxy records of climate from blanket mires: evidence for a Dark Age (1 400 BP) climatic deterioration in the British Isles. *The Holocene* 1, 63–7.

Bohncke, S. 1988. Vegetation and habitation history of the Callanish area, Isle of Lewis, Scotland. In Birks, H. H. et al. (eds), *The Cultural Landscape: Past, Present and Future*. Cambridge: Cambridge University Press, 445–62.

Bridge, M. C., Haggart, B. A. and Lowe, J. J. 1990. The history and palaeoclimatic significance of subfossil remains of *Pinus sylvestris* in blanket peats from Scotland. *Journal of Ecology* 78, 77–99.

Bunting, M. J. 1993. *Environmental History and Human Impact on Orkney*. Unpublished Ph.D. thesis, Cambridge University.

Bunting, M. J. 1994. Vegetation history of Orkney, Scotland: pollen records from two small basins in west Mainland. *New Phytologist* 128, 771–92.

Caseldine, C. J. and Hatton, J. 1993. The development of high moorland on Dartmoor: fire and the influence of Mesolithic activity on vegetation change. In Chambers, F. M. (ed.), *Climate Change and Human Impact on the Landscape*. London: Chapman & Hall, 119–31.

Chambers, F. M. and Elliott, L. 1989. Spread and expansion of *Alnus* Mill. in the British Isles: timing, agencies and possible vectors. *Journal of Biogeography* 16, 541–50.

Chambers, F. M. and Price, S.-M. 1985. Palaeoecology of *Alnus* (alder): early post-glacial rise in a valley mire, north-west Wales. *New Phytologist* 101, 333–44.

Charman, D. J. 1990. *Origins and Development of the Flow Country Blanket Mire, Northern Scotland, with Particular Reference to Patterned Fens*. Unpublished Ph.D. thesis, Southampton University.

Charman, D. J. 1992. Blanket mire formation at the Cross Lochs, Sutherland, northern Scotland. *Boreas* 21, 53–72.

Charman, D. J. 1994a. Late-glacial and Holocene vegetation history of the Flow Country, northern Scotland. *New Phytologist* 127, 155–68.

Charman, D. J. 1994b. Patterned fen development in northern Scotland: developing an hypothesis from palaeoecological data. *Journal of Quaternary Science* 9, 285–98.

Clark, J. S. 1988a. Effect of climate change on fire regimes in northwestern Minnesota. *Nature* 334, 233–5.

Clark, J. S. 1988b. Stratigraphic charcoal analysis on petrographic thin sections: application to fire history in northwestern Minnesota. *Quaternary Research* 30, 81–91.

Clark, J. S. 1988c. Particle motion and the theory of charcoal analysis: source area, transport, deposition and sampling. *Quaternary Research* 30, 67–80.

Clark, J. S., Merkt, J. and Muller, H. 1989. Post-glacial fire, vegetation and human history on the northern alpine forelands, south-western Germany. *Journal of Ecology* 77, 897–925.

Clark, R. L. 1982. Point count estimation of charcoal in pollen preparations and thin sections of sediments. *Pollen et Spores* 24, 523–35.

Coles, J. M. 1976. Forest farmers: some archaeological, historical and experimental evidence relating to the prehistory of Europe. In De Laet, S. J. (ed.), *Acculturation and Continuity in Atlantic Europe mainly during the Neolithic Period and the Bronze Age*. Bruges: De Tempel, vol. 16, 59–66.

Cronon, W. 1983. *Changes in the Land: Indians, Colonists and the Ecology of New England*. New York: Hill & Wang.

Cwynar, L. C. 1978. Recent history of fire and vegetation from laminated sediment of Greenleaf Lake, Algonquin Park, Ontario. *Canadian Journal of Botany* 56, 10–21.

Day, P. 1993. Preliminary results of high-resolution palaeoecological analyses at Star Carr, Yorkshire. *Cambridge Archaeological Journal* 3, 129–40.

Digerfeldt, G. 1988. Reconstruction and regional correlation of Holocene lake-level fluctuations in Lake Bysjon, South Sweden. *Boreas* 17, 165–82.

Dixon, S. B. 1993. *A Critical Assessment of Peat Humification at Achany Glen, Lairg, as a Proxy Climatic Record*. Unpublished B.Sc. dissertation, London University.

Dubois, A. D. and Ferguson, D. K. 1985. The climatic history of pine in the Cairngorms based on radiocarbon dates and stable isotope analysis, with an account of events leading up to its colonisation. *Review of Palaeobotany and Palynology* 46, 55–80.

Durno, S. E. and McVean, D. N. 1959. Forest history of the Beinn Eighe Nature Reserve. *New Phytologist* 58, 228–36.

Edwards, K. J. 1988. The hunter-gatherer/agricultural transition and the pollen record in the British Isles. In Birks, H. H. et al. (eds), *The Cultural Landscape: Past, Present and Future*. Cambridge: Cambridge University Press, 255–66.

Edwards, K. J. 1989. Meso-Neolithic vegetation impacts in Scotland and beyond: palynological considerations. In Bonsall, C. (ed.), *The Mesolithic in Europe*. Edinburgh: John Donald, 143–63.

Edwards, K. J. 1990. Fire and the Scottish Mesolithic: evidence from microscopic charcoal. In Vermeesch, P. and van Peer, P. (eds), *Contributions to the Mesolithic in Europe*. Leuven: Leuven University Press, 71–9.

Edwards, K. J. and Mithen, S. 1995. The colonisation of the Hebridean islands of western Scotland: evidence from the palynological and archaeological records. *World Archaeology* 26, 348–65.

Edwards, K. J. and Ralston, I. 1984. Postglacial hunter-gatherers and vegetational history in Scotland. *Proceedings of the Society of Antiquaries of Scotland* 114, 15–34.

Edwards, K. J., Whittington, G. and Hirons, K. R. 1995. The relationship between fire and long-term heathland development in South Uist, the Outer Hebrides. In Thompson, D. B. A., Hester, A. J. and Usher, M. B. (eds), *Heaths and Moorlands: Cultural Landscapes*. Edinburgh: HMSO, 240–8.

Fossitt, J. A. 1990. *Holocene Vegetation History of the Western Isles, Scotland*. Unpublished Ph.D. thesis, Cambridge University.

Gaillard, M.-J. 1985. Postglacial palaeoclimatic changes in Scandinavia and central Europe: a tentative correlation based on studies of lake level fluctuations. *Ecologia Mediterranea* 11, 159–75.

Gear, A. J. 1989. *Holocene Vegetational History and the Palaeoecology of Pinus sylvestris in Northern Scotland*. Unpublished Ph.D. thesis, Durham University.

Gear, A. J. and Huntley, B. 1991. Rapid changes in the range limits of Scots Pine 4 000 years ago. *Science* 251, 544–7.

Green, D. G. 1981. Time series and postglacial forest ecology. *Quaternary Research* 15, 265–77.

Green, D. G. 1982. Fire and stability in the postglacial forests of southwest Nova Scotia. *Journal of Biogeography* 9, 29–40.

Harrison, S. P. and Digerfeldt, G. 1993. European lakes as palaeohydrological and palaeoclimatic indicators. *Quaternary Science Reviews* 12, 233–48.

Hobbs, J. R. and Gimingham, C. H. 1987. Vegetation, fire and herbivore interactions in heathland. *Advances in Ecological Research* 16, 87–173.

Horn, S. P., Horn, R. D. and Byrne, R. 1992. An automated charcoal scanner for palaeoecological studies. *Palynology* 16, 7–12.

Huntley, B. 1993. Rapid early-Holocene migration and high abundance of hazel (*Corylus avellana* L.): alternative hypotheses. In Chambers, F. M. (ed.), *Climate Change and Human Impact on the Landscape*. London: Chapman & Hall, 205–15.

Huntley, B. 1994. Late Devensian and Holocene palaeoecology and palaeoenvironments of the Morrone Birkwoods, Aberdeenshire, Scotland. *Journal of Quaternary Science* 9, 311–36.

Huntley, B. and Birks, H. J. B. 1983. *An Atlas of Past and Present Pollen Maps for Europe: 0–13 000 Years Ago*. Cambridge: Cambridge University Press.

Ince, J. 1983. Two postglacial pollen profiles from the uplands of Snowdonia, Gwynedd, north Wales. *New Phytologist* 95, 159–72.

Iversen, J. 1941. Landnam I Danmarks Stenalder [Land occupation in Denmark's Stone Age]. *Danmarks Geologiske Undersogelse* Ser. II 66, 1–65.

Jacobi, R. M., Tallis, J. H. and Mellars, P. A. 1976. The southern pennine mesolithic and the ecological record. *Journal of Archaeological Science* 3, 307–20.

Johnson, E. A. 1992. *Fire and vegetation dynamics: studies from the North American boreal forest*. Cambridge: Cambridge University Press.

Keatinge, T. H. and Dickson, J. H. 1979. Mid-Flandrian changes in vegetation on Mainland Orkney. *New Phytologist* 82, 585–612.

Kutzbach, J. E. and Guetter, P. J. 1986. The influence of changing orbital parameters and surface boundary conditions on climatic simulations for the past 18 000 years. *Journal of Atmospheric Science* 43, 1726–59.

Lawson, T. J. and Bonsall, C. 1986. Early settlement in Scotland: the evidence from Reindeer Cave, Assynt. *Quaternary Newsletter* 49, 1–7.

Lowe, J. J. 1991. Stratigraphic resolution and radiocarbon dating of Devensian Lateglacial sediments. In Lowe, J. J. (ed.), *Radiocarbon Dating: Recent Applications and Future Potential*. Cambridge: Quaternary Research Association, 19–26.

Lowe, J. J. 1993. Isolating the climatic factors in early- and mid-Holocene palaeo-botanical records from Scotland. In Chambers, F. M. (ed.), *Climate Change and Human Impact on the Landscape*. London: Chapman & Hall, 67–82.

McLean, D. 1992. *Magnetic and Sedimentological Analyses of Quaternary Lake Sediments from the English Lake District*. Unpublished Ph.D. thesis, CNAA.

McVean, D. N. and Ratcliffe, D. A. 1962. *Plant Communities of the Scottish Highlands*. Edinburgh: HMSO.

Magny, M. 1992. Holocene lake-level fluctuations in Jura and the northern subalpine ranges, France: regional pattern and climatic implications. *Boreas* 21, 319–34.

Mannion, A. M. (1982). Palynological evidence for lake-level changes during the Flandrian in Scotland. *Transactions of the Botanical Society of Edinburgh* 44, 13–18.

Mehringer, P. J., Arno, S. F. and Petersen, K. L. 1977. Postglacial history of Lost Trail Pass Bog, Bitterroot Mountains, Montana. *Arctic and Alpine Research* 9, 345–68.

Mellars, P. 1976. Fire ecology, animal populations and man: a study of some ecological relationships in prehistory. *Proceedings of the Prehistoric Society* 42, 15–45.

Moore, P. D. 1977. Stratigraphy and pollen analysis of Claish Moss, north-west Scotland: significance for the origin of surface pools and forest history. *Journal of Ecology* 65, 375–97.

Morrison, A. and Bonsall, C. 1989. The early post-glacial settlement of Scotland: a review. In Bonsall, C. (ed.), *The Mesolithic in Europe*. Edinburgh: John Donald, 134–42.

Morrison, K. D. 1994. Monitoring regional fire history through size-specific analysis of microscopic charcoal: the last 600 years in south India. *Journal of Archaeological Science* 21, 675–85.

Murray, N. A., Bonsall, C., Sutherland, D. G., et al. 1993. Further radiocarbon determinations of middle and late Devensian age from the Creag nan Uamh Caves, Assynt, NW Scotland. *Quaternary Newsletter* 70, 1–10.

Oldfield, F. 1965. Problems of mid-postglacial pollen zonation in part of north-west England. *Journal of Ecology* 53, 247–60.

O'Sullivan, P. E. 1975. Early and middle-Flandrian pollen zonation in the eastern Highlands of Scotland. *Boreas* 4, 197–207.

Patterson, W. A., Edwards, K. J. and Maguire, D. A. 1987. Microscopic charcoal as an indicator of fire. *Quaternary Science Reviews* 6, 3–23.

Pearson, G. W., Becker, B. and Qua, F. 1993. High-precision ^{14}C measurement of German and Irish oaks to show the natural ^{14}C variations from 7 890 to 5 000 BC. *Radiocarbon* 35, 93–104.

Peglar, S. 1979. A radiocarbon-dated pollen diagram from Loch of Winless, Caithness, north-east Scotland. *New Phytologist* 82, 245–63.

Pennington, W., Haworth, E. Y., Bonny, A. P. and Lishman, J. P. 1972. Lake sediments in northern Scotland. *Philosophical Transactions of the Royal Society of London* B264, 191–294.

Rackham, O. 1980. *Ancient Woodland*. Cambridge: Cambridge University Press.

Rackham, O. 1986. *The History of the Countryside*. London: Dent.

Radley, J. 1965. Significance of major moorland fires. *Nature* 205, 1254–9.

Renberg, I. and Wik, M. 1985. Soot particle counting in recent lake sediments – an indirect dating method. *Ecological Bulletin* 37, 53–7.

Ritchie, W. A. 1966. The post-glacial rise in sea-level and coastal changes in the Uists. *Transactions of the Institute of British Geographers* 39, 79–86.

Robinson, D. E. 1984. The estimation of the charcoal content of sediments: a comparison of methods on peat sections from the island of Arran. *Circaea* 2, 121–8.

Robinson, D. E. 1987. Investigations into the Aukhorn peat-mounds, Keiss, Caithness: pollen, plant macrofossil and charcoal analyses. *New Phytologist* 106, 185–200.

Simmons, I. G. 1975. Towards an ecology of mesolithic man in the uplands of Great Britain. *Journal of Archaeological Science* 2, 1–15.

Simmons, I. G. 1993. Vegetation change during the Mesolithic in the British Isles: some amplifications. In Chambers, F. M. (ed.), *Climate Change and Human Impact on the Landscape*. London: Chapman & Hall, 109–18.

Simmons, I. G., Dimbleby, G. W. and Grigson, C. 1981. The Mesolithic. In Simmons, I. G. and Tooley, M. J. (eds), *The Environment in British Prehistory*. London: Duckworth, 82–124.

Simmons, I. G. and Innes, J. B. 1981. Tree remains in a North York Moors peat profile. *Nature* 294, 76–8.

Simmons, I. G. and Innes, J. B. 1987. Mid-Holocene adaptations and later mesolithic forest disturbance in northern England. *Journal of Archaeological Science* 14, 385–403.

Simmons, I. G., Turner, J. and Innes, J. B. 1989. An application of fine-resolution pollen analysis to later Mesolithic peats of an English upland. In Bonsall, C. (ed.), *The Mesolithic in Europe*. Edinburgh: John Donald, 206–17.

Singh, G., Kershaw, A. P. and Clark, R. 1981. Quaternary vegetation and fire history in Australia. In Gill, A. M., Groves, R. H. and Noble, I. R. (eds), *Fire and the Australian Biota*.Canberra: Australian Academy of Sciences, 23–54.

Smith, A. G. 1970. The influence of Mesolithic and Neolithic man on British vegetation: a discussion. In Walker, D. and West, R. G. (eds), *Studies in the Vegetational History of the British Isles*. Cambridge: Cambridge University Press, 81–96.

Smith, A. G. 1981. The Neolithic. In Simmons, I. G. and Tooley, M. J. (eds), *The Environment in British Prehistory*. London: Duckworth, 125–209.

Smith, A. G. 1984. Newferry and the Boreal-Atlantic Transition. *New Phytologist* 98, 35–55.

Smith, A. G. and Cloutman, E. W. 1988. Reconstruction of Holocene vegetation history in three dimensions at Waun-Fignen-Felen, an upland site in South Wales. *Philosophical Transactions of the Royal Society of London* B322, 159–219.

Smith, A. G. and Pilcher, J. R. 1973. Radiocarbon dates and vegetational history of the British Isles. *New Phytologist* 72, 903–14.

Starkel, L. 1984. The reflection of abrupt climatic changes in the relief and sequence of continental deposits. In Morner, N.-A. and Karlen, W. (eds), *Climatic Changes on a Yearly to Millennial Basis*. Dordrecht: D. Reidel, 135–46.

Starkel, L. 1991. Long-distance correlation of fluvial events in the temperate zone. In Starkel, L., Gregory, K. J. and Thornes, J. B. (eds), *Temperate Palaeohydrology: Fluvial Processes in the Temperate Zone During the Last 15 000 Years*. Chichester: Wiley, 473–96.

Stewart, O. C. 1956. Fire as the first force employed by man. In Thomas, W. L. (ed.), *Man's Role in Changing the Face of the Earth*. Chicago: Chicago University Press, 115–33.

Swain, A. M. 1973. A history of fire and vegetation in northeastern Minnesota as recorded in lake sediment. *Quaternary Research* 3, 383–96.

Swain, A. M. 1978. Environmental changes during the past 2 000 years in north-central Wisconsin: analysis of pollen, charcoal and seeds from varved lake sediments. *Quaternary Research* 10, 55–68.

Tallantire, P. A. 1992. The alder [*Alnus glutinosa* (L.) Gaertn.] problem in the British Isles: a third approach to its palaeohistory. *New Phytologist* 122, 717–31.

Taylor, K. C., Lamorey, G. W., Doyle, G. A., et al. 1993. The 'flickering switch' of late Pleistocene climate change. *Nature* 361, 432–6.

Tight, J. A. 1987. *The Late Quaternary History of Wester Branxholme and Kingside Lochs, South-East Scotland*. Unpublished Ph.D. thesis, Reading University.

Tipping, R. 1991. Climatic change in Scotland during the Devensian Lateglacial: the palynological record. In Barton, N., Roberts, A. J. and Roe, D. A. (eds), *The Lateglacial in North West Europe: Human Adaptation and Environmental Change at the End of the Pleistocene*. London: Council for British Archaeology, 7–21.

Tipping, R. 1993. A detailed early postglacial (Flandrian) pollen diagram from Cwm Idwal, north Wales. *New Phytologist* 125, 175–91.

Tipping, R. (in press). The form and fate of Scotland's woodlands. *Proceedings of the Society of Antiquaries of Scotland*.

Tipping, R. 1995a. Holocene landscape change at Carn Dubh Dubh, near Pitlochry, Perthshire. *Journal of Quaternary Science* 10, 59–75.

Tipping, R. 1995b. Holocene evolution of a lowland Scottish landscape: Kirkpatrick Fleming. I. Peat- and pollen-stratigraphic evidence for raised moss development and climatic change. *The Holocene* 5, 69–81.

Tolonen, K. 1986. Charred particle analysis. In Berglund, B. E. (ed.), *Handbook of Holocene Palaeoecology and Palaeohydrology*. Chichester: Wiley & Sons, 485–96.

Tolonen, M. 1978. Palaeoecology of annually laminated sediments in Lake Ahvenainen, S. Finland. I. Pollen and charcoal analyses and their relation to human impact. *Annales Botanici Fennici* 15, 177–208.

Turner, J., Innes, J. B. and Simmons, I. G. 1993. Spatial diversity in the mid-Flandrian vegetation history of North Gill, North Yorkshire. *New Phytologist* 123, 599–647.

Van Geel, B., Bohncke, S. J. P. and Dee, H. 1981. A palaeoecological study of an upper Late Glacial and Holocene sequence from 'De Borchert', The Netherlands. *Review of Palaeobotany and Palynology* 31, 367–448.

Waddington, J. C. B. 1969. A stratigraphic record of the pollen influx to a lake in the Big Woods of Minnesota. *Geological Society of America Special Paper* 123, 263–83.

Walker, M. J. C. 1984. A pollen diagram from St Kilda, Outer Hebrides, Scotland. *New Phytologist* 97, 99–113.

Wickham-Jones, C. 1990. *Discovery and Excavation in Scotland* 1990, 44. Periodic Publications Council.

Wickham-Jones, C. R. 1994. *Scotland's First Settlers*. Edinburgh: HMSO.

Wickham-Jones, C. and Firth, C. A. 1990. *Discovery and Excavation in Scotland* 1990, 22. Periodic Publications Council.

Wilkins, D. A. 1984. The Flandrian woods of Lewis (Scotland). *Journal of Ecology* 72, 251–8.

Wiltshire, P. A., Edwards, K. J. and Bond, S. 1992. Microbially derived metallic sulphide spherules, pollen and the waterlogging of archaeological sites. *Abstracts of the 8th International Palynological Congress, Aix-en-Provence*, 162.

Winkler, M. J. 1985. Charcoal analysis for palaeoenvironmental interpretation: a chemical assay. *Quaternary Research* 23, 313–26.

4

DAMP SQUIB

HOW TO FIRE A MAJOR DECIDUOUS FOREST
IN AN INCLEMENT CLIMATE

JENNY MOORE

On a wet day in a forest on the West Coast of Scotland, following a week of wet days, a fire must seem as likely as the proverbial flying pig. To suggest that in this environment, particularly during the Mesolithic, people were able to choose to modify their forested environment through the use of fire seems to be entering into the realms of fantasy. This paper will approach the debate (see Edwards, Tipping, this volume) from a different angle; that of forest ecology, forest fire ecology and through the application of ethnographic studies.

The concept of the non-flammability of a deciduous forest is enshrined in Oliver Rackham's famous statement:

'British woodlands (except pine) burn like wet asbestos'

(Rackham 1986: 79)

Rackham (1986) describes woodland history as beginning around 11 000 BC, when the last glaciation ended. The first colonisers were birch, aspen and sallow. They were followed by pine and hazel; then alder and oak; next lime and elm; then holly, ash, beech, hornbeam and maple. The process, Rackham suggests, was like the making of a secondary woodland now. The stability of the climate from about 6 500 to 4 000 BC allowed a series of 'climax' woodland types to develop, which covered the British Isles except for small areas of natural moorland and grassland, high mountains and other extreme environments. This, Rackham (1986) states, was the natural wildwood before the beginning of large-scale human activity. By the Neolithic, at around 4 000 BC, within a period of 200 years, large tracts of wooded country had been converted to farmland or heath. Most British species of tree are difficult to kill by fire. A felled tree will not burn where it lies but has to be cut up and stacked. A log of more than 10 in. diameter is almost fireproof.

Rackham's (1986) description of the lack of fireability of a deciduous forest was reinforced by Rowley-Conwy (1982), who argued that slash-and-burn did not happen in Neolithic temperate Europe, because, amongst other reasons, it was ecologically unlikely. These assertions have become doctrine, an effective bar to evaluation of the potential for human use of fire in the forest. Rackham (1986) creates the impression that, just prior to the Neolithic, Britain was densely forested, except for the areas mentioned above. The term 'climax' suggests that the forest community was in a permanent state of moving towards, or remaining in a state of climax, where a community which was permanent would reproduce itself indefinitely, if undisturbed. This suggests a picture of mature forest forming a canopy across most of Britain, static and undisturbed. This does not seem at all realistic when factors such as windthrow, disease and insect attack, would be occurring, even if natural fire events are entirely discounted. These perturbations were undoubtedly affecting the forest succession, resulting in breaks in the canopy and creating areas of 'edge' and 'patch' dynamics within the forest. Edwards and Ralston (1984: 24) point out that the early postglacial woodland did not everywhere form a continuous canopy, and herb communities were consistently present where such opportunities presented themselves. There is no reason to assume there was any particular variation in this picture.

Tied into this is the desire to see the wildwoods of British prehistory as the virgin forest, the Primeval wilderness undisturbed by human activity and unaltered through aeons of time. Rackham (1986) reinforces this ideology by suggesting that the prehistoric forests of Britain can be understood by reference to the undisturbed wildwoods encountered by the early American settlers, which wildwoods still survive in fragments today. Unfortunately, this completely ignores the activities of Native Americans, who had lived on the continent for thousands of years before European settlers arrived, significantly altering their environment. Fundamental to their management and utilisation strategy of the forest was the use of fire. By the time European settlers arrived, their perceived 'Primeval Forest' was, in fact, the result of careful management over thousands of years. Slightly paraphrasing Jennings (in Cronon 1983) the forests of the Americas were less virgin than widowed.

So, we are invited to understand the wildwoods of prehistory by reference to the forests of America, which had been extensively modified by the time European settlers arrived. In addition, the modifications had largely been undertaken by a method which would ostensibly not be operable by prehistoric people in Britain. A fundamental problem faced by ecologists when endeavouring to define 'climax' and 'succession', is that they are examining an anthropogenically altered environment from which they have to determine what that environment would have been like without human intervention. On this basis, we cannot strictly 'know' what a prehistoric forest would be like, and therefore we cannot dismiss the possibility that fire could be both a part of the natural forest ecology, and also a tool for human management of forest resources. We cannot simply accept that British woodlands burn like wet asbestos (Rackham 1986: 79).

That British woodlands without a high pine component were flammable in the past is evidenced by the presence of macro and microscopic charcoal. The dilemma now faced is: natural fire or anthropogenic fire? The remains of a prehistoric fire are often only microscopic charcoal. This material, which could be described as ephemeral, represents a fire *somewhere* at a particular point in time. There are, however, many ways in which microscopic charcoal could be transported to its depositional environment, away from the source, and no way of determing from the charcoal itself what type of fire lead to its creation. Notwithstanding this, from the earliest palynological work in Scotland to include identification of microscopic charcoal (Edwards 1978), there is a correlation in either the appearance of, or an increase in microscopic charcoal, in the Mesolithic. This occurs across a range of environments. Robinson (1983) and Edwards (1990) inferred Mesolithic activity from microscopic charcoal levels, where there was no direct archaeological evidence. Tipping (this volume) synthesises microscopic charcoal data on a temporal basis, with a view to identifying anthropogenic signals.

Should we take the simplistic view that all microscopic charcoal in this environment results from climatically-induced natural fires? At the other end of the spectrum, it has been suggested that such charcoal could result from large domestic fires burning over long periods (Edwards 1987, Edwards and Ralston 1984, Bennett 1990, Edwards 1990). How is it possible to differentiate between deposition from domestic fires burning over long periods of time and say, small-scale fire clearances of marginal woodland scrub?

On the whole, charcoal results from the combustion of vegetation and the processes involved, particularly in relation to forest fire will now be considered. There are standard requirements for a forest fire, all four of which must be fulfilled for a fire to occur. They are:

1. The accumulation of fuel in the form of plant material, produced by photosynthetic carbon fixation.
2. A climate favourable to plant material reaching a dry enough state, at least seasonally, to ignite.
3. An atmospheric composition in which combustion can occur.
4. Some mechanism of combustion.

(Cope and Chaloner 1985: 257)

The principle natural source of ignition for wildfires is lightning strike, and climate is probably the single most important factor governing the occurrence of wildfire, both directly and indirectly. Climate directly influences the production of potential fuel and ignition source, but also indirectly determines the status of plant communities and hence the likelihood of fire (Cope and Chaloner 1985). This assessment was made in relation to pre-Quaternary fire events, but overall holds for Quaternary incidents. However, the standardisation of requirements for a forest fire tends to lead towards an image of an 'average', or 'normal' forest fire. Each forest fire is unique.

Fires in naturally occurring vegetation fuels are usually unconfined, or free-burning. Even in vegetation fuels accumulated by humans, such as debris from timber harvesting or land clearing, fire spreads from ignition points or lines. Free burning fires establish their own boundaries, and an important factor in this is wind strength and direction. The fire will continue until it encounters a fuel it cannot ignite or a boundary it cannot leap (Albini 1993). The type of fuel tends to define the way in which the fire spreads and therefore the taxonomic grouping of the vegetation fire. A fire which spreads by flaming combustion of vegetation fuels on or near the ground is classified as a 'surface fire'. The fuel combination may include fallen dead vegetation, standing dead fuels, such as grasses or shrubs, or vegetation debris from harvesting or land clearing. A fire which spreads through the crown layer of a stand of trees is called a 'crown fire' (Albini 1993). Crown fires are often dependent on surface fires and are invariably ignited by surface fires (Van Wagner 1977). Heinselman (1981) defined seven types of forest fire regime:

1. No natural fire, or very little.
2. Infrequent light surface fires (more than 25 year return interval).
3. Frequent light surface fires (1–25 year return interval).
4. Infrequent, severe surface fires (more than 25 year return interval).
5. Short return interval crown fires and severe surface fires in combination (25–100 year return interval).
6. Long return interval crown fires and severe surface fires in combination (100–300 year return interval).
7. Very long return interval crown fires and severe surface fires in combination (over 300 year return interval).

The first point to be made here is that perception of a forest fire tends to see the 'crown' fire as exemplifying burning woodland. In other words, the major conflagration outlined in categories 5, 6 and 7 (Heinselman 1981), typifies forest fire events. This ideology leads, unconsciously, to interpretation of peaks in microscopic charcoal as potentially representing a severe fire, with resulting consequences for vegetation. Yet, most forest fires are from surface fuels (categories 2, 3 and 4) and do not always result in burning of tree crowns. The regimes summarised in categories 2, 3 and 4 would be significant for the ecological cycle of the forest, and equally should leave a significant microscopic charcoal record. The second point is that fire regimes as in categories 2, 3 and 4 are also the events which could be readily replicated by humans, manipulating the forested environment for their own purposes. Clearly, in this situation, differentiation between human manipulation of the forest through fire and these 'natural' fire events is problematic.

The above outline of fire events may have created an impression of forest fire ecology being simply a question of categories and requisite fuel. It is not. The role of fire in a modern forest ecosystem is not fully understood. Only relatively recently has the disastrous nature of fire suppression policies become fully apparent in North America. The conditions and influences, the sheer complexity of factors which allow a modern forest fire to take place have not been fully assessed. As Albini (1993) points out, an investigator must get to the fire site when fire activity takes place, and secure a vantage point to make observations and collect data. Unplanned fires are most likely to exhibit poorly understood phenomena, but are likely to be the least accessible. Add to this the necessity for detailed knowledge of pre and post fire conditions, and the scale of the problem becomes apparent.

The prehistory and history of fire represented by charcoal is limited, and biased in nature. The record is distorted geographically and temporally. The most complete records come from environments with suitable sampling areas, and a long tradition of palaeoecological research, which include western and northern Europe and eastern North America. The number and timing of fires represented by microscopic charcoal cannot be specifically defined (Clark and Robinson 1993). Bearing all this in mind, Clark and Robinson (1993) provide a summary of the fire status of Temperate Deciduous Forests in America. Many deciduous forests are dominated by species that depend largely on fire or other disturbance for regeneration. In these forests, few fires appear to occur. Before European settlement, two lines of evidence suggest that fires could have occurred regularly: forest fires occur today in regions of deciduous forest and historic records make frequent reference to fire. While twentieth-century fire regimes cannot be extrapolated into presettlement times, because of the infrequency now there is a tendency to perceive fire events as being similarly rare in the past. The fossil charcoal record is not extensive enough to clarify the significance of fire in deciduous forests in the past, but equally accounts indicate a frequency of fire not currently apparent. From the above summary, it is clear that fire was a component of these Temperate Deciduous Forests. In this relatively well recorded geographical region, it is acknowledged that human populations add a potentially important dimension to past fire regimes in deciduous forests, although this is not well understood. Human ignition has been particularly important along coastlines and river valleys of eastern North America (Patterson and Sassaman 1988), although this area should be more fire-proof with increased atmospheric moisture.

There are many references and studies on Native American use of fire in the forested environment, but one of the best syntheses has been provided by Cronon (1983). In New England, Native Americans cleared land by the simple expedient of setting fire to wood piled around the base of standing trees, which destroyed the bark and so killed the trees. Women could then plant corn amongst the leafless skeletons. During the next few years, many of the trees would topple and could be removed entirely by burning. It was apparently women who undertook this work, one Native American remembered: 'An industrious woman, when a great many logs are fallen, could burn off as many logs in one day as a smart man can chop in two or three days time with an axe' (Cronon 1983: 48).

One of the major reasons for Native Americans moving camp was the lack of

firewood. Big fires burned day and night, yet there are reports of extensive burning of sections of the surrounding forest once or twice a year, as well as utilising
it as a resource for firewood. Colonial observers understood burning simply in
terms of facilitating hunting and travel, failing to observe the subtler ecological
effects. Burning increased the rate at which forest nutrients were recycled into
the soil. The conditions created were favourable to the growth of strawberries,
blackberries, raspberries and other gatherable foods. Effectively, extensive
regions were created which resembled the boundary areas between forests and
grasslands, which was the ideal habitat for a variety of wildlife and in larger
numbers – the 'edge' effect (Cronon 1983). Native Americans used fire as a tool
in the regenerative process of the forest. How they saw the process themselves
is another matter and open to speculation. There is evidence that they did not
always get it right, at Boston and Narragansett Bay the forest was removed
altogether (Cronon 1983). It was, however, a system of forest management which
was largely successful and apparently practised over thousands of years.

At this point, it would seem useful to summarise the position. Is it possible to
fire a major deciduous forest in an inclement climate?

After discussion of concepts of 'forest', forest fire ecology is problematic both
in terms of perception and as a physical process. A 'forest fire' is clearly not a
simply definable event. No two events are the same. Forest fire regimes are highly
variable, both in cyclicity and severity. There is a tendency to see a forest fire as
the most severe events defined by Heinselman (1981), categories 5, 6 and 7. This
predisposes interpretation of past events as falling into these 'severe' categories
– crown fires. Within a forest ecosystem, the events defined in categories 2 to 4
could be essential to the maintenance of that ecosystem. Equally, a mobile human
population could easily replicate these events. It is clear there is a limited understanding of forest ecology and forest fire ecology, and for this reason alone it
should not be assumed that deciduous forests are non-flammable. Work in North
America suggests fire is part of the ecology of some deciduous forests, and
additionally, Native Americans utilised fire in their management of the forest.
Whilst analogies should always be used with caution, it is suggested here that
this evidence opens up spheres for research of prehistoric manipulation of the
woodland in Britain, by the use of fire.

If these arguments are accepted, then it will be apparent there is a potentially
almost insurmountable problem for the palaeoecological record to address. How
would it be possible to differentiate in the microscopic charcoal record, the fire
event in Heinselman's (1981) category 2, prehistoric forest management on the
lines undertaken by Native Americans and say, domestic fires burning over a
long period of time? By referring to data from Scotland, inferences will be made
as to what may be expected from the microscopic charcoal record in identifying
prehistoric forest management.

The sites examined are those referred to by Kevin Edwards in his paper:
'Fire and the Scottish Mesolithic: Evidence from Microscopic Charcoal' (1990).

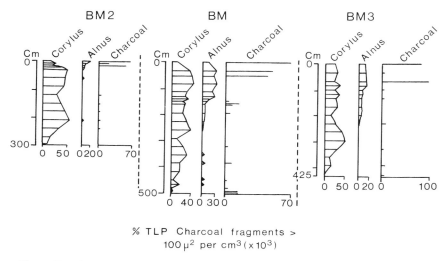

% TLP Charcoal fragments >
100 μ² per cm³ (×10³)

Fig. 4.1. Burreldale Moss.

Geographically, these sites, Burreldale Moss, Black Loch, Loch Davan and Rhoin Farm, fall within Rackham's (1986) Oak-Hazel province of southern Scotland. Rackham (1986) describes this area as having a general mosaic of these trees, with outliers of other woodland types. Edwards's (1990) objective was to see whether any fire-vegetation correspondence can be inferred from the charcoal-pollen records, but particularly examining certain distinctive palynological horizons, namely hazel maxima, the alder rise and the elm decline. The significance of these horizons is that they have been interpreted as resulting from vegetational disturbance, possibly of anthropogenic origin, during the Mesolithic or Mesolithic/Neolithic transition. Hazel is seen as a fire-climax taxon (Smith 1970), the burning of alder can promote its spread (McVean 1956a, 1956b) and the elm decline, that famous marker of the Mesolithic/Neolithic transition, may take on even greater interest if associated with fire.

Briefly, Burreldale Moss is a remnant of raised bog located in a rolling fluvio-glacial landscape 5.5 km north-east of the town of Inverurie. Mesolithic flints are known from nearby uplands. Loch Davan is a large kettle-hole loch lying in the foothills of the eastern Grampian Mountains (Edwards 1978). The nearest Mesolithic find is a microlith 9 km to the south-east. Black Loch is a rock basin site in the Ochil Hills of northern Fife. The nearest Mesolithic finds come from 9 km to the east of the loch. Aros Moss is a raised bog located at the southern end of the Kintyre Peninsula from which the Rhoin Farm sample was taken, at the northern edge of the bog. Lithic material of Mesolithic provenance are known from nearby coastal deposits (Edwards 1990).

Starting with the diagram from Burreldale Moss (Fig. 4.1), this area had been subjected to extensive peat cutting and the cores are undated, but hazel and alder

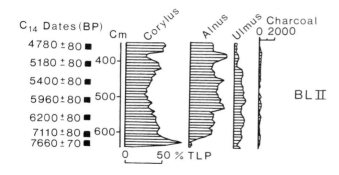

Charcoal in units of 400 μ²
as % TLP

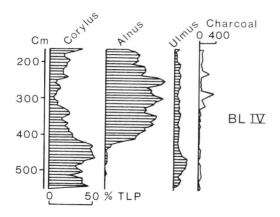

Fig. 4.2.
Black Loch.

rises are apparent in all 3 profiles. The relationship in the cores between charcoal, hazel and alder pollen is almost non-existent, except for the association between alder and charcoal in BM2. The Black Loch core (Fig. 4.2) is dated, but there is no clear correlation in the charcoal:pollen ratios. The core from Loch Davan (Fig. 4.3) is dated, but again there is no sure correlation between hazel, alder and elm pollen with charcoal levels. There does, however, seem to be an increase in alder and elm around 5 800 BP, with a slight increase in charcoal.

The Rhoin Farm diagram (Fig. 4.4) initially shows a hazel curve which is not matched by increases in charcoal. At around 6 910 ± 90 BP, there is a sharp increase in charcoal. This is accompanied by the appearance and steady rise in alder. Charcoal levels are maintained until around 5 000 BP, during which time hazel remains at a constant level, as does alder. Elm continues to be present until around 4 700 BP. The steady levels of hazel and alder, coupled with the

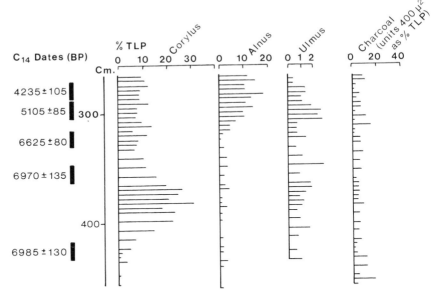

Fig. 4.3. Loch Davan.

continuous presence of microscopic charcoal, a pattern which continues for 2 000 years, could be the sequence which is representative of a human fire-maintained landscape. In other words, instead of looking for great fluctuations in the vegetation sequence to accompany quantities of charcoal, a regularity in the vegetation patterning, particularly that of fire-responsive species could be the indicator of human manipulation of the environment. Of the sites considered here, Rhoin Farm has the strongest archaeological associations. If more sites like this could be examined in detail palynologically, including the recording of microscopic charcoal, then potentially a model could be developed for representation of an anthropogenically fire-maintained landscape. Areas of activity, particularly in the Mesolithic, could be identified without the presence of artefacts.

It is the correlation of maintained levels of species with microscopic charcoal which leads to the interpretation of human fire maintenance. If the charcoal resulted from a sequence of 'natural' fire events, such as under Heinselman's (1981) categories 2 to 4, there could potentially be more variation in the pollen spectra. Further, if the charcoal resulted from domestic fires burning over long periods of time, then other factors might be expected to be reflected in the pollen diagram, rather than the regularity apparent. If the arguments for a fire-maintained landscape at Rhoin Farm are accepted, then it should be pointed out that this data was not the result of an extensive search, and therefore biased. Partly this is because not every palynologist quantifies microscopic charcoal and therefore the correlation of vegetation and charcoal is not possible. Fortunately,

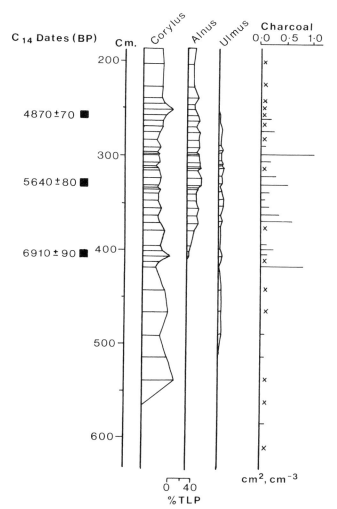

Fig. 4.4.
Rhoin Farm.

Scotland has some of the most extensive data on microscopic charcoal, due to the work of Kevin Edwards and Richard Tipping, which, combined with detailed pollen diagrams, have the potential for proving, or disproving, this theory.

Temperate deciduous forests are not infinitely flammable across time and space, but equally the dismissal of any conflagration possibilities seems somewhat simplistic. Relating forest ecology today to forest ecology of the past is, in ecological terms, problematic, and compounded by the desire of some to see prehistoric forests in the romanticised light of the Forest Primeval. Additionally, perhaps there has been a too simplistic view of what constitutes a 'forest fire'. A forest fire is clearly not a simply definable event, and is unrepeateable in terms of replicability. Fire regimes in the forest are highly variable, both in cyclicity and severity. There is, however, a tendency to see forest fires in terms of the most severe events, which rarely occur, and accordingly interpret past occurrences in this light. Increased levels of charcoal in a sample tend to be equated with a major conflagration, and therefore major changes in the pollen spectra. It may be that a moderate increase and steadily maintained levels of charcoal, with constant patterning in the pollen assemblage, are more informative as to human fire-maintenance activity.

Kauffman et al. (1993) recently defined the criteria within which to understand the role humans play in shaping fire regimes and ecosystem properties. They felt it was important to quantify spatial and temporal variables such as:

1. the areal extent and temporal frequency of burning,
2. fire typology (i.e. surface -v- crown fire),
3. post-fire changes in ecosystem structure or land use,
4. determinants of interactions between humans, fires and ecosystems.

(Kauffman et al. 1993)

Creating models using palynological and microscopic charcoal data, within this framework has the potential to inform on human use of fire in the landscape – how to fire a major deciduous forest in an inclement climate.

ACKNOWLEDGEMENTS

The figures were redrawn by Colin Merrony and reproduced by kind permission of Kevin Edwards.

REFERENCES

Albini, F. A. 1993. Dynamics and modelling of vegetation fires: observations. In Crutzen, P. J. and Goldhammer, J. G. (eds), *Fire in the Environment: The Ecological, Atmospheric, and Climatic Importance of Vegetation Fires.* Chichester: John Wiley & Sons, 39–52.

Bennett, K. D., Simonson, W. D. and Peglar, S. M. 1990. Fire and man in post-glacial woodlands of eastern England. *Journal of Archaeological Science* 17, 635–42.

Cronon, W. 1983. *Changes in the Land: Indians, Colonists, and the Ecology of New England.* New York: Hill & Wang.

Clark, J. S. and Robinson, J. 1993. Paleoecogy of fire. In Crutzen, P. J. and Goldhammer, J. G. (eds), *Fire in the Environment: The Ecological, Atmospheric, and Climatic Importance of Vegetation Fires.* Chichester: John Wiley & Sons.

Cope, M. J. and Chaloner, W. G. 1985. Wildfire: an interaction of biological and physical processes. In Tiffney, Bruce H. (ed.), *Geological Factors and the Evolution of Plants.* Yale: Yale University Press, 257–77.

Edwards, K. J. 1978. *Palaeoenvironmental and Archaeological Investigations in the Howe of Cromar, Grampian Region, Scotland.* Ph.D. thesis, University of Aberdeen.

Edwards, K. J. 1990. Fire and the Scottish Mesolithic: evidence from microscopic charcoal. In Vermeersch, P. M. and Van Peer, P. (eds), *Contributions to the Mesolithic in Europe.* Leuven: Leuven University Press, 71–9.

Edwards, K. J. and Ralston, I. 1984. Postglacial hunter-gatherers and vegetational history in Scotland. *Proceedings of the Society of Antiquaries of Scotland* 114, 15–34.

Heinselman, M. L. 1981. Fire regimes and ecosystem properties. In *Fire Regimes and Ecosystem Properties: Proceedings of the Conference*. US Dept of Agriculture, Forest Service, General Technical Report WO-26, Portland, Oregon, 7–57.

Kauffman, J. B., Christensen, N. L., Goldammer, J. G., et al. 1993. Group report: the role of humans in shaping fire regimes and ecosystem properties. In Crutzen, P. J. and Goldhammer, J. G. (eds), *Fire in the Environment: The Ecological, Atmospheric, and Climatic Importance of Vegetation Fires*. Chichester: John Wiley & Sons.

McVean, D. N. 1956a. Ecology of *Alnus glutinosa* (L.) Gaertn. V: notes on some British alder populations. *Journal of Ecology* 44, 321–30.

McVean, D. N. 1956b. Ecology of *Alnus glutinos* (L.) Gaertn. VI: post-glacial history. *Journal of Ecology* 44, 331–3.

Patterson III, W. A. and Sassaman, K. E. 1988. Indian fires in the prehistory of New England. In Nicholas, G. P. (ed.), *Holocene Human Ecology in Northeastern North America*. New York: Plenum Press.

Rackham, O. 1986. *The History of the Countryside*. London: J. M. Dent.

Robinson, D. E. 1983. Possible Mesolithic activity in the west of Arran: evidence from peat deposits. *Glasgow Archaeological Journal* 10, 1–6.

Rowley-Conwy, P. 1982. Forest grazing and clearance in temperate Europe with special reference to Denmark: an archaeological view. In Bell, M. and Limbrey, S. (eds), *Archaeological Aspects of Woodland Ecology*. British Archaeological Reports International Series 142, 199–215.

Smith, A. G. 1970. The influence of Mesolithic and Neolithic man on British vegetation. In Walker, D. and West, R. G. (eds), *Studies in the Vegetational History of the British Isles*. Cambridge: Cambridge University Press, 81–96.

Van Wagner, C. E. 1977. Conditions for the start and spread of crown fires. *Canadian Journal of Forest Research* 7, 23–34.

5

CLIMATE CHANGE EVENTS AS SEEN IN THE GREENLAND ICE CORE (GISP2)

IMPLICATIONS FOR THE MESOLITHIC OF SCOTLAND

PAUL A. MAYEWSKI, PAUL C. BUCKLAND, KEVIN J. EDWARDS, LOREN D. MEEKER AND SUZANNE O'BRIEN

INTRODUCTION

Traditional interpretations of climatic change have relied heavily upon bio- and litho-stratigraphic data, such as those based on peat stratigraphy, pollen content, tree stumps and sedimentological change (Bell and Walker 1992, Lowe 1993). These described a situation whereby the arctic conditions at the end of the Lateglacial, *c.*10 000 radiocarbon years BP, were followed by a rise in summer temperature to levels warmer than those of today, and cold winters, by *c.*8 000 BP. This 'Boreal' period was succeeded by the 'Atlantic' phase or 'Climatic Optimum', *c.*8 000–6 500 BP, characterised by warm summers, mild winters and abundant precipitation. Challenges to these orthodoxies have come from within palynology itself (Huntley 1988, 1990; MacDonald and Edwards 1991) as well as independently from Coleoptera (beetle) evidence (Atkinson et al. 1987). A fuller understanding of climate change, mediated through a knowledge of northern hemispheric climatic circulation patterns reflected in records of oxygen isotopes from deep sea cores and embedded deep in the ice sheets of Greenland, has revolutionised our thinking concerning climatic change and its rapidity (Imbrie and Imbrie 1979, Dansgaard et al. 1989, Taylor et al. 1993).

This short contribution seeks to examine the evidence from the most recent Greenland Ice Sheet Project (GISP2) and to consider some of the implications for the study of the Mesolithic period in Scotland. In an effort to demonstrate the nature of the long term patterns evident in the ice core record, data covering the last 18 000 years are presented and provide a context for the shorter interlude of the Mesolithic.

Unless indicated otherwise, dates are expressed as calendar years before AD 2 000. Years BP (before present) refer to radiocarbon years where 'present' = AD 1950.

THE GREENLAND ICE SHEET PROJECT

Recent results from the GISP2 ice core (Summit region, central Greenland) have demonstrated the remarkable variety and detail of climate change responses preserved in ice core records over the last 110 000 years (e.g. Taylor et al. 1993; Mayewski et al. 1993a, b, 1994). The Summit region is particularly well-suited as an ice core site because, *inter alia*, it has an approximate mean annual air temperature of −31°C. Dating of the 18 000 years of the GISP2 record discussed in this chapter is based on multi-parameter annual layer counting (Alley et al. 1993; Meese et al. 1994a, b). Continuous, high resolution (approximately bi-annual through the period described here), multivariate samples derived from common sections in the ice core, provide a robust characterisation of environmental change over the North Atlantic region. The focus is upon the GISP2 glacio-chemical series (sodium, potassium, magnesium, calcium, ammonium, chloride, nitrate and sulphate); a measure of more than 95 per cent of the soluble constituents in the atmosphere over Greenland. These series reflect a variety of source and transport histories (e.g. marine and terrestrial sources).

Atmospheric Circulation and the Polar Circulation Index

Records of change in atmospheric chemistry are important for palaeoclimatology because the atmosphere responds more quickly than other components of the Earth system and holds within it measures of both the cause(s) of and response(s) to climate change on all time scales. For example, a major feature of atmospheric circulation, the polar vortex has, in modern times, been linked, through changes in size and shape, to variations in northern hemispheric climatic conditions (Tinsley 1988, Labitzkie and van Loon 1989, Burnett 1993). At longer time scales, modelling studies reveal the influence continental ice sheets have had on tropospheric circulation during the last glaciation (Broccoli and Manabe 1987).

Mayewski et al. (1993a, 1994) have developed a measure of the joint behaviour of glaciochemical series based on empirical orthogonal function (EOF) decomposition (Peixoto and Oort 1992) which facilitates the interpretation of the series as records of atmospheric circulation. The dominant EOF of the suite of eight chemical series explains such a relatively high degree of variance (73 per cent) that it must describe a large-scale feature of northern hemisphere climate. As noted in earlier work (Mayewski et al. 1993a, 1994), it represents a well-mixed atmosphere in which the concentrations of all chemical 'species', except ammonium (Meeker et al. in review), increase or decrease together in fixed proportions. The time series describing the dynamics (i.e. increase and decrease from mean values) of the well-mixed atmosphere represented by the dominant EOF is called the 'polar circulation index' (PCI) (Mayewski et al. 1994). In effect, the PCI provides a relative measure of the average size and intensity of polar atmospheric circulation in the Northern Hemisphere. In general terms PCI values increase (e.g. more continental dusts and marine contributions) during colder portions of the record (stadials) and decrease during warmer periods (inter-stadials and interglacials). It is the PCI series (the dominant feature of the GISP2 chemistry series) which provides an overall view of the last 18 000 years (Fig. 5.1).

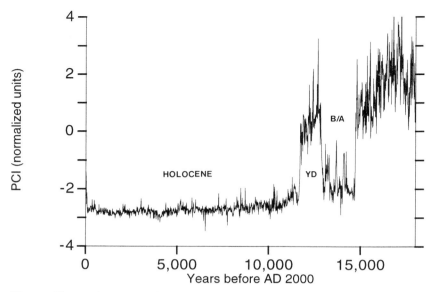

Fig. 5.1. The PCI (50-year sampling, normalised units) over the last 18 000 calendar years. B/A = Bølling/Allerød and YD = Younger Dryas.

The Glacial/Interglacial Transition and the Deglaciation

Changes in Polar Cell Size

The most dramatic changes in the PCI occur at 14 720, 12 940 and 11 640 years ago. The first, a contraction of the atmospheric polar cell that occurs in less than a decade, represents the rapid depletion of sea ice cover over the North Atlantic (Mayewski et al. 1994). The timing of this massive decrease in sea ice cover is consistent with sudden warming at 12 700 ^{14}C years ago (14 908 calendar years ago based on the correction from Bard et al. [1993]) throughout the North Atlantic recorded in oxygen isotopes (Siegenthaler et al. 1984, Lotter and Zbinden 1989), beetle (Atkinson et al. 1987) and pollen (Lotter and Zbinden 1989) records.

The remaining dramatic changes in the PCI are associated with the onset and decline of the Younger Dryas (YD), the most significant rapid climate change event that occurred during the last deglaciation of the North Atlantic region. Previous ice core studies have focused on the abrupt termination of this event (Dansgaard et al. 1989) because this transition marks the end of the last major climate reorganisation during the deglaciation. Most recently the YD has been re-dated and reinterpreted by Alley et al. (1993) as a 1 300 ± 70 year duration event that terminated abruptly, as evidenced by a ~7°C rise in temperature (deduced from the oxygen isotope record developed by Grootes et al. 1993) and a twofold increase in accumulation rate, at ~11 600 years ago.

Changes in Atmospheric Chemistry and Circulation

Using the glaciochemical record it is possible to reconstruct atmospheric conditions during the generally milder period preceding the YD called the Bølling/Allerød (B/A), the YD, and the Holocene (Mayewski et al. 1993a).

During the B/A, levels of crustal and seasalt species over the Greenland ice sheet were generally higher than during the Holocene, but significantly lower than during the YD. These relative levels provide an estimate of storminess (higher concentrations) over continental and marine surfaces. During one portion of the B/A (13 713–13 531 years ago) there is evidence of a massive increase in sulphate in the atmosphere. The size of this increase and the timing relative to other chemical species could suggest a localised source such as marine biogenic sulphur gas production from open water areas in sea ice (polynas) or a prolonged period of volcanism. Ammonium and nitrate concentrations appear to be relatively unperturbed during most of the B/A suggesting relatively stable continental biogenic source strength. However, an increase in ammonium at 12 859–12 786 years ago may signal the destruction of B/A biomass in response to the onset of cooler and drier YD climate conditions.

Seasalt, crustal, and sulphate species increased from B/A to YD levels dramatically over a period of ~10 years. Frequent, massive, short-term (decadal or less) variations in crustal and seasalt levels characterise the yearly YD record, reflecting the significant atmospheric reorganisation produced by this transition.

The Holocene

Although variability in the glaciochemical record is significantly subdued in the Holocene portion of the record (11 640 years ago to present) atmospheric circulation patterns during this period are perhaps the most complex of the entire 110 000 year long GISP2 record. During the Holocene, the high latitudes of the North Atlantic are no longer dominated by one major circulation pattern (the polar cell) but, rather, by the interaction of lower latitude air masses, changing land and sea ice geography and rising sea level. EOF analysis restricted to the Holocene glaciochemical series shows that a smaller, but still substantial, proportion of the variability (41 per cent) in the eight chemical species is explained by the first EOF. In this instance, however, this dominant component represents a well-mixed atmosphere and contains a positive ammonium contribution, reflecting the enhanced importance of mid and low latitude features of the more complex circulation patterns resulting from the northerly retreat of the continental ice sheets.

Total dust (calcium, and equivalent to total of all terrestrial components of the ions measured in this study) and total seasalt (sodium, and equivalent to total of all marine salt components of the ions measured in this study) concentration profiles, displayed as robust spline (~100 year smoothing) versions of the original GISP2 biannual series, are shown for the Holocene (Fig. 5.2). During this time, almost all of the total dust is derived from continental sources and approximately

95 per cent of the sodium is derived from sea salt. Elevated concentrations of total dust and seasalt species in the core result from increased storminess over terrestrial and marine surfaces.

Based on calibration using detailed glaciochemical analyses from snowpits in central Greenland, the presence of these elevated concentrations suggests that present day total dust and total seasalt concentrations peak during mid-winter to early spring (Whitlow et al. 1992). In addition to the general intensification of atmospheric circulation during this season (Erickson et al. 1986), this timing may be a manifestation of late winter cyclonic storms that travel over continental North America incorporating crustal dusts and picking up seasalt species as they cross the North Atlantic. Provided that similar meteorological and environmental conditions generated elevated species concentrations at Summit in the past, this suggests that extended periods of winter-like circulation patterns and storm conditions recurred with some regularity throughout the Holocene.

The total seasalt record displays several notable events of lower concentration interpreted as periods of decreased marine storminess and generally milder conditions (Fig. 5.2). One of these coincides with the timing of the Climatic Optimum (~8 000–6 500 years ago). The total dust record does not display a definitive equivalent of the Climatic Optimum because this record is sensitive to changes in source area; at this time, these were influenced by lower than present sea level (with increased exposure of continental shelves) and remnants of declining European and North American ice cover (with increased outwash surface exposure).

The total dust record displays a prolonged period of increase which ended 5 100 years ago. Another such period starts over 550 years ago and lasts almost until the present. Increased total dust levels in the first half of the Holocene result from enhanced accessibility of dusts due to lower sea level and exposed continental shelves (O'Brien et al. in review). Within this period of heightened dust availability are several periods of increased totals, notably 6 100–5 100 years ago. This period and the period commencing 550 years ago coincide (O'Brien et al. in review) with periods of worldwide glacier expansion (Denton and Karlen 1973) and cool events synthesised from a variety of proxy records. The most recent expansion (550 years ago) accords with the onset of the Little Ice Age (Grove 1988, Mayewski et al. 1993b).

The total seasalt series is fairly similar to the total dust series except that early Holocene increases are more discretely divided. Increased levels are found during the following periods: >11 600–10 700, 9 300–8 100, 6 400–6 200, 5 900–5 500, 3 700–3 400, 3 100–2 800 and 550 to near present. Storminess increased in marine environments during these periods. Unlike the total dust record, the total seasalt series is not affected by changes in sea level. As a consequence, the total seasalt series provides a direct interpretation of climate change.

Estimates of volcanic source sulphate during the Holocene (Fig. 5.2) are provided by the residuals obtained when baseline values (approximated by robust

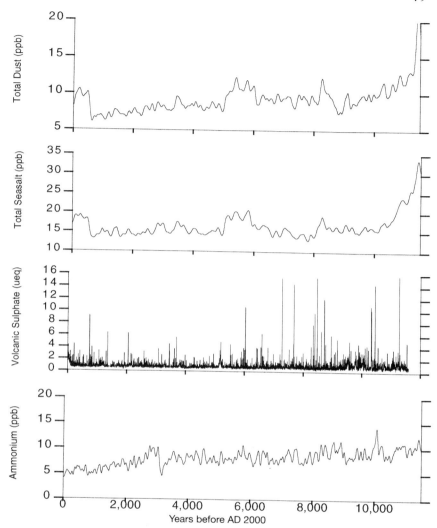

Fig. 5.2. Total dust, total seasalt sodium and ammonium (all reported as spline smooths of the original data, in ppb) and volcanic source sulphate (raw series, in micro-equivalents) over the last 11 500 calendar years.

splines) are subtracted from original biannual series. Volcanic source sulphate appears to be highest in the early Holocene, perhaps in response to unloading of the Earth's crust during deglaciation (Zielinski et al. 1994). Specific volcanic events during this period can be found in Zielinski et al. (1994, in review). This increased period of volcanic activity could have created numerous several year long periods of decreased temperatures in response to sulphate shielding of incoming solar radiation.

Maxima in ammonium concentration have been demonstrated to be an indicator of biomass burning events (Legrand et al. 1992, Taylor et al. 1993, Mayewski et al. 1993b, Whitlow et al. 1994), although the source of these events remains controversial. Ammonium concentrations (presented as ~100 year smoothing of the original biannual series) suggest a marked decline during the Holocene. Ammonium is the only GISP2 chemical species whose concentrations over the past 110 000 years vary inversely with those of the well-mixed atmosphere described by the PCI. Unlike other species, most of its variance (72 per cent) is associated with the second EOF (whose dynamics are statistically uncorrelated with the PCI). Thus, the ammonium series provides a view of palaeoclimate in the northern hemisphere which complements that provided by the PCI. In recent work, Meeker et al. (in review) demonstrated that the primary control on ammonium concentration is solar insolation, in particular the ~21 000 year precessional cycle (Berger 1978). This cycle attains its maxima (in the northern latitudes) when the Earth traverses its perihelion during the northern hemisphere summer and it has been decreasing for the past 11 000 years since this last occurred. From this perspective, the decreasing trend in ammonium concentrations throughout the Holocene is due to reduced continental biogenic production as a result of decreased insolation in northern latitudes.

SCOTTISH TERRESTRIAL BIOTIC DATA AND SOME IMPLICATIONS
FOR THE MESOLITHIC

The ice core evidence shows that the Mesolithic period (in Britain, c.11 640–5 730 calendar years BP [c.10 100–5 000 ^{14}C years BP]), began with a very rapid change of climate – perhaps of the order of 20 years or less – in which arctic conditions were replaced with summer temperatures warmer than those at the present. Conditions then remained fairly stable until about 6 000 cal. BP (5 250 uncal. BP), close to the Mesolithic–Neolithic transition (Edwards 1988).

The pattern of changes during the Lateglacial and early Holocene is supported by the fossil Coleoptera evidence (Atkinson et al. 1987, Buckland 1995) including that from Scotland (Bishop and Coope 1977). It is only from Brighouse Bay, Solway Firth, that early Holocene insect fauna is available (Ibid.). Unfortunately, only a single radiocarbon sample from the site is available (9 640 ± 180, Q-398) and the deposits would appear to cover a restricted period. Nevertheless, the Holocene fauna includes a number of species which do not range as far north as Scotland at the present time (e.g. *Odacantha melanura* L. and *Agonum thoreyi* Dej.) and hence thermal conditions, at least as warm or slightly warmer than today, were established very rapidly in southwestern Scotland.

Palynological data for the Lateglacial and early Holocene are very widespread within Scotland and have tended to reflect vegetational patterns in which a time lag between climate change and a floristic response is evident (e.g. Lowe and Walker 1977, Pennington 1977). Thus, the stadial and interstadial changes indicated by the ice core and insect data appear to be less abrupt in the pollen record, and the transition to warm conditions following the close of the Younger Dryas (Loch Lomond) stadial seems to be more gradual. Recent work, however, indicates sharp changes in environmental conditions during the Lateglacial (Edwards and Whittington 1994) and the pollen–climate curve based on data from Morrone Birkwoods, Aberdeenshire (Huntley 1994) also shows a rapid Postglacial amelioration of climate. Nevertheless, the seeming time-lag between early Holocene climate warming and the appearance of an extensive woodland cover for much of Scotland is not surprising; climate warming and attendant soil development would need to pave the way for colonisation by such woodland taxa as hazel (*Corylus avellana*), elm (*Ulmus*), oak (*Quercus*) and alder (*Alnus*), quite apart from their need to migrate from what may have been distant source areas (cf. Birks 1989, Lowe 1993). Local populations of birch (*Betula*), willow (*Salix*) and juniper (*Juniperus communis*) would, however, have been able to expand rapidly as Holocene warming began. The time-lag for the migration of arboreal pollen taxa would mean that any reflection of a Climatic Optimum is likely to be retarded.

The open landscape of the early Holocene, extending across a North Sea basin dry as a result of low sea level, would have fostered a continuity of hunting technique with the Late Upper Palaeolithic, where drives and large scale kills would be expected to predominate over the hunting of individual animals. Red deer replaced reindeer as the principal herd animal and the increased plant productivity of the temperate landscape may have led to some innovation in terms of available plant foodstuffs (cf. Clarke 1976). There is no unequivocal evidence, however, for a human presence in Scotland prior to the mid-ninth millennium BP (^{14}C years), which provides the earliest Mesolithic dates from Kinloch, Isle of Rhum (Wickham-Jones 1990). The Craig nan Uamh bone caves at Inchnadamph, northwest Scotland, are no longer thought to indicate a Lateglacial occupation (Murray et al. 1993), but the discovery of a tanged point on the island of Islay, together with possible palynological evidence for early (perhaps pre-9 000 ^{14}C years BP) human impact (Edwards and Mithen 1995), may demonstrate that more definite discoveries of early Holocene hunter-gatherers can be anticipated. In the absence of lithic artefacts, pollen and microscopic charcoal evidence provide circumstantial evidence for Mesolithic peoples in parts of Scotland where peat, coastal sands and raised sea levels may hide hunter-gatherer sites (Edwards 1990 and this volume, Edwards et al. 1995). The ameliorated nature of the climate during the Mesolithic period would certainly have enabled plants useful to people to colonise even the extremities of Scotland, including island groups such as the Outer Hebrides and Shetland (Edwards this volume). If the ice core record provides evidence for a prolonged period of drought or warming during the period ~8 000–6 500 BP, this might explain enhanced natural burning and charcoal production (cf. Tipping, this volume), but whether this would have meant microscopic charcoal levels above background levels relative to anthropogenic fires (Edwards this volume) is unknown. As noted above, ammonium concentration values (Fig. 5.2) show an overall sustained decline from the start of the Holocene.

The GISP2 core indicates a period of climatic instability around 6 100–5 100 calendar years ago (c. 5 300–4 500 ^{14}C years BP). This covers the end of the Mesolithic and the early stages of the established Scottish Neolithic. It would be unwise to introduce climatic elements, solely at any rate, into the interpretation of such a cultural change for Scotland – the Meso-Neolithic transition took place much earlier in parts of continental Europe. However, even if changes in the manner in which prehistoric Scottish landscapes have been exploited were driven ultimately by people, those changes were mediated by flora, fauna, soils and climate, any of which could have had a profound or unpredictable influence, especially in marginal areas.

REFERENCES

Alley, R. B., Meese, D. A., Shuman, A. J., et al. 1993. Abrupt accumulation increase at the Younger Dryas termination in the GISP2 ice core. *Nature* 362, 527–9.

Atkinson, T. C., Briffa, K. R. and Coope, G. R. 1987. Seasonal temperatures in Britain during the past 22 000 years, reconstructed using beetle remains. *Nature* 325, 587–92.

Bard, E., Arnold, M., Fairbanks, R. G. and Hamelin, B. 1993. ^{230}Th-^{234}U and ^{14}C ages obtained by mass spectrometry on corals. *Radiocarbon* 35, 191–9.

Bell, M. and Walker, M. J. C. 1992. *Late Quaternary Environmental Change: Physical and Human Perspectives*. London: Longman.

Birks, H. J. B. 1989. Holocene isochrone maps and patterns of tree-spreading in the British Isles. *Journal of Biogeography* 16, 503–40.

Bishop, W. W. and Coope, G. R. 1977. Stratigraphical and faunal evidence for late-glacial and early Flandrian environments in south-west Scotland. In Gray, J. M. and Lowe, J. J. (eds), *Studies in the Scottish Lateglacial Environment*. London: Pergamon, 61–88.

Buckland, P. C. 1995. Origins of Atlantic island biota. *Second Annual PALE Research Meeting (4–6 February 1995)* (Abstract no. 14). Seattle: University of Washington.

Buckland, P. C., Dugmore, A. J. and Edwards, K. J. (in press). Bronze Age myths? Volcanic activity and human response in the Mediterranean and North Atlantic regions. *Quaternary Science Reviews*.

Burnett, A. W. 1993. Size variations and long-wave circulation within the January Northern Hemisphere circumpolar vortex 1946–89. *Journal of Climate* 6, 1914–20.

Clarke, D. L. 1976. Mesolithic Europe: the economic basis. In Sieveking, G. de G., Longworth, I. and Wilson, K. (eds), *Problems in Economic and Social Archaeology*. London: Duckworth, 449–82.

Dansgaard, W., White, J. W. C. and Johnsen, S. J. 1989. The abrupt termination of the Younger Dryas climate event. *Nature* 339, 532–3.

Denton, G. H. and Karlen, W. 1973. Holocene climatic variations – their pattern and possible cause. *Quaternary Research* 3, 155–205.

Edwards, K. J. 1988. The hunter-gatherer/agricultural transition and the pollen record in the British Isles. In Birks, H. H., Birks, H. J. B., Kaland, P. E. and Moe, D.

(eds), *The Cultural Landscape: Past, Present and Future*. Cambridge: Cambridge University Press, 255–66.

Edwards, K. J. 1990. Fire and the Scottish Mesolithic: evidence from microscopic charcoal. In Vermeersch, P. M. and Van Peer, P. (eds), *Contributions to the Mesolithic in Europe*. Leuven: Leuven University Press, 71–9.

Edwards, K. J. and Mithen, S. 1995. The colonisation of the Hebridean islands of western Scotland: evidence from the palynological and archaeological records. *World Archaeology* 26, 348–65.

Edwards, K. J. and Whittington, G. 1994. Lateglacial pollen sites in the Western Isles of Scotland. *Scottish Geographical Magazine* 110, 33–9.

Edwards, K. J., Whittington, G. and Hirons, K. R. 1995. The relationship between fire and long-term wet heath development in South Uist, Outer Hebrides, Scotland. In Thompson, D. B. A., Hestor, A. J. and Usher, M. B. (eds), *Heaths and Moorland: Cultural Landscapes*. Edinburgh: HMSO, 240–8.

Erickson, D. J., Merrill, J. T. and Duce, R. A. 1986. Seasonal estimates of global atmospheric seasalt distribution. *Journal of Geophysical Research* 9, 1 067–72.

Grootes, P. M., Stuiver, M., White, J. W. C., et al. 1993. Comparison of oxygen isotope records from the GISP2 and GRIP Greenland ice cores. *Nature* 366, 552–4.

Grove, J. M. 1988. *The Little Ice Age*. London: Methuen.

Huntley, B. 1988. Europe. In Huntley, B. and Webb, T. III (eds), *Vegetation History*. Dordrecht: Kluwer Academic Publishers, 341–83.

Huntley, B. 1990. European post-glacial forests: compositional changes in response to climatic change. *Journal of Vegetation Science* 1, 507–18.

Huntley, B. 1994. Late-Devensian and Holocene palaeoecology and palaeoenvironments of the Morrone Birkwoods, Aberdeenshire, Scotland. *Journal of Quaternary Science* 9, 311–36.

Imbrie, J. and Imbrie, K. P. 1979. *Ice Ages: Solving the Mystery*. London: Macmillan.

Labitzke, K. and van Loon, H. 1989. Associations between the 11-year solar cycle, the QBO and the atmosphere. Part III: Aspects of association. *Journal of Climate* 2, 554–65.

Legrand, M., DeAngelis, M., Staffelbach, T., et al. 1992. Large perturbations of ammonium and organic acids content in the Summit-Greenland ice cores. Fingerprint from forest fires? *Geophysical Research Letters* 19, 473–5.

Lotter, A. F. and Zbinden, H. (1989). Late-Glacial pollen analysis, oxygen-isotope record and radiocarbon stratigraphy from Rotsee (Lucerne), Central Swiss Plateau. *Eclogae Geologicae Helvetiae* 82, 191–202.

Lowe, J. J. 1993. Isolating the climatic factors in early- and mid-Holocene palaeobotanical records from Scotland. In Chambers, F. M. (ed.), *Climate Change and Human Impact on the Landscape*. London: Chapman & Hall, 67–82.

Lowe, J. J. and Walker, M. J. C. 1977. The reconstruction of the Lateglacial environment in the Southern and Eastern Grampian Highlands. In J. M. Gray and J. J. Lowe (eds), *Studies in the Scottish Lateglacial environment*. London: Pergamon, 101–18.

MacDonald, G. M. and Edwards K. J. 1991. Holocene palynology. I: Principles, population and community ecology, palaeoclimatology. *Progress in Physical Geography* 15, 261–89.

Mayewski, P. A., Meeker, L. D., Whitlow, S., et al. 1993a. The atmosphere during the Younger Dryas. *Science* 261, 195–7.

Mayewski, P. A., Meeker, L. D., Morrison, M. C., et al. 1993b. Greenland ice core 'signal' characteristics: an expanded view of climate change. *Journal of Geophysical Research* 98 (D7), 12 839–47.

Mayewski, P. A., Meeker, L. D., Whitlow, S., et al. 1994. Changes in atmospheric circulation and ocean ice cover over the North Atlantic during the last 41 000 years. *Science* 263, 1 747–51.

Meeker, L. D., Mayewski, P. A., Twickler, M. S. and Whitlow, S. I. (in review). A 110 000-year-long history of change in continental biogenic source strength and related atmospheric circulation.

Meese, D., Alley, R., Fiacco, J., et al. 1994a. *Preliminary Depth-Age Scale of the GISP2 Ice Core.* Special CRREL Report 94-1, US Army Corps of Engineers, Hanover, New Hampshire.

Meese, D. A., Alley, R. B., Gow, A. J., et al. 1994b. The accumulation record from the GISP2 core as an indicator of climate change throughout the Holocene. *Science* 266, 1 680–2.

Murray, N. A., Bonsall, C., Sutherland, D. G., et al. 1993. Further radiocarbon determinations on reindeer remains of Middle and Late Devensian age from the Creag nan Uamh caves, Assynt, NW Scotland. *Quaternary Newsletter* 70, 1–10.

O'Brien, S. O., Mayewski, P. A., Meeker, L. D., et al. (in review). Holocene climate change inferred from a Summit Greenland ice core.

Peixoto, J. and Oort, A. H. 1992. *Physics of Climate.* New York: American Institute of Physics.

Pennington, W. 1977. The Late Devensian flora and vegetation of Britain. *Philosophical Transactions of the Royal Society of London* B280, 247–71.

Siegenthaler, U., Eicher, U., Oeschger, H. and Dansgaard, W. 1984. Lake sediments as continental $\delta^{18}O$ records from the Glacial/Post-Glacial transition. *Annals of Glaciology* 5, 149–52.

Taylor, K. C., Alley, R. B., Doyle, G. A., et al. 1993. The flickering switch of late Wisconsin climate change. *Nature* 361, 432–6.

Tinsley, B. A. 1988. The solar cycle and the QBO influences on the latitude of storm tracks in the North Atlantic. *Geophysical Research Letters* 15, 409–12.

Whitlow, S., Mayewski, P. A. and Dibb, J. E. 1992. A comparison of major chemical species input timing and accumulation at South Pole and Summit Greenland. *Atmosphere and Environment* 26A, 2 045–54.

Whitlow, S. I., Mayewski, P. A., Holdsworth, G., et al. 1994. An ice core based record of biomass burning in North America. *Tellus* 46B, 239–42.

Wickham-Jones, C. R. 1990. *Rhum: Mesolithic and Later Sites at Kinloch, Excavations 1984–1986.* Edinburgh: Society of Antiquaries of Scotland, Monograph Series no. 7.

Zielinski, G. A., Mayewski, P. A., Meeker, L. D., et al. 1994. A continuous record of volcanism (present–7 000 BC) and implications for the volcano-climate system. *Science* 264, 948–52.

Zielinski, G. A., Mayewski, P. A., Meeker, L. D., et al. (in review). A 110 000-year-long record of volcanism from a Greenland ice core.

Part 2
Regional Studies

6

RIVERS, BOUNDARIES AND CHANGE

A HYPOTHESIS OF CHANGING SETTLEMENT
PATTERNS IN THE MESOLITHIC
OF NORTHERN ENGLAND

PENNY SPIKINS

INTRODUCTION

A particularly interesting aspect of the study of past hunter-gatherers is the interpretation of potential resource areas (the total area over which resources are being exploited) or more defined social territories and how these may have changed through time. To date, identification of the 'social territories' of hunter-gatherers in the past have largely depended on stylistic variability in tool types (Rozoy 1978, Jacobi 1979, Price 1983, Gendel 1987, Verhart 1990). Whilst ethnographic analyses sometimes lend support to this (Weissner 1983) there are various limitations to this approach – notably that tool types are not necessarily equivalent to territories (Hodder 1985) and that particularly in the case of certain tool types (such as geometric microliths), it seems probable that group membership would have been displayed through other, more visible means. Raw material source studies have an important role to play in studies of population movement (for the British Mesolithic – Radley and Mellars (1964), Jacobi (1978), Care (1982), with also many relevant applications in the Palaeolithic such as Bahn (1982), Larick (1986), Féblot-Augustins (1993)). However, a major source of evidence, *past landscape features* and *environments*, remains unexploited largely due to practical problems of dealing with large amounts of environmental and topographical data and lack of a theoretical methodology for incorporating this data into models.

An ecological approach to hunter-gatherer resource areas – emphasising the spatial and temporal distribution of exploitable resources, can easily become environmentally deterministic, whilst ethnographic studies have demonstrated that ecological terms such as carrying capacity are not necessarily relevant given the flexibility of hunter-gatherer subsistence strategies and behaviour. Nevertheless, topographic features and differential seasonal distributions of resources do consistently influence hunter-gatherer movements (Jochim 1976). An approach based on a combination of resource availability, topographic features and ethnographic comparison can, at best, only deal in terms of probabilities, possibilities and suggestions, however with these limitations in mind this type of approach may yet yield valuable insight into the interpretation of archaeological evidence.

The first stage of such research was the formulation of a simple model of population movements based on topographic determinants. A combination of ethnographic comparison and archaeological interpretation lead to the conclusion that at a basic level, three main aspects of topography would have been vital in determining population movements in the densely forested environments which would have characterised the British Mesolithic – *rivers, coasts* and *uplands*.

RIVERS AS DETERMINANTS OF MOVEMENT

As well as a water supply, rivers also provide other important resources (most obviously fish can be a vital component in hunter-gatherer diets). River margins, as ecotones, also provide wetland/river edge resources. Casteel (1972) shows that for the Chilcotin, Chipewyan, Montagnais, and Kaska the availability of fish, vital at the times of lowest resources (the winter) is the major limiting factor on population density. Simmons (1980) has emphasised the importance of rivers (which would have steady regimes due to the tree cover) providing brown trout, salmon and pike in the North York Moors in the Mesolithic. Bonsall (1980) has stressed the importance of salmon which may have been harvested in very large quantities on the coastal sites of Cumbria. Other river and river margin resources are also important. The concentration of early Mesolithic sites at Seamer Carr and Star Carr in the Vale of Pickering, at the 25m od elevation at the margin of the ancient lake, (Schadla-Hall 1987, 1985) demonstrates the potential importance of these resources in the early Mesolithic.

Rivers are often important for transport, either through the use of water transport or on foot along river banks. There is little evidence for the use of water transport in the Mesolithic of Northern England (examples include the possible wooden paddle at Star Carr, Clark 1952, 1972), more conclusive evidence for water transport exists in Scandinavia (Andersen 1987) such as dugout canoes and a decorative paddle from Tybrind Vig. Rivers can also be a vital aid to navigation, especially important in the dense rivers of the Mesolithic.

Because rivers become major routeways the territory or resource area pattern becomes defined by the drainage network. This pattern is apparent in many areas such as British Columbia (Brody 1981) and Canada (Rogers 1969), (Jochim (1976) makes the same observation also citing Kroeber 1925, Heizer 1958, Rogers 1969 and Leacock 1973). The importance of the drainage system is also apparent from Watanabe's study of the Ainu (Watanabe 1972) as illustrated by Simmons (1980).

THE COASTAL FACTOR

The sedentary NW coast populations of the US, such as the Kwakiutl (Codere 1990), provide ample evidence of the importance of coastal and estuarine resources. These groups fish for seals, dolphins, whale and also depend on salmon (which can be dried and stored), halibut, rockfish, eulachon and smelt. The British coasts were probably important for these types of coastal resources themselves and littoral resources, furthermore the rapidly fluctuating sea levels (Tooley 1974, 1978) would have made the coastal area rich with early colonising plants. Bonsall (1980) illustrated the year-round availability of marine and estuarine resources in the late Mesolithic of Cumbria, mackerel, skate, mullet, bass, flounders, as well as shellfish, the coast could also be a source of driftwood for populations without technology for felling trees (Bonsall et al. 1985). Coastal resources are particularly important as a year-round resource.

However, the entire coastline of Northern England has been submerged by rising sea levels since the start of the Holocene. Only in the North-West have oscillations of sea level and isostatic uplift resulted in a late Mesolithic coastline being visible, here site distribution clearly demonstrates a coastal basis (Bonsall 1980). Possible evidence for the importance of coastal resources comes from carbon isotope values of bones of dog and wolf from Star Carr and Seamer Carr which demonstrate that the animals' diet must have consisted mainly of seafood (Clutton-Brock and Noe-Nygaard 1990) suggesting that the Mesolithic population spent a substantial amount of time at the sea shore.

THE UPLANDS FACTOR

In areas where movement is defined by rivers (often coastal to inland) boundaries tend to exist at upland watersheds, these locations can be an important focus for social interaction, exchange etc. The Salishan language group of the NW plateau of the NW coast of the USA often demonstrate territories which are defined by rivers, the territory edges are the uplands which are used for hunting, these areas are shared with other groups and are also a focus for trading (Josephy 1993, for further details of this group see Suttles 1990).

The uplands of northern England were originally seen as important in the Mesolithic settlement system as here the dense forest (of birch and pine in the Boreal, mixed deciduous forest in the Atlantic) became thinner. The reduced forest canopy increased the amount of low vegetation and browse thus attracting game animals, especially in summer when the climate of the uplands was milder. Some considerable evidence for later Mesolithic forest disturbance in terms of controlled burning to increase vegetation (Simmons 1975; Jacobi, Tallis and Mellars 1976; Mellars 1976) was interpreted as predominantly to encourage game animals (specifically deer) in summer. Recently the idea of such a heavy dependence on deer has lost favour (Legge and Rowley-Conwy 1985) with an emphasis also on burning to increase plant resources such as hazel (Simmons and Innes 1978). It is particularly the upland margins which seem to have been important with burning especially concentrated at spring heads.

The concentration of Mesolithic sites in the uplands is abundantly clear in Northern England and is the most obvious aspect of the distribution. Much of the archaeological record of Mesolithic sites is composed of surface finds collected from visible scatters, thus the location of peat which is eroding has a major influence in creating this concentration. However Jacobi (1978) highlights that the site distribution is more complex than this with sites being concentrated between 366 m and 488 m (whereas erosion occurs at lower elevations and is widespread at higher elevations). It is also of interest that there is a particular concentration of Mesolithic sites around the Saddleworth Marsden area where the Pennines are narrowest (Barnes 1982).

In reference to the known Mesolithic sites in England and Wales Castleford (1987) identified the above three dominant factors affecting site distribution – riverine, uplands and coastal factors with the greatest emphasis being placed on the first.

A SIMPLIFIED MODEL

To create a much simplified model of population movements in Northern England we must therefore incorporate these factors – movements largely defined by rivers, and the attractiveness of coastal/estuarine resources and upland resources. These simple assumptions may limit the usefulness and reality of any model derived from them but before greater understanding is obtained it is preferable to use simple simulations and hope to arrive at general conclusions. One means of doing this is to use Geographical Information System (GIS) tools, specifically 'network' models to model the movement of people (demand) to resources (supply) along rivers (the network)[1]. Hunter-gatherer resource use is complex, varies annually as well as seasonally and is only partly predictable in terms of available resources, however a very much simplified model of the processes occurring may allow some insight into the situation in Mesolithic Northern England and even the processes by which boundaries of resource areas change.

THE DRAINAGE SYSTEM IN NORTHERN ENGLAND

The first problem with this approach is that much of the drainage system of the early Mesolithic has been submerged. The North Sea basin in particular, but also the Irish Sea, are relatively shallow, falling sea-levels exposed large areas of land during the last glacial so that the topography of Northern England in the early postglacial looked very different from that of today (see Fig. 6.1). Subsequently large areas were submerged as the sea level rose, especially on the west coast of Northern England. As can be seen from Fig. 6.1 the west coast of Northern England was much farther west in the early Mesolithic whilst the east coast approximated the present coastline. The rise in sea level is complex and accompanied by complex phases of isostatic uplift which varies across Britain (Shennan 1987), particularly in the Northwest (Tooley 1974, 1978). The pattern of early Mesolithic drainage is also not reflected directly in the sea-bed topography due to factors such as sea-bed sedimentation and erosion. A very likely

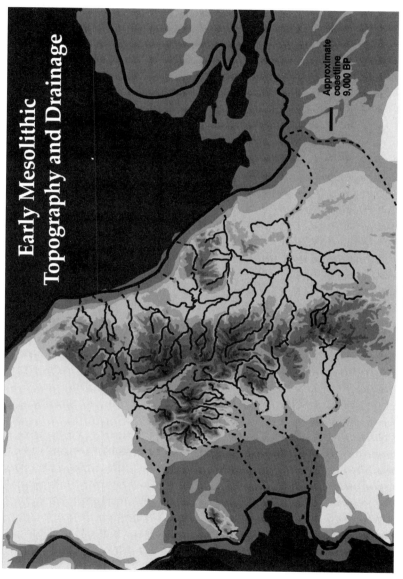

Early Mesolithic Topography and Drainage

Approximate coastline 9,000 BP

Fig. 6.1.

course of the past drainage has been traced using the sea-bed contours (British Geological Survey 1984). The North Sea drainage has been most securely defined but the early postglacial drainage of the Irish Sea remains uncertain.

In order to model population movements we need to specify demand (the population), impedance (the time cost to move along rivers) and supply (the resources). We have little idea of population densities (although it is worth referring to the discussions in Newell and Constandse-Westermann 1986 and specifically for the Mesolithic in England Smith 1992 and Smith and Openshaw 1990). However, since we are interested in the processes of settlement pattern change it is the relative pattern of change in population density and resource availability which is important – rather than the actual numbers.

Price documents a change from three distinct 'technocomplexes' in the Late Upper Palaeolithic of the North European plain to 8–10 distinct Mesolithic groups in the Boreal and at least 15 identifiable groups by the Atlantic (Price 1981). Verhart (1990) demonstrates a change in style zones from 230 000 km² in the late Palaeolithic to 80 000 km² in the middle of the Mesolithic to 30 000 km² in the late Mesolithic of Northwestern Europe. Distinctive zones of material culture exist in Denmark, the distinctive style zones of flake axes in the late Mesolithic in Eastern Denmark, only around 40 km in diameter, are probably explained by a largely sedentary population at this time (Vang Petersen 1984). Smith and Openshaw (1990) and Smith (1992) use the numbers of dated Mesolithic sites in Britain to show a steady increase in the Mesolithic popu-lations in England and Wales at this time. Population densities are obviously difficult to define, in the model a 'dummy' figure of a population density of 0.02 persons per km² was used for the early Mesolithic and five times this density, 0.1 persons per km², for the late Mesolithic (consistent with Newell and Constandse-Westermann 1986), a component of this increase being due to the reduction in land area with sea-level rise.

The maximum time cost which people would be prepared to take can be set in the model and will influence the supply nodes that people (demand) could be allocated to. The time taken to travel was based on walking rather than water transport and was set at 10 km per day – a conservative estimate from Binford's (1983) account of the Numiamuit annual round. This measure has little role to play in the model as the maximum cost to travel right across Britain is approxi-mately 27 days in the early Mesolithic, nearer 20 days in the late Mesolithic. We would expect the distance travelled to have included stops on rivers rather than being a single unbroken trip, as whilst moving along rivers hunter-gatherers would have access to riverine resources. The maximum time cost acceptable to travel to resources was set at 40 days.

The network used consists of the main rivers of Northern England (the minor tributaries may have changed since the early Mesolithic and should be less influential in terms of amount of resources and ease of movement)[2]. The resources (supply) are located as the river network reaches the coast in winter (the estuaries) and the network reaches the upland margins in the summer.

The population is tied to the river system by dividing the estimated population of Northern England (calculated using the land area) by the total of all the river lengths and distributing the population evenly across the river system. This results in a population of 0.33 persons per km of river network in the early Mesolithic and 1.5 persons per km of river in the late Mesolithic.

Winter, the time of greatest resource stress, is the most crucial period for defining Mesolithic populations and it is this period that is most important in our model. In the early Mesolithic it is assumed that, in winter, the most important resources are at the coast. Resources, set somewhat arbitrarily as sufficient to supply 300 people, are set at the points where the river network joins the coast (the estuaries). The model distributes the populations to this supply along the river network.[3] The result of this process is that populations are grouped at points on the coast, which point any person is grouped at depending on their location in the drainage network (Fig. 6.2).

In the summer model the populations disperse throughout the drainage basin from the coast and are distributed to resources which are set on the upland margins (or nodes set in the 400–600 m elevation range if the river head is at a higher elevation than that at which upland resources would have been concentrated) (not illustrated). The upland supply nodes have a supply adequate for 50 persons, this figure is set in relation to the supply at the coast. Actually, Simmons (1975) calculated that each 5 km radius of the Central Pennines could support a group of 25 people, in which case the Central Pennines alone would have supported 625 people! Basically, the model assumes that the resources at the uplands are sufficient to support small groups which have dispersed from the aggregation sites.

IMPLICATIONS

The model produced aggregations of people at main centres during the winter, with the summer dispersal phase defining their resource use area. This pattern could be compared to peoples such as the Central Eskimo (Damas 1972) which gather in large groupings in winter on the coast to exploit mauliqtug seal. Aggregations are vital to cement social relations, important at times of localised resource stress, and to maintain a viable mating network. Various models exist to describe the hierarchical structure of hunter-gatherer society, Wobst's (1976) model is based on 'minimal bands' which aggregate to form 'maximal bands' with populations between 175–475 persons, Constandse-Westermann and Newell (1989), from an analysis of North American Indians, describe bands

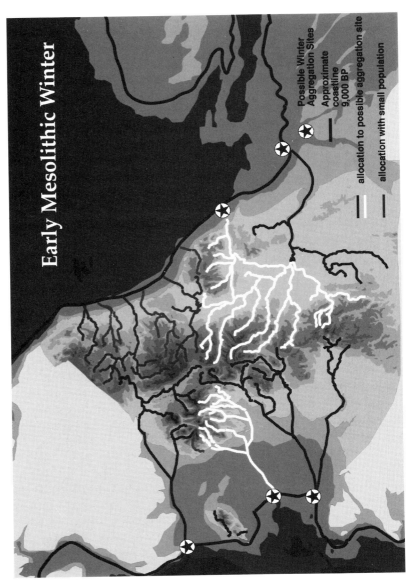

Fig. 6.2.

which form dialectic tribes numbering 142 to 7 242 (average 1 034) in band level societies. Larger 'language groups' or 'technocomplexes' also exist. The aggregations at the west and east of Britain at the coast coming from the Pennines number 300 persons at Holderness and 160 on the Humber with the east coast aggregations all over 140 persons. The resource areas implied by what might be termed the 'population basin' of the coastal aggregation sites are illustrated in Fig. 6.2 (see below for discussion of the North-East).

EARLY MESOLITHIC ARCHAEOLOGY

The importance of the coast is difficult to define from the archaeological evidence as the early Mesolithic coastline of Northern England has been completely submerged. Scandinavian early Mesolithic sites have also largely been submerged but the Sandarna culture of Western Sweden is visible due to isostatic uplift in this area; here most settlements are on the coast and demonstrate a predominantly marine economy (Larsson 1990).

Raw material sources on most of the Pennine sites with an early Mesolithic technology are derived largely from the Lincolnshire and Yorkshire Wolds to the East, specifically around Holderness (Jacobi 1978, for a discussion of the sources see Henson 1985). Southern Pennines sites seem far from the Holderness coast but the model shows that in the early Mesolithic this coast was nearer for many groups than the Humber/North Sea estuary. Jacobi (1978) proposes a model of summer hunting in the uplands and winter on the coast specifically for the groups using the Pennines. Radley and Mellars (1964) describe this association, as well as the similarities between assemblages at Warcock Hill North, a Pennine Mesolithic site and Star Carr in the Vale of Pickering. The high concentrations of early Mesolithic sites at Seamer Carr and Star Carr in the early Mesolithic may be evidence of the importance of this area as populations are funnelled from the drainage basin to the coast.

We could allow a minimum of 140 people to constitute a dialectic tribe or maximal band but smaller populations than this would not be feasible as semi-autonomous groups. Rivers in grey (Fig. 6.2) have population aggregations which are judged too small to constitute a higher level grouping than a band, we can only assume that in this situation bands would aggregate across the river network. An improvement to the model would be to aggregate neighbouring concentrations of population on the coast (by allowing movement along the shoreline) if population numbers were under those necessary to constitute a dialectic tribe. Archaeologically the situation in the North-East confirms that movement must have taken place across the drainage network as 77 per cent of the raw material in the Wear valley (throughout the Mesolithic) comes from the Yorkshire and Lincolnshire Wolds to the South, (Coggins, Laurie and Young 1985; Young 1984, 1987). Very few sites in the Lake District make an archaeological interpretation of the model in this area impossible, especially as the viable upland margin area excludes much of the high elevation relatively barren areas.

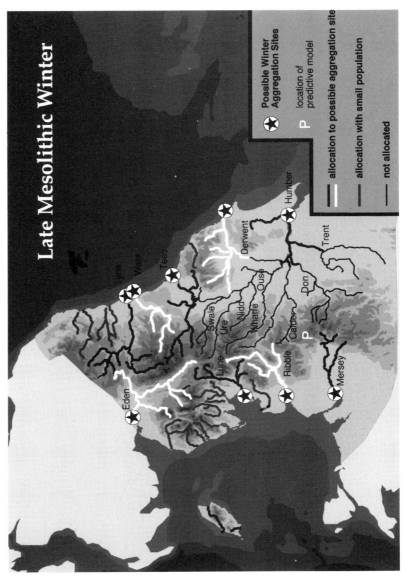

Fig. 6.3.

THE EARLY–LATE MESOLITHIC TRANSITION

As sea level rises (quite rapidly in many cases and certainly largely over a period of under 500 years), the drainage network which has been submerged is 'cut off'. This sea-level change, of itself, would be expected to increase the population density by a half without any rise in actual population. Climate change in this period can be rapid (see Mayewski et al. this volume). Population increase is incorporated into the model using a density of 0.1 persons per km², this population is distributed on the rivers with the same impedance as before. There is likely to have been an increase in coastal resources with the general warming – to model this increase in resources the supply at the centres is increased by a small amount (the supply now being set as supporting 350 people). The relative increase/decrease in lowland and upland resources is difficult to quantify across the Boreal/Atlantic transition. Birch and pine forests are replaced by increasingly diverse deciduous woodland with an increase in understorey vegetation, but the changing environment potentially reduces the herd size and tendency to migrate of ungulates thus making hunting more difficult (see Myers 1989 for a discussion). Thus overall, in the model as upland resources represent a combination of plant and animal foods the supplies are kept constant.

When the population is allocated to the coastal supply areas, the coastal resources at the East (where the large drainage network has caused a large increase in population) cannot support the demand (see Fig. 6.3)[4]. A supply large enough to support the demand at these points would have to be three and a half times that set in the model. The allocation of summer resource locations disperses the 'stranded' populations to the uplands.

IMPLICATIONS

These stranded populations can be seen as 'splinter groups' forming as the aggregations of the early Mesolithic reach too large a population to be supported at the coast. The unallocated population (numbering 1165 in the model) can be grouped into larger groupings or 'dialectical tribes', according to the areas of the network which remain connected (i.e. unallocated), but with no obvious aggregation (Fig. 6.4). The previous Humber group maps onto a group at the coast (350 people) and an unallocated population on the Trent (167 people), the previous Holderness group maps onto a North York Moors based group (of 350) with a large number unallocated (992), of this group the northernmost population (the Ouse and Wharfe, Nidd, Ure, Swale tributaries) are not in contact with the rest of the population and form a larger group/dialectic tribe (553 persons), south of this are two groups the Calder/Aire (224) and the Don (215). The Derwent valley forms it own mini-group (32), (which we might suppose would aggregate with a neighbouring population). The Tyne, Tees and Wear reach sufficient numbers to become feasible aggregation sites but the Tyne and the Eden estuaries are at maximum capacity and the groups would start to splinter given increasing population. Some of the North-East rivers still do not fit a

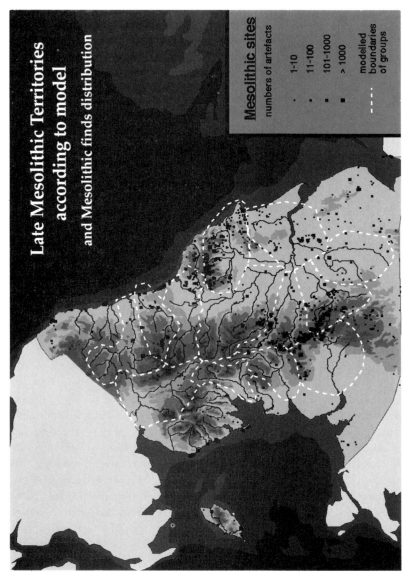

Fig. 6.4.

sensible ethnographic interpretation as the population numbers at the coast are again too small to be viable semi-autonomous groups, the same situation is true for the Lake District and again the aggregation on these small rivers could be united by allowing movement along the coast (which makes sense in terms of Bonsall 1980).

LATE MESOLITHIC ARCHAEOLOGY

In Northern England, late Mesolithic coastal sites are largely only visible in the Lake District, however some coastal sites in Southern England are visible, for example in Cornwall, and also demonstrate the importance of the coast (Castleford 1987). Spratt and Simmons (1976) and Simmons (1980) propose that the settlement pattern on the North York Moors is one of small exploitation camps on the coast in winter/spring, early summer/autumn base camps and upland summer camps (based on a late Mesolithic database). This fits well with the model with different groups exploiting the North York Moors from the North and South, the finds distribution (Fig. 6.4) also shows a concentration of findspots in these uplands at the boundaries of these groups and evidence for mid-Holocene disturbance (see Simmons and Innes 1987 for the distribution of evidence in Northern England).

As for the central area where the territories have divided the archaeological evidence demonstrates a switch from reliance on Yorkshire and Lincolnshire Wold flint towards a variety of flints and cherts (Pitts and Jacobi 1979) probably of more local origin, accompanied by a more intensive use of available raw material (Myers 1989). It is perhaps also relevant that a very high density of cup and ring marked rocks, at Rombalds Moor, a point where the Aire and the Wharfe are close, coincides with a modelled 'boundary' in the Mesolithic which could conceivably have continued to be important through the Neolithic.

LATE MESOLITHIC DISTURBANCE

There appears to be a concentration of both findspots (see Fig. 6.4) and evidence for disturbance events (Simmons and Innes 1987) at upland areas which are the boundaries of groups in our model – the Northern Pennines at the watershed of the Tyne and the Tees, the Yorkshire Moors at the watershed of the Derwent and the Tees and the Central Pennines at the watershed of the Calder and the Ribble. The latter concentration is the most pronounced with the highest density of Mesolithic sites in England and Wales (see Smith and Openshaw 1990). However, some other bias apart from erosion may be influencing the distribution such as proximity to roads or dense populations. If the high density at this point really does reflect a genuine concentration of activity it is possible that, in this case, the summer upland phase may have become particularly significant. In our model groups from the east of the Pennines have no obvious aggregation location and come into contact with other populations at the uplands, we may be seeing upland resources being increased at spot locations to support larger populations.

Disturbance in this context emphasises the social context of the use of the uplands rather than a response to resource stress.

Referring to this area in more detail, the landscape scale distribution (generalised by the predictive model Fig. 6.5) at the highest density point (see Fig. 6.3) show that sites concentrate on either side of the watershed.[5] Excavations in this area have suggested repeated use through the late Mesolithic and revealed several hearths and associated scatters (Spikins 1994, 1995). Interestingly, a hearth at the top of the most prominent hill in this area which has been constructed in a pit, displays at least two phases of use and is partly filled with alder charcoal (which burns slowly and smokily). The hearth appears to be constructed with an opening restricted with large stones (Conneller and Spikins, publication in preparation). Although other interpretations are possible, such as specific cooking activities, the precise landscape location may have been significant given the narrowness of the Pennines (bringing groups from either side into contact) and the extremely wide area of the Pennine uplands from which smoke would have been visible from this spot.

Interestingly, the modelled late Mesolithic territorial pattern is similar in many ways to the territorial patterns of Canadian hunter-gatherers (Rogers 1969) in that the coastal population territories align with rivers perpendicular to the coast, with inland populations assuming more of the hexagonal territory pattern modelled by Wobst (1976) and demonstrated for North American Indians by Newell and Constandse-Westermann (1986).

LIMITATIONS OF THE MODEL

It is not clear how the model relates to ethnographic models in terms of endogamous or exogamous groups. The resource areas which have been modelled may represent the resource areas of a band which forms part of a wider group defined by stylistic or linguistic traits (see Jacobi 1979). Further research is necessary into the possible relevance of the groupings which have been defined in terms of hunter-gatherer social systems. The model might be improved by modelling 'task groups' rather than individuals and by specifying population age and gender and assessing the viability of the aggregations as breeding populations.

The *simplifications* – two seasons, two resource locations, two periods cannot possibly represent the complexity of Mesolithic seasonal resource availability and the mechanisms of population increase, it is also somewhat unrealistic to assume that populations moved only along river networks and did not cross upland areas. The model perhaps fails to adequately explain the movement to the uplands in summer as coastal/estuarine resources may not have been limited to the winter but resources could have been available at the coast nearly year round – with salmon runs in autumn and spring, trout in autumn, saltwater fish possibly mostly shoaling in summer and sea-birds in winter. It is not even suggested that Mesolithic populations had a simple winter–summer bimodal settle-

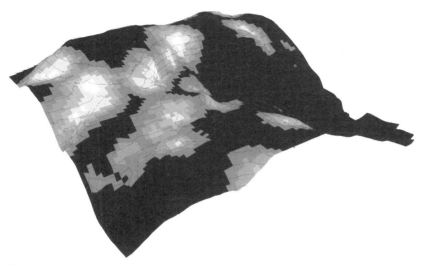

Fig. 6.5.

ment system as more detailed research into resource distributions would be necessary to even approach the likely settlement system.

With seasonal resources of known abundance it would be possible to model the relative attractiveness of the uplands for hunting, gathering certain plant foods such as hazelnuts etc. at specific seasons and further research will follow in this direction. Many improvements could be made using a detailed knowledge of resource availability and seasonality and many variations to the model could be created by incorporating criteria such as fluctuating resources, varied resources at the coast due to tidal currents, an intensification (perhaps through upland management) or diversification of the resource base, exchange across groups etc. However the resolution of the environmental record severely limits the opportunity to test these types of detailed environmental reconstruction.

CONCLUSIONS

The model suggested here is extremely simplistic and is not intended to represent the complexities of real hunter-gatherer settlement systems which involve exploitation of many different locations and resources at different seasons. No attempt has been made to incorporate factors such as information exchange or oscillations of fluctuating environments. The territories seen in Fig. 6.4 are those *according to the model*. Since hunter-gatherer settlement systems are never a direct reflection of their environment, we cannot expect even a more complex model to generate accurately the real boundaries in the Mesolithic. However, some component of the model may relate to the past system, perhaps in particular the changing role of the uplands and thus the model has some usefulness.

This model is only one hypothesis based on a specific set of assumptions, movement along rivers, a dependence on coastal resources in winter, and dispersion to uplands in summer. Many more models drawing on basic assumptions drawn from ethnography should be assessed. A possible model could be based, for example, not on competition for resources generating a divide into different groups, but instead on limitless resources at the coast. Populations would therefore under this model exploit coastal/estuarine resources year round in the early Mesolithic, only moving to the inland areas in the later Mesolithic as overlarge aggregation populations divide because of difficulties in maintaining social ties.

Specifically, the model has given us some insight into possible explanations for the distribution of Mesolithic sites in this area and has hopefully given a social, rather than purely economic, context to Mesolithic site distributions. A strength of the model is that the actual population numbers, resource supplies and minimum viable aggregation estimates are not crucial, rather the process of increasing population, in relation to resources at points of aggregation where movement and resource areas are defined by drainage basins. However, aggregation 'cut off' numbers influence the point where drainage basin populations would be expected to combine to form aggregations.

Generally, the model explores the means by which rivers define territories in these types of environments and how territories might change. GIS has proved a useful tool in terms of generating specific hypotheses and also allowing us to explore the basic principles of settlement system change under this model. It could be suggested on a general note, that, in similar environments with a proximity to the coast and drainage perpendicular to the coast, increasing population density causes the settlement system at each river basin to pass through three phases: with low population, aggregations would cross drainage basins, as populations increase aggregations would be limited to a single drainage basin, further increases would cause aggregations to split according to major arteries of the network. It may be interesting to test these principles in other areas with a higher resolution of the archaeological evidence.

NOTES

1. In ArcInfo release 6.1 ALLOCATE assigns network links to centres based on the available supply at centres and the demand associated with links. Links are assigned to a centre along least impedance cost paths. When a link is assigned to a centre, the available supply at the centre is diminished by the link demand. The allocation ceases when the centre supply is exhausted.

The relevant commands in ARCPLOT are:
NETCOVER
IMPEDANCE {TIME} {TIME}
DEMAND {EMPOPLN}/{LMPOPLN}
ALLOCATE {IN} CENTRES
with a centres file defining a maximum impedance of 40 (days) and a supply of 300 (350 in the late Mesolithic model)

The allocation is displayed graphically using
ROUTELINES {river_network} {em_allocation_route}

2. The tributaries of the Rye and the Ure very nearly connect in the North York Moors, the connection has been made in the model as Mesolithic populations would undoubtedly have crossed the watershed, the impedance of the link is doubled relative to the river network.

3. Early Mesolithic allocation (centres clockwise from the North-East)

estuary	*time in days*	*population*
CENTRE	MAX. IMPEDANCE ALLOCATED	TOTAL DEMAND ALLOCATED
3	5.607	30.920
11	5.083	43.862
24	11.143	83.479
35	9.917	44.838
41	12.198	79.031
53	4.045	13.414
99	22.855	300.000
150	26.672	160.876
155	17.365	214.267
133	12.832	156.078
84	23.500	145.092

*3 – Late Mesolithic allocation (centres clockwise from the North-East)

estuary	*time in days*	*population*
CENTRE	MAX. IMPEDANCE ALLOCATED	TOTAL DEMAND ALLOCATED
103	2.430	36.429
122	4.516	67.702
107	3.814	100.289
104	3.493	52.372
11	9.701	350.000
20	8.911	187.642
29	10.035	324.863
60	2.926	43.870
154	8.556	350.000
141	7.686	350.000
93	6.450	173.320
77	7.082	191.903
80	3.424	51.327
150	6.847	171.314
65	2.586	88.901
67	1.870	28.032
144	1.425	21.369
134	1.647	24.699
118	1.498	22.454
136	1.759	26.374
116	2.197	32.936
69	2.926	43.875
35	9.744	350.000

5. The predictive model was generated in ArcInfo 6.1 using grids of aspect, slope, distance to major rivers, distance to minor rivers and elevation as attributes. Findspot locations taken from West Yorkshire Archaeology Service Sites and Monuments Record are

compared to random locations on the basis of these attributes using forward stepwise logistic regression in SPSS/WIN. The function displayed is prob= $1/1 + e^z$
where $z = -18.2411 + (0441 *B) + (0.09 * C) + (0.0014 * F)$
where B–elevation, C–slope, F–distance to rivers
from 365 cases

ACKNOWLEDGEMENTS

The idea for the model began as a network analysis project as part of an MA in Geographical Information Systems at Leeds, where I am indebted to Graham Clarke for his help and comments. Todd Whitelaw and Paul Mellars at Cambridge have provided valuable comments and Colin Shell and Melanie Leggart technical support. I would also like to thank John Castleford, Rob Young and West Yorkshire Archaeology Service but above all Horacio Ayestaran has provided invaluable help and support.

REFERENCES

Bahn, P. G. 1982. Inter-site and inter-regional links during the upper Palaeolithic: the Pyrenean evidence. *Oxford Journal of Archaeology* 1, 247–65.

Barnes, B. 1982. Mesolithic evidence. In Barnes, B. (ed.), *Man and the Changing Landscape*. Merseyside County Council/Merseyside County Museums, University of Liverpool Department of Prehistoric Archaeology, Work Notes 3.

Binford, L. R. 1983. *In Pursuit of the Past*. London: Thames & Hudson.

Bonsall, C. 1980. The coastal factor in the Mesolithic settlement of north-west England, *Veröffentlichungen des Museums für Ur- und Frühgeschichte Potsdam* 14/15, 451–72.

Bonsall, C., Sutherland, D., Tipping, R. and Cherry, J. 1989. The Eskmeals Project: Late Mesolithic settlement and environment in north-west England. In Bonsall, C. (ed.), *The Mesolithic in Europe*, Papers presented at the Third International Symposium, Edinburgh. Edinburgh: John Donald, 175–206.

British Geological Survey, 1984. Sea Bed Sediments around the UK 1:1 000 000 series and Sea Bed Sediments and Quaternary 1:250 000 series.

Brody, H. 1981. *Maps and Dreams: Indians and the British Columbian Frontier*. Vancouver: Douglas & Macintyre.

Care, V. 1982. The collection and distribution of lithic materials during the Mesolithic and Neolithic periods in southern England. *Oxford Journal of Archaeology* 1, 269–85.

Castleford, J. 1987. *Spatial Analysis of Mesolithic Site Patterning in England and Wales*. MA Dissertation, University of Victoria, Canada.

Clark, J. G. D. 1954. *Star Carr*. Cambridge: Cambridge University Press.

Clark, J. G. D. 1972. *Star Carr: A Case Study in Bioarchaeology*. Cambridge: Addison Wesley Modular Publications 10, 1–42.

Clutton-Brock, J. and Noe-Nygaard, N. 1990. New osteological and C-isotope evidence on Mesolithic dogs: companions to hunters and fishers at Star Carr, Seamer Carr and Kongemose. *Journal of Archaeological Science* 17, 643–53.

Codere, H. 1990. Kwakiutl: traditional culture. In Suttles, W. (ed.), *Handbook of North American Indians*, vol. 7: *The North-West Coast*. Washington: Smithsonian Institute.

Coggins, D., Laurie, T. and Young, R. 1989. The late upper Palaeolithic and Mesolithic of the North Pennine Dales in the light of recent fieldwork. In Bonsall, C. (ed.),

The Mesolithic in Europe. Papers presented at the Third International Symposium, Edinburgh. Edinburgh: John Donald, 164–75.

Constandse-Westermann, T. S. and Newell, R. R. 1989. Social and biological aspects of Western European Mesolithic population structure: a comparison with the demography of North American Indians. In Bonsall, C. (ed.), *The Mesolithic in Europe*. Papers presented at the Third International Symposium, Edinburgh. Edinburgh: John Donald, 106–15.

Damas, D. 1972. The Copper Eskimo. In Bicchieri, M. G. (ed.), *Hunters and Gatherers Today*. New York: Holt.

ESRI 1992. *Network Analysis, Modelling Network Systems* ArcInfo 6.1 Users Guide. ESRI. Redlands. CA. USA.

Féblot-Augustins, J. 1993. Mobility strategies in the Late Middle Palaeolithic of Central Europe and Western Europe: elements of stability and variability. *Journal of Anthropological Archaeology* 12, 211–65.

Gendel, P. 1987. Socio-stylistic analyses of lithic artefacts from the Mesolithic of northwestern Europe. In Rowley-Conwy, P., Zvelebil, M. and Blankholm, H. P. (eds), *Mesolithic Northwest Europe: Recent Trends*. Dept of Archaeology and Prehistory, University of Sheffield, 65–74.

Heizer, R. F. 1958. *Aboriginal California and Great Basin Cartography*. Berkeley: University of California Archaeology Survey Report 41.

Henson, D. 1985. The flint resources of Yorkshire and the East Midlands. *Lithics* 6, 2–9.

Hodder, I. 1985. Boundaries as strategies: an ethnoarchaeological study. In Green, S. W. and Perlamon, S. M. (eds), *The Archaeology of Frontiers and Boundaries*. 141–59. Orlando.

Jacobi, R. M. 1978a. Northern England in the eighth millennium BC: an essay. In Mellars, P. A. (ed.), *The Early Postlgacial Settlement of Northern Europe*. London: Duckworth 295–332.

Jacobi, R. M. 1978b. Early Flandrian hunters in the South-West. *Proceedings of the Devon and Cornwall Archaeological Society* 37, 48–89.

Jacobi, R. M., Tallis, J. H. and Mellars, P. A. 1976. The Southern Pennine Mesolithic and the ecological record. *Journal of Archaeological Science* 3, 307–20.

Jochim, M. A. 1976. *Hunter-Gatherer Subsistence and Settlement: A Predictive Model*. New York: Academic Press, 86–8.

Josephy, A. M. 1993. *America in 1492: The World of the Indian Peoples before the Arrival of Columbus*. New York: Vintage Books.

Kroeber, A. L. 1925. *Handbook of the Indians of California*. Washington: US Government printing office.

Larick, R. R. 1986. Perigordian cherts: an analytical frame for investigating the movement of Palaeolithic hunters and their resources. In Sieveking, G. de G. (ed.), *The Scientific Study of Flint and Chert*. Cambridge: Cambridge University Press.

Larsson, L. 1990. The Mesolithic of southern Scandinavia. *Journal of World Prehistory* 4, 257–309.

Leacock, E. 1973. The Montagnais–Naskapi Band. In Cox, B. (ed.), *Cultural Ecology*. Carleton Library 65.

Legge, A. J. and Rowley-Conwy, P. A. 1989. Some preliminary results of a re-examination of the Star Carr fauna. In Bonsall, C. (ed.), *The Mesolithic in Europe*, Papers presented at the Third International Symposium, Edinburgh. Edinburgh: John Donald, 225–31.

Mellars, P. A. 1976. Fire ecology, animal populations and man: a study of some ecological relationships in Prehistory. *Proceedings of the Prehistoric Society* 42, 15–45.

Myers, A. M. 1989. Reliable and maintainable technological strategies in the Mesolithic of mainland Britain. In Torrence, R. (ed.), *Time, Energy and Stone Tools.* Cambridge: Cambridge University Press: 78–91.

Newell, R. R. and Constandse-Westermann, T. S. 1986. Testing an ethnographic analogue of Mesolithic social structure and the archaeological resolution of Mesolithic ethnic groups and breeding populations. *Proceedings of the Royal Academy of Sciences, Amsterdam* 89, 243–400.

Pitts, M. W. and Jacobi, R. M. 1979. Aspects of change in flaked stone industries of the Mesolithic and Neolithic in southern Britain. *Journal of Archaeological Science* 6, 164.

Price, T. D. 1981. Regional approaches to human adaptation in the Mesolithic of the north European plain. *Veröffentlichungen des Museums für Ur- und Frühgeschichte Potsdam* 14/15, 217–34.

Price, T. D. 1983. The European Mesolithic. *American Antiquity* 48, 4.

Radley, J. and Mellars, P. A. 1964. A Mesolithic structure at Deepcar, Yorkshire, England and the affinities of its associated industries. *Proceedings of the Prehistoric Society* 30, 1–24.

Rogers, E. S. 1969. *Band Organisation among the Indians of Eastern Subarctic Canada.* National Museum of Canada Bulletin 228.

Rozoy, J.-G. 1978. *Les Derniers Chasseurs: L'Epipalaeolithique en France et en Belgique.* Bulletin de la Société Archéologique Champenoise, special issue. Charleville: Chez L'auteur.

Schadla-Hall, R. T. 1989. The Vale of Pickering in the Early Mesolithic in context. In Bonsall, C. (ed.), *The Mesolithic in Europe*, Papers presented at the Third International Symposium, Edinburgh. Edinburgh: John Donald, 218–25.

Shennan, I. 1987. Holocene sea level changes in the North Sea. In Tooley, J. and Shennan, I. (eds), *Sea Level Changes.* Oxford: Blackwell 109–52.

Simmons, I. G. 1975. Towards an ecology of Mesolithic man in the uplands of Britain. *Journal of Archaeological Science* 2, 1–15.

Simmons, I. G. 1980. Late Mesolithic societies and environment of the uplands of England and Wales. *University of London Institute of Archaeology Bulletin* 16, 111–29.

Simmons, I. G. and Innes, J. B. 1987. Mid-Holocene adaptations and later Mesolithic forest disturbance in northern England. *Journal of Archaeological Science* 14, 385–403.

Smith, C. 1992. The population of Late Upper Palaeolithic and Mesolithic Britain. *Proceedings of the Prehistoric Society* 58, 37–40.

Smith, C. and Openshaw, S. 1990. Mapping the Mesolithic. In Vermeesch, P. M. and Van Peer, P. (eds), *Contributions to the Mesolithic in Europe.* Leuven: Leuven University Press 17–22.

Spikins, P. A. 1994. *West Yorkshire Mesolithic Project: Site Report.* Wakefield internal publication, West Yorkshire Archaeology Service.

Spikins, P. A. 1995. *West Yorkshire Mesolithic Project: Interim Report.* Wakefield internal publication, West Yorkshire Archaeology Service.

Spratt, D. A. and Simmons, I. G. 1976. Prehistoric activity and environment on the North York Moors. *Journal of Archaeological Science* 3, 193–210.

Suttles, W. 1990. *Handbook of North American Indians*, vol. 7: *The North-West Coast*. Washington: Smithsonian Institute.

Tooley, M. J. 1974. Sea-level changes during the last 9 000 years in north-west England. *Geographical Journal* 140, 18–42.

Tooley, M. J. 1978. *Sea Level Changes in North-West England during the Flandrian Stage*. Oxford: Clarendon Press.

Vang Petersen, P. 1984. Chronological and functional variation in the late Mesolithic of Eastern Denmark. *Journal of Danish Archaeology* 3, 7–18.

Verhart, L. B. M. 1990. Stone age bone and antler points as indicators for 'social territories' in the European Mesolithic. In Vermeesch, M. and Van Peer, P. (eds), *Contributions to the Mesolithic in Europe*. Leuven: Leuven University Press, 139–52.

Watanabe, H. 1972. *The Ainu Ecosystem Environment and Group Structure*. Seattle and London: University of Washington Press.

Wobst, H. M. 1976. Locational relationships in Palaeolithic society. *Journal of Human Evolution* 5, 49–58.

Young, R. 1984. Potential sources of flint and chert in the north-east of England. *Lithics* 5, 3–9.

Young, R. 1987. *Lithics and Subsistence in the North-East of England*. British Archaeological Reports (British Series) 161. Oxford: British Archaeological Reports.

7

THE CONTRIBUTION OF TOM AFFLECK
TO THE STUDY OF THE MESOLITHIC
OF SOUTHWEST SCOTLAND

KEVIN J. EDWARDS

If seeds in the black earth can turn into such beautiful flowers, what
might not the heart of man become in its long journey towards the
stars?

G. K. Chesterton

Two communications bracket my experience of Tom Affleck. A first letter was
written by him to me on 25 May 1983. This letter of introduction noted that he
had 'been told by both Mike Ansell and Alex Morrison ... that you are possibly
undertaking palynology work in Dumfries and Galloway ... I am presently
researching the Mesolithic evidence in the area, may I offer any assistance?'
The second letter was written by me on 14 March 1987. It was addressed to
Isabel, Tom's widow of three days, and expressed my sorrow to Isabel and their
children Jim and Jan; my failure to leave a contact telephone number in Amsterdam, where I had been lecturing, meant that I was unaware of the tragedy unfold-
ing back in Scotland, and I remember walking the streets in a state of disbelief.
Tom (Fig. 7.1) was more than a research colleague – both he and Isabel had made
me feel that I was an honorary member of their family. The four-year interval
in the writing of those letters is eclipsed by the eight years which have elapsed
since Tom's death; but for many who knew him, the loss is as keenly felt today
as it was back in 1987.

The address at the top of Tom's letter was The Old Bank House, Moniaive.
The Old Bank House evoked images of a building fittingly aged; Moniaive I had
never heard of and knew even less how to pronounce. Both places were to become
familiar to me as Tom, often accompanied by Isabel, joined myself and others
in the hunt for evidence of Mesolithic peoples in southwest Scotland (Fig. 7.2).
Tom's first letter not only offered assistance, but also expressed interest 'in
observing and learning at first hand something of your field of study'. This was
somewhat disingenuous, for he was a very fine naturalist, trained as an agricultural botanist, who was well aware of the value of integrated studies in archaeology. Indeed, he often remarked that he could not see how meaningful studies

Fig. 7.1. Tom Affleck.

of the Mesolithic could be carried out without a full consideration of the environmental context.

In his short archaeological life, Tom carried out some of the finest small-scale
excavations in southwest Scotland and threatened to put the area on the archaeological and geoarchaeological map of Britain. In his excellent critical review of
the Scottish Mesolithic, Peter Woodman (1990: 7) said that 'in this region, the
untimely death of Tom Affleck has unfortunately brought to an end a potentially very promising contribution to Scottish prehistory'. It might be argued
that the potential was in very great measure realised, and that Tom's contribution will become appreciated over the coming years as more of his work is
published. This offering is presented in the belief that Tom's memory deserves
to be more than that of a name on a few papers.

BEFORE ARCHAEOLOGY

Thomas Lamb Affleck was born on 19 July 1926 in Lesmahagow, Lanarkshire.
His father was a horticulturalist and Tom grew up in the town. In 1944 he entered

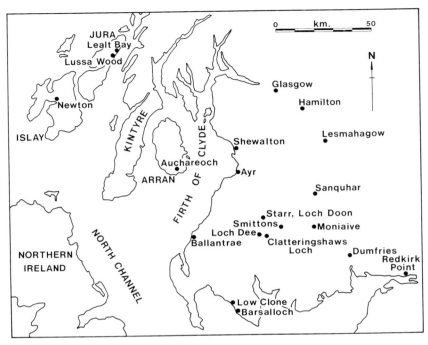

Fig. 7.2. Loch Dee and Clatteringshaws Loch.

the University of Glasgow to study engineering, successfully completing the first
two years of his course. There he followed-up a childhood interest in aviation
by joining the university air squadron and undergoing pilot training. In 1946 he
succumbed to a near-fatal virus which led to kidney failure. Tom was reduced
to five stones in weight and for 12 months he was wheelchair-bound. The reflection attendant upon the slow path to recovery convinced Tom that a temporary
break from engineering would be more conducive to recovery, and rather than
returning to Glasgow, he entered the West of Scotland Agricultural College at
Auchincruive near Ayr, with the intention of studying horticulture as an interim
measure. At Auchincruive, Tom realised that he had a passion for botany and he
left the college three years later with a diploma in horticulture, along the way
acquiring a medal as best student. At this stage, his father was in ill-health, and
Tom felt keenly that he had an obligation as the only son to help run the family
business. He was to pursue a career as a market gardener for some 28 years
in Lesmahagow, successfully expanding the enterprise (mainly the growth of
tomatoes and pot plants) by intensifying output. Tom managed to fit in some
teaching in rural science at Lesmahagow High School as well as making a number
of appearances on the gardening programme broadcast by BBC Radio Glasgow.
At college he had met a Glasgwegian, Isabel Hiddleston, whom he had had the
good sense to marry in 1952.

ARCHAEOLOGICAL BEGINNINGS

Tom had long had an interest in archaeology and ancient history. This translated itself into membership of local historical and archaeological societies. In 1977, after the death of Tom's mother (his father had died in 1972), Isabel urged Tom to study his great hobby, archaeology, more seriously. Taking matters into her own hands, she informed Tom that he had to meet someone in Glasgow. It was only when Isabel had deposited Tom outside a door at Glasgow University that she told him he was to go inside and discuss the requirements for an archaeological career with the University enrolment officer. Tom reappeared glum-faced – the officer was encouraging, but said that some suitable Highers had to be procured. Not to be thwarted, Isabel phoned their son, Jim, who ascertained that Bell College in Hamilton was an appropriate centre for adult education. Tom was duped into a trip to Hamilton, had a successful interview with a well-primed lecturer, and emerged one year later with A-grade passes in Higher English and French, having often studied late into the night under the greenhouse lights. Leaving market gardening behind him for good, Tom obtained practical experience of excavation in the summer of 1978, when he participated in the excavation of Lesmahagow Priory. A month or so later, with Isabel's full encouragement, and with children Jim and Jan already away following their own studies in higher education (Jim reading biochemistry at Herriot-Watt University and Jan enrolled at Auchincruive, which was clearly becoming an Affleck family training centre), Tom began a four-year degree course in archaeology at the University of Glasgow.

He lodged in Glasgow during the week and travelled back to Lesmahagow at weekends. In his final year, the Afflecks moved to Moniaive, the Dumfriesshire village where Isabel had family connections. At the start of his course, Tom was 52 years of age, but he found little difficulty in adapting to degree work and was readily accepted by his much younger contemporaries, many of whom remained staunch friends long after graduation and, indeed, were to participate in his excavations.

His undergraduate dissertation was a study of the Mesolithic environment and occupation of the Lower Irvine valley in Ayrshire. This was prompted by Lacaille's (1930, 1954) discussion of lithic material from the coastal sand dunes at Shewalton, later discoveries of lithics slightly further inland (cf. MacNeill 1975), and the fact that palynological investigations by Bill Boyd were underway (Boyd 1982). Tom became especially aware of the neglect of research into the potential Mesolithic utilisation of inland areas. He graduated with his MA Honours degree in 1982 and elected to continue researching the Mesolithic of Scotland for a part-time Ph.D. under the supervision of Alex Morrison. In notes prepared for his unfinished doctorate, Tom remarked:

> By coincidence, or subconscious design, the writer took up residence in Galloway just prior to undertaking postgraduate research in the inland

Mesolithic in Scotland. Here was an area ideally suited to the purpose. Already there was a partial and tantalising record of lithic scatters in inland Galloway that appeared to suggest a pattern; to augment this, an appreciable amount of palaeoenvironmental fieldwork in the area had been published, and there was a current palynological research programme being initiated. The fortuitous discovery of chert and flint lithics of Mesolithic type on a former river terrace, now part of the writer's garden, could only be regarded as the ultimate incentive!

THE MESOLITHIC OF SOUTHWEST SCOTLAND

Apart from work at Low Clone (Cormack and Coles 1968), Barsalloch (Cormack 1970) and Redkirk Point (Masters 1981), little recent work had been done on the Mesolithic of southwest Scotland. Power station engineer Mike Ansell had done a great deal of field-walking and had revealed many spot sites where flint and chert lithics of Mesolithic aspect were to be found and I, along with colleagues in the School of Geography at the University of Birmingham, had found new sites while engaged in projects to ascertain the impact of Mesolithic communities upon the environment of southwest Scotland. Our work was concentrating on inland sites, theretofore considered to be of little importance compared to the apparent dominance of coastal sites (cf. Morrison 1980). Tom's follow-up letter to my response, which had detailed our inland focus, was a pleasant surprise. He there declared that 'my main subject of study [is] the inland Mesolithic of Dumfries and Galloway' (letter undated, probably July 1983). He added:

> I feel that, while surface collecting is of great value, a genuine excavation of an inland site must be carried out to obtain a true assemblage ... At present I have my eye on a site near the R. Ken, found by Mike [Ansell]. It is situated on what I think is a shingle or gravel raised ridge or strand, presently surrounded by marshy ground. I surmise that formerly this area may have been occupied by a braided stream system.

Smittons, Water of Ken

This concern with the need for excavation to complement distributional studies resulted in the two season study at Smittons in 1983 and 1986. Tom's concern with the wider environmental context also extended to the site stratigraphy and his excavation notes and diagrams are meticulous in recording all pertinent site details.

The Smittons excavations (Fig. 7.3) produced, *inter alia*, flint and chert lithics including microliths, and a series of fire spots for which reliable AMS dates of 6 260 ± 80 (OxA-1 595) and 5 470 ± 80 BP (OxA-1 594) were obtained on charred hazelnut shells from trenches T1 and T3 respectively. Tom noted that many of the microliths (which included rods, crescents and isosceles triangles) were remarkable for their minute dimensions (averaging 12.7 mm, but with the smallest

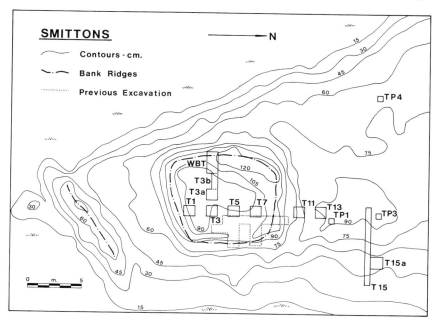

Fig. 7.3. Excavation trenches at Smittons.

at 9 mm) and delicate retouch. He considered that the stratigraphy indicated the dynamic nature of a seasonally-flooded riverine environment. This supposition may be supported from the evidence in trench T15a, where birch wood charcoal from within a silty matrix containing lithics produced a date of 1 910 ± 100 BP (OxA-1 593); the lithics probably moved downslope as a result of fluvial action, or, equally likely, they may have been moved by surface runoff, facilitated by burning and laying bare of the ground surface in the Iron Age.

Of particular interest was Isabel's discovery, in 1986, of a hearth-like structure on a bluff overlooking the Smittons site. Tom had urged Isabel to investigate this potentially promising area, and the stone setting (Fig. 7.4) is reminiscent of one of the stone rings from Lussa Wood, Jura (Mercer 1980), albeit it at a smaller scale. Eleven microliths were recovered from here. The site was backfilled and Isabel and I attempted to rediscover the site in August 1987, but unsuccessfully.

Starr, Loch Doon

During the first season at Smittons, Tom visited Loch Doon with Alex Morrison. Alex encouraged him to carry out some excavations at Loch Doon, where the Birmingham team had already been working on environmental sites and had discovered a lithics scatter away from the loch edge (Edwards et al. 1984). Tom

KEVIN J. EDWARDS

Fig. 7.4. Stone setting from Smittons, 1986.

wrote (12 September 1983) expressing an interest in a Loch Doon shore site.
Mike Ansell had informed him that the water level at Loch Doon would be
artificially-lowered the following summer, thus increasing the likelihood of new
find sites as well as assisting excavation. The immediate problem, however, was
finance. Tom had himself paid for the Smittons excavations, and a larger-scale
endeavour at Loch Doon would be a more costly affair. Limited assistance was
forthcoming from the Glasgow Archaeological Society and the Dumfries and
Galloway Natural History and Antiquarian Society, and a trial excavation took
place in August 1984 (Affleck 1985).

The excavation site was on the southwestern loch shore where fluctuating
water-levels had eroded peat, beneath which lithic spreads were frequent
(Edwards et al. 1983). The name of the site – Starr – suggested itself; it was only
150 m from Starr Cottage, owned by the Coylton Boy's Brigade, where excavators could be housed, and the name bore a delicious similarity to a rather
famous Mesolithic site in Yorkshire (Clark 1954). The trial excavation at Starr I
involved the opening of four trenches (Affleck 1985). In each case, a complex
stratigraphy was found with lithics *in situ* upon an old land surface which immediately underlay the peat cover. Within trench 3, a gully was found within
which was an apparent setting of greywacke cobbles with charcoal, birch bark
and three microliths in close association (Figs 7.5 and 7.6). Tom considered that
this possible hearth setting may denote seasonal occupation during drier summer
or autumn months. Mapped lithics distributions in trench 5 revealed two distinct

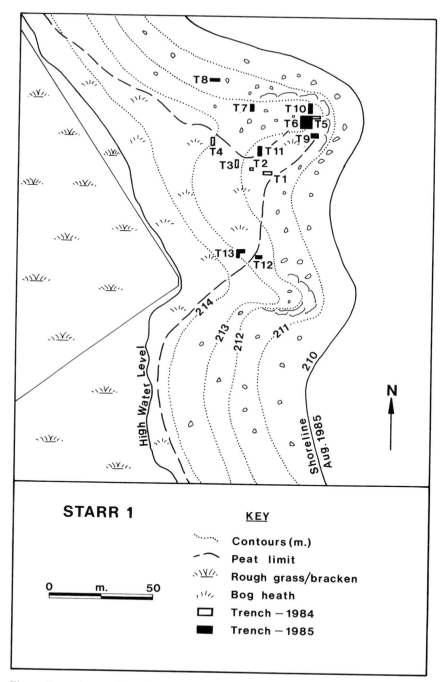

Fig. 7.5. Excavation trenches at Starr 1, Loch Doon.

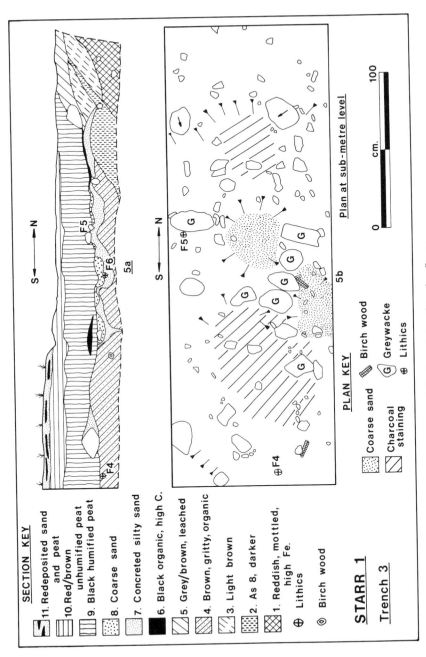

Fig. 7.6. Section and plan of trench 3, Starr 1.

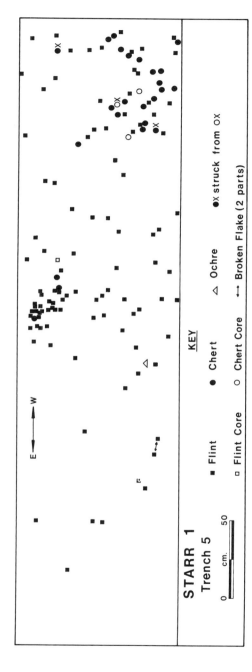

Fig. 7.7. Lithics distributions in trench 5, Starr 1.

knapping locales, one represented almost exclusively by chert debitage, including cores, and the other by flint (Fig. 7.7). This plan, in matching some of the lithic fragments, also reveals a characteristic attention to detail.

A second phase of excavation took place in July 1985, with some funding secured from Glasgow Archaeological Society and the Society of Antiquaries of Scotland on the strength of the report of the 1984 season. With Mary Kemp Clarke and Jim MacDougall as able supervisors, a further six trenches were opened (Affleck 1986). Trench 6 revealed a series of stakeholes associated with pits, gullies and lithics and some kind of shelter suggested itself. The amount of work achieved in three weeks was surprisingly great considering the appalling weather. Continuous rain led to a steady but increasingly rapid rise in the water level of Loch Doon until all trenches were inundated. A series of photographs shows frantic efforts to retrieve information from trench 6 on one darkening evening. The battle was finally lost, bailing and recording ceased and the trench was left to its own fate; volunteers willingly assisted Tom in the dire conditions – and only the hot soup prepared by supercook Anne Johnston back at Starr Cottage was able to temper the disappointment felt by all. Next morning, insular spoil tips were the only sign that the trench had existed (Fig. 7.8). It is a mark of the respect in which Tom was held that volunteers were willing to tolerate rain, water, midges and a cottage without power or running water, in order to participate on the Starr digs.

The only useful radiocarbon dating evidence from Starr came from hazel charcoal 10 cm within a firespot ringed by a setting of rotted granite boulders. This was located on the loch shore 38 m south of 1985 trench 2 and an AMS date of 6 230 ± 80 BP (OxA-1 596) was obtained. This date is indistinguishable from that of 6 260 ± 80 for a hazelnut shell from the firespot in trench 1 at Smittons (Edwards 1989a). Two dates of 2 415 ± 25 (GrN-13 135) and 2 395 ± 25 BP (GrN-13 136) obtained from the base of peat in 1984 trenches 1 and 3 respectively clearly post-date the Mesolithic levels at Starr.

Auchareoch, Arran

In June 1985, immediately prior to beginning the second season of excavation at Starr, Tom, assisted by Isobel Hughes and Ann Clarke, travelled to Arran to carry out a survey of lithic distributions at a Mesolithic pitchstone and flint site. I blame myself for this distraction from doctoral activities! In 1984, I had been shown an eroding quarry site close to Auchareoch Farm in southern Arran by a local geography teacher Chris Allen. Both he and archaeologist Peter Strong had collected over 1 800 lithics from the site. The geography students from Birmingham carried out a site survey and I collected environmental samples. I enthused about the site to Tom and expressed concerns about its chances of survival. Tom managed to obtain financial assistance from the Department of Archaeology at the University of Glasgow and the lithic survey of his team produced another 2 600 artefacts. The narrow blade assemblages bore significant parallels with

Fig. 7.8. Flooded trenches, Loch Doon, 1985.

other west coast ones such as Newton, Islay (McCullagh 1991), Lealt Bay, Jura (Mercer 1968) and Kinloch, Rhum (Wickham-Jones 1990). An AMS date of 8 060 ± 90 (OxA-1 601) for a charred hazelnut shell at Auchareoch (Affleck et al. 1989) adds to the corpus of sites from western Scotland which suggests that a classsic narrow blade technology was established at or before 8 000 BP (cf. Woodman 1990).

Garleffin, Ballantrae

With a growing reputation for quality work, Tom was engaged by Noel Fojut of the Scottish Development Department to carry out a survey of a site at Garleffin, 1 km southeast of Ballantrae, Ayrshire, in advance of a projected road construction. An intended fieldwalking exercise turned into an excavation as 18 (1 m²) test pits were opened with the aid of six Glasgow students in five days just before Christmas 1985. Assisted by Tony Pollard, Tom aligned his trenches in relation to the juxtaposition of the road line with the so-called '50-foot' raised beach. Lithics were found in all 18 pits, with a density varying between 1 and 18 artefacts per pit and a total of 100 finds (94 flint, 3 chert and 3 pitchstone; 92 per cent of the total being débitage). More than half of the flint at Garleffin appeared to have been burned (surface crazing), but no firespots, hearths or structures were found. The records from Garleffin, like those previously reported from the Ballantrae area (Lacaille 1930, 1945), come from the downslope side of the 50-foot beach and would seem to confirm this topographic element as a major zone of activity during the Mesolithic.

Other Mesolithic Studies

In addition to the excavation work and the analysis of results, Tom also saw the value in continued additions to our knowledge of lithic distributions. He added find spots around Loch Dee and Clatteringshaws Loch (Fig. 7.2), but a long-cherished notion of searching for finds along a possible routeway from the Solway to the east and west coasts was never realised:

> I have plans to fieldwalk the upper stretches of the R. Nith north of Thorn-hill and especially the broader stretches of the valley near Kirkconnel and Sanquhar. In this northern stretch of the Nith system we are getting close to the headwaters of the Clyde and Tweed – the well-known Biggar Gap (letter dated 15 February 1984)

ENVOI

In a letter dated 9 February 1985, Tom acknowledged that 'keyhole' excavation could only result in a partial picture; he was fully aware that long trench or extensive areal excavation was superior. He was, however, working with relatively little help, and his use of many small trenches represented an essential compromise given the nature of assumed Mesolithic evidence and the requirements of a field- and excavation-based doctoral project in which environmental evidence was to play a major role. In July 1984, he had written:

> ... it seems important that there should be as much integration of our respective [research] programmes as possible. To this end I propose, at Starr, to arrange my trial trenches, where convenient, to include exposed 'soil', shallow partly-eroded peat overlay, and the apparently deeper layers of peat which occur in the small channels or gullies between the more exposed areas. This should show an overall stratigraphy, and hopefully serve both our purposes.

Parts of the environmental work have appeared (Affleck et al. 1989, Edwards 1989b, Newell 1990, Edwards et al. 1991), as well as tantalising glimpses of the archaeology (Affleck 1983, 1984, 1985, 1986; Edwards 1989a). Tom also placed his lithic collections at the disposal of Bill Finlayson (1989) who was able to carry out use-wear analysis on them as part of his doctoral research.

Throughout these all too brief years, Tom gave extra-mural classes in archaeology and botany; he carried out an excavation at the early Christian site of St Connel's chapel, Tynron, close to Moniaive in March and July, 1983 and in September 1985; and he still found the time to help with the lambing on daughter Jan's farm in Northumberland. Tom and Isabel provided superb hospitality at The Old Bank House and even now it is easy to conjure up an image of Tom standing before a peat fire in Moniaive, stroking his beard thoughtfully, beginning another story, while Isabel tries to usher him into the adjacent dining room where he would take his place at the head of the table. It is impossible to forget

Tom's humour, openness, generosity, spontaneity and his conscientiousness, all packed into a striking tall, lean frame. His grave in Glencairn churchyard, close to Moniaive, contains a flint and a piece of coarseware, and his headstone bears a Pictish motif – gestures he would have appreciated, if only to puzzle future generations of archaeologists!

ACKNOWLEDGEMENTS
Thanks are due to Isabel, Jim and Jan for sharing their thoughts, memories, kindnesses and homes over the years; and Anne Johnston, Mary Kemp Clarke and Tony Pollard for their encouragement.

Environmental and radiocarbon dating research was supported by grants from the Science and Engineering Research Council to the author.

In order to fulfill a promise, I would like to place on record the fact that this paper is the first written upon the author's new desk – a leaving present from colleagues at the University of Birmingham. This would have amused Tom whose response might have been: 'Why did you wait so long before writing this, and why did they wait so long before getting rid of you?'

REFERENCES
Affleck, T. 1983. Loch Dee, flints; Clatteringshaws Loch, flint; Moniaive, flints; St Connel's Chapel, early ecclesiastical site; Smittons, enclosure, Mesolithic flints. *Discovery and Excavation in Scotland*. Council for British Archaeology, Scotland, 4–6.

Affleck, T. 1984. Loch Dee, Mesolithic flint and chert artefacts; Clatteringshaws Loch, Mesolithic site. *Discovery and Excavation in Scotland*. Council for British Archaeology, Scotland, 6.

Affleck, T. L. 1985. Excavation at Starr 1, Loch Doon. August 1984. *Glasgow Archaeological Society Bulletin* 20, 4–6.

Affleck, T. L. 1986. Excavation at Starr, Loch Doon 1985. *Glasgow Archaeological Society Bulletin* 22, 10–21.

Affleck, T. L., Edwards, K. J. and Clarke, A. 1989. Archaeological and palynological studies at the Mesolithic pitchstone and flint site of Auchareoch, Isle of Arran. *Proceedings of the Society of Antiquaries of Scotland* 118 (1988), 37–59.

Clark, J. G. D. 1954. *Excavations at Star Carr*. Cambridge: Cambridge University Press.

Cormack, W. F. 1970. A Mesolithic site at Barsalloch, Wigtownshire. *Transactions of the Dumfriesshire and Galloway Natural History and Antiquarian Society* 47, 63–80.

Cormack, W. F. and Coles, J. M. 1964. A Mesolithic site at Low Clone, Wigtownshire. *Transactions of the Dumfriesshire and Galloway Natural History and Antiquarian Society* 41, 67–98.

Edwards, K. J. 1989a. Meso-Neolithic vegetational impacts in Scotland and beyond: palynological considerations. In Bonsall, C. (ed.), *The Mesolithic in Europe*. Edinburgh: John Donald, 143–55.

Edwards, K. J. 1989b. Comment on dates from S.W. Scotland. In Hedges, R. E. M., Housely, R. A., Law, I. A. and Bronk, C. R., Radiocarbon dates from the Oxford AMS system: Archaeometry datelist 9. *Archaeometry* 31, 217–18.

Edwards, K. J., Ansell, M. and Carter, B. A. 1983. New Mesolithic sites in south-west Scotland and their significance as indicators of inland penetration. *Transactions of the Dumfriesshire and Galloway Natural History and Antiquarian Society* 58, 9–15.

Edwards, K. J., Hirons, K. R. and Newell, P. J. 1991. The palaeoecological and pre-historic context of minerogenic layers in blanket peat: a study from Loch Dee, southwest Scotland. *The Holocene* 1, 29–39.

Finlayson, B. 1989. *A Pragmatic Approach to the Functional Analysis of Chipped Stone Tools*. Unpublished Ph.D. thesis, University of Edinburgh.

Lacaille, A. D. 1930. Mesolithic implements from Ayrshire. *Proceedings of the Society of Antiquaries of Scotland* 64, 34–48.

Lacaille, A. D. 1945. The stone industries associated with the raised beach at Ballantrae. *Proceedings of the Society of Antiquaries for Scotland* 79, 81–106.

Lacaille, A. D. 1954. *The Stone Age in Scotland*. London: Oxford University Press.

McCullagh, R. 1991. Excavation at Newton, Islay. *Glasgow Archaeological Journal* 15, 23–51.

MacNeill, M. 1975. Small finds, Dreghorn and Drybridge. *Discovery and Excavation in Scotland*. Council for British Archaeology, Scotland, 58.

Masters, L. J. 1981. A Mesolithic hearth at Redkirk Point, Gretna. *Transactions of the Dumfriesshire and Galloway Natural History and Antiquarian Society* 56, 111–14.

Mercer, J. 1968. Stone tools from a washing-limit deposit of the highest Post-glacial transgression, Lealt Bay, Isle of Jura. *Proceedings of the Society of Antiquaries of Scotland* 100, 1–46.

Mercer, J. 1980. Lussa Wood I: the Late-glacial and early Post-glacial occupation of Jura. *Proceedings of the Society of Antiquaries of Scotland* 110, 1–32.

Morrison, A. 1980. *Early Man in Britain and Ireland*. London: Croom Helm.

Newell, P. J. 1990. *Aspects of the Flandrian vegetational history of south-west Scotland, with special reference to possible Mesolithic impact*. Unpublished Ph.D. thesis, University of Birmingham.

Wickham-Jones, C. R. 1990. *Rhum: Mesolithic and Later Sites at Kinloch, Excavations 1984–1986*. Society of Antiquaries of Scotland Monograph Series no. 7.

Woodman, P. C. 1990. A review of the Scottish Mesolithic: a plea for normality! *Proceedings of the Society of Antiquaries of Scotland* 119, 1–32.

8

THE SOUTHERN HEBRIDES
MESOLITHIC PROJECT

RECONSTRUCTING MESOLITHIC SETTLEMENT
IN WESTERN SCOTLAND

STEVEN MITHEN AND MARK LAKE

The Southern Hebrides Mesolithic Project (SHMP) was established in 1988 to undertake survey and excavation on Islay and Colonsay for Mesolithic settlement. These are two of the islands which comprise the archipelago of the southern Hebrides (Fig. 8.1). Previous Mesolithic research in this region has been on the two other major islands of the southern Hebrides, Oronsay (Mellars 1987) and Jura (Mercer 1968–76). By acquiring new data from Colonsay and Islay, and integrating this with data from previous research, the SHMP aims to develop a regional perspective on early postglacial settlement. By so doing, the project hopes to be able to address a range of outstanding problems concerning the early prehistory of Scotland, including the process of colonisation, inter-assemblage variability during the Mesolithic, and the transition to the Neolithic. The character of such problems has been reviewed by Woodman (1989).

The first phase of the project lasted until 1992 and involved survey work on Colonsay by fieldwalking and test-pitting, together with excavations at the sites of Bolsay Farm and Gleann Mor on Islay. The second phase, 1992–5, has involved survey work and test excavations on Islay, combined with the excavation of the site of Staosnaig on Colonsay and programmes of experimental archaeology, palaeoenvironmental studies and computer modelling. The fieldwork was completed in the summer of 1995. Post-excavation, artefact, palaeoenvironmental and quantitative studies will continue for a further two years, during which time a monograph describing the work and results of the project will be prepared, to be published by the McDonald Institute for Archaeological Research, Cambridge. This paper will provide a broad overview of the project, describing the range of research it encompasses and summarising the new Mesolithic sites excavated by the project.

PROJECT STRUCTURE

The research of the SHMP is multidisciplinary and can be divided into five general categories: archaeological fieldwork, post-excavation studies, artefact studies,

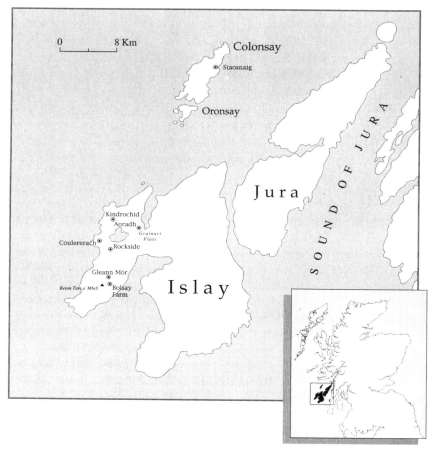

Fig. 8.1. Location of the Southern Hebrides, marking the sites and places referred to in the text.

palaeoenvironmental studies and quantitative and computer studies. The following provides a brief summary of the work within each of these categories.

Archaeological Fieldwork

Fieldwork has involved a variety of survey and excavation methods on Colonsay
and Islay, ranging from fieldwalking to area excavation. In addition to the three
principle excavations at the sites of Gleann Mor, Bolsay Farm and Staosnaig,
test excavations have been carried out at locations on Islay (Rockside,
Coulererach, Kindrochid and Aoradh) and several other locations have been test-
pitted. In the next section of this paper we will discuss the methodologies of this
fieldwork and provide brief site summaries.

Post-Excavation Studies

The principle element of post-excavation studies is the analysis of the chipped stone assemblages from the fieldwork, largely undertaken by Dr B. Finlayson (Edinburgh University) and Nyree Finlay (Reading University) (see Finlayson, Finlay & Mithen, this volume). Due to the soil conditions of the Hebrides faunal remains only survive in substantial amounts in shell middens, a type of site the project has not excavated. In addition to the chipped stone assemblages there is a substantial assemblage of coarse stone artefacts from the sites, and at Bolsay Farm a large, but poorly preserved, pottery assemblage from later prehistoric occupation on the site. In addition to these artefact studies, there is a range of post-excavation work being undertaken on the soils and sediments including micromorphological studies of soils from Bolsay Farm and Gleann Mor by Dr C. French (Cambridge University) and for Staosnaig by Dr S. Carter (AOC, Scotland).

Artefact Studies

The SHMP includes a series of artefact research projects which extends the analysis of material beyond the requirements of post excavation. Dr B. Finlayson is undertaking a microwear study of selected artefact classes from the Gleann Mor and Bolsay Farm chipped stone assemblages. A particular interest within this study is the analysis of microliths as both assemblages provide large samples which are suitable for wear analysis. Moreover, these microliths show a wide degree of morphological variability. Consequently this research is exploring the relationship, if any, between microlithic morphology and wear traces. For this study low power microscopy is being used, the aim being to simply establish the presence of wear traces and general attributes of these, such as hard/soft material and direction of motion, rather than attempting to make detailed reconstructions of past use.

A series of experimental studies are also being undertaken. Nyree Finlay is conducting replication experiments concerned with the manufacture of microliths with particular emphasis on variation between individual knappers. She will also be constructing multi-component tools using replicated microliths, such as arrows and vegetable graters, and exploring microlith breakage patterns from their use. This work is being undertaken within a general context of re-evaluating widespread interpretations of the Mesolithic with regard to the types of activities likely to have been undertaken by men and women.

Experimental knapping is also being used to explore the spatial patterning of debitage, and how this varies with raw material and knapping methods (e.g. platform versus bipolar cores). Experimental artefact use has also involved 'limpet hammers'. These are elongated pebbles, often having a bevelled end, which vary in size from a few centimetres to over 25 cm in length. Such artefacts have been particularly prominent in shell middens, although they are also found within the sites excavated by the SHMP. Whether they were used for detaching limpets has always remained unclear. Consequently the SHMP has undertaken a series of experiments using replica artefacts. These experiments have involved the use of such artefacts for a range of tasks, such as removing limpets, as hammer stones in knapping and for cleaning hides. Initial results suggest they are indeed effective at removing limpets and that this creates wear and breakage patterns similar to those found on artefacts from Mesolithic sites. Although they are generally ineffective as hammerstones, this also appears to create similar wear/breakage patterns.

Palaeoenvironmental Studies

The most important element of the palaeoenvironmental studies being undertaken by the project is a study of changing sea levels in the southern Hebrides during the late glacial and early postglacial. Understanding this is of upmost importance when studying the Mesolithic due to the importance of coastal resources and the significance of travel costs between islands for influencing settlement patterns.

The geomorphological evidence on the islands in the form of raised beaches is principally informative about two periods of high sea level: that of the late glacial when it reached $c.25$ m OD and the maximum transgression of $c.6\,500$ BP when the sea level reached $c.10$ m OD. This last transgression has essentially destroyed any geomorphological evidence for the location of the sea level during the principle period of Mesolithic settlement studied by the SHMP, that is $8-7\,000$ BP. Consequently a project has been established under the aegis of the SHMP directed by Dr A. Dawson (Coventry University) to establish the sea level curve for this intervening period.

The principle means of doing this is by locating buried land surfaces beneath the sediments of the $6\,500$ BP transgression. An analysis of the pollen and diatoms from these sediments is then being used to establish the sequence of environmental change. This sequence is in turn being dated by acquiring a series of dates on the buried land surfaces. In 1993 a programme of coring was undertaken in the area of Gruinart flats on Islay which successfully located a peat horizon sandwiched between marine silts at a depth of $c.5.0$ m. A series of cores were taken and current research is establishing the diatom sequence within these cores, interpreting this with regard to environmental changes and acquiring radiocarbon dates. This work is integrated with completion of the mapping and interpretation of the geomorphological features on Islay, especially in the vicinity of the Loch Gorm region.

With regard to reconstructing the early postglacial vegetation on Islay, the SHMP has been fortunate due to the work undertaken by Professor K. Edwards (Sheffield University) at Lochá Bhogaidh. This is adjacent to two of the SHMP excavated sites in the Rhinns of Islay and Professor Edwards has recently published a pollen sequence from the Loch covering the early postglacial period (Edwards and Berridge in press, Edwards and Mithen 1994). Further palaeoenvironmental information concerning vegetation is available from the Sorn Valley on Islay published as part of the excavations at Newton (McCullagh 1988). To supplement this existing information Elaine Carp (Reading University) is working on a series of pollen cores from the vicinity of Loch Gorm, around which the SHMP is exploring three Mesolithic sites, Rockside, Coulererach and Kindrochid. One of these cores was taken during the course of excavations at Coulererach and provides a fine pollen sequence for part of the later prehistoric period, between *c.* 4 700 and 4 000 BP. Additional cores have been taken from the edge of Loch Gorm but how far these extend back into prehistory remains to be established.

A third element of the SHMP palaeoenvironmental studies concerns raw material distribution (Mithen 1995). Understanding the distribution and character of raw materials is an essential part of interpreting lithic assemblages from Mesolithic sites. The manner in which cores are worked, and consequently the character of debitage assemblages, is likely to vary with the availability and quality of raw material. Consequently prior to interpreting assemblages with regard to factors such as function and style, the influence of raw material characteristics on assemblage variability must be established. This requires an understanding of the location and character of raw material sources.

In the southern Hebrides the principle lithic raw material used during the Mesolithic was flint beach pebbles. Initial survey work in 1988–1990 established that these were found at highly variable densities around the coast of Islay. Consequently in 1993 a research project was set up to explore this distribution in detail by Gilbert Marshall (Southampton University). His initial work has involved a systematic survey of the coastlines of the southern Hebrides and adjacent mainland to identify the general distribution of flint pebbles. This has been followed by a series of detailed surveys at a sample of beaches aimed at establishing the variability in the density, quality and sizes of pebbles. The preliminary results indicate that the principle raw material location during the Mesolithic would have been the west coast of Islay. The source of these pebbles appear to be a glacial marine deposit in this area which includes nodules of flint which are likely to have originated fron Northern Ireland. The erosion of this glacial-marine deposit results in flint nodules being washed up on the beaches.

Gilbert Marshall is acquiring quantitative data on the character of the modern beaches as a raw material source which will then facilitate the interpretation of the excavated assemblages. Prior to this, however, one must make allowances for the changes in the coastline since the Mesolithic and how this may have effected the patterns of erosion and deposition of flint pebbles. Consequently, there is a close link between this aspect of palaeoenvironmental reconstruction and that concerning past sea levels.

Quantitative and Computer Studies

One of the initial aims of the SHMP was to acquire data in a systematic fashion to allow a quantitative analysis of the lithic assemblages and associated material, in an attempt to introduce a greater degree of objectivity into prehistoric studies than is often the case. Three aspects of the quantitative and computer work are briefly described here: intra-site spatial analysis, predictive modelling of settlement location and computer simulation.

While there has been a considerable development of intra-site spatial analysis during the last decade in archaeology, this continues to play a very limited role in British archaeology. With regard to the Scottish Mesolithic, intra-site spatial analysis may help in identifying the location of specific activities on sites, unravelling palimpsests of artefacts which have arisen from multiple occupations, and distinguishing between knapping floors and artefact 'dumps'. If such studies are to be undertaken it is essential that data is recorded in an appropriate fashion, especially with regard to consistency at different sites to allow inter-site comparisons.

The majority of spatial analyses to be undertaken by the project will involve use of data recorded in quadrats, rather than point data, simply because of the vast resources required to record adequate amounts of data for the latter method, although this has been undertaken at Gleann Mor. Excavations have either used 25 cm or 50 cm square quadrats. This will allow a variety of spatial analytical methods to be used, such as unconstrained cluster analysis as described by Whallon (1984).

With regard to the distribution of sites in the landscape the problem that the SHMP faces is the very limited amount of the landscape that is available for survey due to peat, blown sand, and the limited amount of arable farming. Indeed, as Mesolithic sites rarely leave any surface features the problem of locating sites is one of the major reasons for the long history of neglect of Mesolithic studies in Scotland. At present, it is simply unclear to what extent the distribution of Mesolithic sites in the landscape reflect past settlement patterns rather than being simply a function of modern farming practice and archaeological activity.

To tackle this problem the SHMP is building a predictive model for Mesolithic settlement on Islay, from which it is hoped a general understanding of Mesolithic settlement location and the biased nature of the archaeological record will arise. This research is being undertaken by Paddy Woodman (Reading University). Her overall approach is to develop a series of expectations for Mesolithic site locations on Islay by drawing on a series of archaeological and ethnographic case studies in which both site locations and topographic features are known. By using these to establish statistical relationships between site location and topography, and using the known topography of Islay, a probability surface for site distribution will be created on the island. This work draws on three archaeological case studies: the Tweed Valley, which provides a sample of $c.100$ lithic scatters; the west coast of Scotland stretching from Redkirk Point on the Solway Firth to An Corran on the Isle of Sky; and the vicinity of Loch Doon which provides a sample of $c.60$ lithic scatters. Supplementing these is information from two ethnographic case studies: the Haida Indians of the Queen Charlotte islands off the North West coast of America, and the Alacalut/Yahgan Indians of Tierra del Fuego. These two areas have been chosen as they bear a topographic similarity to the southern Hebrides and provide adequate ethnographic data describing the settlement location of the local hunter-gatherers. The probability surface for Islay will be generated by implementing the ethnographically and archaeologically derived settlement model as a Geographical Information Systems (GIS) model for Islay. The GIS model will be constructed using GRASS software.

This computer study is essentially working from known data sets to predict settlement location. Supplementing this study is a NERC funded post-doctoral research project at Reading University which integrates GIS and computer simulation modelling to explore Mesolithic settlement. This is being undertaken by Mark Lake who is developing a model for the colonisation of the islands by hunter-gatherers. In essence, this involves the construction of a GIS model for the southern Hebrides using GRASS software. The landscape described in the GIS is dynamically updated to model the environmental changes of the early postglacial. Multi-agent simulation modelling is then used to populate this landscape with foragers who will make decisions about where and when to move. By combining GIS and multi-agent simulation it will be possible to add a spatial dimension to the study of hunter-gatherer decision-making undertaken by Mithen (1990). As with Mithen's previous models this project will simulate the creation of the archaeological record. Consequently it is expected to facilitate both the interpretation of data from fieldwork and the development of new fieldwork strategies.

Summary

These brief summaries of the five project elements provides an overview of the range of research required to understand early postglacial settlement in a landscape such as the southern Hebrides. We now want to focus on the methodologies adopted for just one of the research components referred to above: archaeological fieldwork.

FIELDWORK METHODS AND SITE SUMMARIES

This section will provide a brief summary of the fieldwork undertaken by the project, focussing on the survey and excavation methodologies it has adopted. It will offer preliminary interpretations of each of the sites discussed.

The Landscape as Site

The starting point for a summary of the fieldwork is to note that the project has attempted to conceive of the landscape as a single site with a continuous distribution of archaeological material across it, rather than adopting a site-oriented approach to fieldwork. In practice, of course, excavations, and indeed past activity, are inevitably focused at specific locations in the landscape: the notion of 'landscape as site' is of more significance for interpretation rather than the practice of fieldwork itself. The exception to this would be if one was working with an enormous budget that allowed a true systematic sampling of the whole landscape.

Survey Methodologies

Three methods of survey have been employed. The most important of these is fieldwalking. In an area such as the southern Hebrides, where the extent and precise timing of ploughing from year to year is unpredictable, fieldwalking must be undertaken on a more reactive basis than in areas such as southern England. Whereas in the latter a proper campaign of survey can be planned, with a carefully devised sampling strategy for different soils and topography, in the southern Hebrides the most appropriate military analogy is a war of attrition. Since only a small percentage of the landscape is ploughed it is only possible to make decisions about which areas to walk, and with what intensity, when one is actually in the field. In spite of this handicap, persistent fieldwork over a number of years can be very rewarding: the SHMP has now amassed a considerable amount of information from fieldwalking on Islay and Colonsay.

The main strategy for acquiring this information has been to walk fields as complete units making a subjective note of possible artefact concentrations. If these appear to be of interest the initial investigation is followed up with a gridded collection over part or all of the field. This strategy is particularly appropriate because the project has had to work with inexperienced fieldwalkers and a wide range of weather and soil conditions. Consequently keeping the walking method as simple as possible has been a priority. Fortunately the fieldwalking survey on Islay has been directed for three years by Margaret Mathews (Reading University) who has ensured consistency of collecting in spite of a new team of inexperienced fieldwalkers each fieldseason. The gridded collections have been undertaken to map the spatial distribution of artefacts, partly to assess whether below surface investigation should be undertaken.

The second method of survey is by test-pitting. This is labour intensive but an essential method to adopt when working in highland regions with such limited amounts of ploughing. While test-pitting can never provide a detailed understanding of a site, it can provide a sample of the lithic assemblage at a site from a relatively small investment as compared to full excavation. The SHMP has adopted test-pitting in two contexts. The first is when a concentration of artefacts has been identified by gridded fieldwalking (or other means as discussed below) and further information is required, such as regarding the lithic assemblage, the spatial distribution of artefacts, or the soil profile. This additional information is often required to make a decision about whether excavation is warranted, and if so the form that this should take.

The second context for test-pitting is when a part of the landscape needs to be examined and there is simply no other means to explore whether traces of Mesolithic settlement exist. Many of the potential locations for Mesolithic settlement are in locations which are not used for arable farming, and these are often covered in peat or blown sand. Other then attempting to find areas of erosion which may expose underlying sediments, there is no choice but to undertake a test-pitting exercise. The development of a predictive model for settlement location, as described above, will hopefully facilitate this type of survey work.

In several cases, test-pitting by the SHMP has been undertaken due to finds by the third survey method of the project: drawing on local knowledge and encouraging farmers to collect arterfacts from their fields. This is not difficult. Indeed in several cases farmers have been so enthusiastic that the amount of material collected from their fields has threatened to destroy an artefact scatter. Drawing on local knowledge is essential for work in the Hebrides when ploughing times are so irregular and many of the finds come from contexts such as ditch sections which are cleaned at unpredictable times during the year.

Excavation Methodologies

Excavations by the the SHMP have been undertaken at three scales: test-pitting (which has been discussed as a survey method), trial trenching used to expose long sections and to search for features, and area excavation ranging from small trenches (4 × 4 m) to relatively large trenches (15 × 20 m). To explain how these different scales of excavation have been used, and how the survey and excavation methodologies interact, this section provides brief summaries about the sites excavated by the SHMP. This section also introduces the range of contingent factors that influence the practice of fieldwork. The emphasis in this section is with the aims and methods of excavation, rather than the results.

Gleann Mor

The site of Gleann Mor was located by following reports of microliths eroding from the edge of a disused quarry on Gleann Mor in the Rhinns of Islay (Fig. 8.2). A visit to the site in 1988 confirmed this, and indicated that erosion of the quarry face was occurring rapidly. The artefacts were derived from a thin soil horizon sandwiched between the base of the peat and an iron pan composing a gleyed podzol. At this stage it was, of course, unclear what the artefacts represented. They could have derived from a discrete artefact scatter that had been largely destroyed by the quarry; alternatively just the edge of the site may have been disturbed. A third possibility was that the artefacts represented a low density artefact scatter covering this area of moorland with no clear spatial boundaries.

To resolve this the initial work at the site consisted of test-pitting around the immediate vicinity of the site in 1988 (Mithen 1990) and in a 50 m radius in 1990. This work demonstrated that the second of the above possibilities was correct: there was a well-preserved, discrete and high density artefact scatter which had been clipped by the edge of the quarry. As such, this was located on a shoulder from which excellent views are available in two directions, although whether this would have also been the case with greater tree cover is unclear.

Fig. 8.2. The Sand quarry at Gleann Mor and the excavation cover marking location of the 1989 excavation (photo: Mark Lake).

The initial excavation at Gleann Mor was concerned with recovering a larger sample of the lithic material, acquiring material for absolute dating, and attempting to locate features which may help identifying the function of the site.

In 1989 a 4 × 4 metre trench was excavated. This was located within the heart of the artefact scatter and employed a meticulous recovery method for artefacts (Fig. 8.3). The site was excavated in four 5 cm spits and within each spit an attempt was made to plot any artefact greater than 1 cm in two dimensions. The excavated sediment from each 0.5 m square across the site was washed through a 3 mm wet sieve and the remaining artefacts picked from the residue. A charcoal fragment from within the artefact scatter has been radiocarbon dated to 7 100 ± 125 BP.

This method of excavation had mixed success. The poor finances of the project in 1988 prevented an adequate cover being constructed across the site and the wet and freezing cold weather during the excavations had inevitable effects on the efficiency of recovery. Nevertheless c.12 000 artefacts were plotted in three dimensions on the site and a further 1 000 recovered from the sieve residues and located to within a 50 cm quadrat. Not surprisingly there was considerable variability between different artefact classes in the extent to which piece plotting occurred, with the best results coming from cores for which 91 per cent (143) were plotted to their 3D locations. Whether this meticulous, and highly labour intensive recovery method was worthwhile remains to be seen. The spatial

Fig. 8.3. Excavation at Gleann Mor 1990, illustrating piece plotting of artefacts (photo: Mark Lake).

analysis of the data will explore whether it has provided information about artefact distribution patterns that could equally have been acquired by recovery in,
say 10 cm or 25 cm quadrats.

In addition to this trench, two additional 4 × 2 m trenches were excavated in
1989 away from the high density artefact scatter itself. These were specifically
aimed at locating features, as none had been identified within the initial trench.
These were excavated much more rapidly by recovering artefacts to 0.5 m
quadrats alone and with no wet sieving of sediments. They failed to locate any
features. It remains unclear as to whether no features were created during the
Mesolithic occupation, or whether these have become archaeologically invisible
due to the pedogenesis of the site.

Our current interpretation of this site is that it was a hunting camp located
with views down two adjacent valleys to watch for the movement of game. The
initial results from the microwear studies indicate that some of the microliths
at the site had been used as projectile points, although others had been used as
part of cutting and drilling implements. The small spatial extent of the site, and
very discrete distribution of material, suggest that it was occupied on just one
or two occasions. We suspect that similar discrete scatters of artefacts would be
found on other rises and shoulders surrounding Loch á Bhogaidh, each reflecting a short term event involved with monitoring the changing resources in this
vicinity of the Rhinns. As such, we suspect that each of these would be satellite
camps from larger residential sites. One of these may be the next site we will
describe, Bolsay Farm.

Bolsay Farm

While excavating at Gleann Mor in 1988 our attention was drawn to Bolsay Farm.
This is a disused farm approximately 3 km west of Gleann Mor, the fields of
which were tenanted to Craigfad Farm (Fig. 8.4). Although these fields were in
pasture in 1988 we were informed by the farmer, Mr Clark, that when under
plough flint had been quite prominent. This was confirmed by the artefacts that
Mr Clark had collected which included a series of blade cores similar to those
currently being excavated at Gleann Mor.

The possibility of a site at Bolsay was of considerable interest not only due to
its vicinity to Gleann Mor, but also because Boslay Farm is adjacent to Loch á
Bhogaidh from which Kevin Edwards had extracted a pollen sequence. Consequently in 1988 we undertook a test-pitting exercise. This was very limited in
scope due to the limited resources of the project. It was undertaken by digging
0.5 m test-pits on a 20 m grid across about 25 per cent of the total area. A 20 m
grid is of little value, as the whole of the Gleann Mor site could easily have fitted
between test-pits. Yet, having a little luck on this occasion, a high density artefact scatter was located in the western area of the fields at Bolsay. Test-pits
excavated on a 10 and 5 m grid in this area served to define the boundaries of
the artefact scatter, in terms of marked changes in artefact densiites.

Fig. 8.4. View of Bolsay Farm with the 1990 excavation marked by the poly-tunnel (photo: Mark Lake).

In 1989 a 7 × 4 m trench was excavated in the eastern half of the site with the same aims of the initial excavation at Gleann Mor: to recover a larger artefact assemblage, to acquire material for absolute dating and to attempt to locate features. In addition to these, the excavation had the intention of attempting to understand the stratigraphy of the site. Whereas that within the test-pits at Gleann Mor was constant and relatively simple, at Bolsay Farm the test-pits indicated a deep and complex stratigraphy that could not be understood from the test-pits themselves.

Excavation of this trench proceeded by stratigraphic levels, and by 5 cm spits when these were required, with artefact recovery to 0.5 m squares. Spoil from the ploughsoil was handsorted, while that from sealed contexts was wet sieved, followed by a picking of artefacts from the residues. This excavation method proved to be extremely slow due to the very high density of artefacts at the site. Consequently it was only in one 0.5 m wide strip at the eastern edge of the trench that all contexts to the underlying glacial marine sediment were excavated. This was supplemented by a 2 × 2 m area at the north end of the trench where a series of stake holes were located, and a 2 × 2 metre trench at the southern end where a pit had been identified.

This excavation provided the SHMP with a large sample of artefacts from Bolsay Farm, material for dating and evidence for features at the site. Radiocarbon dating of charcoal from the southern pit gave a date of 7250 ± 145 BP, which is consistent with TL dating of flint artefacts at 7.93 ± 0.59 Kyr BP. An interpretation of the stratigraphy indicated that the site consisted of an *in situ* horizon, sealed

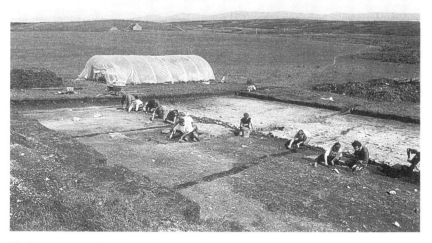

Fig. 8.5. 1992 excavation at Bolsay Farm (photo: Mark Lake).

by colluvium and a plough soil. All of these levels had a very high density of artefacts. It appeared likely, therefore, that a relatively large area of *in situ* occupation
deposits survived at Bolsay Farm (Mithen et al. 1992).

The 1992 excavation was designed to acquire data for a study of the spatial
distribution of artefacts within this *in situ* horizon at the site. Consequently it
aimed to expose and excavate as large an area as possible with the limited resources of the project. Obviously this required a compromise between the spatial
extent excavated and the spatial resolution at which artefacts could be recovered.
Drawing on our experiences from Gleann Mor – the other on-going fieldwork
– we chose an area of 20 × 15 m and recovered artefacts from a 5 cm spit in 0.25 m
quadrats (Fig. 8.5).

This required the excavation of over 4 000 quadrats. Excavation in this case
involved shovelling up all the sediment from the quadrat, wet sieving it and picking artefacts from the residue. The exception to this occurred when features
were identified, which were primarily located at the northern end of the trench.
Artefacts picked from the sieve residues consisted of chipped stone, fragments
of coarse stone tools, burnt plant material and pottery fragments. The latter were
unexpected as none had been identified during the 1990 excavation and they
appear to reflect a later prehistoric occupation on the site. Prior to the sediment
fill from each quadrat being wet sieved a sample was taken for geochemical
analysis, and the fill was weighed to facilitate adjustments for human error in
the thickness of the deposit removed. Using these weights, the quantity of each

Fig. 8.6. View of the east coast of Colonsay, showing the locations of Staosnaig (Queen's Bay) (photo: Mark Lake).

artefact type from each quadrat can be converted to a density per unit of sediment volume. The sorting of sieve residues continued throughout two fieldseasons. The resulting pottery assemblage is being catalogued and interpreted by Dr Ann McSween (Edinburgh), the burnt plant material by Jamie Kaminski (Reading) and the coarse stone assemblage by Gilbert Marshall and Steven Mithen. The chipped stone assemblage, estimated to be at least 300 000 pieces, has been catalogued by Nyree Finlay and is currently being entered on a computer database in preparation for spatial analysis. Geochemical and micromorphological studies of soils from Bolsay are being undertaken in Reading and Cambridge.

The large spatial extent and the high density of material at Bolsay Farm suggest that this may be the remains of a residential settlement of the Mesolithic period, in contrast to the small hunting camps, such as at Gleann Mor. However, we must remain cautious about this interpretation as the site could be no more than many 'Gleann Mors' stacked on top of each other; in other words a palimpsest of many small occupations. We are hoping that the spatial analysis of artefact distributions and study of tool type diversity may help resolve this issue.

The site of Bolsay Farm certainly appears very well located with regard to exploiting the resources in the vicinity of Loch á Bhogaidh. At present red deer and roe deer feed around the margins of the lake and then pass behind Ben Tart a Mhill to northwest facing grazing pastures on the Rhinns. The Bolsay Farm site is very well located for watching and stalking such deer and the site lies down wind from these grazing and movement areas (prevailing winds will always principally have blown off the Atlantic), and is secured behind a small rise. Indeed, the area at Bolsay farm is still regularly used for stalking deer (which is one of the reasons we never started work at 5.00 am in the morning!).

Staosnaig

Staosnaig is the only location on Colonsay from which *in situ* Mesolithic artefacts have been recovered (Fig. 8.6). The site is located within a sheltered bay on the east coast of the island. It was indeed this topographic location that drew the SHMP's interest to Staosnaig. In 1987 the field had been ploughed for reseeding for grass, but fieldwalking failed to locate any artefacts. When the fieldwalking excercise was repeated in 1988, on a surface in which grass had effectively failed to grow, a single small blade core was recovered. In the autum of 1989, however, following a summer of heavy rains, the surface of the field was littered with artefacts, and an assemblage of *c*.400 pieces of worked flint and quartz was recovered by fieldwalking.

Having recovered this assemblage the field was then test-pitted during the same season. This excercise indicated that the artefacts were concentrated in two main loci, although artefact densities were very low as compared to Gleann Mor and Bolsay Farm (Mithen & Finlayson 1991). The initial excavation at Staosnaig was undertaken in 1991 to acquire a larger lithic assemblage, to explore whether *in situ* deposits survived and to acquire material for dating (Fig. 8.7). To this end a 7 × 4 m trench was excavated in the southernmost artefact concentration. This was undertaken in six 5 cm spits through the plough soil and underlying deposits with a recording of finds in 0.5 m quadrats. This method was adopted as we wished to explore the distribution of artefacts in the plough-soil itself. The lowermost spit cut into a raised beach deposit, which has since been suggested to date to approximately 13 000 BP (Dawson, pers comm.).

This excavation exposed a series of small, ephemeral features, the nature of which seemed appropriate to the character of the low density lithic assemblage. To explore the possibility of additional features at the site a series of test trenches was rapidly excavated during one week of fieldwork in poor weather conditions in March 1992. These trenches were 1 m wide, and were rapidly excavated to the plough soil with no collection of artefacts. One of these located part of what appeared to be a feature: a cut with a fill containing high densities of burnt hazelnuts, chipped stone and coarse stone artefacts.

In 1994 an excavation was undertaken to explore the nature of this, and any possible associated features. As with Bolsay Farm in 1992, the intention was simply to excavate as large an area as possible within the limited resources of the project. The cut identified in the 1992 test trench proved to be part of a large feature, which was fully excavated along with four smaller adjacent features (Fig. 8.8). As there was little clear stratigraphic division within this feature, the fill was principally excavated in four 5 cm spits. The fill from each 0.5 m quadrat for each spit was collected and 75 per cent wet sieved, with 25 per cent kept for

Fig. 8.7. Excavation at Staosnaig, 1991 (photo: Mark Lake).

flotation – in the manner illustrated in Fig. 8.9. Of the additional features, one of these contained a stone, cist-like structure, while the others were small pits and the remains of a hearth. The function of the features excavated during the 1994 season remains unclear at present, but will hopefully be clarified once the artefacts and burnt plant material from their fills have been analysed. The current working hypothesis is that the large feature is the base of a dwelling, while the features with stone linings/structures are storage pits.

Fig. 8.8. Feature 24, Staosnaig, 1994 (photo: Mark Lake).

The size and nature of these features is quite unusual for Mesolithic sites in Scotland and they were sufficiently substantial to have been identified by geophysical methods. Consequently, to explore whether any further features existed at Staosnaig, a geophysical survey was undertaken in January 1995. The intention had been to use both resistivity and magnetometry. The latter proved impossible as the constant strong wind prevented the magnetometer being held at an angle of more than 45 degrees to the horizontal.

The resistivity survey covered 7 300 square metres, representing approximately 85 per cent of the total field area. A total of 29 200 readings were logged over three days using an RMI5 resistivity meter. These were then analysed using Contours Geospan software. The results highlighted two areas of interest. Interpretation of an area of low resistance to the south of the 1994 excavation is made difficult by water run-off from the adjacent hillside. However, a second area of low resistance to the west may represent a feature on the same scale as that excavated in 1994.

During this survey there was time to excavate a further feature at Staosnaig. This was in the northern part of the site where rocks were exposed at the surface. Resistivity indicated abnormally high readings around these rocks. Removal of the turf in a 1.75 m square centred on the exposed rock uncovered a stone lined feature. This was sectioned and half of the fill removed for sieving.

Reflecting on the work at Staosnaig since 1987 one can see a logical sequence from fieldwalking, through test-pitting and initial excavation to the relatively

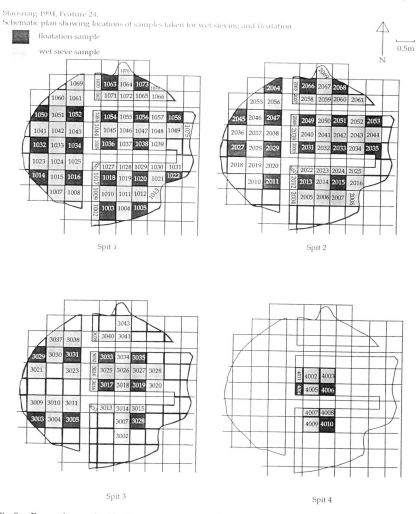

Fig. 8.9. Excavation method for feature 24, Staosnaig, showing the sampling procedure for wet sieving and flotation.

large scale excavation of 1994. Of course, with the benefit of hindsight, it would have been appropriate to have undertaken a geophysical survey at the site in 1988, and our failure to do this reflects the general expectation of no more than ephemeral features at Mesolithic sites. Indeed had we not undertaken the week's trial trenching in 1992 the site would still be described as an ephemeral occupation.

There can be no doubt that Staosnaig is a very important Mesolithic site, not just for Scotland but for the whole of Britain. Interpretation of the features must

await the results from the analysis but preliminary ideas suggest that we are dealing with the remains of a hut and storage pits. The processing of hazelnuts
appears to have been very intensive and on a substantial scale. There is also the
possibility that at least one of the features, that with what looks like a stone cist,
could have been a burial. This feature is indeed similar to the type of graves at
Téviec and Hoëdic in Brittany. Unfortunately no faunal remains survive at the
site (except for tiny fragments in the largest feature). Of all the sites excavated
by the SHMP Staosnaig deserves further excavation, which will hopefully be
undertaken in a follow up project focussing on this site.

Coulererach

Coulererach is the name of a small croft on the narrow stretch of land between
the western edge of Loch Gorm and the Atlantic ocean. The possible presence
of Mesolithic occupation in this vicinity was brought to our notice by the crofter,
Susan Campbell. When earlier living on Jura she had become acquainted with
John Mercer who taught her how to identify flint artefacts. While working
Coulererach during the 1980s she had collected numerous of these from her
ditches and field drains and passed them on the Islay Museum, who drew them
to the project's attention in 1988.

    It was not until 1993 that part of a fieldseason on Islay could be devoted to
Coulererach (Mithen 1993). The artefacts collected by Mrs Campbell had principally come from a ditch between two fields so we undertook a test-pitting
exercise across these. Only a restricted area could be examined due to rapid waterlogging and the slow rate of work caused by the the thick peat cover, averaging
1.5 m. Most of the test-pits produced an assemblage of artefacts from below the
peat, although in some artefacts were also recovered from within the peat itself.
This created an interesting problem as there appeared to be no clear technological or typological differences between the artefacts from below and within
the peat, although the small size and depth of the test-pits, together with the
very wet conditions, made the separation of these assemblages difficult. Consequently a test trench was excavated bisecting the area from which artefacts
appeared to be most dense (Fig. 8.10). The peat from this was rapidly removed
and samples of the underlying sediments taken for wet sieving. The within-peat
artefact horizon was evident at c.0.12 m below the surface (Fig. 8.11). An area
of 2 × 2 m was excavated in order to expose the scatter of artefacts in plan, and
the sediment in which these were located was then taken for wet sieving. The
result of this indicated that the assemblage from within the peat was techno-
logically indistinguishable from that coming from below the peat.

    In addition to using the section to locate the artefact horizon within the peat,
a series of monoliths were also taken for palaeoenvironmental studies. One of
these has since been sampled for pollen and a sequence of AMS radiocarbon dates
taken from the basal peat to above the within-peat artefact horizon. These indicate that the initiation of peat formation began at c.4700 BP and the 1.75 m of

Fig. 8.10. Excavation of the trial trench at Coulererach, 1993 (photo: Mark Lake).

peat in this monolith formed in *c.*1 000 years. Charcoal from amongst the arte-facts below the peat, which had a morphology indicative of coming from a hearth, was dated by AMS to 7 500 ± 110 BP. On this basis the within peat artefact horizon should date to *c.*4 000 BP – if it is an *in situ* occupation. If this is correct it indicates that a microlithic technology, indistinguishable from that being made 7 500 BP, continued into the Neolithic. The alternative, is that the artefact horizon is redeposited by down slope soil movement. A study of the pollen within this layer has proved inconclusive, and it is hoped that current micromorphological study will be able to differentiate between an *in situ* or a redeposited artefact horizon.

It is very desirable to undertake further work at Coulererach. There appears to be a considerable amount of re-fitting of artefacts from individual test-pits, suggesting that the occupation remains are undisturbed. The artefacts are very fresh and include some fine blade work and tanged microliths which have not been seen in any other assemblage recovered by the SHMP. Moreover, the location of the site is close to a wide range of resources: raw materials on the west coast of Islay, coastal resources (in 1994 a sperm whale was beached close to Coulererach) and terrestrial game in the vicinity of Loch Gorm. For these reasons Coulererach is likely to have been an attractive settlement location during the early postglacial, and the lithic remains of such settlement appear to be well preserved.

Fig. 8.11. Section of the north face of the Coulererach trial trench, 1993, showing artefact horizons below and within the peat (photo: Mark Lake).

Fig. 8.12. Location of Rockside (photo: Mark Lake).

These are sealed, however, below 1–2.0 m of peat, and any excavation of these results in severe drainage problems. Consequently it is unlikely that any substantial further work at Coulererach can be undertaken by a future project. Further small-scale work is also of little value: Coulererach requires/deserves a large area excavation. This could only be undertaken with substantial funding to allow removal of peat from the whole field and the installation of an efficient drainage system.

With regards to interpretation, the most important feature on Coulererach is its vicinity to the west coast of Islay which we believe to be the principal source of raw materials. The high frequency of cores and pebbles with single flakes detached indicates that Coulererach was a location where preliminary flint knapping activity took place. We also suspect that the site acted as a hunting camp for exploitation of the resources in what would have been highly productive margins of Loch Gorm. Indeed, Coulererach has provided microliths with tanged ends which may well have been dedicated to some specialised fishing or fowling activity in this area.

Rockside

The site of Rockside is located at the southern edge of Loch Gorm, approximately 1.5 kilometres from Coulererach (Fig. 8.12). Between 1992–4 a series of fields at Rockside were walked. Two of these provided assemblages which appeared Mesolithic in date due to a relatively high frequency of blades and low frequency of scrapers in comparison to assemblages from elsewhere on Islay.

Fig. 8.13. Excavation of Rockside, 1995, showing stable horizon sandwiched between two layers of hill wash (photo: Mark Lake).

In the spring of 1994 a test-pitting exercise was undertaken in a field of pasture that lay midway between the two which had been fieldwalked. This identified a concentration of artefacts distributed through a stratigraphic sequence of almost 2 metres in depth. As at Bolsay Farm in 1989, it proved impossible to understand this stratigraphy from the test pits alone and consequently a 20 × 1 m trench was cut to expose a section. This revealed a sequence from glacial gravel deposits at the base, an organic rich layer above this, and then a series of layers reflecting periods of slope washed soils, and periods of soil stability until the uppermost plough soil was reached. As Mesolithic artefacts were in all layers above the glacial deposit, field observations alone could not indicate when the major period of soil movement occurred: it may have been due to early prehistoric clearances, as evident from the pollen sequence in the core at Coulererach, or farming practices during Historic periods.

Further study of this section was undertaken in the spring of 1995 (partly due to the atrocious weather conditions during the 1994 spring field season). A small excavation was undertaken into the section of this trench to acquire charcoal for dating from two periods of soil stability on either side of the major period of hill wash (Fig. 8.13). Unlike Coulererach, the value of further work at Rockside is very limited. Although Mesolithic artefacts are very dense in certain areas, very few of these appear to be an undisturbed context. No evidence for features were identified by the test pitting, although the lesson from Staosnaig warns against drawing any conclusions from this about the nature of the site. At present the

Fig. 8.14. Excavation at Kindochid, 1995 (photo: Mark Lake).

lithic assemblage from Rockside is being entered onto a computer data base for comparison with that from the other SHMP excavated sites. Initial observations suggest that the assemblage is much more similar to those from Bolsay Farm and Gleann Mor, rather than Coulererach, in spite of its vicinity to the latter. It will be difficult to arrive at any specific interpretation for the site of Rockside. The site is poorly preserved and lacks any distinguishing features. The contrast with Coulererach is, however, striking, Although Rockside is no no more than 1.5 km from Coulererach, the assemblages are strikingly different. Rockside lacks evidence for high frequency of preliminary flint knapping as would be expected for a site so close to raw material sources. Whether this reflects a chronological difference between the site, and hence a different technological organisation, or does indeed reflect that raw material effects are only felt over very short distances remains to be seen.

Kindrochid

The site of Kindrochid is located at the northen edge of the Loch Gorm Basin. During 1994 the local farmer, Sue Bignall, collected lithic assemblages from several of her fields. The largest of these (3 526 pieces) came from a field approximately 450 m west of the River Leoig and c.30 m OD. During the 1995 spring field season a team from Southampton University directed by Gilbert Marshall working under the auspices of the SHMP undertook a test-pitting exercise and trial trenching within this field (Fig. 8.14). The aim of this work was to collect a spatially controlled artefact assemblage, to acquire material for dating and to assess the liklihood and condition of any *in situ* occupation.

The test-pitting involved 119 0.5 m square test-pits dug on a 10 metre grid. These confirmed Sue Bignall's impression that artefacts formed two clusters, one in a low lying area adjacent to a marsh, and another on a slight rise *c*.50 m to the northeast. All test-pits, with the exception of those in the low lying areas, have a simple stratigraphy of a 10–30 cm thick plough soil onto an orange/red iron pan. In the low lying area the soil profile was *c*.1 m thick with a series of horizons marking levels of hill wash and waterlogging. A series of trenches was excavated which acted to connect these two clusters and remove as much plough soil as possible.

These trenches exposed a series of features. In trench two a discrete area of burning located within three large rocks was identified, which may have been a hearth. This was associated with a scatter of burnt flint and a discrete cluster of microliths. In area 2, trench 3, a series of stake holes were located, the largest of which reached 25 cm deep and had a fill containing flint and charcoal inclusions. A shallow, stone-lined pit was also located in this area, which had been sealed by a large stone slab. The fill of this contained flint artefacts, charcoal fragments and a single piece of prehistoric pottery. While the date of these features remains unclear at present, their location coincides with the clustering of artefacts from the original field collection and test-pitting.

The topographic location of Kindochid is striking as it is placed with excellent views to the northeast and the southwest towards Loch Gorm. Any interpretation of the site must await dating of the features and a comparison of the lithic assemblage with that from the other SHMP excavated sites.

Aoradh

The site of Aoradh lies immediately to the southwest of Loch Gruinart at *c*.25 m OD. It was located in April 1995 as a result of the on-going process of fieldwalking (Fig. 8.15). Further gridded field collection revealed one of the three scatters initially identified to be discrete and of reasonably high density (*c*.82 pieces per 5 m grid). It was felt that this merited further investigation to provide additional comparative data for the project, especially given the proximity of Aoradh to an area which would have offered rich marine resources during the Mesolithic. Consequently further fieldwork was conducted during two weeks in July 1995. This comprised a test-pitting excercise and trial trenching.

The test-pitting excercise was designed to provide material for inter-assemblage comparisons and as elsewhere involved the digging of 0.5 m square test-pits on a 10 metre grid. Artefacts were collected by hand-sorting the spoil from each pit. A total of sixty pits were dug and in most cases revealed a simple stratigraphy of a 0.1–0.3 m thick ploughsoil overlying an orange/pink clayey gravel containing a variable proportion of larger clasts. The easternmost test-pits differed by virtue of an additional *c*.5 cm thick remnant peat horizon lying

Fig. 8.15. Excavation at Aoradh (photo: Mark Lake).

immediately below the plough soil and sealing a yellow/brown sandy silt which appeared to represent a buried land surface. This deposit roughly co-occurred with the greatest density of flint recorded from the ploughsoil.

In light of the stratigraphy revealed by the test-pitting trial trenches were dug to explore the possibility that Mesolithic features might survive, either in the buried land surface, or cut into the underlying marine-glacial deposit further away from the centre of the lithic scatter. Six 1 m wide trenches were dug to the surface of the deposits below the ploughsoil. Typically 30 m long these trenches formed a grid centred north to south on the lithic scatter and extending uphill. They revealed several substantial linear features which clearly related to recent agricultural drainage and a number of more ephemeral roughly circular features. Given the lack of a discrete fill many of these can almost certainly be attributed to the plough catching stones and boulders. However, several small features (typically less than 20 cm in diameter) cut into the possible buried land surface did contain a discrete fill, and charcoal was recovered from one of these.

The most striking feature of Aoradh is the view from the site looking across Gruinart estuary and flats. We suspect that it is no coincidence that the site is located so close to a current RSPB reserve and hide: the Mesolithic foragers of Islay must have been as interested in the movements of the ducks and geese of the island as the current ornithologists (although the reason for their interest may have differed somewhat!).

SUMMARY

This chapter has only given the briefest of details about the Mesolithic sites discovered by the SHMP which have been subjected to either trial trenching and/or
area excavation. Further sites (or potential sites) have been explored by test-
pitting, such as at Bowmore and Laggan on Islay, and Machrins and Scalasaig
on Colonsay. The fieldwork of the project was completed by the small scale
excavations at Aoradh in July 1995. But this was, of course, only the beginning
of the end of the project for there remains a substantial amount of post-excavation
and research studies to be completed. The largest task facing the project is the
completion of the cataloguing, analysis and interpretation of the lithic assemblages. The methodology for this is described in the companion chapter to this
one within this volume by Finlayson, Finlay and Mithen.

As should be apparent from this brief overview of the *Southern Hebrides
Mesolithic Project*, it is an interdisciplinary exercise to address outstanding problems regarding the early postglacial settlement of Scotland. In scope it ranges
from detailed descriptions of stone tools to the development of computer simulation models for hunter-gatherer behaviour. In addition to addressing problems
concerning the Scottish Mesolithic, it also hopes to make a significant methodological contribution to early prehistoric studies. As such it hopes to join other
current research projects in Scotland to remedy the neglect of the Scottish
Mesolithic that has been an unfortunate feature of British archaeology for much
of the last forty years.

ACKNOWLEDGEMENTS

We would like to thank Tony Pollard for organising the 'Stone Age in Scotland' conference and for inviting the Southern Hebrides Mesolithic Project to present a summary
of its current research. Since 1988 the Southern Hebrides Mesolithic Project has been
supported by grants from: The British Academy, The Society of Antiquaries of Scotland, The Society of Antiquaries of London, The Russell Trust, The Robert Kiln Trust,
The McDonald Institute for Archaeological Research, Reading University, and Historic
Scotland. The current research of Mark Lake is funded by a grant from NERC. For help
in writing this paper we would like especially to thank Paddy Woodman, Gilbert Marshall
and Elaine Carp. We would also like to once again thank the landowners, managers and
farmers on Islay and Colonsay who have allowed us to work on their land, and the many
individuals who have provided help with our work. In this regard we would particularly
like to thank Lord Strathcona for permission to work on Colonsay and John Clark for
permission to work on his land at Staosnaig. Scottish Nature gave permission to work at
Gleann Mor and Aoradh. We thank Mr Clark of Craigfad, Mr and Mrs French of Rockside Farm, Sue Campbell of Coulererach and Eric and Sue Bignell of Kindrochid for
permission to work on their land. We are also grateful to the Islay and Laggan Estates on
Islay for permission to undertake fieldwalking on their land.

REFERENCES

Edwards, K. J. and Berridge, J. M. A. (in press). The Late Quaternary vegetational history of Loch á Bhogaidh, Rhinns of Islay sssi, Scotland. *New Phytologist*.

Edwards, K. J. and Mithen, S. J. 1995. The colonisation of the Islands of western Scotland: evidence from the palynological and archaeological records. *World Archaeology* 26, 348–65.

McCullagh, R. 1989. Excavation at Newton, Islay. *Glasgow Archaeological Journal* 15, 21–53.

Mellars, P. A. 1987. *Excavations on Oronsay: Prehistoric Human Ecology on a Small Island*. Edinburgh: Edinburgh University Press.

Mercer, J. 1968. Stone tools from a washing-limit deposit of the higher Postglacial transgression, Lealt Bay, Isle of Jura. *Proceedings of the Society of Antiquaries of Scotland* 102, 1–46.

Mercer, J. 1969. Flint tools from the present tidal zone, Lussa Bay, Isle of Jura, Argyll. *Proceedings of the Society of Antiquaries of Scotland* 102, 1–30.

Mercer, J. 1974. Glenbatrik Waterhole, a Microlithic site on the Isle of Jura. *Proceedings of the Society of Antiquaries of Scotland* 105, 9–32.

Mercer, J. 1980. Lussa Wood I: the late glacial and early postglacial occupation of Jura. *Proceedings of the Society of Antiquaries of Scotland* 110, 1–32.

Mithen, S. J. 1990. *Thoughtful Foragers: A Study of Prehistoric Decision Making*. Cambridge: Cambridge University Press.

Mithen, S. J. 1990. Gleann Mor: A Mesolithic site on Islay. *Current Archaeology* 119, 376–7.

Mithen, S. J. 1993. Islay and Coulererach. *Discovery and Excavation in Scotland*. Periodical 68–9.

Mithen, S. J. 1995. Mesolithic settlement and raw material availability in the southern Hebrides. In Fischer, A. (ed.), *Man and Sea in the Mesolithic*. Copenhagen: The National Forest and Nature Agency.

Mithen, S. J. and Finlayson, B. 1991. Red deer hunters on Colonsay? The implications of Staosnaig for the interpretation of the Oronsay middens. *Proceedings of the Prehistoric Society* 57, 1–8.

Mithen, S. J., Finlayson, B., Finlay, N. and Lake, M. 1992. Excavations at Bolsay Farm, A Mesolithic site on Islay. *Cambridge Archaeological Journal* 2, 242–53.

Whallon, R. 1994. Unconstrained clustering for the analysis of spatial distributions in archaeology. In Hietala, H. (ed.), *Intrasite Spatial Analysis in Archaeology*. Cambridge: Cambridge University Press, 242–77.

Woodman, P. 1989. A review of the Scottish Mesolithic: a plea for normality! *Proceedings of the Society of Antiquaries of Scotland* 119, 1–32.

9

ARCHAEOLOGY ON THE EDGE

LEARNING TO FEND
FOR OURSELVES

PETER C. WOODMAN

Countries on the edge of North Western Europe often have common problems in their search for an 'older' stone age. Therefore it is not surprising that there is an historic similarity in the way Mesolithic studies developed in countries such as Ireland, Scotland and Norway.

Various prejudices have always coloured the approach to research in these areas. There is often an assumption that the first human settlement was either quite late or else made up of the most remarkable amalgam of earlier Palaeolithic survivals. Until the 1950s, given the absence of a radiocarbon chronology, typological comparisons and geological dating formed the mainstay of Mesolithic research. In this context the manner in what we now consider Mesolithic research developed in Ireland, Scotland and Norway is remarkably similar. Therefore Armand Lacaille was only one of several scholars who were attempting to make sense out of what in these regions could be considered an 'Older Stone Age'.

In Ireland, William Knowles had made his contribution at an earlier date but Claude Blake Whelan was to have a major influence, so much so that it is possible to see how Whelan's research interests (1938) coloured Hallam Movius's choice of sites and typology (Movius 1942). In fact Whelan had already explored some of the locations which Movius was to excavate. In Norway, Anders Nummedal, again as an amateur archaeologist, made a major contribution to the Mesolithic of Norway in the decades before the Second World War. The problem for all workers was to tread a very narrow line between either a simple minimalist explanation or exorbitant claims for Palaeolithic components. In fact it was often possible to be on both sides of the argument at the same time! These problems were also compounded by poor independent dating, therefore typological comparisons had to be relied upon. In the context of a diffusionist view of archaeology, there was, particularly between the two world wars, a reliance on typological sequences of regions, such as France or England. In some cases battles over the interpretation of material in these core regions spilled over into the so called periphery; like the Williamite wars in Ireland, i.e. other peoples battles were fought in these regions.

While, by the time of the publication of *The Stone Age in Scotland*, it is possible to suggest that Lacaille's work was beginning to appear a little dated, its strength was that he never succumbed to some of the more outlandish interpretations that were being suggested for other regions (Lacaille 1954). In fact the periphery of North West Europe could be described in Mesolithic studies in a number of different ways.

FROM ULTIMA THULE TO SHANGRI LA

Regions on the edge of Europe tended to encourage a range of attitudes based on views that they were so far from 'core' regions that the abnormal should be expected – Ultima Thule. Again there was a common assumption that elements from earlier stone age technologies would survive indefinitely in these regions – Shangri La.

In Ireland the strength of Movius's *Irish Stone Age* (Movius 1942) was that it firmly placed most of the known pre-Neolithic material in the Holocene. This was achieved with the aid of a series of archaeological excavations which were backed up by palynological investigations carried out by Jessen, Mitchell and others. In spite of other weaknesses, such as the degraded nature of the material, there has been a consistent recognition that the material which Movius excavated came from Holocene contexts. Yet within the preceding 30 years there had been various suggestions that Ireland had a Palaeolithic.

William Knowles had argued throughout his life that there were traces of a Palaeolithic in Ireland and in a series of articles culminating in his 1914 paper, he claimed that earlier artefacts found in the raised beaches could be paralleled with artefacts from the Lower Palaeolithic of other regions. This was long since the rebuttal of his claim that the Ballyrudder mammoth tooth showed that raised beaches were of 'Ice Age' date. Again he claimed in a little known paper that Irish Neolithic leaf-shaped arrowheads were the product of communities descended from those using the Solutrean leaf points in France (Knowles 1897).

This desire to fit artefacts into French Palaeolithic typologies continued into the 1950s when Mitchell (1955) saw some Aurignacian elements in the material from his excavations at Toome on the shores of Lough Neagh. It was not that Mitchell would ever have believed that Irish Mesolithic artefacts were of Aurignacian age but rather, following on the opinion of Movius, it was felt the Irish Mesolithic or 'Larnian' owed its origins to groups of Upper Palaeolithic hunters from regions such as Creswell Crags in Derbyshire. Its apparent non-microlithic component was therefore explained by assuming that the Irish Larnian was a last relic survival of an Upper Palaeolithic community which found its way to Ireland and did not receive the technological innovations which were supposed to characterise the European Mesolithic. However, as noted earlier, Movius was the first person to first place the Irish Older Stone Age material in a Holocene context. In the 1930s and 40s this was a comparatively rare phenomenon. Others also sought a typological validation for the antiquity of certain assemblages.

Claude Blake Whelan (1933) searched for an Irish Tardenoisian which was to be similar to assemblages found by Lacaille in Scotland. These he claimed to have found in the Castlereagh Hills above Belfast. There is now a realisation that most of this material is natural. Similarly his espousal of terms such as Campignian for certain industrial forms found on the Antrim coast caused more harm than good (Whelan 1934). In particular a spurious set of so-called tranchet arrowheads was identified and a series of flake axes – 'tranchet axes' – which we now know to be Mesolithic, were also placed in this so called Campignian. Whelan suggested the curious term 'fish tail scraper' for flakes that simply expand at their distal end. Movius (1942) picked up this term and similarly Lacaille (1954) took over the term from Movius. For example see Lacaille 1954 (Fig. 115: 39) from Ballantrae.

In some regions the desire to tie a Mesolithic chronology to the accepted sequence of adjacent regions also had the effect of minimising the apparent age of assemblages. The existence of flake axes in the Mesolithic of Bohuslan in Sweden (the Hensbecka Culture) and in Southern Norway (the Fosna Culture) was a constant source of contention between Danish archaeologists, and, on the other side, many Swedish and Norwegian archaeologists. Essentially while local archaeologists argued that these assemblages were early Holocene, based on the fact that in many areas they only occurred on high (early) Holocene strandlines, many Danish archaeologists felt that because somewhat similar flake axes were found in the Late Mesolithic of Denmark, it was highly improbable that they could exist several thousand years earlier further north (see Moberg 1963, Boplatsproblem vid Kattegatt och Skagerack). If anything there was a presumption that any technological innovation in regions such as North Norway should be later, not earlier, than innovations in the Baltic.

This was not the only region to focus on the chronological significance of flake axes. The author initially saw parallels between Irish flake axes from sites such as Mount Sandel and their existence in the Ertebølle, and therefore suggested (Woodman 1974) that Irish microlithic assemblages, which were clearly associated with flake axes, had to be considered as late in the Mesolithic, after 6 000 BP, an error of 3 000 years! Only a footnote in that paper points towards the fact that it was becoming apparent that these assemblages were early.

There was of course good reason for the reluctance of many south Scandinavians to accept an early Holocene date for certain assemblages. The Komsa Culture of North Norway had provided an object lesson in the belief in far flung analogies. Anders Nummedal may be unique in that he discovered and documented two distinct Mesolithic complexes, namely the Fosna of Southern Norway and, over 1 000 kilometres away to the north, the Komsa culture of the Province of Finnmark. As has been noted by Woodman (1992) Nummedal, through his early excavations around Komsa Mountain at Alta, felt that his assemblages showed some similarity to the later phases of the Magdelanian (1928). However as the material accumulated it was felt that a more substantial and definitive international publication was necessary. This was produced jointly with Bøe as *Le Finnmarkien* (Bøe and Nummedal 1936). In this case much greater emphasis was placed on the discovery of artefacts which were thought to resemble Mousterian points, Chatelperonian knives or Aurignacian scrapers. These larger macrolithic forms soon came to dominate the perceived wisdom about the Komsa. Certain aretefacts were re-illustrated on a number of occasions, particularly the larger points from Storbukta (Clark 1975, Fig. 53) and Indrelid (1978, Fig. 2). The normal forms of tanged points such as those illustrated by Woodman (1992) were ignored, as were several other implement types. Long range typological comparison of individual pieces was again substituting for an overall analysis of assemblages and the result was a general impression of a Komsa culture made up of residual Palaeolithic elements surviving at the top of Europe.

The reality was of course that the massiveness of the artefacts chosen to illustrate the Palaeolithic character of the Komsa was a product of surface collecting, in regions where frost sorting often leaves the larger elements on the surface. This phenomenon was observed during the 1993–4 excavations at Smellroren near Vardø (Engelstad and Woodman in prep.). The typical Komsa assemblages of course only represent one portion of the Mesolithic of North Norway – the earliest, and in its earliest phases they may closely resemble the Fosna which, as Bjerck (1986) has shown, are equally early. There would also appear to be reason to believe that a narrow blade technology appeared well before 8 000 BP. These fine blades may have been used in the same manner as those in the slotted points of the Baltic which began to appear at the same date. Technology, when it was advantageous, was transferred virtually instantaneously to North Norway.

Obviously in the case of Scotland the Highland Zone time-lag factor set the agenda for expectations. In the Mesolithic a very superficial resemblance between the Star Carr and Morton assemblages, in particular, led to the belief that the so called 'non-geometric' microlithic assemblages either only occurred late or survived chronologically later in Scotland than elsewhere in Britain. The author was one of those who accepted the view that non-geometric assemblages survived late in Scotland (Woodman 1978). In retrospect, in the context of the dates from Morton (Coles 1971), and a late date for a presumed non-geometric assemblage at Lussa Wood (Mercer 1980), it is possible to see how these errors were made. However I suspect that the problem really was that in spite of the indicators from Mount Sandel (Woodman 1985), we are all too ready to believe in a time lag in both Scotland and Wales. Therefore any suggestion of relic survivals or time lags should be looked at with suspicion. The work in Ireland at Mount Sandel (Woodman 1985) and Rhum in Scotland (Wickham-Jones 1990) has shown that the microlithic rod/scalene triangle technology was established in the west and north as early as in England. Similarly David (1990) has shown that the non-geometric phase of the Mesolithic of South Wales was of a comparable age to that in England.

FILLING IN THE EMPTY SPACES

Coping with minimalist attitudes where there are time lags and survivals is one problem. The assumption that, if there is no known Mesolithic in a region, then it does not exist is another. In an Irish context the periphery was not only Ireland itself but areas to the south and west within Ireland were also thought to be marginal. Therefore when O'Riordain (1948) found a fine example of a scalene triangle during the excavation of a ring barrow in Co. Limerick, it was ignored as there was at that stage no reason to believe that the southwest of Ireland was occupied during the Mesolithic. Much of the research in southwest Ireland was instead driven by the study of megalithic tombs. There was an attitude that because there were few presumed early megalithic tombs in southwest Ireland then there was no stone age settlement. The idea developed that the first traces of human settlement were those associated with the building of wedge tombs which were thought to have been built by so called 'Beaker Folk' searching for sources of copper ores (De Valera and O'Nuallain 1982). This of course implied that the southwest of Ireland was left unoccupied until 4 000 BP. It was only with Lynch's research in 1980 that the first indicators of early human settlement began to appear (Lynch 1980) while Mesolithic settlement was not identified until the early 1980s (Woodman 1989a). Instead the lack of investigation for a Mesolithic was rationalised with suggestions that there were no flint sources in Munster therefore settlement could not exist.

Obviously the discovery of the Komsa of Finnmark created an entirely different situation. It was studied as much for its curiosity value but the other Arctic provinces of Troms and Nordland were left without a Mesolithic of any significance and the Komsa was left in splendid isolation until the 1980s (Sandmo 1986).

The obvious question about Scotland is whether the apparent absence of Mesolithic settlement in the north has become so much of a self evident truth that there will continue to be a presumed absence of Mesolithic settlement in any region, until incontrovertible proof is discovered. There can be many reasons why sites are not being discovered (Woodman 1989) but it would be more reasonable to assume that the Outer Hebrides, Orkney and maybe Shetland had a Mesolithic. The alternative is to accept a proposition that some areas of Scotland were the only regions in Northern Europe to remain unoccupied during the Mesolithic.

DEALING WITH THE ODDITIES

It is reasonable to have an expectation that Mesolithic settlement in peripheral regions could be as early as in regions where primary research on the Mesolithic was carried out, i.e. England, France and Denmark. The problem is the line between valid indicators that even earlier traces of settlement remain to be found and a too willing acceptance of some very slight indicators. In retrospect it is easy to dismiss some of the previous efforts to extend the Palaeolithic to Scotland

and Ireland. Perhaps the Rev. Frederick Smith's (1909) *The Stone Ages in North Britain and Ireland* represent a particularly extreme and optimistic view of the potential for a Palaeolithic in Scotland and Ireland. However it does represent an extrapolation of the English argument in favour of eoliths as human artefacts. Similarly the Burchell claim for an Irish Mousterian (Burchell et al. 1929) was an extension again of the argument for the antiquity of humanely created artefacts from the sub-Crag contexts in Suffolk (Reid Moir 1927).

In the case of the Rosses Point material the argument that the material was Mousterian rested on the identification of certain pieces as being typical Mousterian artefacts. A re-examination of some of the Rosses Point material suggest that again, as with the Komsa Culture, there is a preference for the illustration of pieces which looked Palaeolithic. Some of the classic artefacts illustrated (Mousterian side scrapers or hand axes) are actually natural, but at the same time the significance of the other simple large flakes was virtually ignored (Woodman in prep.). These pieces showed that some stone tool manufacturing of unknown age had taken place. In this case, because of the perceived Palaeolithic nature of the material a convoluted argument was advanced to explain why in Co. Sligo a Palaeolithic assemblage could survive beneath the Midlandian ice.

Strange assemblages can exist. This has been the lesson of the excavations at Ferriter's Cove, Co. Kerry (Woodman and O'Brien 1993). Here a range of metamorphosed silt stones and volcanic rocks were used to produce a range of Later Mesolithic artefacts, many of which parallel Mesolithic artefacts found elsewhere in Ireland, but some of which were stranger than anything previously seen in an Irish Mesolithic context. Equally the apparent anomalous nature of some of the assemblages in North Norway was not due to the coarse quartzite raw materials used but rather were the exaggerated product of a particular method of collecting, namely from frost sorted contexts. In both cases the few rather odd looking artefacts can be understood in the context of excavated assemblages which provide a less spectacular range of artefacts which fit more easily into a Mesolithic context.

Therefore in a Scottish context some of the assemblages found in Western Scotland could be worthy of re-examination rather than being consigned to the dubious category of Mesolithic survivals. As noted by Woodman (1989), the failure to follow up the buchite or vitrified shale assemblages from the head of Lough Snizort Beag is again a sign of a reluctance to go beyond the traditional norm. Even a cursory examination of Lacaille (1954, Fig. 135) must lead to a conclusion that this material pre-dates the Neolithic. A recognition of the significance of the Lough Snizort assemblages during the 1950s might well have revolutionised Mesolithic studies in the North of Scotland but as noted earlier, we only find significant what we have already decided is of significance.

Obviously there is, as in the case of the Rosses Point material, a reluctance to return to anomalous assemblages, particularly those which have been described as Epi Mesolithic or Mesolithic survivals. Many of these assemblages in Lacaille's chapters 8 and 9 are probably not to be classified today in the same manner as Lacaille but instead of focusing on the fact that they are not 'Epi Mesolithic' etc., it is important to remember that anomalous stone assemblages from areas such as Ardnamurchan in Argyll do represent an obvious prehistoric presence and are worth studying in their own right. In fact, at the risk of being too adventurous not all the Rev. Frederick Smith's artefacts should be dismissed as natural (Smith 1909). Three flakes (Figs 164–6) from Dalmuir appear convincing. They are unlikely to be Palaeolithic but if the illustrations genuinely reflect what was found then they could be prehistoric.

The question of the date of the earliest settlement will always exist in regions such as Ireland, Scotland and Norway. However from this short history it should be apparent that typology has often been more a hindrance than a help. Over the years we have had Azilian harpoons in Oban (Clark 1956), Chatelperronian knives in North Norway and hand axes on the River Bann! In the long run all that has stood the test of time are the carefully collected assemblages. In this context recent suggestions that there are indications that Scotland, and perhaps Ireland, were occupied in the Late Glacial should be treated with caution. Occasional large backed blades in Ireland, such as that from the Blackwater near Youghal, Co. Cork (Woodman 1989a) or some pieces from Cushendun (Movius 1940), could indicate an earlier human presence. The author was one of those who encouraged an examination of the significance of the Scottish tanged points (Woodman 1986a, Morrison and Bonsall 1989) but really those items, including some from Islay (Edwards and Mithen 1995) are only tempting indicators of a reasonable proposition that Ireland and Scotland may have had a Late Glacial human settlement. However are they ultimately any better indicators than the Azilian harpoons in the Obanian or the Komsa Chatelperronian knives. They may be outliers of something, but extending the Palaeolithic to Scotland and Ireland will ultimately depend on more than a few typological analogies. The ideas of the 1930s that there could be residual Palaeolithic elements surviving north of the Last Glacial maximum Ice sheet of Scandinavia today seems naive. When therefore today we identify individual artefacts as, for example, Ahrensburgian points, then it is essential that these pieces are treated as no more than indicators of early settlement. We could be suggesting that hunters were expanding up the North Irish Sea during the Loch Lommond re-advance when the European Atlantic edge was particularly cold. Human settlement was possible at that date but occasional type fossils are an unreliable indicator. It is also possible that, as with the Hamsburgian points found throughout Denmark, they represent outliers from Hamsburgian settlement which is confined to the southernmost parts of Denmark (Holm and Rieck 1982, Fischer 1991). Finally the possibility should be considered that as it is difficult to identify Ahrensburgian points in much of England (Barton 1991), these pieces may only fortuitously resemble Ahrensburgian points. Some rather strange tanged points were found in a Mesolithic context at Cass Ny Hawin in the Isle of Man (Woodman 1986).

SUMMARY

The attraction of working on the 'edge' is that there are opportunities for speculation, but in the long run the archaeology of any of these regions is best served through the creation of their own typological and chronological framework. History has shown that external typological validation of one's theories is no substitute for an independently derived scheme, whether based on excavation, fieldwork or museum studies. The strength of Armand Lacaille's contribution is that while the terms he used for certain types of assemblages have changed, the assemblages are still there. Minimalist perspectives for the Scottish Mesolithic were to a great extent a product of our expectations for Scotland, not his.

REFERENCES

Barton, N. 1991. Technological innovation and continuity at the end of the Pleistocene in Britain. In Barton, N., Roberts, A. J. and Roe, D. A. (eds), *The Late Glacial in North West Europe*. London: CBA Research Report 77, 234–45.

Bjerck, H. 1986. The Fosna–Nøstvet problem: a consideration of archaeological units and chronozones in the south Norwegian Mesolithic period. *Norwegian Archaeological Review* 19, 103–21.

Bøe and Nummedal, A. 1936. *Le Finnmarkien: les origins de la civilisation dans l'extrême nord de l'Europe*. Oslo: Institutet for sammenlignende Kultturforskning, Ser. B XXXII.

Burchell, J. P. T., Moir, J. R. and Dixon, E. E. L. 1929. Palaeolithic man in north west Ireland. *Proceedings of the Prehistoric Society of East Anglia*. Occasional Paper no. 1.

Clark, J. G. D. 1956. Notes on the Obanian. *Proceedings of the Society of Antiquaries of Scotland* 89, 91–107.

Clark, J. G. D. 1975. *The Earlier Stone Age of Scandinavia*. Cambridge: Cambridge University Press.

Coles, J. 1971. The early settlement of Scotland: excavations at Morton, Fife. *Proceedings of the Prehistoric Society* 38, 284–366.

David, A. 1990. *The Mesolithic of South West Wales*. Unpublished Ph.D. thesis, University of Lancaster.

DeValera, R. and O'Nuallain, S. 1982. *Survey of the Megalithic Tombs of Ireland, IV: Counties Cork, Kerry, Limerick and Tipperary*. Dublin: Stationery Office.

Edwards, K. and Mithen, S. 1995. The colonisation of the Hebridean Islands of western Scotland: evidence from the palynological and archaeological records. *World Archaeology* 26, 348–65.

Fischer, A. 1991. Pioneers in deglaciated landscapes: the expansion and adaption of Late Palaeolithic societies in southern Scandinavia. In Barton, N., Roberts, A. J. and Roe, D. A. (eds), *The Late Glacial in North West Europe*. London: CBA Research Report 77, 100–21.

Holm, J. and Rieck, J. 1983. Jels 1. The first Danish site of the Hamsburgian culture: a preliminary report. *Journal of Danish Archaeology* 2, 7–11.

Indrelid, S. 1978. Mesolithic economy and settlement patterns in Norway. In Mellars, P. (ed.), *The Early Post Glacial Settlement of Northern Europe*. London: Duckworth, 147–76.

Knowles, W. J. 1897. Survivals from the Palaeolithic Age among Irish Neolithic implements. *Journal of the Royal Historical and Archaeological Association of Ireland* 7, 1–18.

Knowles, W. J. 1914. The antiquity of man in Ireland, being an account of the older series of Irish flint implements. *Journal of the Royal Anthropological Institute* 44, 83–121.

Lacaille, A. D. 1954. *The Stone Age in Scotland.* Oxford: Oxford University Press.

Lynch, A. 1981. *Man and Environment in South West Ireland 4 000 BC – AD 800: A Study of Man's Influence on the Development of Soil and Vegetation.* Oxford: BAR, British Series, 85.

Mercer, J. 1980. Lussa Wood 1: the late glacial and early post glacial occupation of Jura. *Proceedings of the Society of Antiquaries of Scotland* 110, 1–31.

Mitchell, G. F. 1955. The Mesolithic site at Toome Bar, Co. Derry. *Ulster Journal of Archaeology* 18, 1–16.

Moberg, C. A. 1963. Boplatsproblem vid Kattegatt och Skagerack. *Studier i Nordisk Arkeologi*, no. 5.

Moir, J. R. 1927. *The Antiquity of Man in East Anglia.* Cambridge: Cambridge University Press.

Morrison, A. and Bonsall, C. 1989. The early post-glacial settlement of Scotland: a review. In Bonsall, C. (ed.), *The Mesolithic in Europe: Papers Presented at the 3rd International Symposium.* Edinburgh: John Donald, 134–42.

Movius, H. L. 1940. An early post-glacial archaeological site at Cushendun, Co. Antrim. *Proceedings of the Royal Irish Academy* 46, 1–84.

Movius, H. L. 1942. *The Irish Stone Age.* Cambridge: Cambridge University Press.

Nummedal, A. 1928. *Stone Age Finds in Finmark.* Oslo: Institutet for sammenlignende Kultturforskning, Ser. B XIII.

O'Riordain, S. P. 1948. Earthen barrows at Rathjordan, Co. Limerick. *Journal of the Cork Historical and Archaeological Society* 53, 19–23.

Sandmø, A. K. 1986. *Råstoff of redskap mer enn teknisk hjelpemiddel.* Unpublished Magistergrad thesis, University of Tromsø.

Smith, F. 1909. *The Stone Ages in North Britain and Ireland.* Glasgow: Blackie & Sons.

Whelan, C. B. 1933. Post glacial prehistory in Northern Ireland: three chronological indicators, no. 2 Castlereagh. *Irish Naturalists Journal* 4, 201–2.

Whelan, C. B. 1934. Studies in the significance of the Irish Stone Age: the Campignian question. *Proceedings of the Royal Irish Academy* 42, 121–43.

Whelan, C. B. 1938. Studies in the significance of the Irish Stone Age: the culture sequence. *Proceedings of the Royal Irish Academy* 44, 115–36.

Wickham-Jones, C. 1990. *Rhum: Mesolithic and Later Sites at Kinloch. Excavations 1984–86.* Edinburgh: Society of Antiquaries of Scotland, Monograph Series no. 7.

Woodman, P. C. 1974. Settlement patterns of the Irish Mesolithic. *Ulster Journal of Archaeology* 36–7, 1–16.

Woodman, P. C. 1978. *The Mesolithic in Ireland.* Oxford: BAR, British Series, 58.

Woodman, P. C. 1985. *Excavations at Mount Sandel 1973–1977.* Archaeological Research Monographs no. 2. Belfast: HMSO.

Woodman, P. C. 1986a. Excavations at Cass Ny Hawin. *Proceedings of the Prehistoric Society* 53, 1–22.

Woodman, P. C. 1986b. Why not an Irish Upper Palaeolithic? *Studies in the Upper Palaeolithic of Britain and North West Europe*. Oxford: BAR, British Series 296, 43–54.

Woodman, P. C. 1989a. The Mesolithic of Munster: a preliminary assessment. In Bonsall, C. (ed.), *The Mesolithic in Europe: Papers Presented at the 3rd International Symposium*. Edinburgh: John Donald, 116–24.

Woodman, P. C. 1989b. A review of the Scottish Mesolithic: a plea for normality! *Proceedings of the Society of Antiquaries of Scotland* 119, 1–32.

Woodman, P. C. 1992. The Komsa culture: a re-examination of its position in the Stone Age of Finnmark. *Acta Archaeologica* 63, 57–76.

Woodman, P. C. and O'Brien, M. 1993. Excavations at Ferriter's Cove, Co. Kerry: an interim statement. In Shee-Twohig, E. and Ronayne, M. (eds), *Past Perceptions*. Cork: Cork University Press, 25–34.

Part 3
Marine Adaptations

IO

IT IS THE TECHNICAL SIDE OF THE WORK
WHICH IS MY STUMBLING BLOCK

A SHELL MIDDEN SITE ON RISGA
RECONSIDERED

TONY POLLARD, JOHN ATKINSON AND IAIN BANKS

INTRODUCTION

This paper provides a preliminary statement on work recently carried out on the 'Obanian' shell midden site on the island of Risga, Loch Sunart, Ardnamurchan, Argyll (NGR NM 611 599 – Fig. 1). The site had previously been investigated on two occasions, by Ludovic Mann in 1920 and more thoroughly by Keith MacKewan in 1921–2. Other than a brief newspaper article written by Mann (1920) – reprinted here as an appendix – no full report on these excavations has ever appeared, although later assessments of the artefactual assemblages have been carried out (Lacaille 1951, 1954; Coles 1963; Stevenson 1978; Foxon 1991). The most important documentary archive of MacKewan's work is a series of letters written by him to Henderson Bishop, under whose patronage the excavation was carried out. These letters are quoted here at length in order to provide an essential background to the present work, which has so far consisted of the limited re-investigation of the shell midden site and the excavation of an area immediately outside the midden mound. The preliminary results of this on-going work suggest an alternative explanation to those previously proposed for the presence of a substantial quantity of lithics on this site and their appearance in only relatively small numbers on shell midden sites in Oban and on Oronsay.

RISGA AND ITS PLACE IN THE 'OBANIAN'

The shell midden on the island of Risga is the most northerly of the three locations traditionally identified with the so-called 'Obanian', the others being Oronsay and Oban. Investigation of the site on two occasions in the early twentieth century resulted in the recovery of a substantial artefactual assemblage, which included organic (bone and antler) and lithic components. It is perhaps ironic that the site which has provided the most extensive artefact assemblage is the one we know the least about, with even the earlier investigations in Oban being well reported for their time (Anderson 1895, 1898; Turner 1895).

The first 'investigation' of the site by Ludovic Mann appears to have consisted of little more than a couple of days spent casually turning over the ground and riddling the loose created.[1] MacKewan, who was to work on the site a year or so later, did not look kindly on this earlier disturbance of the site, writing, 'Have been obliged to open a new cutting as some persons unknown had, before I started here, riddled here and there giving the ground the appearance of having been gone over thoroughly ... Truly the evil that men do lives after them and no mistake' (n.d.). Though his labours do not appear to have represented a controlled excavation, Mann did report on his findings. He published an article in the *Glasgow Herald* on 21 August 1920 (see appendix), in which he compared the many animal bones to those recovered by Bishop during his earlier excavation of the Oronsay shell middens.

It may well have been Mann's article which prompted Henderson Bishop to employ D. Keith MacKewan to single-handedly carry out the most intensive investigation of the site. Work began in August 1921 and continued at least until the November of the same year. A gap in the correspondence between MacKewan and Bishop, between late November and the following summer, appears to represent a break from the work which was completed by the end of June 1922. The failure of this work ever to reach publication is largely to blame for our present lack of understanding of the site.

One component of the assemblage includes organic forms which have come to epitomise the idea of the 'Obanian' as a spatially and temporally specific cultural adaptation to a marine environment. These artefacts include fragments of bone and antler barbed points similar in form to complete and partial examples recovered from several of the Oban cave sites and the Oronsay shell middens. Also recovered was at least one antler beam mattock, which again has close parallels with examples from Oban and Oronsay. It has been proposed that these implements were used in the processing of marine mammals (Clark 1947, 1956), a correlation further suggested by the discovery of several examples associated with whale remains in the Carse of Stirling (Morris 1925). However, it has more recently been proposed that these artefacts may have served a number of purposes; macroscopic analysis suggests that digging, perhaps for roots or shellfish, was among them (Smith 1989). The organic assemblage also included bevel-ended tools, which have elsewhere been interpreted as 'limpet scoops' used to remove the flesh from the shell of the limpet (e.g. Mann 1920 [appendix this paper], Lacaille 1954). Although similar forms have been recovered from the majority of the shell middens so far excavated in western Scotland their exact function is somewhat uncertain, with suggestions including working flint (Breuil 1922), working skin, polishing harpoons (Grieve 1923: 54–55) and removing limpets from rocks (Bonsall this volume).

Many of the organic elements recovered by Mann and MacKewan therefore have close parallels with other 'Obanian' sites. However, the same cannot be said for the extensive assemblage of worked stone, which numbers around 14 000 pieces of flint, quartz and bloodstone (Stevenson 1978). The reasons for this presence on Risga and the marked absence of a sizeable lithic component from the other 'Obanian' sites have never been adequately explained. Perhaps the most common explanation for the presence of flints at Risga and their relative absence elsewhere has been the proximity of the island to one of the few sources of drift flint in Scotland (Lacaille 1954: 234, Stevenson 1978, Morrison 1980: 161). Alternatively, it has been suggested that the majority of lithics were deposited prior to the formation of the shell midden (Woodman 1988; Foxon 1991: 115) and so by implication may not be associated with the 'Obanian' organic artefacts. The question of context is therefore an important one. However, without the support of a comprehensive excavation report it is difficult to establish contextual relationships between artefacts and the deposits from which they were recovered. It was the desire to resolve these contextual uncertainties which provided a strong motivation for the current programme of fieldwork. However, prior to presenting the initial results of this work it is necessary to more fully introduce the documentary evidence upon which, up until now, the most informed discussions of Risga have been based, namely the MacKewan letters.

HENDERSON BISHOP AND KEITH MACKEWAN: THE CORRESPONDENCE

Henderson Bishop played a vital role in the development of archaeology in Scotland in the earlier part of this century[2] and carried out excavations on the Oronsay shell mounds, which for their day were highly accomplished (Bishop 1914). However, Bishop was also a keen collector and in this regard was as much an antiquarian as an archaeologist. One means by which he obtained artefacts and information on newly discovered sites was to retain agents, who would keep their eyes open and send him anything of interest. Keith MacKewan was one of these agents, corresponding with Bishop over a period of about fifteen years between the wars, during which he provided Bishop with finds from places as far removed as Coll off the west coast and Culbin sands to the east. MacKewan appears to have been more than equal to his task, with a passage in his letters to Bishop suggesting that his quest for information at times took on some of the characteristics of a 'cloak and dagger' operation: 'The postmaster here (Coll) knows a bit so I hear so I shall subject him to a gentle course of pumping. I am a holiday maker curious to see the isles. Dr Johnson up-to-date and possibly a trifle more careful of treading on local corns' (11/7/22).

Having excavated the Oronsay shell mounds, Bishop was eager to further establish the presence of a specific Obanian culture – or 'Oransay (sic) culture' as he termed it (the term Obanian was not introduced until 1940 when Movius [1940] used it in his comparison of Mesolithic material from the Northern Irish 'Larnian' and sites in western Scotland). Bishop decided to hire MacKewan, for a monthly fee of £20 16s 6d, to carry out the work on his behalf rather than excavate the site himself; this decision appears to have caused many of the problems relating to our current lack of understanding of the site. MacKewan had little or no excavation experience and in one letter states: 'It is the technical side of the work which is my stumbling block so far, as it's simply the lack of necessary knowledge, which practice will give, which keeps me back' (11/6/22). Bishop's failure to even visit the site did little to help the situation. In the same letter MacKewan notes, 'I was sorry to see you were not able to get north and have been obliged to start on the reserve as the soot layer is rapidly thinning elsewhere.' Thus, by the summer of 1922 the work was drawing to a close and Bishop had lost his last opportunity to visit the site.

Though we know from his letters that MacKewan kept a notebook account of his work and also made a number of drawings:[3] all attempts to trace these have so far met with disappointment. It does appear that Bishop intended to produce a report, as MacKewan replies to a letter from him in 1934: 'Re Risga I shall be very glad to assist in any way I can. I did submit a report of sorts to you but I am afraid it was an amateurish production' (15/10/34). However, the proposed collaboration came to nothing and in a letter to the Hunterian Museum, written by Henderson Bishop in 1950 during his retirement in Switzerland, he states: 'Among the letters from Mr McKewan (sic) you will find the only records of the Sunart Island shell heap' (27/8/50). It would therefore appear that the notebook, the drawings and the 'amateurish' report have been lost.[4] The letters to which Bishop refers usually accompanied parcels of finds from Risga which MacKewan posted to him at his Lanarkshire home, where they became part of his impressive private collection (these items now reside in the Hunterian Museum, Glasgow, along with the rest of Bishop's collection). MacKewan used these opportunities to report on the progress of his work, noting changes in the nature of the deposits or puzzling over the character and function of an artefact. It is from these tantalising snippets that we are able to piece together at least a very basic idea of the stratigraphy of the mound as observed by MacKewan.

Before further considering MacKewan's Risga investigation, reference to the letters will help to cast a little more light onto the life of this enigmatic character and his working relationship with Henderson Bishop.

MacKewan undoubtedly enjoyed working for Bishop, writing of his days on Risga as 'happy days … and Risga was an experience I wouldn't have missed for anything' (15/10/34). However, the two did not always see eye to eye and MacKewan actually resigned in August 1922, quite soon after finishing his work on Risga. Though he cites poor health as the reason for this move, it is difficult to dissociate it from the rather acrimonious tone used earlier in the same letter: 'I am, however puzzled as to your meaning when you imply that I am not frank with you. As I said before, I did return to Howard St. on that Wednesday afternoon though half an hour after the arranged time. Also I waited for a considerable time but finally concluding that you had gone I caught the afternoon train for Oban' (8/8/22). This misunderstanding therefore appears to have put paid to more than a planned visit to Coll and Tiree, though MacKewan did proceed on his own. A break in their professional relationship is suggested by the apparent cessation of correspondence between the two from that date (8/8/22) until

October 1924 (though it cannot be said for certain that the letters currently held in the Hunterian Museum represent the sum of MacKewan's correspondence).

In the later letters MacKewan expresses something of his outlook on life, giving here and there the briefest of glimpses into what, had it been written, would have been a fascinating autobiography. In one of these letters MacKewan touches upon his experiences as a soldier on the western front during the First World War, writing: '... my memory of detail is very vivid and oddly enough never more so than in respect to digging or anything connected with labour on land. I do not pretend to account for it but think it likely that trench experiences – still as vivid in my memory as ever – reflect their vividness through any similar work, one thing recalling the other – through association of ideas. Thus if I dig I recall Flanders. If I recall Flanders I recall incidents connected with digging I have done for you' (15/10/34). It was perhaps the war which bequeathed MacKewan his itinerant lifestyle. He never appears to have settled down and spent a lot of time in temporary lodgings. He wrote fondly of his days as a lodger with a Mrs Kennedy in Forres, who upon his confessing to liking ham and eggs proceeded to 'serve them for breakfast, dinner and tea until I rebelled, much to the old lady's surprise' (n.d.).

MacKewan undoubtedly felt happiest outdoors and he spent at least part of his life as a forester, working for a time in the 1930s at the Key Moss saw mill in Forres. From there he wrote: 'I must close here and get back to the woods again. The tent is doing grandly and believe me it's been well tested. I honestly think that I shall never live in a house again, except temporarily of course. Not that I'm a misanthrope. Simply that "the lure of the open's in my blood"' (25/6/38). When not working in the woods he took great pleasure from the landscape and the many cerebral experiences it had to offer; 'I have a notion to delve into geology ... I have so many various interests – trees, birds, flowers, moths, butterflies, to mention only a few – that I always find myself in close agreement with Shake-speare's lines:- "We are such as dreams are made of and our own little life is rounded with a sleep". "Little" indeed! What a wonderful mind that man had. His works are yet another interest, though I read whatever's worth reading, a pretty wide field. Apart from the poets most of the modern output leaves me cold' (25/6/35). It was also during this time that he collected many artefacts from the Culbin sands and forwarded them to Bishop.

Despite his many travels throughout Scotland it is always to Risga that MacKewan returns in his musings, 'I was so fond of that islet that Simpson, a friend on a geological survey, used to chide me to the effect that when I ulti-mately figured on the Honours list I should be Baron MacEwan of Risga!' (n.d.).

MACKEWAN AND RISGA

Although MacKewan's excavation was never published, the artefacts he re-covered have been the subject of a number of studies (Lacaille 1951, 1954; Clarke 1956, Coles 1963, Stevenson 1978, Foxon 1991). Despite the fact that this assemblage is largely unprovenanced, a number of writers have proposed that both stratigraphic and chronological differentiation are implied by its typological variation. Ritchie (P. R.) went as far as to suggest that these artefacts suggest two phases of occupation; the first took place during the Mesolithic prior to 3 000 BC, resulting in the deposition of the organic tools, while the second phase took place during the Neolithic and was evidenced by the deposition of stone knives and pottery similar to those from chambered cairns on Arran (1968: 119).

There is little evidence to back up Ritchie's rather sweeping interpretation and Foxon (1991) has taken a more measured approach, recognising that the finds 'must be considered as a collection of unstratified objects' (ibid. 88), but also concluding that '... most of the finds seem to have come from a sooty earth deposit beneath the shell midden rather from the shell midden itself' (ibid. 115). Woodman (1989) was less circumspect and, citing a personal communication from Mellars, asserted that the microliths from Risga came from a deposit beneath the shell midden (ibid. 15). According to Woodman's argument, the absence of microliths within the later deposit (shell midden) adds credence to his hypothesis that the use of composite barbed points comprising microliths set into organic armatures was abandoned in the very late Mesolithic – to which the Obanian was, until recently, usually assigned – in preference for single-piece barbed points of bone and antler (ibid. 16). However, this argument has since suffered a serious set-back with the publication of early radiocarbon dates obtained from organic barbed points from Oban and Risga (see Bonsall, this volume). Clearly then, these organic points can no longer be regarded as a purely very late Mesolithic phenomenon, with the dates also demonstrating their contemporaneity with microlith assemblages from various parts of western Scotland.

The basal deposit to which both Foxon (1991) and Mellars (1988) allude is what MacKewan refers to as the 'soot layer' in his letters. Though these letters do not, by any stretch of the imagination, represent a detailed record of the site, reference to them may cast some light on the nature of the site and its stratigraphy, containing as they do scattered references to the appearance of the site and the artefacts recovered from it.

Mackewan describes the appearance of the mound quite soon after the commencement of excavation thus: 'The centre of the mound is a core of boulders, sandstone, burnt earth, bones and fire fractured stones are the rule here, the shell layer being well defined. In other places it is very intermittent and rather difficult to locate. I always sink holes here and there till I am satisfied where the shell layer does occur. This saves time and labour as it is futile to move a hillock only to find the layer petered out a bare yard or so from where it started' (22/10/21). The mound therefore appears to display a complex stratigraphic sequence. There is only limited reference to the types of artefacts recovered from the shell layer, though Mackewan does note 'The point and barb of the harpoon I found practically at the centre of the mound where the shell layer is dense' (ibid.). The presence of a barbed point within the shell midden is in keeping with the relationship between marine resources and barbed points suggested by the shell midden sites in Oban and on Oronsay. However, it is apparent that lithics were also recovered from the shell midden: 'Am through the shell-bearing area in parts but there is still a good deal yet to do. Flints – worked and otherwise – are still occurring, mostly white' (2/11/21). The shell midden, then, appears to have contained both stone tools and the waste created in their manufacture. This picture contrasts somewhat with that in Oban and on Oronsay, where the small quantities of lithics which have been recovered are generally characterised by unworked pieces or waste.[5]

It is unfortunate that Mackewan's description provides little insight into the type of stone tools recovered from the shell midden deposits, though we know from the museum collection that a wide range of types was recovered from the excavation, including microliths, scrapers, burins, etc. (Stevenson 1978). Similarly, the letters provide only veiled references to the stratigraphic relationship between the shell midden and soot layer but these do suggest that, at least in places, the former does overlie the latter.[6] More specific reference is made to artefacts recovered from the soot layer and Mackewan writes that 'The finer specimens of flint are invariably found in the soot layer' (2/11/21). One piece from this deposit is described as a 'whitey grey flake chipped very minutely on one side, and pointed, then chipped on the other side, but on its underside' (n.d.). MacKewan wonders whether this may be a drill but it is possible that he is describing a microlith, though making positive identifications from descriptions alone is very difficult. Although MacKewan notes that the 'finer pieces of flint' (whatever that phrase is taken to mean) came from the soot layer, it would certainly be stretching his words too far to state for certain that microliths were found only in the soot layer.

The soot layer was also found to contain an artefact type recovered from the majority of 'Obanian' shell middens: 'I had a large number of bone gouges, I call them shell scoops, today some used at both ends, all from the soot layer' (23/10/21). This point of similarity between the soot deposit and shell middens elsewhere[7] may indicate that, though the shell midden and soot layer are clearly the result of different processes of deposition, the clear-cut sequence of soot deposit overlain by shell midden may not be as straightforward as has been previously suggested. The soot deposit, rather than being a homogenous layer, displayed some variation in its make-up; at one point a flint artefact was recovered from '… a sooty deposit, on a layer of stone, which I am well into – the hearth area' (23/10/21). Also within the soot layer MacKewan came across 'another pocket of fine quartzite gravel' (n.d.). Like the shell midden the soot deposit varied in depth and extent, in places being 'remarkably thick', while it 'Looks like petering out at the north side' (n.d). Differential deposition was further visible in a section cut through layers which are described as 'up-and-down every few feet or so' (23/10/21). On the basis of these observations, it is perhaps more reasonable to view both the shell midden and the soot deposits as the result of prolonged periods of differential deposition rather than two homogenous layers representing discrete acts of deposition. MacKewan's mention of a 'hearth area' (ibid.) may suggest that the soot layer bears some similarity to the ash-rich deposits which appear in other shell middens, including those on Oronsay, and appear to represent the sweepings from hearths (Smith 1992: 153).

One further detail casts doubt on any suggestion that the soot layer, at least in its entirety, represents an early Mesolithic deposit. Relatively little attention has been paid to the sherds of pottery recovered by MacKewan, though it has been noted that the evolutionary sequence suggested in the letters, with coarse sherds giving way to finer sherds, is the reverse of that suggested by recent re-examination of this material which revealed that the coarse sherds are probably Iron Age and the fine sherds Neolithic (Pollard 1990). In referring to the pottery MacKewan states that 'the soot layer is rapidly thinning elsewhere. However flints are fairly numerous yet, some very good specimens. Fragments of pottery are among the finds.' Thus at least some of the pottery appears to have originated in the soot layer, a presence clearly at odds with the formation of this deposit prior to the formation of an 'Obanian' shell midden. The recovery of pottery from the soot deposit therefore adds weight to the suggestion that we are dealing with a number of deposits laid down intermittently over a prolonged period of time rather than two deposits, one superimposed over the other, each relating to a specific period in the history of the site's use. The overall picture is of a complex series of deposits displaying patterns of differential deposition and discontinuity.

THE CURRENT PROGRAMME OF WORK

The initial phase of the Risga project had several aims:
1. To relocate and survey the site.
2. To investigate the potential for the survival of elements of the site in order to provide further contextual information on the previously recovered artefactual assemblage.
3. To investigate the possibility that archaeological remains existed outside the area occupied by the midden mound.

PRELIMINARY RESULTS

The first phase of the project took place in the early summer of 1993, with the location and survey of the site the primary aim. The site manifested itself as a low, irregular, grass-covered mound,[8] situated at around 15 m OD at the rear of a rock terrace on the eastern tip of the island.

A stone-lined trough, which MacKewan described in his letters as a 'cromlech', is cut into the mound at its southern end and may represent a much later kelp-burning kiln. Though Mackewan's letters suggested that he completely 'cleared' the mound, the first real evidence of this was provided by his working

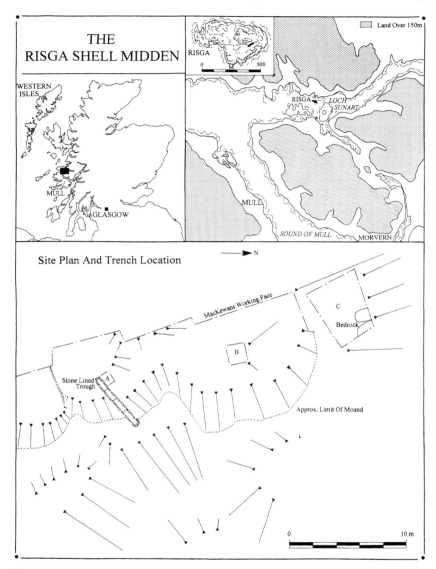

Fig. 10.1.

face, which could be seen cutting into the east facing section of the hill to the rear (west) of the mound (Fig. 10.1). Mackewan, after 'carving out a practical working face' (2/10/21) along the eastern side of the mound, appears to have worked his way through the mound to the west. By 23 October 1921 his working face was '20 yds from end to end. Distance penetrated would be 15 yds'. With reference to his advancement into the mound he further notes: 'Any future investigator here will be puzzled by the occurrence of turf walls, my method being to build these behind me to separate the riddlings from the to-be-riddled mass' (30/10/21). MacKewan obviously didn't anticipate that a future investigator would read his letters prior to commencing work! The turf walls were clearly visible in the sections created by the trial pits cut through the mound, which also revealed extensive disturbance of the deposits, which consisted of marine shells and dark organic soil, with the mound now representing little more than MacKewan's spoil. Samples of the spoil were removed for analysis and it appears that MacKewan missed some animal bones and lithics. Despite the extensive disturbance, it is possible that lower deposits may remain relatively undisturbed in places, but these have yet to be located.

Outside the mound the results of the trial pitting excercise were more promising, with the pits located to the north of the mound all containing flints, clearly suggesting activity outside the area defined by the mound. On the basis of these results it was decided to concentrate on this area during the second season of work. This investigation took place in the summer of 1994 and involved the excavation of an area measuring some 5 m × 5 m (trench A in Fig. 10.1). Further investigation of the mound and the stone-lined trough was also carried out, but the results of this work must await a later report.

EXCAVATION OUTSIDE THE MOUND

Immediately upon the lifting of turf (Fig. 10.2), lithics were revealed caught in the bracken roots and humic topsoil. Large quantities of lithics were removed from a series of surface cleans, with finds initially bagged by grid square. Once onto the sub-surface finds were, where possible, individually bagged and plotted, though in places they appeared in such high densities that multiple bagging was unavoidable. It quickly became apparent that features existed in the sub-soil, with charcoal patches in some places suggesting firespots. Also identified were a number of curvilinear features which contained water-rolled stones and lithics. In the time available it was only possible to sample a few of these features, the excavators having much sympathy with MacKewan's cry that 'the day is all too short' (23/10/21). However, the preliminary results do suggest that we are dealing with a largely undisturbed structural complex, with foundation slots, hearths and pits. One of the curvilinear features was sectioned and found to represent a shallow trench into which water-rolled stones had been packed, apparently for structural support. These may well represent the foundations for small, temporary structures. Parallels for similar structures have been found both on Rhum (Wickham-Jones 1990) and at Kirkhill Farm (Pollard 1993), with structures in the order of 3 m by 5 m recorded at the latter.

In the region of 2 000 pieces of worked quartz, flint and bloodstone were recovered during the excavation and are currently undergoing characterisation and analysis. The majority of the assemblage appears to represent debitage, strongly suggesting that knapping was taking place on the site.

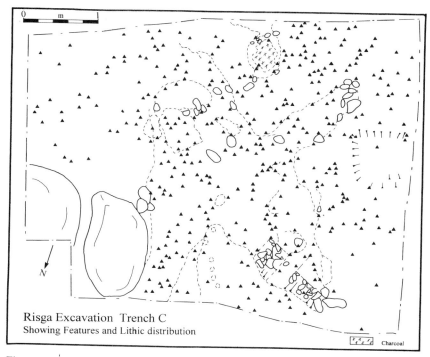

Risga Excavation Trench C
Showing Features and Lithic distribution

Charcoal

Fig. 10.2.

A number of short blades have been identified, some having been snapped to produce microliths, most of them flint, though some fine work on quartz is evident. The microburin technique also appears to have been used in the production of a small number of triangular microliths. A number of scrapers were also recovered, suggesting that a variety of activities were taking place on the site. A single leafed-shaped arrowhead of bloodstone was recovered from the northern end of the trench.

From the limited excavation carried out so far, it appears that trench A corresponds to the site of a small temporary settlement or camp-site. Its location, immediately outside the northern perimeter of the mound, may suggest that the two features are at least partly contemporary, with the camp representing the living space of those responsible for the accumulation of the midden deposits. However, radiocarbon dates must be obtained before this can be stated with confidence.

CONCLUSIONS

Clearly there is much work still to do on the site and at least two further seasons of fieldwork are planned. Analysis of the lithic assemblage recovered over the last two seasons is also at a preliminary stage. It would therefore be highly inappropriate to draw firm conclusions on the basis of the work at this stage. However, the results achieved so far may provide at least a limited insight into the reasons for the presence of numerous lithics on the Risga site and their general absence on the other classic 'Obanian' sites.

As noted previously in this chapter, it has been claimed that the 'Obanian' sites relate to a period during which microliths were not utilised, with preference given to other materials such as bone and antler. Woodman has suggested that this change was motivated by the desire to reduce the time and labour required to manufacture and repair barbed points, with single piece bone or antler points requiring less input than microlith forms (1989: 16). A lack of local stone sources has also been noted in the consideration of the relatively lithic-free 'Obanian' sites, while the availability of flint in Morvern has been cited as a possible explanation for the presence of numerous lithics on Risga (Lacaille 1954, Morrison 1980). It was important to Woodman's argument that the microliths from Risga were deposited prior to the formation of the shell midden deposit. However, as argued above, there is only limited evidence for this and for the soot layer representing an earlier deposit.

An alternative explanation for the general absence of lithics in the 'Obanian' shell middens to that proposed by Woodman (1989) is that they represent specific 'task sites' dedicated to the processing of marine resources (Pollard 1987, Finlayson 1990, Pollard 1994). The limited range of activities carried out on these sites may not have required an extensive kit of stone tools, which during the Mesolithic usually included microliths. Instead, the majority of marine-related tasks appear to have been carried out with organic artefacts such as bone and antler barbed points and mattocks. The specialised nature of these shell midden sites is further emphasised by the possibility that they were only utilised at certain times of the year; this is suggested by the results of examination of saithe otoliths from the Oronsay sites (Mellars and Wilkinson 1978). It is also possible that the use of these sites varied according to a daily schedule dictated by the turn of the tides (see Pollard, this volume). At other times it is likely that activities were centred on other parts of the landscape, in areas perhaps further inland.

In Oban the midden sites may well have existed away from settlement sites, with the narrow raised beach terrace and high sea levels making the location of settlements or camps impractical on the shore front; these same reasons also make the caves in which the majority of middens were located unsuitable for use as living quarters (Pollard 1994). The recent excavation, by Clive Bonsall, of a major lithic scatter possibly related to structural remains at Lón Mór behind Oban, on the shore of a former sheltered embayment, appears to add credence to the idea that the Oban midden sites represent specific task sites. This site may represent the settlement of those responsible for the accumulation of the shell midden deposits some distance away (see Bonsall, this volume). The same may prove to be true on Oronsay, where Mellars has suggested that settlements were located away from the middens, perhaps toward the centre of the island (1987: 3). On Risga the picture seems to be somewhat different, with evidence for settlement, albeit of a temporary nature, located in close proximity to the shell midden. This proximity may in part have been dictated by the topography of the island, with the shelf upon which the shell midden and camp are located providing one of the few sheltered locations on the island, even at times of higher sea-level. It should be noted that structural remains were located beneath the Cnoc Coig midden, Oronsay, but their later submergence beneath the midden suggests a change in settlement patterns over time, with the stakehole-defined structures having been abandoned prior to this submergence. The possibilty that a similar shift may have occurred on Risga should also be considered; though MacKewan did not locate any sign of structures beneath the shell midden, writing: 'I have failed to spot any post holes' (30/10/21).

Judging from the varied artefact assemblage the site appears to have been used over a considerable period of time. The reasons for this continued use may include not only the ideal siting of the island for fishing but also its temporary occupation by red deer. Deer bones were recovered during MacKewan's excavation and red deer can still be seen on the island today, having swum across the channel from the mainland to the north. At least some of the lithic assemblage, including the microliths, the scrapers and the leaf-shaped arrowhead, may be related to the hunting of these animals. Relatively small quantities of terrestrial animal bones were recovered from the other 'Obanian' shell middens, but these may have been brought to those sites from settlements elsewhere to be used as a source of raw material for the manufacture of marine procurement equipment (Grigson and Mellars 1987, Pollard 1994 and this volume). Although it cannot be denied that terrestrial animal bones were used for the same purpose on Risga it is possible that the midden also accumulated bones which represent food waste dumped from the adjoining camp. It is this dumping of refuse which originated in the camp which may account for the presence of the large quantity of terrestrial animal bones noted by Mann (1920).

The midden deposits on Risga therefore appear to represent not only the residues resulting from the specialised extraction and processing of marine resources, but also the place at which material from the nearby settlement or camp was dumped. The lithics recovered by MacKewan may well have originated within the settlement, where lithic manufacture was being carried out, but were later dumped on the midden as they fell out of use. It can also be suggested that at least some of the material which went to make up the 'soot layer' may also have originated in the camp, representing material removed from hearths. The close proximity of the camp to the midden has therefore brought together a number of activities elsewhere spatially separated, combining, on the one hand, deposition related to settlement activities, which included stone tool manufacture, and on the other, deposition related to the execution of specialist marine resource extraction and processing tasks.

The on-going programme of work will provide more information on the issue of site history and longevity. This programme will also include a wider ranging survey of the Ardnamurchan peninsula, which Lacaille himself noted as an area of particular interest (1954). In the meantime, however, it is hoped that the preliminary results outlined in this paper have gone some way to casting fresh light on a site which has for so-long languished in the dark.

APPENDIX

Oronsay period discoveries at Risga

by Ludovic McL Mann

reprinted from the *Glasgow Herald*, 21 August 1920

The rocky island of Risga is the central isle of the little archipelago which guards the entrance to the serpentine sea loch of Sunard (sic) which divides Ardnamurchan from Morven. For long centuries no man has dwelt upon the island and no crofter has ever turned up its soil, though rich black and deep in places. The natives of the mainland consider the island useless for man and beast, but once upon it was a small flock of the thin-legged deer-like, large-horned Soay sheep put there by a previous proprietor many years ago. An old ewe was the last of the flock and she survived alone on the island for two years.

The island, roughly oval, measures 500 yards east and west by 400 yards north and south, and has rocky and at places precipitous shores possessed of neither sand nor shingle. The hard, grey metamorphic schistose sandstone, streaked with little wavy veinlets of quartz, outcrops through wiry grass in bald glacial rounded knolls near the summit. In the lower reaches the visitor, when he is not knee-deep in spongy mosses has to struggle in a maze of splintered rocks, weathered into high obliquely set slabs partly hidden by a luxurious vegetation chiefly of very tall heather. Pushing aside the heather he may see in the dark mossy crevices patches of the smallest British fern, and other botanical curiosities, the Tunbridge filmy fern, and other botanical curiosities.

A KITCHEN MIDDEN

Obeying a summons to visit the island, and tempted to do so by a number of humanly-worked bones which had been transmitted to me after their accidental discovery in a shell mound on the eastern side of the island some 30 feet above high water mark and about 60 feet from the shore, I proceeded to the island and was favoured by two of the best days of this unseasonable August.

On removing the turf which covered a cumulation of soil anciently washed down upon the shell mound evidence was forthcoming which confirmed the testimony of the relics already detected – that a new 'locus' had been established for that very rare and interesting phase of human industry, the 'Azilian' or 'Oronsay' (sic) period, an epoch intermediate between the Palaeolithic and Neolithic ages. No more ancient human period has been so far discovered in Scotland excepting perhaps that represented by a few heavily patinated, water-rolled flint tools of Palaeolithic appearance from Western Wigtownshire. It is estimated that the 'Oransay' period has an antiquity of between 28 000 and 30 000 years. Relics of that age were first disclosed in Scotland by Mr Galloway and Mr Symington Grieve during exploration of three shell-mounds on the island of Oronsay, near Colonsay, but the significance of this discovery was not fully understood until 1895 when similar relics found in a cave at Oban came under close scrutiny. Another Oban cave or shelter containing the same class of remains was found in 1898. Traces of Oransay man have been detected in Inchkeith, Colonsay and Tiree. A single harpoon head characteristic of the period was found in the river Dee, Kirkudbright: another in the Victoria Cave, Settle, Yorkshire: a third on the shore at Whitburn, Durham and various implements on a shore site near Dale, Pembrokeshire.

THE PRE-HISTORIC LARDER

Oransay man had no knowledge of domestic animals, agriculture, pottery, textiles, of metals, but he was a skilled fisher, hunter and boatman. In Scotland his dietary consisted chiefly of products of the sea. His kitchen middens contain remains of crabs, including the fiddler crab, haddock, conger eel, skate, grey mullet, bream (both sea and black), wrasse, angel fish, tope, ray, and the now despised spiny dogfish. He ate limpets in large quantities also peri-winkles, cockles, scallops, mussels, and oysters. Before eating the dog whelks he broke the shell upon little flat stones which show traces of the abrasions thus made. Pecten valves he employed as scoops and spoons and pieces of antler he made into tools like shoe horns. Among the bones scattered about his dwelling place, as if thrown aside at his meals, are those of the marten, red deer, boar, otter, rorqual, common and grey seal and a large number of birds which he perhaps snared or trapped, such as the guillemot, gannet, razorbill, gull, tern, water rail, goose, shag, cormorant and red-breasted merganser.

Oransay man seems to have clothed himself in skins, for neatly made bone pins and piercers have been found at Risga, Oban and Oransay. He or his children, had necklaces of perforated cowrie shells and he used a red pigment. Fire-injured stones, charred and burnt animal bones testify that he had fires and roasted his venison and other flesh secured in the chase. Some shellfish he ate raw. With finger-like implements of bone horn and stone he gouged the limpet mollusc from its shell, the peculiar contour of the inside of that shell giving the end of the gouge a characteristic facet. The function of these tools was obscure until, in 1912, Mr A Henderson Bishop put forward the explanation of their use, which has met with general acceptance. He used club-like stones, and with these he could readily kill the gare-fowl or great awk when it was met with on the shore. The abortive condition of its wings did not permit it to fly, and it fell an easy victim. I picked up a leg bone of this bird on the shell-mound on Risga, and many of its remains have been found on Oransay. It must have been common at the time of shell-mound men, though it has now been hunted to extinction, the final acts of destruction taking place in Iceland by organised expeditions to supply museums in Europe. The bird was nearing extinction in Scotland early last century and seems to have disappeared finally from St Kilda about 1820. Oransay man lived in caves and in sheltered nooks along the shore just above high water where he built little huts of wooden standards about seven inches in diameter, which supported a structure perhaps of thatch and plastered wattle. The climate from these days differed but little from that of modern times. His most common implement was the flattish harpoon head of bone or horn, occassionally decorated with incised lines and having several barbs on one side or more usually on both sides of the stem. Sometimes it has a perforation at the base to hold a cord, by which it was loosely attached to the shaft. With pumice stone and other stone rubbers he finished the surface of the pins and harpoon heads.

Oransay man, expert in many things, was very poor as a worker in flint, simple crude chippings of which he used with flakes of quartz in the scraping of hides and in the cut-ting of shells, wood, bone and horn. His predecessors, and probably also certain of his contemporaries in Europe were more skilled in flint working.

GEOLOGICAL CHANGES

The preliminary scrutiny of Risga tends to confirm the evidence of the other Scottish sites of the same period, that at the time of Oransay man the land stood relative to sea-level 25 to 30 feet lower than it now does. On the continent relics extraordinarily similar to those found in (?)Hte Garonne, Ariege, Lourdes, Lot, Gard, Laugerie Basse and in the Dordonne.

While no human osseous remains without doubt of that period have so far been dis-closed in Britain, at Ofnet, Wurtemburg, on a supposed identical archaeological horizon, have been found human skulls set to face the setting sun and covered with powdered ochre, in groups like eggs in a nest, one 'nest' had 27 and another 6 skulls and were both asscociated with remains of necklaces of perforated shells and otters teeth. The absence of the trunk and limbs, the strange setting and the presence of ochre point to some ritual so obscure that one scarcely dares to offer a suggestion as to its character.

Risga thousands of years after Oransay man lived on it, but centuries before the advent of Christianity, appears to have been a sacred isle. On certain rocky platforms upon the east shore, and one upon the north shore, were found very old sculptorings – these mysterious carvings which were the work of the astronomer priests of the late neolithic and Bronze ages. Covered by turf and heather the carvings have been protected perfectly. Rubbings of them and their bearings have been carefully noted and from these meaning may be interpreted after much study.

NOTES

1. The full extent of Mann's work on the island is difficult to ascertain. Though a period of two days is mentioned in his *Glasgow Herald* article of 21 August 1920 (see above), there is reason to suspect that he devoted more time to his investigations. A brief note in the *Glasgow Herald* of 8 September 1920, reported on a visit by several archae-ologists to inspect 'the excavations being carried out on the scene by Ludovic McL Mann'. It would therefore appear that Mann's excavations were more extensive than they first seemed. It is hoped that continued research into Mann's personal papers will further our understanding of his work on the island.

2. The senior author is currently researching and writing a more extensive work con-cerned with the contribution of Bishop, Mann and other early twentieth-century figures to the development of archaeology in Scotland.

3. MacKewan appears, upon Bishop's advice, to have drawn numerous sections during his excavation. However, he also states: 'I note your comments on the sections and, now that I see the force of their positions being shown on a ground plan, I am calling myself all sorts of a damn fool for not seeing the idea before' (11/6/22).

4. Bishop may simply mean that the reports etc. are among the letters, perhaps in the same box, but unfortunatetly it is only the letters which have so far been located.

5. Coles (1963: 95) states that over 1 100 retouched lithics were recovered from the Risga site, while 900 displayed utilisation and waste pieces numbered 11 800. Outside Risga the largest lithic assemblage comes from Cnoc Sligeach, Oronsay, and consists of over 500 pieces of which only 26 were retouched and 4 displayed utilisation, the rest being waste (Mellars' more recent excavations on Oronsay may well provide a different picture but as yet the data is unavailable).

6. The few references to the stratigraphic position of the the soot layer are rather vague and nowhere does he specifically state that it underlay the shell midden. However, in describing the earlier disturbance of the mound he states: 'they'd forgotten the soot

layer' (n.d), which does suggest that it underlay the shell midden, at least in the area where the shell midden had been disturbed.

7. Though the passage quoted specifically states that the shell scoops in question came from the soot layer, MacKewan is refering only to the examples recovered that day. Although this is the only reference made to shell scoops there is no reason to believe that they were not also recovered from the shell midden deposit. Mann also reports similar artefacts from Risga (1920 – appendix) and it is very likely that these came from the shell midden.

8. A number of relatively fresh spade-size pits scattered over much of the mound were noted during the first season of work in 1993. To our knowledge there is no record of any work recently carried out on the island and MacKewan's phrase 'the evil that men do' again springs to mind.

ACKNOWLEDGEMENTS

The authors would like to thank the Society of Antiquaries of Scotland and Highland Regional Council for their financial support of this project. The owner of the island, Mr Rich, kindly allowed work to take place, while the staff at Glenborrodale House were most accommodating and kindly allowed the use of their boat. Special thanks goes to those who have put in hard time on the island, braving the plagues of tics and the variable weather over the past two seasons: Mike Donnelly, Andrew Jones, Gavin MacGregor and Kevin Taylor – Barons of Rigsa all! Peter Madden of Forest Enterprise kindly assisted and introduced us to local sites of interest. Thanks to Olivia Lelong for proof-reading a draft version.

REFERENCES

Anderson, J. 1895. Notice of a cave recently discovered at Oban, containing human remains and a refuse-heap of shells and bones of animals and humans and stone implements. *Proceedings of the Society of Antiquaries of Scotland* 29, 211–30.

Anderson, J. 1898. Notes on the contents of a small cave or rock-shelter recently discovered at Druimvargie, Oban; and of 3 shell mounds in Oronsay. *Proceedings of the Society of Antiquaries of Scotland* 32, 298–313.

Bishop, A. H. 1914. An Oronsay shell mound – a Scottish pre-Neolithic site. *Proceedings of the Society of Antiquaries of Scotland* 48, 52–108.

Bishop, A. H. 1950. Unpublished letter to A. Robertson. The Bishop collection, Hunterian Museum, University of Glasgow.

Breuil, H. 1922. Observations on the pre-neolithic industries of Scotland. *Proceedings of the Society of Antiquaries of Scotland* 56, 261–81.

Clark, J. G. D. 1947. Whales as an economic resource. *Antiquity* 21, 84–104.

Clark, J. G. D. 1956. Notes on the Obanian with special reference to the antler and bone work. *Proceedings of the Society of Antiquaries of Scotland* 89, 91–106.

Coles, J. M. 1963. New aspects of the Mesolithic settlement of western Scotland. *Transactions of the Dumfriesshire and Galloway Natural History and Antiquarian Society* 41, 67–99.

Finlayson, B. 1990. Lithic exploitation during the Mesolithic in Scotland. *Scottish Archaeological Review* 7, 41–58.

Foxon, A. D. 1991. *Bone, Antler, Tooth and Horn Technology and Utilisation in Prehistoric Scotland.* Ph.D. thesis, University of Glasgow.

Grieve, S. 1923. *The book of Colonsay and Oronsay.* Edinburgh.

Grigson, C. and Mellars, P. 1987. The mammalian remains from the middens. In Mellars, P., *Excavations on Oronsay*. Edinburgh: Edinburgh University Press, 243–390.

Lacaille, A. D. 1951. A stone industry from Morar, Inverness-shire; its Obanian (Mesolithic) and later affinities. *Archaeologia* 94, 103–41.

Lacaille, A. D. 1954. *The Stone Age in Scotland*. Oxford: Oxford University Press.

MacKewan, D. K. 1921–34. Unpublished correspondence to A. Henderson Bishop. The Bishop collection, Hunterian Museum, University of Glasgow.

Mann, Mc.L. 1920. Oronsay period discoveries at Risga. *Glasgow Herald*, 21 August 1920, 9.

Mellars, P. A. and Wilkinson, M. R. 1980. Fish otoliths as indicators of seasonality in prehistoric shell middens: the evidence from Oronsay. *Proceedings of the Prehistoric Society* 46, 419–44.

Morris, D. B. 1925. The whale remains of the Carse of Stirling. *The Scottish Naturalist*, 137–40.

Morrison, A. 1980. *Early Man in Britain and Ireland*. London: Croom Helm.

Movius, H. L. 1940. An early post-glacial archaeological site at Cushedun, Co. Antrim. *Proceedings of the Royal Irish Academy* 46, 1–84.

Pollard, A(T). 1991. Down through the ages: a review of the Oban Cave deposits. *Scottish Archaeological Review* 7, 57–84.

Pollard, T. 1993. *Kirkhill Farm: Excavation of a Mesolithic Flint Scatter*. GUARD monograph report 130. University of Glasgow.

Pollard, A(T). 1994. *A Study of Marine Exploitation in Prehistoric Scotland, with Special Reference to Marine Shells and Their Archaeological Contexts*. Ph.D. thesis, University of Glasgow.

Ritchie, P. R. 1968. The stone implement trade in third-millenium Scotland. In *Essays Presented to Stuart Piggott*. Leicester: Leicester University Press, 117–36.

Smith, C. 1989. British antler mattocks. In Bonsall, C. (ed.), *The Mesolithic in Europe*. Edinburgh: John Donald, 272–84.

Stevenson, R. D. 1978. *Risga: The Mesolithic Industry*. Unpublished undergraduate dissertation, University of Glasgow.

Wickham-Jones, C. R. 1990. *Rhum: Mesolithic and Later Sites at Kinloch, Excavations 1984–1986*. Edinburgh: Society of Antiquaries monograph series 7.

Woodman, P. C. 1989. A review of the Scottish Mesolithic: a plea for normality! *Proceedings of the Society of Antiquaries of Scotland* 119, 1–32.

I I

THE 'OBANIAN PROBLEM'

COASTAL ADAPTATION IN THE MESOLITHIC OF WESTERN SCOTLAND

CLIVE BONSALL

INTRODUCTION

Direct evidence for the exploitation of coastal resources in the Mesolithic of western Scotland is restricted to a small number of sites on which shell midden deposits are preserved. These sites are generally referred to as 'Obanian' after the initial discoveries around Oban Bay in Argyll (Fig. 11.1).

The Obanian sites share a number of features: faunal assemblages dominated by the shells of marine molluscs but including crustacean remains and bones of fish, sea birds, sea mammals, and wild land mammals such as red deer and pig; lithic assemblages of flint and quartz in which retouched tools are often rare or absent and bipolar cores and débitage well represented; and a distinctive range of implements made from antler or bone which include bevelled tools, points ('awls') and, occasionally, harpoon-heads and perforated mattock-heads.

A contrast is often drawn between the artefact assemblages from the Obanian middens and the microlithic industries recovered from a large number of Mesolithic sites in western Scotland. The latter are invariably surface sites where soil conditions are unsuitable for the preservation of organic materials and Mesolithic activity is indicated mainly by the occurrence of one or more lithic scatters. Compared to Obanian toolkits, the lithic scatters are often characterised by a higher incidence of platform cores and blade débitage and the presence of microliths, scrapers and other retouched tools regarded as typical of Mesolithic sites. This contrast in assemblage types is at the heart of long-standing debate in Scottish archaeology between those workers who believe the evidence justifies the recognition of an Obanian culture or phase within the west Scottish Mesolithic, and those who consider that the assemblage types are most readily explained in functional terms.

This paper examines the background to this debate and offers a possible solution to the 'Obanian problem'.[1]

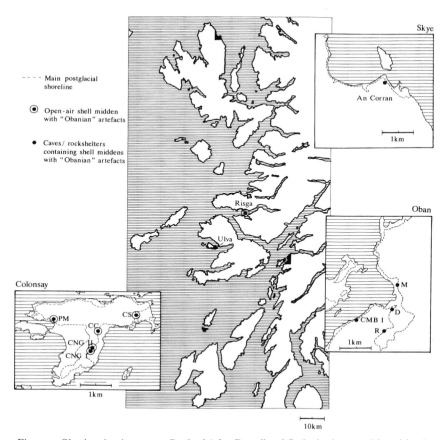

Fig. 11.1. Obanian sites in western Scotland (after Bonsall and Sutherland 1992, with revisions): CC, Cnoc Coig; CMB, Carding Mill Bay; CNG, Caisteal nan Gillean; CS, Cnoc Sligeach; D, Druim-vargie Rockshelter; M, MacArthur's Cave; PM, Priory Midden; R, Raschoille Cave.

OBANIAN SHELL MIDDENS: THE DEVELOPMENT OF IDEAS

Early work on the Obanian between 1881 and 1926 focused on small caves and rockshelters around Oban Bay and a series of open-air sites on the islands of Oronsay and Risga.

Anderson, in his account of the excavations at Druimvargie Rockshelter in Oban, was in effect the first to suggest that the Obanian sites were sufficiently distinctive to warrant their isolation as a distinct 'culture' (Anderson 1898) – although the term 'Obanian culture' did not come into general usage until several decades later (Movius 1940).

Most subsequent workers have followed this interpretation, although there have been disagreements over the origins of the Obanian. Anderson (1898), Breuil (1922) and Clark (1956) interpreted the style of the barbed points as evidence of a link with the Azilian, while Movius (1942) and Lacaille (1954) favoured an origin in the Irish Mesolithic.

Further work on the Oronsay middens was undertaken by Paul Mellars in the 1970s designed primarily to recover information on the economic basis of the Obanian occupation of the island (Mellars 1987). Mellars' excavations also provided the first radiocarbon dates for Obanian sites – multiple dating of each of the five excavated sites indicated that the Oronsay middens had been deposited between *c*.6 200 and *c*.5 400 BP. Radiocarbon determinations for microlithic industries available at that time ranged from *c*.8 200–6 000 BP.

From this evidence, several authors have concluded that the Obanian sites are a very late manifestation of the Mesolithic in western Scotland, post-dating the sites with microlithic industries and possibly overlapping in time the earliest Neolithic sites. Woodman (1989) argued that the use of microlithic armatures in hunting equipment had been abandoned in favour of the production of barbed projectile points of bone and antler (see also Woodman 1990). Jacobi (1982) suggested that the adoption of barbed points, mattock-heads and other elements of the Obanian toolkit was the result of contact with the earliest farming communities of the region. Mellars (1972: 92) reserved judgement on the relationship between the Obanian and microlithic sites, but suggested that the Obanian artefact assemblage represented 'a highly specialised toolkit adapted to the intensive exploitation of coastal economic resources'.

THE OBANIAN IN PERSPECTIVE

Most previous interpretations of the Obanian are underpinned by five basic assumptions:

1. The Obanian has a limited geographical distribution, occurring only in coastal areas of Argyll.
2. The Obanian middens belong to a very late stage in the development of the Mesolithic in this part of western Scotland, after *c*.6 500–6 000 BP.
3. The manufacture of microliths was not characteristic of the human groups responsible for the Obanian middens.
4. Certain artefact types found in Obanian assemblages are not characteristic of other coastal Mesolithic sites in Scotland.
5. Obanian sites are found only on coasts where sites with microlithic industries do not occur, and vice versa.

Results of recent research on shell midden and microlithic sites in western Scotland, coupled with a reassessment of existing evidence, raise doubts about the validity of most, if not all, of these assumptions.

It has long been recognised that certain artefact types regarded as characteristic of the Obanian are not confined to shell midden sites on the west coast of Scotland. Isolated finds of flat harpoon-heads and perforated mattock-heads are

Table 11.1. Radiocarbon determinations for Obanian shell middens and sites with antler and bone artefacts of Obanian form. The ¹⁴C ages quoted are as reported by the laboratory, with errors expressed at the ± one sigma level of confidence. Dates on marine shell have been 'adjusted' for the marine reservoir effect by subtracting 405 ± 40 years (Harkness 1983). All dates have been calibrated using the CALIB 3·03 program – Macintosh version, 12/03/93 (Stuiver and Reimer 1993).

Site	Lab. Ref.	Stratigraphic Context	Material	¹⁴C Age BP	cal BC age	Age range (1σ)	Age range (2σ)
Druimvargie Rockshelter (Oban)	OxA-4608	Midden	Bone artefact	8340 ± 80	7423	7486 – 7291	7533 – 7067
	OxA-4609	Midden	Bone artefact	7890 ± 80	6645	6696 – 6596	7032 – 6478
	OxA-1948	Midden	Bone artefact	7810 ± 90	6598	6696 – 6474	7001 – 6426
Ulva Cave	GU-2704	Midden (residual, cave interior)	Soil matrix (humic acid)	7800 ± 160	6595, 6573, 6569	6993 – 6453	7043 – 6252
	GU-2600	Midden (entrance): lower	Marine shells (*Patella* spp.)	7655 ± 65	6457	6477 – 6415	6595 – 6372
	OxA-3738	Midden (entrance): upper	Antler artefact	5750 ± 70	4581	4712 – 4505	4780 – 4457
	GU-2602	Midden (entrance): upper	Marine shells (*Patella* spp.)	5685 ± 65	4512	4583 – 4459	4711 – 4361
An Corran (Skye)	OxA-4994	Midden, C36	Bone artefact	7590 ± 90	6416	6463 – 6267	6552 – 6189
MacArthur's Cave (Oban)	OxA-1949	Midden	Antler artefact	6700 ± 80	5583	5621 – 5522	5693 – 5441
Cumstoun	OxA-3735	Unassociated find	Antler artefact	6665 ± 70	5574, 5543, 5528	5594 – 5479	5638 – 5439
Morton (Fife)	Q-981	Midden: lower, T50/T57	Charcoal	6382 ± 120	5290	5435 – 5226	5564 – 5059
	Q-988	Midden: lower, T50	Charcoal	6147 ± 90	5062	5219 – 4940	5266 – 4839
	Q-928	Midden: upper, T50/T59	Charcoal	6115 ± 110	5046	5215 – 4869	5268 – 4780
	OxA-4612	Midden: upper, T59	Bone artefact	5790 ± 80	4681, 4635, 4624	4771 – 4534	4833 – 4461
	OxA-4611	Midden: lower, T59	Bone artefact	5475 ± 60	4338	4356 – 4255	4455 – 4165
	OxA-4610	Midden: T65	Bone artefact	5180 ± 70	3977	4038 – 3950	4221 – 3799
Caisteal nan Gillean I (Oronsay)	Q-3008	Midden: Tr. C, layer 4 (base)	Charcoal	6190 ± 80	5201, 5176, 5136	5229 – 5003	5275 – 4927
	Q-3007	Midden: Tr. C, layer 4 (base)	Charcoal	6120 ± 80	5051	5206 – 4933	5250 – 4836
	Q-3009	Midden: Tr. C, layer 4 (upper)	Charcoal	6035 ± 70	4932	5036 – 4839	5196 – 4780
	Q-3010	Midden: Tr. C, layer 3	Charcoal	5485 ± 50	4341	4356 – 4264	4453 – 4238
	SRR-1458b	Midden (redeposited)	Marine shells	5485 ± 81	4341	4440 – 4250	4466 – 4108
	Q-3011	Midden: Tr. C, layer 3	Charcoal	5450 ± 50	4331	4346 – 4248	4361 – 4162
Risga	OxA-2023	Midden	Antler artefact	6000 ± 90	4905, 4872, 4865	4963 – 4787	5198 – 4711
	OxA-3737	Midden	Antler artefact	5875 ± 65	4773	4809 – 4695	4907 – 4571

186

Site	Lab. Ref.	Stratigraphic Context	Material	¹⁴C Age BP	cal BC age	Age range (1σ)	Age range (2σ)
Meiklewood	OxA-1159	Unassociated find	Antler artefact	5 920 ± 80	4 793	4 905 – 4 719	4 952 – 4 591
Priory Midden (Oronsay)	Q-3001	Midden: CT, layer 19	Charcoal	5 870 ± 50	4 770	4 795 – 4 711	4 896 – 4 604
	Q-3000	Midden: CT, layer 19	Charcoal	5 825 ± 50	4 714	4 774 – 4 612	4 800 – 4 540
	Q-3002	Midden: CT, layer 18	Charcoal	5 717 ± 50	4 539	4 664 – 4 470	4 712 – 4 458
	Q-3003	Midden: CT, layers 9/10	Charcoal	5 510 ± 50	4 348	4 435 – 4 333	4 458 – 4 252
	Q-3004	Midden: CT, layer 7	Charcoal	5 470 ± 50	4 337	4 352 – 4 257	4 448 – 4 230
Shewalton	OxA-1947	Unassociated find	Antler artefact	5 840 ± 80	4 719	4 794 – 4 593	4 906 – 4 504
Cnoc Coig (Oronsay)	Q-3006	Pre-midden	Charcoal	5 675 ± 60	4 502	4 549 – 4 458	4 685 – 4 361
	Q-3005	Pre-midden	Charcoal	5 650 ± 60	4 466	4 536 – 4 401	4 672 – 4 353
	Q-1353	Midden: Tr E, unit 8	Charcoal	5 645 ± 80	4 465	4 544 – 4 365	4 690 – 4 340
	Q-1354	Midden: Tr E, unit 6	Charcoal	5 535 ± 140	4 536	4 502 – 4 245	4 711 – 4 008
	Q-1351	Midden: Tr E, unit 2	Charcoal	5 495 ± 75	4 344	4 445 – 4 257	4 466 – 4 160
	Q-1352	Midden: Tr E, unit 3	Charcoal	5 430 ± 130	4 323, 4 281, 4 262	4 433 – 4 086	4 520 – 3 973
Cnoc Sligeach (Oronsay)	GX-1904	Midden	Mammal bone fragments	5 755 ± 180	4 587	4 805 – 4 368	5 048 – 4 245
	Birm-465	Midden (redeposited)	Marine shell (*P. maximus*)	5 605 ± 156	4 456	4 597 – 4 330	4 792 – 4 049
	BM-670	Midden: Tr B, layer 7	Charcoal	5 426 ± 159	4 321, 4 284, 4 261	4 452 – 4 042	4 574 – 3 949
	GX-1903	Midden	Marine shell (*O. edulis*)	4 610 ± 214	3 360	3 637 – 2 929	3 897 – 2 703
Caisteal nan Gillean II (Oronsay)	Q-1355	Midden: Tr B, layer 4 (base)	Charcoal	5 460 ± 65	4 334	4 353 – 4 245	4 454 – 4 151
	Birm-347	Midden: Tr B, layer 4 (base)	Charcoal	5 450 ± 140	4 331	4 453 – 4 091	4 546 – 3 973
	Birm-348	Midden: Tr B, layer 4 (base)	Marine shells (*Patella* spp.)	5 445 ± 313	4 329, 4 271, 4 269	4 592 – 3 958	4 946 – 3 636
	Birm-346	Midden: Tr B, layer 3 (upper)	Charcoal	5 150 ± 380	3 965	4 354 – 3 535	4 788 – 2 928
Carding Mill Bay I (Oban)	OxA-3740	Midden: lower, XV	Antler artefact	5 190 ± 85	3 981	4 211 – 3 948	4 229 – 3 791
	GU-2796	Midden: upper, XIV	Charcoal	5 060 ± 50	3 930, 3 875, 3 808	3 950 – 3 786	3 970 – 3 713
	GU-2899	Midden: lower, XV	Marine shells (*Patella* spp.)	5 035 ± 65	3 894, 3 887, 3 798	3 946 – 3 729	3 972 – 3 693
	GU-2898	Midden: upper, XIV	Marine shells (*Patella* spp.)	5 005 ± 73	3 785	3 938 – 3 702	3 966 – 3 646
	GU-2797	Midden: lower, XV	Charcoal	4 980 ± 50	3 772	3 892 – 3 701	3 939 – 3 653
	OxA-3739	Midden: upper, XIV	Bone artefact	4 795 ± 65	3 621, 3 580, 3 533	3 639 – 3 383	3 691 – 3 367

known from a number of coastal locations in northern Britain (Movius 1942, Mellars 1972), while a shell midden excavated at Morton on the east coast of Scotland produced bevelled tools of bone similar to those from the west coast middens (Coles 1971). Stone bevelled tools have a wide distribution along the western seaboard of Britain, and have recently been reported from a microlithic site at Kinloch on the island of Rhum in western Scotland (Wickham-Jones 1990).

Bone tools of typical Obanian form have been found recently at An Corran on the Isle of Skye in apparent association with a lithic assemblage which contains microliths, scrapers and other retouched tools (Rees et al. 1994, Saville and Miket 1994), and at Ulva Cave on an island off the west coast of Mull in conjunction with platform cores and blade débitage (Bonsall et al. 1994). The An Corran site also extends the distribution of known Obanian middens along the western seaboard to significantly north of the 'core area' in Argyll.

Knowledge of the chronology of the Obanian has been vastly improved by the use of AMS ^{14}C dating to obtain direct dates on individual antler and bone artefacts from sites that were previously undated (Bonsall and Smith 1990, 1992; Bonsall et al. in press). A large series of AMS and conventional radiocarbon determinations are now available for sites with Obanian artefacts (Table 11.1). These dates range from c. 8 350 to c. 4 750 BP and can be compared with (reliable) dates for sites with microlithic industries of between c. 8 600 and c. 5 450 BP (Morrison and Bonsall 1989, Hedges et al. 1989). The radiocarbon evidence therefore demonstrates a substantial chronological overlap between Obanian and microlithic assemblage types in western Scotland. The dates from Carding Mill Bay I (the latest of the Obanian sites) are similar to those for the earliest dated Neolithic sites in western Scotland and suggest that the economic system represented by the Obanian middens persisted until, and possibly after, the adoption of farming in the region.

Until recently, no microlithic sites were known to occur in close proximity to any of the known Obanian shell middens. At Lón Mór, near Oban, microlithic and shell midden sites have been recorded on the margins of a former marine embayment (Bonsall and Robinson 1992, Bonsall et al. 1993), while research on the island of Colonsay has revealed several sites with microlithic industries within 6–8 km of the Oronsay shell middens (Mithen and Finlayson 1991).

Results of recent research, therefore, do not support the view that Obanian and microlithic assemblage types were the product of populations that were differentiated culturally or chronologically. Other possible explanations need to be considered. It can be argued that much of the variability exhibited by Mesolithic sites in western Scotland is a consequence primarily of the conditions of preservation at the sites and the nature of the activities undertaken there.

SHELL MIDDENS AND SITE FUNCTION

Shell middens will accumulate where refuse from shellfish gathering is deposited on a regular basis. They will only survive, however, under favourable circumstances. In western Scotland shell midden deposits are preserved mainly in two geological situations – in coastal caves and rockshelters the entrances to which were sealed by talus accumulations, and on open-air sites where the middens were subsequently buried beneath blown sand deposits.

Among ethnographically-known shellfish gatherers, shellfish are rarely the principal source of food. But shellfishing is a regular activity, often undertaken by women and children, which normally is integrated with other economic tasks such as fishing, hunting (of land and sea mammals) and plant gathering.

In her study of the Anbarra of the north coast of Australia, Meehan (1982) described three types of site at which shellfish remains accumulate: home bases, processing camps and 'dinnertime' camps. Processing and dinnertime camps are normally located near to the shell beds; the former being special-purpose sites where shellfish are gathered and cooked, and the flesh carried back to the home base; and the latter 'small campsites used during the middle of the day while people are engaged in [collecting] trips away from their home base' (Meehan 1982: 26), where food procured up to that time is cooked and eaten – some of the food prepared at these sites may also be carried back to the home base for later consumption.

The existence of special-purpose 'processing camps' has been reported for other contemporary shellfish gatherers in different parts of the world (Waselkov 1987), and they may be assumed to have archaeological counterparts in a similarly wide range of coastal situations.

From ethnographic evidence, archaeological 'processing camps' can be hypothesised to exist where the main habitation sites are some distance from the shell beds, and to occur close to the contemporaneous shoreline; they are also likely to lack evidence of substantial structures, and to be characterised by a more restricted range of cultural equipment than at residential base camps (cf. Waselkov 1987: 145).

Ethnographically-known 'dinnertime camps' are typically small and were often used on only a single occasion; it follows that their prehistoric open-air equivalents are likely to be less visible archaeologically than either base camps or processing sites. However, if dinnertime camps were located in coastal caves, the chances of survival and discovery would be greatly enhanced; and if such locations were used repeatedly over a long period of time, then significant amounts of food refuse can be expected to have accumulated there.

SHELL MIDDENS IN THE MESOLITHIC OF WESTERN SCOTLAND

These observations drawn from ethnographic data can serve to guide interpretation of Mesolithic shell middens in western Scotland. Mesolithic coast-dwelling communities in western Scotland had access to abundant and varied shellfish resources, and it is probable that most groups were in some degree shellfish gatherers. It is also likely that women and children played an important role in this economic activity. Shellfish on the rocky coasts that characterise much of western Scotland constitute a highly dispersed resource (see below). It is un-likely, therefore, that shellfishing activities would have been confined to base camps. Thus, it may be suggested that in addition to residential camps the use of processing camps and dinnertime camps was a feature of the Mesolithic settle-ment-subsistence system, and that individual middens will relate to one or other of these site categories.

The quality of the data from the Obanian sites is highly variable, but a number of general features can be discerned which have a bearing on the question of site function:

1. All of the known shell middens (whether within caves or in the open air) appear to have been deposited in close proximity to the contempor-aneous shoreline; and at two sites, MacArthur's Cave (Oban) and Cnoc Sligeach (Oronsay) the midden deposits were interstratified with storm beach gravels (Anderson 1895, Mellars 1987).

2. The sites often occur on open, relatively exposed coasts; and six of the 12 known sites are on small islands (Oronsay, Risga) that could not have sustained resident populations of deer or other large herbivores, and where access to land-based resources generally would have been limited. Conversely, such locations maximise access to shellfish and other shore-based resources.

3. In contrast to Mesolithic coastal shell middens in some parts of Europe, the Obanian sites are very small – rarely exceeding 25 m across or 1.5 m in thickness. Yet radiocarbon dating and stratigraphic evidence from several recently excavated sites suggest that they were used repeatedly over long periods – on Oronsay this use appears to have followed a seasonal pattern (Mellars and Wilkinson 1980, see below). At Druim-vargie Rockshelter in Oban and Caisteal nan Gillean I and Priory Mid-den on Oronsay midden accumulation occurred over several hundred radiocarbon years, while the Ulva Cave midden (only 8 m across) was deposited over 2 000–3 000 RC yr (Russell, Bonsall and Sutherland n.d.).

4. Although the faunal evidence indicates that seals, otters and sea birds were sometimes procured from the sites, the processing of shellfish and fish appears to have been the main economic activity undertaken. Bones of wild land mammals (principally red deer and pig) occur in all of the middens, but there is no unequivocal evidence that these were procured from the sites, or that major processing of their carcasses or hides occurred there (but see Finlayson n.d.). From a study of the Cnoc Coig assemblage, Grigson concluded that antlers and bones of red deer and bones and tusks of wild boar had been introduced to the site primarily as a source of raw material for tool manufacture (Grigson and Mellars 1987).

5. None of the sites has produced convincing evidence of dwelling structures or storage facilities. The only site with extensive structural remains is Cnoc Coig on Oronsay, where two stake-hole settings and a series of hearths, small pits and concentrations of heat-affected stones were associated with a former land surface underneath the midden (Mellars 1987). These features appear to have resulted from frequent reuse of the site, and their occurrence with burnt shells and fish bones suggests that they were connected essentially with food preparation activities.

6. Many of the artefacts recovered from the Obanian middens appear to reflect 'expediency' in design, manufacture and raw material procurement. Reduction strategies applied to flint and quartz frequently involved use of the bipolar technique. At the majority of sites nearly all of the lithic artefacts, and most of those made from bone, antler or shell, are simple, easily made (and hence 'disposable') items which were probably manufactured at the sites for immediate use – as such they offer an interesting parallel to the 'situational gear' of the Nunamiut which tends to be well represented at their special-purpose sites (Binford 1979).[2] The frequent absence of retouched pieces, such as microliths and scrapers, commonly found at other Mesolithic sites in western Scotland, implies that activities (production, use, maintenance) involving such artefacts were not normally undertaken at the shell midden sites. Occasionally, elaborate artefacts such as harpoon- and mattock-heads made of bone or antler are represented in the middens. These are items that can be expected to have been 'heavily curated' (cf. Binford 1979). In some cases, they may have been brought to the sites for use there. In many instances, however, they were probably introduced as broken items intended for recycling. Some of the broken harpoon heads from MacArthur's Cave, for example, appear to have been converted into bevelled tools.

From the similarities in their location and in the character of their artefactual and faunal assemblages, it can be argued that the known Obanian sites fulfilled a specific role in the Mesolithic settlement-subsistence system of the region. The absence of major architectural features and the lack of certain categories of industrial and food refuse that can be expected to have been discarded inside residential camps, suggest that the middens do not represent the disposal of refuse from nearby base camps. From the available evidence it can be inferred that they mark the locations of special-purpose processing camps associated with the exploitation of sea food resources, principally fish and shellfish, and that food prepared at the sites was carried back to residential camps located some distance away. As noted above, it is likely that women and children played a dominant role in this economic activity and at some sites, perhaps, an exclusive one.[3]

Processing of shellfish and other food items occurred at all of the known Obanian sites. However, differences in the content of the midden deposits suggest that there was significant variation in the frequency, range, scale and intensity of the processing activities undertaken. The midden in Ulva Cave is substantially smaller than those on Oronsay, is unusually heavily dominated by shells of marine molluscs, and contains comparatively few artefacts or mammalian bones (Russell, Bonsall and Sutherland n.d.). Yet evidently it represents refuse from numerous visits to the site over several millennia, implying that the site was used less frequently than those on Oronsay, or for shorter periods, or that particularly small amounts of material were processed during individual occupations. Such differences suggest that the Obanian sites perhaps represent a spectrum of human activities between dedicated processing camps and repeatedly-used dinnertime camps.[4]

SHELL MIDDENS AND SITE LOCATION

It was noted above that Mesolithic shell middens in western Scotland occur in coastal caves/rockshelters and on open-air sites. Among ethnographically-known shellfish gatherers the processing of shellfish for food often involves cooking (roasting or boiling) 'in, over, under or around open fires' (Waselkov 1987: 100). If climatic conditions in Scotland during the Mesolithic were similar to today – with high rainfall and strong winds – then processing activities would necessitate the frequent use of some form of shelter. It follows that where caves existed near to the shell beds they would have been used occasionally for processing activities (Russell, Bonsall and Sutherland n.d.), and that construction of artificial shelters is likely to have occurred on open-air processing sites. The existence of stake-hole settings, hearths and pits in association with shell refuse at Cnoc Coig on Oronsay (Mellars 1987) is consistent with this hypothesis.[5]

The shell middens on Oronsay and around Oban Bay occur at intervals along the shoreline that was formed at the maximum of the Main Postglacial Transgression, c.6 000–7 000 BP (Fig. 11.1). Radiocarbon dating and stratigraphic evidence indicate that most of the sites post-date or are contemporaneous with the maximum of the transgression. Since the middens are likely to have been deposited in close proximity to the contemporaneous shoreline, it is highly probable that many sites predating the maximum of the transgression (and possibly some that were contemporaneous with it) are likely to have been destroyed during that event (Bonsall and Sutherland 1992). Therefore, the known sites are most probably only a partial record of shellfish-gathering activities along those coasts during the Mesolithic.

From a study of the length distributions of otoliths in the Oronsay middens, Mellars and Wilkinson (1980) have shown that fish were procured from the different sites at specific times of the year. Equivalent seasonality data are not available for the shellfish, but it seems reasonable to assume that they were collected and processed at the sites at the same times of year. Although shellfish probably contributed less to the overall food supply than either fish or sea mammals, it may be suggested that they exercised a significant influence on site location. Oronsay (like many coasts in western Scotland) has a rocky shoreline. As Waselkov (1987: 115) has observed, shellfish associated with such shorelines constitute a dispersed resource which can be exploited most effectively at numerous points. Thus, the choice of location for the processing sites on Oronsay may have been determined primarily by the need for seasonal scheduling of the shellfish resources.

From the ethnographic and archaeological evidence discussed, it can be predicted that remains of Mesolithic processing camps will occur at numerous points around the coasts of western Scotland, around or above the level of the Main Postglacial Shoreline. Unlike Oronsay, many coasts have no blown sand deposits which could preserve open-air shell middens. The former locations of such middens, however, can be expected to be represented by residual scatters of lithic artefacts similar in character to those from known shell midden sites. Such sites are likely to be of limited extent, and hence difficult to locate. Moreover, in the absence of microliths or other diagnostic artefacts, it is doubtful if they would be immediately identifiable as Mesolithic. In a recent survey of the Isle of Ulva, several such scatters were recognised (Russell, Bonsall and Sutherland, in press: Fig. 2). None of he sites, however, has been investigated further and their ages are unknown.

CONCLUSIONS

In this paper it has been argued that the contrast between Obanian sites and sites with microlithic industries evident in the Mesolithic of western Scotland cannot be explained satisfactorily in cultural or chronological terms, but is primarily a reflection of differences in the conditions of preservation at the two types of site and the nature of the activities undertaken there.

A case can be made for interpreting most, and possibly all, of the known Obanian sites as remains of special-purpose processing camps associated primarily with the exploitation of shellfish and fish. The use of such logistic camps appears to have been an integral part of an economic system that operated in western Scotland (if not more widely in northern Britain) throughout the greater part of Mesolithic and into the period after *c*. 5 000 BP and the widespread adoption of farming in the region. The model proposed explains a number of 'unusual' features of Obanian sites, such as their frequent occurrence on open coasts and on small islands which lacked resident populations of large land mammals, and the prevalence in the middens of expediently designed and manufactured tools.

The existing evidence, however, has obvious limitations. Although there has been a marked increase in research activity over the past 25 years, with new excavations at sites on the islands of Oronsay, Skye and Ulva, and on the mainland around Oban Bay, the full results of this research are not yet available. Consequently, there is a lack of detailed information on the faunal composition of the majority of Obanian sites and on functional and technological aspects of the

Obanian toolkit. There is also a need for additional research, including studies to determine the seasonality of shellfish gathering at individual sites like those conducted by Margaret Deith (1983, 1985, 1986) at sites in eastern Scotland and northern Spain, and for more extensive excavations to expose areas adjacent to middens in order to test for associated architectural features and to recover information on site structure in general.

The interpretation of the Obanian sites presented in this chapter, therefore, should be viewed as a 'working hypothesis' which can be tested, and modified, as new data become available.

NOTES

1. A version of this paper was presented at the international conference on *The Mesolithic of the Atlantic Façade*, held in Santander, Spain, in July 1994 (Bonsall 1994).

2. The principal categories of artefacts with an 'expedient' aspect occurring in Obanian sites are unretouched flakes of flint and/or quartz often produced by the bipolar technique, bevelled tools, and small bone points. There has been little systematic research on the possible uses of these artefacts. Finlayson (in Connock et al. 1993) has observed that a bipolar reduction strategy applied to small pebbles of flint or quartz produces numerous flat, sharp flakes which could be used without further modification as 'knives' for processing fish. Experimental studies of bevelled tools and bone points are being undertaken at the University of Edinburgh. Pending the results of this research, the present writer favours the view advocated by some previous workers (e.g. Grieve 1885, Bishop 1914) that the bevelled tools were used in the processing or collection of limpets. (In this context it is worth noting that 'Asturian picks' from Mesolithic shell middens along the north coast of Spain, usually interpreted as 'limpet hammers', often exhibit a degree of bevelling at the tip.) The small bone points which occur in large numbers in some Obanian middens may also have been used in the processing of shellfish, e.g. for removing the soft parts of periwinkles and dog-whelks from their shells, and for piercing shellfish/fish meat so that it could be strung up for drying.

3. The age/sex composition of the task group occupying a site is likely to have some influence on the character of the resulting artefact assemblage. The incidence of bipolar débitage is likely to be greater where women and children were more actively involved than men in the use of the site, on the assumption that generally they were less skilled flint knappers. Similarly, items traditionally made and used by men (e.g. remains of hunting equipment) ought to be poorly represented at sites where men and teenage boys were not present or only occasionally participated in the activities of the site.

4. The midden at An Corran (Skye) is unusual in possessing what Saville and Miket (1994) have termed a 'conventional' Mesolithic assemblage with blade débitage, microliths and other retouched artefacts. But the site is also unusual in respect of access to lithic resources. Compared to other Obanian sites a wider range of materials was available locally, including large pieces of high-quality volcanic rock; a significant proportion of the microliths and blade débitage are apparently made from this volcanic material. In addition to 'normal' processing activities, therefore, An Corran was possibly important for raw material procurement, and stages in the production of lithic items related to the manufacture or repair of personal gear may have been undertaken there. Such tasks are likely to have involved men, and could have been performed in conjunction with the processing of fish and shellfish or at other times.

5. A similar interpretation can be placed on the structural remains excavated at Morton on the east coast of Scotland.

ACKNOWLEDGEMENTS

The author wishes to thank Bill Finlayson for sight of an unpublished paper, Douglas Harkness for advice on radiocarbon dates and calibration, and László Bartosiewicz and Nicola Murray for their comments on an earlier draft of this paper.

REFERENCES

Anderson, J. 1895. Notice of a cave recently discovered at Oban, containing human remains and a refuse heap of shells and bones of animals, and stone and bone implements. *Proceedings of the Society of Antiquaries of Scotland* 29, 211–30.

Anderson, J. 1898. Notes on the contents of a small cave or rock shelter at Druimvargie, Oban; and of three shell mounds on Oronsay. *Proceedings of the Society of Antiquaries of Scotland* 32, 298–313.

Binford, L. R. 1979. Organisation and formation processes: looking at curated technologies. *Journal of Anthropological Research* 35, 255–73.

Bishop, A. H. 1914. An Oransay shell-mound – a Scottish pre-Neolithic site. *Proceedings of the Society of Antiquaries of Scotland* 48, 52–108.

Bonsall, C. 1994. The 'Obanian problem': coastal adaptation in the Mesolithic in western Scotland. Paper presented at the International Conference on The Mesolithic of the Atlantic Façade, Santander 6–9 July 1994.

Bonsall, C. and Robinson, M. R. 1992. *Archaeological Survey of the Glenshellach Development Area, Oban: Report to Historic Scotland*. Edinburgh: University of Edinburgh Department of Archaeology.

Bonsall, C., Robinson, M. R., Payton, R. and Macklin, M. G. 1993. Lón Mór, Oban. *Discovery and Excavation in Scotland* 76.

Bonsall, C. and Smith, C. 1990. Bone and antler technology in the British Late Upper Palaeolithic and Mesolithic: the impact of accelerator dating. In Vermeersch, P. M. and Van Peer, P. (eds), *Contributions to the Mesolithic in Europe*. Louvain: University Press, 359–68.

Bonsall, C. and Smith, C. 1992. New AMS ¹⁴C dates for antler and bone artefacts from Great Britain. *Mesolithic Miscellany* 13, 28–34.

Bonsall, C. and Sutherland, D. G. 1992. The Oban caves. In Walker, M. J. C., Gray, J. M. and Lowe, J. J. (eds), *The South-West Scottish Highlands: Field Guide*. Cambridge: Quaternary Research Association, 115–21.

Bonsall, C., Sutherland, D. G., Russell, N. J., et al. 1994. Excavations in Ulva Cave, western Scotland 1990–91: a preliminary report. *Mesolithic Miscellany* 15, 8–21.

Bonsall, C., Tolan-Smith, C. and Saville, A. (in press). Direct Dating of Mesolithic antler and bone artefacts from Great Britain: new results for bevelled tools and red deer antler mattocks. *Mesolithic Miscellany*.

Breuil, H. 1922. Observations on the Pre-Neolithic industries of Scotland. *Proceedings of the Society of Antiquaries of Scotland* 56, 261–81.

Clark, J. G. D. 1956. Notes on the Obanian with special reference to antler- and bone-work. *Proceedings of the Society of Antiquaries of Scotland* 89, 91–106.

Coles, J. M. 1971. The early settlement of Scotland: excavations at Morton, Fife. *Proceedings of the Prehistoric Society* 37, 284–366.

Connock, K. D., Finlayson, B. and Mills, C. M. 1993. Excavation of a shell midden site at Carding Mill Bay near Oban, Scotland. *Glasgow Archaeological Journal* 17, 25–38.

Deith, M. R. 1983. Molluscan calendars: the use of growth-line analysis to establish seasonality of shellfish collection at the Mesolithic site of Morton, Fife. *Journal of Archaeological Science* 10, 423–40.

Deith, M. R. 1985. Seasonality from shells: an evaluation of two techniques for seasonal dating of marine molluscs. In Fieller, N. R. J., Gilbertson, D. D. and Ralph, N. G. A. (eds), *Palaeobiological Investigations: Research Design, Methods and Data Analysis*. British Archaeological Report, S266. Oxford: British Archaeological Reports, 119–30.

Deith, M. R. 1986. Subsistence strategies at a Mesolithic campsite: evidence from stable isotope analysis of shells. *Journal of Archaeological Science* 13, 61–78.

Finlayson, B. 1995. Complexity in the Mesolithic of the western Scottish seaboard. In Fischer, A. (ed.), *Man and Sea in the Mesolithic: Coastal Settlement above and below Present Sea Level*. Oxford: Oxbow Books/Danish National Forest and Nature Agency, 261–4.

Grieve, S. 1885. *The Great Auk or Garefowl (Alca impennis, Linn.): Its History, Archaeology and Remains*. London: Jack.

Grigson, C. and Mellars, P. A. 1987. The mammalian remains from the middens. In Mellars, P. A., *Excavations on Oronsay*. Edinburgh: Edinburgh University Press, 243–89.

Harkness, D. D. 1983. The extent of natural ^{14}C deficiency in the coastal environment of the United Kingdom. In Mook, W. G. and Waterbolk, H. T. (eds), *Proceedings of the First International Symposium ^{14}C and Archaeology* (PACT 8). Strasbourg: Council of Europe, 351–64.

Hedges, R. E. M., Housley, R. A., Law, I. A. and Bronk, C. R. 1989. Radiocarbon dates from the Oxford AMS system: archaeometry datelist 9. *Archaeometry* 31, 207–34.

Jacobi, R. M. 1982. Lost hunters in Kent: Tasmania and the earliest Neolithic. In Leach, P. E. (ed.), *Archaeology in Kent to AD 1500* (CBA Research Report 48). London: Council for British Archaeology, 12–24.

Lacaille, A. D. 1954. *The Stone Age in Scotland*. Oxford: Oxford University Press.

Meehan, B. 1982. *Shell Bed to Shell Midden*. Canberra: Australian Institute for Aboriginal Studies.

Mellars, P. A. 1972. The Palaeolithic and Mesolithic. In Renfrew, C. (ed.), *British Prehistory: A New Outline*. London: Duckworth, 41–99.

Mellars, P. A. 1987. *Excavations on Oronsay: Prehistoric Human Ecology on a Small Island*. Edinburgh: Edinburgh University Press.

Mellars, P. A. and Wilkinson, M. R. 1980. Fish otoliths as indicators of seasonality in prehistoric shell middens: the evidence from Oronsay (Inner Hebrides). *Proceedings of the Prehistoric Society* 46, 19–44.

Mithen, S. J. and Finlayson, B. 1991. Red deer hunters on Colonsay? The implications of Staosnaig for the interpretation of the Oronsay middens. *Proceedings of the Prehistoric Society* 57, 1–8.

Morrison, A. and Bonsall, C. 1989. The early post-glacial settlement of Scotland. In Bonsall, C. (ed.), *The Mesolithic in Europe: Papers Presented at the Third International Symposium, Edinburgh 1985*. Edinburgh: John Donald, 134–42.

Movius, H. L. 1940. An early post-glacial archaeological site at Cushendun, County Antrim. *Proceedings of the Royal Irish Academy* 46, 1–84.

Movius, H. L. 1942. *The Irish Stone Age: Its Chronology, Development and Relations.* Cambridge: Cambridge University Press.

Rees, T., Kozikowski, G. and Miket, R. 1994. Investigation of a shell midden at An Corran, Staffin, Isle of Skye. Unpublished report.

Russell, N. J., Bonsall, C. and Sutherland, D. G. 1995. The exploitation of marine molluscs in the Mesolithic of western Scotland: evidence from Ulva Cave, Inner Hebrides. In Fischer, A. (ed.), *Man and Sea in the Mesolithic: Coastal Settlement above and below Present Sea Level.* Oxford: Oxbow Books/Danish National Forest and Nature Agency, 273–88.

Saville, A. and Miket, R. 1994. An Corran rock-shelter, Skye: a major new Mesolithic site. *PAST* no. 18, December 1994, 9–10.

Stuiver, M. and Reimer, P. J. 1993. Extended ^{14}C data base and revised CALIB 3.0 ^{14}C age calibration program. *Radiocarbon* 35, 215–30.

Waselkov, G. A. 1987. Shellfish gathering and shell midden archaeology. In Schiffer, M. B. (ed.), *Advances in Archaeological Method and Theory*, vol. 10. New York: Academic Press, 93–210.

Wickham-Jones, C. R. 1990. *Rhum: Mesolithic and Later Sites at Kinloch. Excavations 1984–86.* Edinburgh: Society of Antiquaries of Scotland, Monograph 7.

Woodman, P. C. 1989. Ireland and Scotland: the Mesolithic of Europe's western periphery. Paper presented at the Conference on Scottish–Irish Links, Edinburgh 1989.

Woodman, P. C. 1990. A review of the Scottish Mesolithic: a plea for normality! *Proceedings of the Society of Antiquaries of Scotland* 119, 1–32.

12

TIME AND TIDE

COASTAL ENVIRONMENTS, COSMOLOGY AND RITUAL PRACTICE IN EARLY PREHISTORIC SCOTLAND

TONY POLLARD

> On the beach,
> our shells are left behind,
> like a library,
> like a memory
> of our ghost-written lives.
>
> from *Shell* by Peter Hammill

INTRODUCTION

The coastal environment has proved a rich hunting ground for both antiquarian and archaeologist alike. It is here, on the boundary between land and sea, that the constant battering of waves against the shore has brought to light all manner of archaeological sites, ranging from deserted villages to the graves of those long buried. Though it is true that this same processs of marine erosion has resulted in the permanent loss of many archaeological sites (Ashmore 1983) it cannot be denied that the action of waves breaking against the land has revealed many sites which would otherwise have remained concealed. It is not always the sea which has been responsible for this exposure, the wind too has played its part, uncovering sites previously buried and preserved beneath sands which themselves had been transported from the sea-bed by both wave and wind action. However, many of these sites, including the Neolithic settlements of Knap of Howar and Skara Brae on Orkney, did not always sit in immediate proximity to the shore or require the protection of specially constructed sea walls, as they do today. Here, rising sea levels have submerged much of the land which had at one time separated these sites from the beach and the sea beyond it. These continually rising sea levels are in part the long lasting result of the worldwide increase in sea levels which followed the melting of the Devension ice sheets some 10 000 years ago. Not having suffered glaciation to the same extent as mainland Scotland these locations did not benefit from the resulting isostatic rebound, which followed the release of the downward pressure of ice, and instead lost territory to the sea.

As yet the effects of global warming, which may have accentuated this relative rise in sea level, are poorly understood.

In contrast to those previously land-locked sites which today exist on the immediate shore are those which now sit some distance inland from the shore they occupied in the prehistoric past. Undoubtedly the best known examples of this latter type of site are the shell middens, many of which are to be found at the rear of raised beach terraces. The result of isostatic rebound has been a relative reduction in sea level, with beaches lifted up and away from the waters which had once nurtured the shellfish now represented by the sometimes substantial deposits of empty shells located on their landward fringes.

It is apparent that the coastal environment is a dynamic one, associated with a number of dramatic shifts and transformations. These changes occur both on a regular daily basis, with the ebb and flow of the tide, and over much longer periods of time, as demonstrated by the changes in sea level and the formation of raised beaches. These changes will be further considered in a discussion of evidence for early prehistoric coastal activity which follows.

RECENT APPROACHES TO SHELL MIDDENS

Archaeology has been studied in Scotland for well over 150 years and throughout that time shell middens have been the subject of investigation and speculation. Their optimum preservation levels, promoted through the alkaline qualities of marine shells, made them an attractive prospect for those eager to recover artefacts, often of bone and antler, while large quantities of animal bones and other dietary components helped to provide an insight into past lifeways not possible on other types of archaeological site.

The same reasons which made shell middens a target for early collectors and antiquarians also made them an obvious testing ground for the processual sampling techniques developed as part of the so-called New archaeology in the 1960s and 1970s. They were largely viewed as 'fact mines' from which raw empirical data could be extracted and refined through the application of various statistical forms of analyses in order to produce information on prehistoric diet, processing techniques, resource availability, seasonality, and other issues related to the food quest. A number of Scottish shell midden excavations have been published over the last ten years, with the most notable of these being the work of Paul Mellars on Oronsay (1987).

All of these relatively recent works are characterised by the contributions of various specialists, with a multidisciplinary approach being at the core of the processual ethos. They include reports on artefacts, with stone, bone and pottery (in the case of later sites) all requiring particular specialisms. Likewise, the faunal remains, such as fish, mammal and bird bones, are all subject to detailed scrutiny. Marine shells are often counted, and measured, with metrical analysis utilised to determine the parts of the beach from which they were collected, while the calculation of calorific content through quantitative analysis is used to calculate the number of people supported by this particular dietry component.

Though concerned with sites located on the eastern seaboard of the United States 'Deciphering a shell midden' edited by Julie K. Stein (1992) provides a similarly detailed insight into the types of analysis carried out on shell middens. However, in a review of this book Bell criticises it because: 'we are not told what is special about a shell midden and why we should go to such lengths to decipher them and what it all means in terms of past human activity' (1994: 134). It can certainly be argued that one shortcoming of such closely focused studies is that they rarely pull back to consider the people responsible for these deposits. Though detailed scientific excavation has a vital role to play in any study of shell middens (see Pollard, Atkinson and Banks, this volume) it is equally important that we take a step back and view these sites within their wider context as elements of a complex cultural landscape; only then will we have any hope of moving beyond the sometimes stereotypical image of these features as straightforward heaps of food waste.

SHELL MIDDENS AND SCOTTISH ARCHAEOLOGY

The serious study of shell middens in Scotland was encouraged through advances made in the field in Denmark, where as early as 1869, the 'Kjokkenmodding' or Kitchen-Midden Committee had excavated no less than 40 such features (Munro 1884). The Danish shell middens, which Munro felt 'had been forced to disclose the salient features in the social life of a bygone people' (1884: 216), provided evidence for a previously unrecognised period in that country's prehistory, during which people did not practise agriculture but obtained their subsistence from the natural environment, which included the sea and its littoral. This mode of existence was seen to correspond to the earlier part of what had come to be known as the 'Stone Age'. It was Thomsen who first conceived the 'Three Age System' but its wider acceptance was largely due to its refinement by Warsaae, who himself was a member of the Kitchen Midden Committee. The results of the Danish excavations soon prompted researchers, such as Anderson, Grieve, Lubbock, and Laing to turn to shell middens in an attempt to establish the applicability of this chronological scheme to the prehistory of Scotland.

As had been the case in Denmark a number of the shell middens discovered in Scotland during the latter part of the nineteenth century appeared to represent the residues of groups exploiting the natural environment at a time prior to the adoption of agriculture. However, there was a tendency to regard all shell middens as Mesolithic, or previous to the introduction of the term as early Stone Age. This was a blinkered attitude largely due to the perception of shellfish as an impoverished and primitive resource. Among the factors which these earlier researchers failed to take on board were the large quantities of fish bone present in many shell middens – a presence which may indicate at least in some cases that shellfish were merely used as bait to catch fish or eaten alongside other foodstuffs. So strong was this perception that Laing, following his excavations in the 1860s, concluded that an Iron Age broch was in fact constructed during a much earlier pre-agricultural period, largely on the basis of a lack of artefacts and the presence of large quantities of marine shells (Laing and Huxley 1866: 56–57). Laing even went as far as to suggest that disarticulated human remains within the shell layers, which included a child's jaw, represented the left-overs from a cannibal feast! (ibid. 28–29).

Though such dramatic misinterpretations are unlikely to be made today there is still a tendency to assume, prior to excavation, that a shell midden is Mesolithic. The recent excavation of a shell midden at Culbin in eastern Scotland revealed what had been assumed to be a Mesolithic site to be no older than the Pictish period, accumulating some time during the eighth or ninth century AD (Wickham-Jones 1992). More relevant to this paper are the large oyster dominated middens in the Forth estuary which upon excavation produced not only bones from domestic cattle and pottery but also a series of late radiocarbon dates, all of which indicated activity stretching well into the period traditionally regarded as the Neolithic (Sloan 1982, 1984).

Among the best known shell middens in Scotland are the so-called 'Obanian' sites in Oban itself and on the islands of Risga and Oronsay (see Bonsall, this volume for location maps). During the latter half of the nineteenth century the small crofting and fishing village of Oban began to grow into a town. The construction of the railway from Glasgow in the 1880s not only transformed the town into a thriving stock-market (Hunter 1984: 26), but also ensured it a lasting place in the new industry of tourism. The earliest parts of the village were located on the raised beach, and it was also upon this terrace formed by a reduction in sea levels, that arable agriculture was practised. As will be made clear later, these raised beaches play an important role in our understanding of prehistoric economic and social change in this region. At the rear of the raised beach sandstone cliffs rose up to provide a dramatic but restrictive backdrop to the village. As the village developed into a town so it began to encroach on its immediate environment and when the talus of tumbled rocks and earth was removed from the base of these cliffs a number of caves containing shell middens were discovered. Several apparently similar sites were recovered from the 1860s onwards, but it was not until the discovery of the MacArthur cave in 1895 that a thorough archaeological excavation took place.

Recovered from the shell deposits were a number of artefacts of bone and antler, the most striking of which are the antler barbed points, which were probably used in the procurement of marine mammals and large fish. Similar artefacts were also recovered from open shell middens on the island of Oronsay to the southwest, and Risga to the northwest. It was the similarity between the nature of these sites and the material culture recovered from them which prompted the application of the 'Obanian' cultural label (by Movius in 1940), appearing as they did to represent the residues of a specific cultural group, which practised a highly specialised mode of subsistence geared towards the exploitation of the marine environment.

A number of Obanian sites have been subject to excavation over the past two decades. Some of these sites, such as the shell middens on Oronsay (Mellars 1987) and the site on Risga (Pollard et al. this volume), had been subject to earlier investigations, while others, such as those at Carding Mill Bay, were centred on sites newly discovered in Oban, as a consequence of those same processes of urbanisation responsible for the first discoveries during the nineteenth century. Some of these more recent investigations have resulted in the recovery not only of the bones of various animals, but also human remains, predominantly those of the hands and feet. Human remains were recovered from some of the earlier excavations but these have been largely ignored in the consideration of these sites, usually being written of as later intrusions unrelated to the build-up of shell midden deposits. The Iron Age radiocarbon dates recently obtained from a number of human bones recovered in the nineteenth-century excavations in the MacArthur Cave (Saville and Hallen 1994) certainly appear to suggest that this was the case with some bones.

It is has been suggested by the present author that the presence of post-Mesolithic human remains in shell middens represent the later use of these sites as a focus for marine exploitation. The absence of large areas of suitable agricultural land in northwest Scotland would ensure an important role for marine resources in 'agriculutral' economies and so the use of shell middens as places of burial may reflect the need to legitimate and reinforce a particular group's access to the stretch of coastline adjacent to the shell midden (Pollard 1990).

However, it can also be suggested that there was another set of motivations at work here, some of them perhaps not so obvious but just as important as the need to secure access to marine resources. It is in exploring this further set of motivations that this chapter will hopefully cast fresh light upon shell middens and their role within the social practices of those responsible for their accumulation.

THE SHORE AS A LIMINAL ZONE

The shore is an environment subject to constant change, being neither land nor sea, but a transitional zone between the two. Twice a day the sea advances and retreats, at times of low tide giving access to land that was previously sea and at high tide submerging these same places beneath breaking waves. The exploitation of many of the resources evidenced in shell middens is only practical at times of low tide, when the rocks which accommodate mussels and limpets, or the sands within which cockles and razor shells are buried, are temporarily exposed by the withdrawn sea. Fish traps also do their job at this time, with the recession of the tide not only making them accessible but also providing the mechanism by which fish are drawn into the trap.[1] Low tide occurs every day, twice a day, and it is these temporary windows which provide the cue for the intensification of activity on the shore, with people perhaps setting aside other tasks and moving from areas removed from the shore in order to reap the harvest of these temporary forests of kelp and fields of mussels.

Though the window provided by changing tides is predictable it is also a moving window, with times of low tide moving forward an hour every day, on a regular monthly cycle. This system differs somewhat to the time cycles which dictate non-marine based activities, such as agriculture and hunting, where work is dictated by the available hours of daylight[2] and the turn of the seasons. Time for the agriculturalist or hunter is marked by the sun, while for the fisher it is marked by the effect of the moon on the movement of the sea. When agricultural-ists or hunters are also fishers the two systems mesh, marine time acting as a rolling counterpoint to land time.

It is not suggested that the earlier prehistoric inhabitants of the coast were aware that the mutual gravitational pull of heavenly bodies was responsible for the movement of the tides; that was not realised until 1687, when Isaac Newton developed his laws of graviation. However, it is not unlikely that these people were aware of the intimate relationship between the phases of the moon and tidal action. As the moon reaches both ends of its cycle twice a month, so the tides reach their extremes. The full moon coincides with the lowest or ebb tide, while the waning moon equates with the highest, or spring tide, when the sea extends its reach further up the beach than at any other time.

Shell middens exist on the very edge of this moving world, at times of very high tide or during storms they may well have been touched by the sea, which washed material onto the beach before reclaiming the fragmented remains of creatures previously removed from its depths by human hand. It is doubtful whether people lived in such exposed environments, usually prefering to locate their camps or settlements a little further inland (but see Pollard et al. this volume). Generally, shell middens appear to represent specialised task sites at which marine resources were transformed into the cultural product which is food. This food may have been consumed at the site of the shell midden but it is equally likely to have been moved inland to be consumed at settlement sites. Although the bones of terrestrial fauna have also been recovered from Scottish Mesolithic shell middens they appear to be limited in quantity, and it has been suggested that they were brought to these sites with the intention of using them in the manufacture of tools, as in the case of the harpoon points of red deer antler (Grigson and Mellars 1987: 253). The shell midden therefore represents a place of transformation, where terrestrial resources were transformed into tools prior to their deployment in the marine envronment and marine resources transformed into food prior to its consumption or movement into the terrestrial zone.

The special nature of the littoral environment is made nowhere more obvious than in the case of marine mammals, which belong fully to neither land or sea. Scottish oral tradition is rife with stories about seals, which can be seen both offshore, bobbing in the waves, and also in land, basking on the beach. They are known as 'selchies' and depending on location may be held to represent the souls of the damned, the bewitched or the reincarnation of those lost at sea (Thomson 1965).

It is proposed here that the shell midden represents a place of mediation between land and sea, the meeting of the two being a liminal zone which was perhaps negotiated via the shell midden. The special status of this zone and the location of shell middens within it, or at least on its landward boundary, may be one reason why these sites were selected as a place to deposit the remains of the dead. Many cultures identify the corpse with pollution, danger and fear, and in order to ensure its safe passage from the world of the living to the world of the dead rely upon a variety of ritual mechanisms (Huntington and Metcalf 1979: 12).

The predominance of the bones of the hands and feet on some of the sites in Oban (Lorimer 1992) and on Oronsay (Meiklejohn and Denston 1987: 298) may provide further support to this argument. It is these small bones which are usually lost when bodies are excarnated, with the flesh allowed to decay to reveal clean, and perhaps 'safe' bones. This practice, which represents one means of negotiating the dangerous liminal phase between death and the safe disposal of the body, appears to characterise many of the insertions in Neolithic chambered tombs. However, as the remains on Oronsay suggest the practice may have had a Mesolithic origin. In this case the shell middens, which themselves exist within a liminal environment, appear to have represented the place where corpses were left to decay, after which time the bones may have been collected, moved and deposited elsewhere, leaving the smaller bones of the hands and feet behind. Thus, shell middens appear to represent a location at which the dangerous transformation between life and death was negotiated.

The association of the beach itself with the transformation between life and death would have been more than metaphorical; it is here that dead animals, and perhaps more rarely even humans, would periodically be washed ashore after dying at sea. Dead animals were also brought to the shell midden after being captured at sea and prior to their transformation into food. A number of whale remains in the Firth of Forth apear to be associated with antler mattocks which may have been used to remove their blubber. Although hunting whales, perhaps by driving them ashore, would have been well within the capabilities of Mesolithic coastal groups it should also be recognised that even accidental strandings would provide an important social focus, with the sharing of spoils perhaps being controlled through ritual feasting.

SHELL MIDDENS, CHAMBERED TOMBS AND RAISED BEACHES

Chambered tombs represent one of the most striking features of the Neolithic in Scotland, their monumental construction guaranteeing their survival long after the majority of settlements became totally denuded. In western Scotland several of these tombs appear to have been constructed directly on top of earlier shell middens. The best example of this juxtaposition is to be found on the island of Bute, in the Firth of Clyde, where Bryce's early excavation of the chambered tomb at Glecknabae revealed an uneven deposit of marine shells stratified beneath the tomb (Bryce 1904). Fragments of ox bone were found to be sparsely distributed through the shell deposit and may suggest a Neolithic provenance for at least some some of the activity evidenced by the midden, though it is possible that they represent wild ox.[3] The more recent discovery of a flint blade core eroding from a rabbit burrow in the tomb mound may provide very limited evidence for a Mesolithic element (Cormack 1986: 26).

Rabbit activity has also provided evidence for a similar stratigraphic relationship at Cladh Aindreis, in northern Ardnamurchan, where Henshall reported marine shells eroding from rabbit scrapes in the cairn (1972: 315). Scott has also compared a deposit of marine shells found beneath the floor of the chamber of the tomb at Crarae, on the shores of Loch Fyne, Argyll, to a shell midden stratified beneath a nearby Bronze Age cairn known as the Fairy Knowe. Although the smaller deposit within the chambered tomb appears to have been placed there as part of a ritual, rather than representing the build-up of a shell midden (Scott 1961: 16), it is possible that it carried with it a series of metaphors similar to those identified with shell middens.

It has been suggested by Renfrew (1973, 1976) that chambered tombs may have served a function as territorial markers, while Chapman has made a more explicit correlation between these monuments and important resources, which may have included agricultural land (1981). In western Scotland a number of chambered tombs are situated on or near raised beaches, many of which represent the best agricultural land in this part of the world; the interior being dominated by steep hills or mountains. It has been estimated that some 20 000 hectares of new land were created through the formation of raised beach terraces following the recession of the main postglacial maximum sea level (Price 1983: 182). The correlation between raised beaches and chambered tombs may add further credence to the idea that the tombs represent territorial markers, legitimising access to a valuable new resource; that being agricultural land.

It should not be forgotten that raised beaches represent land which had once been sea, and this in itself have imbued these areas with a special meaning. The period of time taken for sea levels to receed to their present levels and correspondingly for raised beaches to be formed is difficult to assess, with the effects of warping and bending in the earth's crust causing variation in land recovery from one area to another. However, it is thought that sea levels in the Oban area were falling around 4 500 BC (Gray 1972), while the present washing limit at Lealt Bay on Jura was reached some time between 3 200 BC and 2 800 BC (Mercer 1971). Sissons has suggested that land recovery following the postglacial maximum may have been in the region of six feet per century (1962), while Mercer has suggested a rather slower rate of recovery of around one foot per 25–35 years in northern Jura (1971).

Though in human terms the rate of recovery was very slow, and is a phenomenon usually regarded to have taken place outside human experience, the relative flatness of these areas would mean that a drop of even a few feet would be enough to reveal entire terraces. This may have taken place over a period as brief as several human generations. Though not observable by individuals it is not unreasonable to suggest that people were aware of this dramatic change, possibly through stories being passed down from one generation to the next, perhaps in the form of creation myths, with the giving up of new lands by the sea or the turning of the tide on a grand scale marking an important change in the way that people lived their lives. Now those who had previously lived exclusively through recourse to gathering, hunting and fishing had the opportunity to add the growing of crops to their subsistence reportoire.

Some shell middens may have served a similar, and perhaps earlier, function to that suggested above for chambered tombs, some of them representing equally striking components of the cultural landscape.[4] Here, the presence of the ancestors, in the form of human remains, may have served to secure a group's access to the sea and the littoral, both of which represented an important resource base. However, Hughes has pointed out that the territorial model is oversimplistic and has pointed to the influence of past practices (Mesolithic), which included hunting and gathering, on the placement of later (Neolithic) monuments (1988: 51). Similarly, it can be suggested that the placement of chambered tombs over shell middens, which after all denies the continued use of the shell midden in marine exploitation practice, may have been equally motivated by the function of the shell midden as a mediator between two worlds, be they land and sea or life and death. A similar motive may therefore lie behind the presence of human remains in shell middens themselves, with the Iron Age bones in the MacArthur Cave (Saville and Hallen 1993) and the possible cist insertion into the top of the Carding Mill Bay midden (Connock et al. 1992) being of special note.

THE ENGENDERING SHORE

From the foregoing it can be suggested that the marine environment played a vital role in constructing cosmologies and influencing the way people made sense of the world around them and their role within it. This becomes even more apparent if we consider Classen's claim that despite the acknowledgement of the woman's consistant role in shellfishing within anthropological works, it is a role largely overlooked in the archaeological literature (1991). However, to limit women to this role is to perpetuate stereotypical images of the female as gatherer and it may be more appropriate to envisage an active role in many aspects of the marine based economy, which would include the manufacture and maintenence of procurement equipment, preparation of bait, control of fish traps, processing and butchery etc. One important consequence of the presence of women on the foreshore and littoral is their accompaniment by young children. Though Suaer's paper on the role of the seashore as 'the primitive home of man' (1962) has been rightly criticised for its extreme stance (Palsson 1991), there may be something to his statement that 'The sea, in particular the tidal shore, presented the best opportunity to eat, settle, increase and *learn*' (1962: 309 – my emphasis). The possibility that children in coastal communities spent much time during their formative years on or near the shore, would certainly suggest that its influence in moulding their world views and its function as an environment within which knowledge was gained would have been an important one.

If shell middens represent the places of mediation between land and sea then those people utilising shell middens may well have been recognised as the active agents of that mediation, being responsible for many of the transformational shifts identified with the shell midden. Woman and perhaps children may have been strongly identified with this role and here it is appropriate to at least draw attention to the role of the moon in ordering activity on the beach and the cycle of menstruation which in some cases may exactly mirror the lunar cycle.[5] However, gender is defined on more subtle criterea than biological sex and it is suggested here that anyone, regardless of sex, spending periods of time on the beach carrying out activities related to the shell middens may have been equally engendered by this environment.

It is not implausible that the identification of women and children, among others, with shell middens and the acts of transformation related to marine exploitation carried out within the liminal littoral may have led to their playing a central role in the treatment of the dead, which in some cases at least appears to be linked directly with shell middens. Although much of this discussion has been concerned with chambered tombs located over shell middens it is noteworthy that, as at Crarae, the inclusion of marine shells within a number of chambered tombs, generally regarded as offerings for the dead (e.g. Corcoran 1966; Henshall 1962: 36, 1963: 96), provides a further link between death, the shore and those identified with both (Pollard 1994).

Sassaman has suggested that the increasing economic importance of shellfish collection in Woodland period southeast America brought about a marked transformation of the social position of women, enabling 'greater decision-making power among women with regard to settlement choices, production schedules, marriage, and conflict resolution' (1992: 73). He also envisages 'that women increasingly occupied central roles in ceremonial activities at coastal shell rings and other locations of social aggregation' (ibid. 73). The present paper has also placed women within a central role in ritual activity, but rather than explaining this through their control of a specific resource, albeit one procured from the littoral zone, has instead stressed the importance of a wider cosmological system, which constantly drew upon metaphors centred upon the littoral zone and the daily activities taking place there.

CONCLUSION

This chapter has sought to demonstrate that the coastal environment represented much more to prehistoric peoples than a rich a source of food. Without reverting to environmentally deterministic arguments it has been proposed that the marine environment and the activities related to its exploitation played an important role in structuring social practice, which included the rituals related to the disposal of the dead. The foregoing discussion has demonstrated some of the ways in which our understanding of these residues of past activity can be broadened by standing a little way back from the detailed work which has so far characterised shell midden studies; though of course, detailed analyses will always have a valuable contribution to make. Hopefully, the approach adopted here has demonstrated some of the ways in which shell middens are special and in doing so has succeeded where Bell felt Stein's book to have failed (Bell 1994: 143).

NOTES

1. Fish traps can still be seen on the northwest coast, usually appearing as low cresentic barriers of piled stones. They are normally located in the upper reaches of lochs or inlets which demonstrate a wide tidal range. It is likely that the majority of those still visible today post-date the Medieval period, with many of them being used at least as late as the mid-nineteenth century. Prehistoric examples, some of which may have been constructed from timber, have yet to be identified in Scotland but may well survive submerged beneath marine silts, possibly in locations removed from the contemporary shoreline.

2. A number of species of fish move closer to the sea's surface at night and there is plentiful evidence from more recent times for their capture outside the hours of daylight.

3. The author has elsewhere suggested that cattle bones, which may have symbolised a relatively new lifestyle, i.e. pastoral agriculture, may have been purposefully integrated within shell middens, some of which, like those in the Firth of Forth, may have had a much longer tradition of use, as a means of negotiating the transformation between the old and the new (Pollard 1994).

4. Heaps of marine shells, such as scallops, can sometimes be seen in the corner of modern farm fields, where they await ploughing into the soil as fertiliser (Pollard 1994). These deposits reflect sunlight and provide some idea of the visual effect of bleached shells within the landscape – the visibility of prehistoric middens may have been enhanced by the smoke from fires lit upon them.

5. The present author is not the first to make a connection between the tides, the moon and menstruation. In *The Old Man and the Sea*, Hemingway wrote 'the old man always thought of her [the sea] as feminine and as something that gave or withheld great favours, and if she did wild or wicked things it was because she could not help them. The moon affects her as it does a woman, he thought' (1952: 23).

ACKNOWLEDGEMENTS

I would like to thank Olivia Lelong for her constant encouragement and assistance in the writing of this paper and the Ph.D. thesis upon which it is based.

REFERENCES

Ashmore, P. J. 1993. *Archaeology and the Coastal Erosion Zone: Towards a Historic Scotland Policy.* Edinburgh: Historic Scotland.

Bell, M. Review of deciphering a shell midden (ed. Stein, J. K.). *Journal of Archaeological Science* 21, 143–4.

Chapman, R. W. 1981. The emergence of formal disposal areas and the 'problem' of megalithic tombs in prehistoric Europe. In Chapman, R. W., Kinnes, I. A. and Randsorg, K. (eds), *The Archaeology of Death.* Cambridge: Cambridge University Press.

Claasen, C. P. 1991. Gender, shellfishing, and the shell mound archaic. In Gero, J. M. and Conkey, M. W. (eds) *Engendering Archaeology.* Blackwell. 162–3.

Connock, K. D., Finlayson, B. and Mills, A. C. M. 1992. The excavation of a shell midden site at Carding Mill Bay, near Oban, Scotland. *Glasgow Archaeological Journal* 17, 25–39.

Corcoran, J. 1966. Excavation of 3 chambered tombs at Loch Calder, Caithness. *Proceedings of the Society of Antiquaries of Scotland* 98, 1–76.

Fenton, A. 1978. *The Northern Isles: Orkney and Shetland.* Edinburgh: John Donald.

Grigson, C. and Mellars, P. 1987. The mammalian remains from the middens. In Mellars, P., *Excavations on Oronsay.* Edinburgh.

Hamill, P. 1986. 'Shell'. From the album *Skin.* Virgin Records.

Hemingway, E. 1952. *The Old Man and the Sea.* London: Arrow Books (1993).

Henshall, A. 1963. *The Chambered Tombs of Scotland*, vol. 1. Edinburgh: Edinburgh University Press.

Henshall, A. 1972. *The Chambered Tombs of Scotland*, vol. 2. Edinburgh: Edinburgh University Press.

Hughes, I. 1988. Megaliths: space, time and the landscape – a view from the Clyde. *Scottish Archaeological Review* 5, 41–56.

Hungtington, R. and Metcalf, P. 1979. *Celebrations of Death.* Cambridge: Cambridge University Press.

Lacaille, A. D. 1954. *The Stone Age in Scotland.* Oxford: Oxford University Press.

Laing, S. and Huxley, T. H. 1866. *Prehistoric remains in Caithness.* London: Williams & Norgate.

Lorimer, D. 1992. The burials. In Connock, K. D. et al. *Glasgow Archaeological Journal* 17, 28–9.

Mellars, P. 1987. *Excavations on Oronsay.* Edinburgh: Edinburgh University Press.

Mercer, J. 1971. A regression-time stone workers camp, 33 ft OD Lussa River, Isle of Jura. *Proceedings of the Society of Antiquaries of Scotland* 103, 1–32.

Mieklejohn, C. and Denston, C. B. 1987. The human skeletal material: inventory and initial interpretation. In Mellars, P., *Excavations on Oronsay.* Edinburgh: Edinburgh University Press, 290–301.

Movius, H. L. 1940. An early postglacial archaeological site at Cushendun, County Antrim. *Proceedings of the Royal Irish Academy* 46, 1–84.

Munro, R. 1884. Danish Kjokkenmoddings, their facts and inferences. *Proceedings of the Society of Antiquaries of Scotland* 18, 216–66.

Palsson, G. 1991. *Coastal Economies, Cultural Accounts: Human Ecology and Icelandic Discourse.* Manchester University Press.

Pollard, A(T). 1990. Down through the ages: a reconsideration of the Oban cave sites. *Scottish Archaeological Review* 7, 57–84.

Pollard, A(T). 1994. *A Study of Marine Exploitation in Prehistoric Scotland, with Special Reference to Marine Shells and Their Archaeolgical Contexts.* Ph.D. thesis, University of Glasgow.

Price, R. J. 1983. *Scotland's Environment During the Last 30 000 Years.* Edinburgh: Scottish Academic Press.

Sassaman, K. E. 1992. Gender and technology in the Archaic–Woodland transition. In Claasen, C. (ed.), *Exploring Gender through Archaeology.* Madison, Wisc.: Prehistory Press.

Saville, A. and Hallen, Y. 1995. The 'Obanian Iron Age': human remains from the Oban cave sites, Argyll, Scotland. *Antiquity* 68, 715–23.

Sissons, J. B. 1962. A re-interpretation of the literature of lateglacial shorelines in Scotland with particular reference to the Forth area. *Transactions of the Edinburgh Geological Society* 19, 83–99.

Sloan, D. 1982. Nether Kinneil. *Current Archaeology* 84, 13–16.

Sloan, D. 1984. Shell middens and chronology in Scotland. *Scottish Archaeological Review* 3, 73–9.

Thomson, D. 1965. *The People of the Sea: A Journey in Search of the Seal Legend.* New York:

Wickham-Jones, C. R. 1992. *Excavations at Scotscraig Burn, Tayport, Fife, September 1992.* Preliminary report. Fife Regional Council.

Part 4
Material Culture

13

LACAILLE, MICROLITHS
AND THE MESOLITHIC
OF ORKNEY

ALAN SAVILLE

INTRODUCTION

A. D. Lacaille, in common with other prehistorians of his generation, found it hard to rationalise the contradictions created by apparent indications of Meso-lithic activity in northern Scotland. His interest and expertise in Mesolithic tech-nology and typology drew him percipiently to study certain microlithic and related forms of flint artefacts from Orkney in the national collections and else-where, but he could not quite come to terms with their implications, about which he remained hesitant and ambiguous. Thus in his first publication on the sub-ject, he concluded that: 'Reason to assign these implements to a pre-Neolithic culture seemed to be wanting despite recognition of shapes found in certain Mesolithic industries' (Lacaille 1935a: 259).

Essentially this remained his view, and in his *magnum opus* of 1954, Orkney flints were firmly restricted to the chapter on 'Post-Mesolithic Developments' and given short shrift, being dismissed as 'reminiscent of decadent Upper Palaeo-lithic workmanship' (1954: 270). To judge from the minimal treatment in 1954, Lacaille had actually paid little attention to Orkney material in the intervening period. The Orkney flints illustrated in the 1954 book are mostly those from his 1935 article, though in some cases redrawn (see below).

Microburin technique, the significance of which had attracted Lacaille early on (1935b), is said to have been absent in Orkney (Lacaille 1942: 108, 1954: 270). Since he does not refer to it in his book, Lacaille seems to have overlooked his own contribution to Rendall's 1937 article on the surface finds from South Ettit, mainland Orkney, where he was quoted as describing one artefact as follows, the implication being that it was manufactured by microburin technique:

> ... a true microlith in that it is fashioned in [sic] a truncated flake, the batter-trimming being characteristic but not delicate. In view, however, of the position of our studies of the Mesolithic, I am disinclined to use the term Tardenoisian. Microliths, as you know, appear in many industries, even very late ones. (Rendall 1937: 48)

This view, that microliths may in some sense be culturally but not chrono-
logically Mesolithic, occurring in Neolithic and even Bronze Age contexts and
thereby demonstrating 'archaising', 'decadent', or 'backwater' tendencies, was
a very persuasive one at the time. In the 1930s Lacaille was in step on this with
Gordon Childe (1935: 20) and it was the dominant explanation followed by most
archaeologists into the 1960s. For example, Livens (1956), in his discussion
of two 'tanged points' from Orkney (one of which, his Fig. 1: 2 from Brodgar,
Stenness, appears to be a straightforward microlith), concluded that:

> ... the points which have been discussed here all seem to demonstrate the
> survival of a lingering, degenerate, Upper Palaeolithic tradition of flint-
> working in the remoter areas of Scotland, long after such a tradition had
> been supplanted or absorbed elsewhere in the British Isles. (Livens 1956:
> 443)

The credibility of such notions was of course bolstered by the prevailing short
chronology in use in the pre-radiocarbon era. As with Piggott's 'Secondary Neolithic' of Mesolithic ancestry (1954: 277), these concepts were far more plausible
while it was generally accepted that the whole of the Neolithic period lasted only
500 years.

It is curious, however, that this model has continued to be a very persistent
one in writings on Scottish prehistory in the radiocarbon era, when not only has
the true length of the Neolithic period been realised, but also the antiquity of
Mesolithic settlement in other parts of Scotland has become apparent. For
example: 'This material [Lacaille's Orkney flints] is insufficient as evidence of
a truly mesolithic phase of activity and is best seen ... as an archaic survival in
a post-mesolithic context' (Ritchie 1985: 36–7).

Even in her most recent general publication on Orkney prehistory, Ritchie
remains sceptical about the presence of Mesolithic hunter-gatherers, and, with
specific reference to the Knap of Howar, reiterates the view that: '... flintwork
that looks Mesolithic can turn up on Neolithic sites ... where it is more likely
to indicate the survival of old-fashioned ideas in toolkits than pre-Neolithic
activity' (Ritchie 1995: 20). Thus, at least in the prevailing popular view of Scottish prehistory, Lacaille's model is alive and well.

Woodman, in his recent overview of the Mesolithic in Scotland (1989) was
admittedly much more circumspect, taking the view that the absence of Mesolithic occupation in Orkney was 'anomalous and ... unbelievable' (1989: 20), but
he nevertheless categorised Lacaille's 1935 artefacts as 'rather odd' and took the
hard line that 'only coherent assemblages containing a range of artefacts should
be accepted as a clear indication of a Mesolithic presence' (1989: 25–7).

Among specialists, the caution exhibited by Woodman has been typical, though
more recently Wickham-Jones has stated quite firmly that Mesolithic hunters
did, on the basis of lithic artefactual evidence, inhabit Orkney (1994: 74). However, her statement was published in a popular survey without any supporting

evidence, so the academic jury has been unable to evaluate this and deliver a verdict.

The purpose of this note is critically to review the evidence published by Lacaille, to present what other information is available from the national collections, and thereby to reach a reassessment of the current position on Mesolithic Orkney.

LACAILLE'S FLINTS

In Fig. 1 of his 1935(a) article, Lacaille illustrated ten Orkney flint implements 'with battered back'. Six of these (Fig. 1: 1, 4, 5, 8, 9 & 10) were said to be from the private collection of Thomas Omand, of Stenness (see Appendix II below), and the remaining four (Fig. 1: 2, 3, 6 & 7) were from the national collection. Exactly the same illustration was reproduced to accompany Lacaille's Glasgow article of 1937 (Fig. 4). In the 1954 book, fourteen Orkney implements were illustrated in Fig. 119. These included the previous ten pieces from 1935, though differently numbered (see Appendix I below).

The four items in the national collection (formerly the National Museum of Antiquities, now the National Museums of Scotland - abbreviated hereafter to NMS) were reproduced in 1954 exactly as in 1935, but the Omand flints were all redrawn, in some cases so that the character of the piece is strikingly different (compare especially Fig. 1: 5 with Fig. 119: 10, or Fig. 1: 10 with Fig. 119: 4), while the cross-sections all changed alarmingly from 1935 to 1954. Two of the other 1954 pieces, supposedly gravers (Fig. 199: 12 & 14), were previously illustrated by crude line-drawings and photographs in Rendell (1937: Figs. I & II on page 50 and in the lower photograph facing page 54), and also by Lacaille in 1938 (Fig. 2: 2 & 4).

Lacaille in 1954 gave no details of provenance within Orkney for the flints in his Fig. 119, and I have not yet been able to trace the origin of two of the pieces, nos. 2 and 13; the former described as an edge-retouched flake, the latter as a graver.

The four pieces Lacaille published from the NMS collections have all been redrawn for the present note (Fig. 13.1). To facilitate comparison they are described individually. (The dimensions, weight, provenance, and acquisition details of all the illustrated pieces are listed in Appendix II. The NMS artefacts are referred to throughout by their registration numbers.)

AB 1293 (Lacaille 1954: Fig. 119: 7). Edge-blunted (LHS) microlith with some inverse trimming.

AB 1294 (Lacaille 1954: Fig. 119: 5) . Edge-blunted (RHS) microlith with some LHS trimming. Rolled condition.

AB 1297 (Lacaille 1954: Fig. 119: 8). Edge-blunted (RHS) microlith, with some thinning removals across the dorsal surface and inverse bilateral trimming at the tip. The retouched areas are slightly less densely corticated

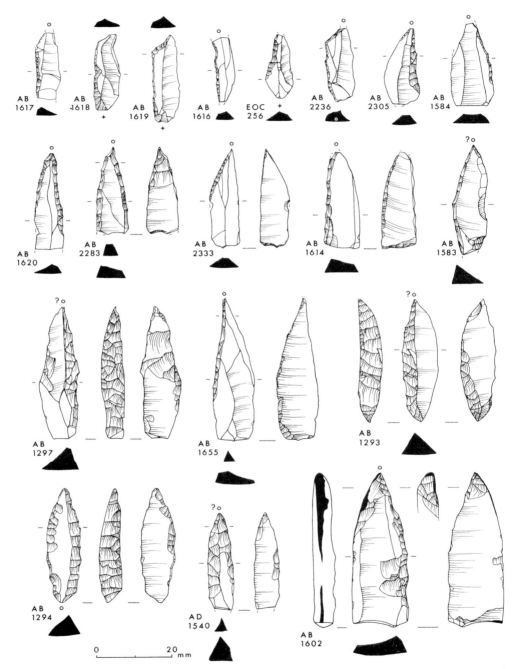

Fig. 13.1. Flint microliths and related forms from Orkney in the National Museums of Scotland (see Appendix II for details). Scale 1:1. Drawn by Marion O'Neil.

than the flake surfaces of the blank, indicating reuse of a previously manufactured flake.

These three microliths are all atypically thick forms, with some retouch on
the blunted edge struck from the dorsal ridge as well as from the bulbar
surface.

> AB 1602 (Lacaille 1954: Fig. 119: 1). Edge-blunted (RHS) implement with
> some retouch at upper LHS and inversely at tip. As with AB 1297, the re-
> touched areas are less densely corticated than the flake surfaces of the blank.
> Apart from its large size, this piece is exceptional in that it is worn smooth
> on much of the LHS edge, especially at the tip, and slightly at the base and
> on other areas at the tip.

It is extremely interesting that Lacaille should have selected these particular
pieces for illustration. All are somewhat atypical as microliths or are otherwise
anomalous, as in the case of AB 1602. The latter piece seems to exemplify Lacaille's
model, in that it shows a combination of 'polish' (= Neolithic) and blunted back
(= Mesolithic). However, his description of this piece (1935a: 256) makes no
mention of the edge-smoothing (despite previous recognition of this by Callander
1931: 84), and he mistakenly says the blunting of the edge is only partial. He
further undermines his own case by describing it as approaching a form well
known in the Neolithic and Bronze Age (though it is not clear what he meant
by this). AB 1297 is described as being much thinner than both AB 1293 and 1294,
which is not actually the case.

What is to be made of these pieces? AB 1602 is the kind of complex, idiosyncratic form which challenges classification. A large flake blank, probably a blade,
has been reused after breakage to make the present tool. The main retouch, down
the RHS, is extensive and of classic blunting character, all of it struck from the
bulbar surface. The edge-smoothing post-dates the retouch wherever the two
impinge. 'Polish' caused by wear in use, as must be the case here, is a relatively
common Mesolithic phenomenon (Saville 1977), but not on an implement
formed by such extensive retouch and presumably designed to have a piercing
or cutting function. One would have to conclude that this implement is so far
from resembling any recurrent type that, regretfully, it is not helpful to the
present discussion.

The other three implements are acceptable as microliths of a rather special
type, which there is some justification in regarding, as did Lacaille, as a local
Orkney variant. AB 1583 and AD 1540 are two other examples of the same type
illustrated here; there is at least one more in the NMS (AB 2282: Midhowe, Rousay);
and there are other related forms (e.g. AB 1296: Stennis [Stenness]; AB 2332: Ring
of Brodgar, Stenness), which are short pointed forms with blunted backs, but
which have other attributes that disqualify them as microliths. The true
cultural/chronological status of these forms is unclear but, despite Lacaille's

comments about association with later forms in surface collections (1937: 65), an important point is that they do not appear to occur among assemblages from excavated Neolithic/Bronze Age sites. In the context of this article one hesitates to mention that there may perhaps be some value in exploring typological relationships with another 'Orkney special', the narrow, but thick and dorsally-ridged, lenticular leaf-shaped arrowhead, to which attention was drawn by Callander (1930: 220, 1931: 79) and for which a good context is also required.

Of the pieces in private collections illustrated by Lacaille, one (1954: Fig. 119: 6) is clearly of the same type as the variant identified above, and this might also be true for Fig. 119: 10 & 11, which certainly appear to have ridge-flaking on their blunted edges. Ignoring Fig. 119: 2, which seems to be an edge-trimmed blade with no microlithic features, and Fig. 119: 12–14, the supposed gravers, this leaves Fig. 119: 3, 4, & 9. At least in the 1954 versions of the drawings, these all seem acceptable as standard edge-blunted microliths (though 9 is atypical in being fashioned on a bladelet which retains its bulb and platform, and 3 is apparently exceptionally thick in cross-section).

In 1935 Lacaille came close to describing two of his pieces (1954: Fig. 119: 9 & 10) as microliths (1935a: 257–8), but on balance he preferred a designation as knives for the group as a whole. The 1937 article does not describe any of the illustrated flints, but refers generally to Orcadian microliths [sic] falling into two classes, on the one hand knives, and on the other hand a '… second category, till now represented by a few specimens only, [which] resembles the microliths from sites south of the Pentland Firth' (1937: 65). These Lacaille appeared to be accepting as true microliths in 1937, because he went on to say that: 'Isolated artefacts of different forms and geometric shapes, which have turned up in some Orkney parishes, seem to be components which served to barb harpoon points' (1937: 65).

In 1954 only Fig. 119: 1 is described as a knife; Fig. 119: 3–5 are described as armatures (presumably meaning microliths, though 5 is equally as thick as 7); while Fig. 119: 6–11 are simply described as abruptly blunted flakes and blades. The distribution map from 1937, showing the findspots of 'isolated microliths' around Stenness and on Rousay, has no equivalent in the 1954 book.

All this is very inconsistent and confusing. It may be surmised from his sketchy illustration and description of the NMS pieces that Lacaille studied them very briefly before the 1935 and 1937 articles and did not re-examine them prior to the 1954 book. The redrawing of the flints from the private collection between their illustration in the articles and in the book may indicate that Lacaille had retained those pieces, or they may have been drawn again from original sketches. The most intriguing question, however, is why Lacaille selected the particular implements he did, when there were more typical microliths from Orkney of which he was obviously well aware, including examples already in the national collection before 1935?

OTHER ORKNEY MICROLITHS IN THE NMS COLLECTION

The NMS has relatively few flint artefacts from Orkney obtained from surface collection, and these are all early finds (Callander 1931: 78, and see Appendix II). The collections are obviously multi-period in terms of their diagnostic forms, and are clearly selective, with retouched implements such as arrowheads and scrapers featuring prominently. The present note publishes almost all the microliths and related forms from among these surface finds (Fig. 13.1) .

The microliths comprise some examples of classic British later Mesolithic types (cf. Saville 1981). For example: the elegant obliquely blunted points with inverse basal retouch (AB 1655, AB 2333); the simple obliquely blunted point (AB 1584); edge-blunted forms (AB 2283, AB 2305); and scalene triangles (AB 1619, AB 2236). Other fragmentary microliths (AB 1616, AB 1617, AB 1620) or idiosyncratic forms (AB 1618; EOC 256) can readily be paralleled from within many large Mesolithic assemblages elsewhere in Britain. AB 1583 and AD 1540 are of the thick, edge-blunted type with some ridge flaking, as mentioned in the previous section. All these implements have single-phase cortication, leaving as the exception AB 1614. This piece, which is edge blunted (LHS) with inverse blunting across the straight base and inverse trimming on the RHS, is anomalous because all the retouch is uncorticated through a densely corticated surface, indicating reuse of a suitable blank of considerably earlier date.

Many other flaked lithic finds in the NMS derive from the numerous excavations of Orkney chambered tombs and from settlement sites of Neolithic and later date. Only one specific microlithic form has been noted from such contexts (EOC 256), the artefact from the Knap of Howar previously published by Henshall (in Ritchie 1983: 86). This is a small obliquely blunted (LHS) point, formed on a bladelet which retains its bulb and platform. The pinkish raw material is problematic; it was originally identified as a quartzite but has a very fine conchoidal fracture, as evidenced by the dorsal negative flake scars. As an isolated find on unusual raw material, this piece is hard to evaluate.

The fairly large flint assemblage from the Knowe of Yarso does not include any microliths, and previously suggested artefacts of 'Mesolithic type' (Henshall 1963: 217, Davidson and Henshall 1989: 139) cannot be accorded much significance because they are not diagnostic forms; the same is true in the case of the Quanterness assemblage (Henshall 1979: 81). Occasional pieces which may appear to exhibit some potentially Mesolithic features, for example a steeply bilaterally retouched flint flake amongst the large flint assemblage from Rinyo (Childe and Grant 1948: Fig. 8: 17), when examined prove to be of convincing Neolithic character.

Work currently in progress on the Barnhouse, Links of Noltland, and Skara Brae lithic collections will provide a much-needed clarification of the presence or absence of residual earlier implements within the Orkney later Neolithic assemblages, and will create a yardstick for use in the analysis of surface collections.

DISCUSSION

In the author's opinion, the publication here of several examples of absolutely classic microlith types, to which can be added the few previously published by Lacaille (1954: Fig. 119: 4), Livens (1956: Fig. 1: 2), and Rendall (1937: 47), leaves no doubt of the existence of a fully Mesolithic presence on Orkney. There is simply no evidence from anywhere else in prehistoric Britain of microliths like AB 1584, AB 1655, AB 2236, AB 2305, or AB 2333, occurring as manufactured items in a post-Mesolithic context. Such a type-fossil approach may appear anachronistic, but its essential veracity cannot be gainsaid. It is true that ideally, as Woodman (1985: 27) has emphasised, coherent assemblages are required to document Mesolithic settlement. Such assemblages, however, will only become available from Orkney as a result of the excavation or repeated fieldwalking of actual Mesolithic sites, and these have yet to be identified. This is a *Catch 22* situation, therefore, and in the meantime it would be wrong to ignore the evidence provided by the implements already available for study.

Almost all of the microliths described in this note are old finds, which cannot now be attributed to specific findspots. Indeed, in most cases the provenance is only to parish level. On the other hand, there is no reason to doubt their genuineness as Orkney finds or to suspect any modern importation of antiquities by the collectors involved. Taken at face value they indicate Mesolithic occupation on Rousay as well as the western Mainland. The implement from Papa Westray, though not in itself conclusive, hints that Mesolithic presence on the outer islands should also be considered.

Is there any reason at all why Orkney should not have been inhabited before the Neolithic period? The antiquity of Mesolithic settlement on the islands off the west coast of Scotland is well established. Indeed, the earliest radiocarbon date for Mesolithic occupation in Scotland comes from the island of Rum (Wickham-Jones 1990: the calibrated radiocarbon determinations indicate settlement from the 8th millennium BC). Apart from Rum, there is Mesolithic settlement on Arran, Colonsay/Oronsay, Islay, Jura, and Skye, and other islands, though the Outer Hebrides, like Shetland, have signally failed to produce any convincing Mesolithic finds. (The position of the Fair Isle core-tool (Cumming 1946), which is certainly of Mesolithic type, remains enigmatic: for further discussion see Saville, 1994.)

Thus Mesolithic sea passage off the Scottish coast is well established and the crossing to Orkney need have presented no huge problems. The resources necessary for human existence were there on Orkney in abundance - in terms of natural food supplies probably more so than in later prehistoric times - while obtaining the raw material for lithic technology was also not a problem, even if its precise origin and availability are unresolved (Brown 1992). Admittedly, little is known about Mesolithic presence in adjacent Caithness and Sutherland, but the NMS collection includes three microliths from Freswick (AB 2284–5: see *PSAS* 69 (1934–35) 438; and HD 553: see *PSAS* 70 (1935–36) 358; cf. Lacaille 1937: 63);

microliths and microburins are recorded from Camster Long (Davidson and Henshall 1991: 101); and a major site has been reported from Bettyhill (Wickham-Jones 1994: 65).

This note has been restricted to microliths for the obvious reason that these (and microburins) are the most diagnostic and conclusive indicators of Mesolithic presence, and because the collections available in the NMS are biased in favour of readily recognisable retouched implements. Examination of existing lithic collections in Orkney will inevitably reveal further examples of microliths and probably other Mesolithic artefact types, while the encouraging trend towards fieldwalking in Orkney will provide the basis for identifying Mesolithic sites with the potential to produce the full range of lithic tools and by-products. Within the next few years it should be possible to gain a much clearer picture of the Mesolithic evidence from Orkney and finally to escape from the currency of Lacaille's 1930s-based views. Whatever the territorial imperatives were that made Mesolithic peoples so colonially adventurous, there now seems no reason to doubt that Orkney was a part of their empire.

APPENDIX I

Concordance between illustrated flints in Lacaille 1935a: Fig. 1(= Lacaille 1937: Fig. 4); Lacaille 1954: Fig. 119; and this note.

1935a: Fig. 1	1954: Fig. 119	Present note
1	6	—
2	7	AB 1293
3	5	AB 1294
4	9	—
5	10	—
6	8	AB 1297
7	1	AB 1602
8	11	—
9	3	—
10	4	—

APPENDIX II

Catalogue of flints illustrated in this note.

NMS no.	Length	Breadth	Thickness	Weight	Provenance
		(dimensions in mm)		(in grams)	
AB 1293	34.2	9.4	5.8	1.7	Stennis
AB 1294	31.0	9.3	5.7	1.7	Stennis (illustrated by Callander 1930: Fig. 4: 4, described as a leaf-shaped arrowhead)
AB 1297	36.3	10.8	6.0	2.0	Stennis
AB 1583	29.8	9.3	5.3	1.0	Stenness
AB 1584	22.7	11.4	2.5	0.7	Stenness

NMS no.	Length	Breadth	Thickness	Weight	Provenance
		(dimensions in mm)		(in grams)	
AB 1602	41.9	14.9	5.9	4.0	Heddle Hill, Firth
AB 1614	26.5	9.5	3.5	1.0	Bookan, Stenness
AB 1616	17.5	5.3	2.1	0.2	Stenness
AB 1617	17.8	5.9	2.0	0.2	Stenness
AB 1618	20.3	7.0	2.4	0.3	Stenness
AB 1619	23.8	6.9	2.9	0.5	Stenness
AB 1620	26.2	7.4	2.9	0.6	Stenness
AB 1655	38.9	11.4	3.8	1.5	Bockan, Sandwick
AB 2236	19.9	7.2	3.1	0.5	Hullion, Rousay
AB 2283	23.5	8.6	3.5	0.7	Field above Midhowe Broch, Rousay
AB 2305	20.5	9.2	2.7	0.4	News (Newhouses), Hullion, Rousay
AB 2333	26.7	7.8	2.8	0.5	Quinni Moan, Stenness
AD 1540	27.0	7.0	5.9	0.9	Stenness or Stromness or Sandwick (illustrated by Callander 1931: Fig. 2: 3, described as a leaf-shaped arrowhead)
EOC 256	17.1	7.0	3.0	0.3	Knap of Howar, Papa Westray

Provenances are given in the form in which they are recorded in the NMS registers. The majority (10) are simply recorded as from Stenness [or Stennis: alternative spelling] parish on Mainland, though in some cases there may be confusion between Stenness and Stromness (see below). Another two are from more specific locations at Stenness: Bookan and Quinni Moan. Two other Mainland finds are from Hill of Heddle, south of Finstown, and Bockan, Sandwick, respectively, while a final Mainland find is provenanced only to the Sandwick/Stenness/Stromness region. Three are from the island of Rousay, two of them from Hullion on the south coast, one from Midhowe on the west coast. The final piece is from Papa Westray.

The raw material is predominantly flint or very closely related silicious stone, mainly greyish in colour but with three pieces (AB 1293, AB 1294 and AB 1614) on brown flint. The exceptions are EOC 256, already mentioned above, AD 1540 on coarse 'quartzy' flint(?), and AB 1583 on what may actually be quartz. The acquisition information about these finds is as follows:

> AB 1293, AB 1294 and AB 1297 donated by J. Grant in 1909: see PSAS 43 (1908–9) 268–9 (provenance here given as Parish of Stromness, not Stenness).
> AB 1583 and AB 1584 donated by Revd Dr Murison in 1928: see PSAS 63 (1928–9) 16.
> AB 1602 donated by A. Wood, per J. M. Corrie, in 1928: see PSAS 63 (1928–9) 17.
> AB 1614 donated by P. Irving or Irvine, per J. M. Corrie, in 1928: see PSAS 63 (1928–9) 17.
> AB 1616, AB 1617, AB 1618, AB 1619 and AB 1620 donated by T. Oman, per J. M. Corrie, in 1928: see PSAS 63 (1928–9) 19.
> AB 1655 purchased in 1928: see PSAS 63 (1928–9) 21.
> AB 2236 purchased in 1935: see PSAS 69 (1934–5) 323 (gives provenance as: small field at Newhouse, Hullion).
> AB 2283 donated by W. Grant in 1935: see PSAS 69 (1934–5) 438.
> AB 2305 donated by W. Grant in 1935: see PSAS 70 (1935–6) 16–17.
> AB 2333 purchased in 1935: see PSAS 70 (1935–6) 24.
> AD 1540 donated by W. Brough, per J. M. Corrie, in 1928: see PSAS 63 (1928–9) 17.
> EOC 256 part of the 1973–5 excavation assemblage (Ritchie 1983).

NB: The Mr Tom Oman of Stenness, who donated AB 1616–19 in 1928, could well be the same person as Mr Thomas Omand of Mayfield, Stenness, whose flints were lent to Lacaille (1935a: 253) but, as explained above, those pieces figured by Lacaille do not appear to be in the national collection.

ACKNOWLEDGEMENTS

I am most grateful to Marion O'Neil for undertaking the artefact illustrations accompanying this chapter, and to Annette Carruthers and Ann MacSween for reading the text in draft.

REFERENCES

Brown, J. F. 1992. Flint as a resource for Stone Age Orcadians. *Orkney Field Club Bulletin*, 21–8.

Callander, J. G. 1930. Pointes de flèches et petits outils de pierre en roches autres que le silex, en Ecosse. *Bulletin de la Société Préhistorique Française* 27, 213–20.

Callander, J. G. 1931. Notes on (1) certain prehistoric relics from Orkney, and (2) Skara Brae: its culture and its period. *Proceedings of the Society of Antiquaries of Scotland* 65, 78–114.

Childe, V. G. 1935. *The Prehistory of Scotland*. London: Kegan Paul, Trench, Trubner & Co.

Childe, V. G. and Grant, W. G. 1948. A stone age settlement at the Braes of Rinyo, Rousay, Orkney (second report). *Proceedings of the Society of Antiquaries of Scotland* 81, 16–42.

Cumming, G. A. 1946. Flint core axe found on Fair Isle, Shetland. *Proceedings of the Society of Antiquaries of Scotland* 80, 146–8.

Davidson, J. L. and Henshall, A. S. 1989. *The Chambered Cairns of Orkney*. Edinburgh: Edinburgh University Press.

Davidson, J. L. and Henshall, A. S. 1991. *The Chambered Cairns of Caithness*. Edinburgh: Edinburgh University Press.

Henshall, A. S. 1963. *The Chambered Tombs of Scotland*, vol. 1. Edinburgh: Edinburgh University Press.

Henshall, A. S. 1979. Artefacts from the Quanterness cairn. In Renfrew, C., *Investigations in Orkney*. London: Society of Antiquaries of London (Research Report 38), 75–93.

Lacaille, A. D. 1935a. The small flint knives of Orkney. *Proceedings of the Society of Antiquaries of Scotland* 69, 251–64.

Lacaille, A. D. 1935b. The Tardenoisian micro-burin in Scotland. *Proceedings of the Society of Antiquaries of Scotland* 69, 443–5.

Lacaille, A. D. 1937. The microlithic industries of Scotland. *Transactions of the Glasgow Archaeological Society* 9, 56–74.

Lacaille, A. D. 1938. Scottish gravers of flint and other stones. *Proceedings of the Society of Antiquaries of Scotland* 72, 180–92.

Lacaille, A. D. 1942. Scottish micro-burins. *Proceedings of the Society of Antiquaries of Scotland* 76, 103–19.

Lacaille, A. D. 1954. *The Stone Age in Scotland*. London: Oxford University Press.

Livens, R. G. 1956. Three tanged flint points from Scotland. *Proceedings of the Society of Antiquaries of Scotland* 89, 438–43.

Piggott, S. 1954. *The Neolithic Cultures of the British Isles*. Cambridge: Cambridge University Press.

Rendall, R. 1937. The South Ettit flint industries. *Proceedings of the Orkney Antiquarian Society* 14, 45–56.

Ritchie, A. 1983. Excavation of a Neolithic farmstead at Knap of Howar, Papa Westray, Orkney. *Proceedings of the Society of Antiquaries of Scotland* 113, 40–121.

Ritchie, A. 1985. The first settlers. In Renfrew, C. (ed.), *The Prehistory of Orkney BC 4000–1000 AD*. Edinburgh: Edinburgh University Press, 36–53.

Ritchie, A. 1995. *Prehistoric Orkney*. London: Batsford/Historic Scotland.

Saville, A. 1977. Two Mesolithic implement types. *Northamptonshire Archaeology* 12, 3–8.

Saville, A. 1981. Mesolithic industries in Central England: an exploratory investigation using microlith typology. *Archaeological Journal* 138, 49–71.

Saville, A. 1994. A possible Mesolithic stone axehead from Scotland. *Lithics* 15, 25–8.

Wickham-Jones, C. R. 1990. *Rhum: Mesolithic and Later Sites at Kinloch, Excavations 1984–86*. Edinburgh: Society of Antiquaries of Scotland, Monograph 7.

Wickham-Jones, C. R. 1994. *Scotland's First Settlers*. London: Batsford/Historic Scotland.

Woodman, P. C. 1989. A review of the Scottish Mesolithic: a plea for normality! *Proceedings of the Society of Antiquaries of Scotland* 119, 1–32.

14

THE ROUGH AND THE SMOOTH

AXE POLISHERS OF THE MIDDLE NEOLITHIC

KEVIN J. TAYLOR

How would we classify the material world without the senses? With our eyes we break the world down into classes of colour, shape, brightness and darkness. What we hear can be separated into loud and quiet, harmonious, and cacophonous. Smells and tastes can be bitter or sweet, salty, spicy, strong or mild. And by touch we divide the world into hard and soft, hot and cold, blunt and sharp, rough and smooth.

By combining these sensory perceptions we create both simple and complex categories with which we classify the material world encountered via personal experience. But also, due to the general similarity of anatomy that exists between individuals, we can, through the negotiation of a common understanding of words and the senses to which they connect, convey tangible knowledge beyond our immediate experience.

These forms of classification are so basic and generally universal that they naturally become the means by which individuals negotiate an understanding of abstract concepts beyond the tangible realm. So, for example, if we think of many contemporary concepts we can observe that sensory classification, and specifically the discourse of roughness and smoothness, plays an important role in shaping and maintaining our generalised perceptions of the world. Many of these abstract categorisations negotiate our own position and also the status of others, for example, gender, age and class.

Traditionally men have been regarded to some extent as rough, perhaps even a degenerate form of their smoother female equivalent. In some ways, there may be physically tangible reasons for this, for example, facial hair or the roughening of the hands as a product of some forms of 'traditionally' male labour. Essentially, however, this classification is merely a subjective construct employed to add a tangible depth to an arbitrary division of the sexes.

The classification of people by age also involves attributing particular sensory qualities to distinguishable groups. Think of the expression 'as smooth as a baby's bottom' and then juxtapose this with the label 'old hag' and without much need for elaboration we can see how the discourse of roughness and smoothness enters into our perceptions of age and ageing.

Our understanding of class, even in a classless society, is also shaped by such basic notions. On a general level the working classes are regarded as a rougher form of their smoother, richer, upper class counterparts.

Even concepts of the present and the past are formed and maintained within this discourse. In contemporary western society the future is often dominated by visions of technology. The images with which we are regularly bombarded, leave us in no doubt as to its smoothness and slickness, and by implication the smooth running of the future. Furthermore, these images of our future reflexively determine the nature of the present, and what we expect of technology today. These images are contrasted sharply with those of the past, from cavemen, to nineteenth-century slums, we are often offered images of roughness and degeneracy.

Of course often this perception of our future is inverted in apocalyptic visions of what is to come, but these are often associated with catastrophic events (e.g. nuclear holocaust, etc.) which imply a usurpation of the natural order of the future.

But again, as with gender, all these classifications are essentially subjective and arbitrary.

Although these statements may appear as exaggerated, even questionable generalisations, a crude structuralism betraying the infinite subtlety of differ- ences and distinctions the senses allow, they do offer an indication of how common understandings of the world are actively created and maintained by association with, and analogy to, the senses. We can see also that these simple, sensual distinctions between rough and smooth take on a whole series of con- notations that both reflect and determine their appropriateness in particular contexts. Measures of smoothness are often taken to reflect connotations of order, tranquillity, easiness, optimism, pleasure, femininity, even almost of goodness itself (or perhaps disguised or insincere good, e.g. smoothies and smooth-talkers). Whilst levels of roughness become associated with degrees of degeneracy, disorder, chaos, immorality, anger, and 'bad' things in general.

Similar discourses of the senses were undoubtedly employed in the past in establishing similarities and differences within socially constructed concepts such as time and also between specific intra-social groups, perhaps based on age or gender. But is it possible to link these sensual discourses to specific social groups in the Neolithic?

During the Neolithic we witness the emergence of early agricultural com- munities, possibly practising a mixture of pastoral and agrarian farming, yet still dependent on more traditional methods of food acquisition, i.e. gathering and hunting. These communities may have been relatively sedentary but were prob- ably relatively mobile, insomuch as land, even if minimally exploited, may have become exhausted and fresh areas of land cleared for cultivation and habitation.

It is hardly surprising in these circumstances that the polished stone axe, already in use from the later Mesolithic (Woodman 1978), emerges as a fundamental item of material culture at this time – a tool essential to the clearance of woodland, for the construction of permanent dwellings, and for the collection of firewood – sources of deadwood and driftwood having diminished as mobility declined (Bradley 1978).

In addition, perhaps within the relatively small hunter-gatherer groups of the Mesolithic and earlier Neolithic, relationships between individuals belonging to a group were potentially highly personalised, that is to say, each individual could potentially have been familiar with every other member of the group. Whilst in later, larger, less mobile communities it is possible to envisage an increasing depersonalisation/formalisation of intra-communal relations. Relationships may no longer have been negotiated on a personal level but rather established on a group basis using predefined and accepted discourses such as gender, age, kinship – discourses also witnessed in contemporary societies.

This may be supported by contemporary evidence. Woodburn (1982) has observed that some modern hunter-gatherer groups lack complex funerary rituals, a form of rite of passage during which the status of both the living and the deceased is formally renegotiated (van Gennep 1960). Potentially hunter-gatherer intra-social relations can be personalised and informal enough to dispel the need for a formal statement or renegotiation of an individual's status. In larger communities, like those appearing in the later Neolithic however, changes in relations, and therefore status, must be endorsed and validated formally in rites of passage to ensure a common acceptance of the new position.

Is it possible, that the polishing, the smoothing off, of the rough stone axe in the Neolithic creates, maintains, and actively engenders it to, a specific formalised intra-social group?

A couple of reasons have traditionally been proposed as to why a stone axe may have been polished. One is that the polishing of the axe enhances its use in a functional respect:

> A sharp flaked edge, for example, is very vulnerable to damage during use as the pressures produced are very similar to those applied during manufacture and can cause flaking. A ground edge, however, presents a less vulnerable but still efficient surface ... Axes were often ground all over to reduce wear, not only upon the edge, but also on other areas such as those in contact with the haft (Wickham-Jones 1985: 168).

Alternative, yet complementary, explanations have suggested that the polish may have enhanced the value of the axe in gift exchanges (Olausson 1983), and it is important to remember in this respect that polishing is not merely a particular kind of finish but also a decorative technique occasionally employed in megalithic art (Shee Twohig 1981).

These are of course perfectly valid explanations, however, the evidence indicates that many of the most beautifully polished axes of the early Neolithic such as the jadeite axes may never have been intended to be employed practically

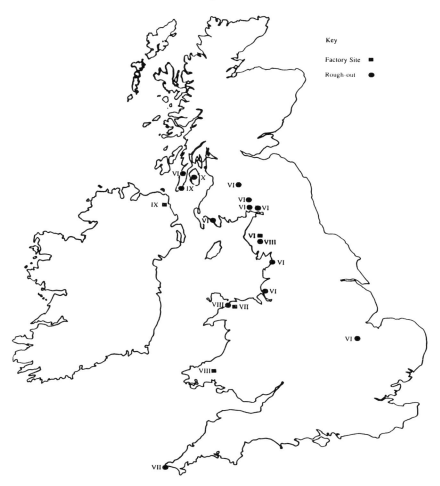

Fig. 14.1. The distribution of axe rough-outs recovered outwith their local contexts in relation to their place of production. It is likely that these represent only a mere fraction of those originally exchanged in this form, the majority having been subsequently polished (information derived from Clough and Cummins 1988).

(Bishop et al. 1977). In addition, in the middle Neolithic it appears that some axes were actually exchanged over considerable distances in rough-out form (see Fig. 14.1) and, as we shall see, it may be the case that these were more highly valued in formalised exchanges than the finished, polished artefact (it is also possible that axes were exchanged merely with unpolished blades, like those noted by Manby (1965), at present however the evidence is unclear).

The evidence from Scotland shows that polishing may have taken two essentially different forms. Fairly large polished areas on both mobile and immobile stone probably indicating the primary reduction of the rough-out to its final polished form, and smaller pebble rubbers and grinders occasionally found in association with axes probably utilised for secondary work, such as more detailed polishing or for the repolishing of minor worn areas.

Only a few of the more substantial polishers probably used in primary reduction of the rough-out, have been noted from Scotland. For example, the polisher of red sandstone found with an axe within it's worn and polished hollow from Stoneykirk, Glenluce, Wigtownshire (Wilson 1881). Williams (1970: 112) records the presence of axe-polishing grooves on the west portal stone of Cairnholy I chambered cairn. In addition a large polisher was recovered from the working gallery at Northmaven, Shetland – the source of Group XXII axes (Scott and Calder 1952).

Although perhaps it is not immediately obvious, these polishers all have one thing in common – death.

The axe polishing grooves from Cairnholy I are clearly directly contextualised within a monument preoccupied with the dead. The polisher from Stoneykirk, Glenluce was recovered along with fragments of bone and a tooth, the author concluding that it was therefore 'connected with an interment' (Wilson 1881). The Shetland polisher was found within a working gallery, which in terms of construction, reflects the architecture of a chambered tomb only 150 yards away (i.e. the dry-stone walling, lintelled roofing, one wall formed by rock-face, access by roof). Curiously, the chambered tomb, in plan, forms the shape of a hafted axe (as also noted of some tombs in Brittany, see Thomas and Tilley 1993). The tomb therefore, in its construction also, seems to be reflexively referencing the presence of the working site.

These few Scottish examples, all three of which may potentially be of a middle to late, rather than early, Neolithic date, seem to reflect patterns evident elsewhere in Wales, England and Ireland in the mid to later Neolithic. For example the polisher recovered from a pit within Henge A at Llandegai had been interred with a cremation (Houlder 1968) dated to 2 790 ± 150 bc from an internal fire trough (Houlder 1976). Also a polisher was recovered from the cairn matrix of Bryn-yr-Hen-Bobl chambered cairn (Hemp 1936) and another from the basal layer of the cairn at Gwernvale, dated to after *c.*3 100 BC but before *c.*2 440–2 640 bc (Britnell and Savory 1984). Piggott (1962) recorded the presence of axe polishing grooves on the sarsen uprights in the forecourt, in the passage, and within the western chamber of the chambered tomb at West Kennet, the skeletal material being dated to *c.*2 800 bc (Piggott and Atkinson 1986). Another was recorded from the flooring of the earlier barrow at Wayland's Smithy (Atkinson 1965) (dated to some time within the 50 years preceding 2 820 ± 130 bc). At least two of the uprights in the Avenue at Avebury show evidence of having been used to polish axes, and several others seem to have had partial or complete inhumations at their bases (Smith 1965). One of the corbels from Newgrange bears similar evidence (O'Kelly 1982, Bradley and Edmonds 1993) – a tomb appearing as a hafted axe in plan.

Even Scottish examples of smaller rubbers/grinders found in direct association with stone axes from Drumour, Glenshee (Neish 1871) and Harelaw Dam,
Forfarshire (Hay 1990), may be making symbolic reference to this context of
death via the use of quartz as the polishing material – a type of stone deliberately
deposited both within, and amongst the cairn matrix of many chambered tombs
in Scotland (Henshall 1963 and 1972).

It seems possible, therefore, that in the mid to later Neolithic, in some areas
at least, contemporary factory products may have been exchanged beyond the
local contexts of their production in roughout form to be polished down within,
or at the very least symbolically referencing and being referenced within,
'ceremonial' contexts generally associated with the dead.[1] This would appear to
be indirectly supported by the evidence from Langdale (the source of Group VI
axes) where, at this time (after 3300 cal BC), the extractive techniques become
more formalised with increased emphasis on the production of more axiform
roughouts (Bradley and Edmonds 1993) presumably more appropriate for exchange into communities unfamiliar with the appropriate lithic expertise. This
general picture appears to be in sharp contrast with the evidence from the earlier
Neolithic where it appears that axes for local use were worked and/or polished
at sites relatively near to their local sources, e.g. Ehenside Tarn near Langdale
(Darbishire 1872), Llandegai (Houlder 1968) and Bryn-yr-Hen-Bobl (Hemp
1936, Piggott 1954, Lynch 1969) near Graig Llywd (the source of Group VII
axes), Carn Brea (Mercer 1981) close to the Cornish sources, and Maiden Castle
(Edmonds and Bellamy 1991) and other causewayed enclosures in the south
associated with flint mining (Bradley and Edmonds 1993).

But what is the relevance of these contexts of death in the middle Neolithic?

The events that surround death often involve a formal renegotiation of the
status of the deceased and of the mourners, i.e. a rite of passage (van Gennep
1960). Not only that, rites of passage involving a change of status of the living,
for example initiation, often make symbolic and sometimes physical reference
to the dead and to dying (Turner 1969). Of course symbolically the polishing of
a rough-out, or merely the presence of a polisher, is particularly appropriate in
both contexts for, like a rite of passage itself, polishing represents an act of
irreversible transformation of status, in the case of the axe a transformation from
rough to smooth.

It is possible therefore that the reduction of rough-outs to their final polished
form may occur during formal rites of passage. But if this is the case, what change
of status is it related to?

In a few of the examples discussed it would appear that the presence of the
polisher rather than the production of the polished axe itself, directly refers to
the change of status from life to death, e.g. Bryn-yr-Hen-Bobl, Llandegai, Glen
Luce, Gwernvale, Wayland's Smithy, and Newgrange – smoothing the bed of
death so to speak. In these examples, the incorporation of the polishers appears
to have made it impossible for them to have continued in use. Of course it is

possible, however, that when they were in use they may have been employed within contexts of death thus perhaps partially determining the context of their final deposition. In addition at least two of the polishers (those at Bryn-yr-Hen-Bobl and Llandegai) post-date early working of local axe-factory products on the same site, and both of these were recovered in close association with axes. The axes associated with these two are, in contrast to earlier material from the sites, not of local factory stone (Houlder 1968, Clough and Cummins 1988). So this also appears to be a dramatic statement of the change in use of these sites from the local production of axes to the import of foreign axes for polishing with an emphasis on mortuary contexts.

In the other examples (i.e. Shetland, Cairnholy, West Kennet, Avebury) however, the polishers may have been intended for reuse,[2] and the final product, the smoothed and polished axe, carried from the site – the emphasis resting on the production of the finished artefact. In these examples it is the presence of the dead that appears to reflect upon the process of polishing, and the trans-formation involved.[3] If this transformation from rough to smooth potentially reflects a change in personal status of the bearer within a rite of passage in these few overt examples from the middle and later Neolithic, what specific change could it reflect?

Perhaps in this respect it may be appropriate to consider who was using the stone axe in the Neolithic.

Amongst the Yir Yoront of the Cape York Peninsula of Australia, Sharp (1952) noted that the stone axe was a tool predominantly employed by women. This is hardly surprising because the axe is a tool that lends itself favourably to a multi-tude of tasks in the domestic arena including the gathering and preparation of foodstuffs, but most importantly, to the collection of firewood, essential for both warmth and cooking – activities traditionally considered as areas of female labour. It is not unreasonable to expect, therefore, that this may have also been the case in many societies in the recent and more distant past (see also Gero 1991).

Of course axes may have also been employed in the traditionally male pastimes of chopping down trees, making weapons, hunting, chopping down more trees, etc. But it is fairly safe to assume that, relative to daily domestic activities, these forms of use were relatively infrequent.

There have been vague rumblings in the past that the axe may have been a potent male fertility symbol, having the appearance of a phallus. But of course, given that the anatomy of humans has not altered dramatically in the last few thousand years this is clearly a fallacy, considering the wide range of available evidence. It could just as easily be argued that many axes in plan symbolise the mons pubis and that the blade in section is representative of the labia. In fact it may be this symbolic ambivalence that was so fundamental to its role.

In addition, the role of the axe in facilitating the provision of food, shelter, and warmth – essentially a provider of the basic elements essential to life itself – whilst also being a potential taker of life in hunting, and possibly warfare, enables it to transcend its practical role to become a potent symbol of death and re-generation, which Bloch and Parry (1982) have argued is, in many societies, directly associated with female fertility.

It is possible therefore that the polished stone axe may have been potentially, not only a predominantly female tool, but also a potent female symbol.

This is interesting because both women and death are in many societies re-garded as both polluted and polluting and, in this respect, dangerous (Douglas 1966). So it seems, on reflection, most appropriate that this female tool should be prepared, in the Neolithic, in the polluting environment of death. But almost paradoxically if a rough-out is thought to have been appropriate both within and referencing this polluted, potentially female context, then its transformation may imply a change from a rough female status to a smooth 'other', a transfiguration of this potent female symbol, perhaps a male appropriation of female power, and by possible implication, a change in status of the bearer from female to male. A change in status acknowledged in many societies during the transformation of the androgynous/female child to the adult male (Meigs 1984).

Indeed if rough-out axes (or axes with unpolished blades) were acquired via bridewealth exchange, as they were by the Tungei of Papua New Guinea (Burton 1987), it seems highly probable that both would have potent female connotations.

In this way the labour of polishing a rough-out axe, or perhaps simply sharp-ening the blade, may not have been recognised as a mere affirmation of what was surely already known, that is, that the axe was a tool that was both a predominately female symbol and tool. Instead the polishing of an axe, in its nullification of its feminine roughness, may have actively engendered it to a specific social group, and this may have been adult men – symbolically enabling it to transcend gend-ered roles.

And if we return to the Yir Yoront we are told by Sharp (1952: 19) that although the axe was employed mainly by women only a male could own an axe. The necessity of *borrowing* an axe, therefore, constantly defined and maintained the relationship of the sexes.

The evidence from the middle Neolithic however need not indicate a formalised regime of practice concerning purely the polishing of rough-outs during initiation but also perhaps a range of practices involving the sharpening of blades or worn areas as part of other forms of 'life-crisis' rites (Turner 1969) such as during periods of ill-health.

Perhaps the secondary polishing of these axes once they had become rough-ened and worn, using, in areas of Scotland at least, pebbles of quartz, may have represented both a re-affirmation of status, and a re-invigoration of the axe and its bearer, by employing an item associated with the dead.

In reconstructing, from our deconstructed past, some kind of generalised frame-work of less functional motivations within which the more subtle manoeuvrings and manipulation of this obsolete material culture were, and perhaps can be, understood, the uniqueness and diversity of the available evidence has inevitably been diminished. There is perhaps some justification for this universalising approach when examining axes, in the middle Neolithic at least, for it is at this time that we first see definite evidence for their exchange beyond local contexts (Bradley and Edmonds 1993, Smith 1979). For these socially embedded exchanges to have happened at all there must have been at least some similarity in practice, at least in terms of the actual mechanisms of exchange, between communities. Furthermore it may have been these very exchanges that, by bringing about cultural contact, may have led also, even if unintentionally, to the exchange of ideas and potentially practices.

In the early Neolithic the polished stone axe seems to operate within a localised context of production, polishing and use (Bradley and Edmonds 1993). This seems to have been associated with infrequent exchanges of finely polished axes beyond local contexts, such as jadeite axes (Bishop et al. 1977), which may have been chosen for exchange specifically because of the beautiful polish they could acquire and perhaps representing some form of extra-social display. In the middle Neolithic, however, the axe seems to become more important in emphasising *within group* status – not necessarily in terms of its *ownership* but by a differentiation in the appropriate participation of individuals in particular practices involving perhaps its acquisition and production but almost certainly in its polishing and use. This general change in role would also seem to be reflected in a change in the nature of production at Langdale at this time for Bradley and Edmonds (1993) note that after *c.* 3 300 cal BC areas of working become physically more inaccessible. In addition it may be at this time also that the working face at Northmaven in Shetland becomes enclosed, the walling appearing to follow the artificial contours produced on the rockface during earlier activity.

It seems obvious that, in the middle Neolithic, the choice, and referencing, of special places for the practice of polishing, and also the referencing of polishing at these special places by the interment of polishers, implies that we cannot simply understand these activities in purely functional terms. These ritualised contexts of polishing also suggest that this polish was not merely produced to enhance the axe's aesthetic image for prestige exchange. Indeed the evidence for the exchange of rough-outs, combined with the discovery of special finds such as the Group VIII rough-out, originating in South Wales, from Langdale, and also the polisher made from a rough-out of Group VIII rock found at Llandegai in the North of Wales, suggests that rough-outs may have been as, if not more, valued as artefacts of exchange. Perhaps this may have been partially due to the difficulties in acquiring them, rather than polished finished axes which may have been relatively abundant through exchange, inheritance, fortuitous recovery, theft, etc.

Finally, if we offer the people of the past the humanity of the people of the present, we can appreciate that a complex sensual discourse was used to tangibly distinguish, amongst other things, between the sexes and will have been actively employed in the production of contemporary material culture. Of course the polishing of the axe may have enhanced its functional use and improved its visual impact but more importantly the evidence from the middle Neolithic suggests that it also created a platform upon which social relationships could be negotiated with reference to it. Almost ironically it may have been the polished axe, the very tool that transcended and potentially bound together discrete gendered activities, that may have been so crucial in their division. Still more importantly, the varying degrees of polish produced, combined with the diversity of stone axe-types, sizes, and materials employed, which seem to defy satisfactory classification, are not simply indicative of specific social groups in silent bondage to these crude structural discourses. They also represent the infinite variety of foibles, neuroses, eccentricities, fetishes and phobias of their makers and users bound by the force of their own individuality.

NOTES

1. The polisher within the working gallery in Shetland is obviously not associated with the polishing of non-local axe factory products. This may be an exception due to the relative isolation of this area in terms of the potential networks of exchange. Perhaps this partially accounts for the more indirect referencing of a mortuary context.

2. The patches showing evidence of axe-polishing at West Kennet, Avebury, and Cairnholy I may have been produced prior to their integration into these monuments as the evidence is presently unclear. If this was the case, however, it still emphasises the importance of axe-polishing symbolically to the continuing practices at these sites whilst still allowing the possibility that axes were actually polished in these contexts using the more typical portable polishers of which no tangible evidence remains. This possibility also applies to those other sites where the interred polishers could not have possibly continued in use.

3. Of course it could be argued that the evidence of axe production in the earlier Neolithic at causewayed enclosures in the South also suggests an association with ceremonial contexts associated with the dead and therefore also with rites of passage. However, there appears to be a distinction between what would appear to be more communal activity in these large open enclosures in the earlier Neolithic (perhaps also reflected in the evidence from the other more 'domestic' sites, i.e. Ehenside Tarn, Llandegai and Bryn-yr-Hen-Bobl) and later contexts. Perhaps the type of ceremonial activity observed at causewayed enclosures may be more akin to the 'calendrical rites' observed by Turner (1969) which emphasise social cohesion rather than in the later Neolithic where the emphasis seems to have shifted to the role of the individual, or a small group, in polishing. Even if the two examples from henges, areas of potentially communal activity in the later Neolithic, are considered we see that the polisher from within Henge A at Llandegai is interred with an individual cremation and can no longer be utilised within the communal activities potential taking place whilst the polishing grooves from Avebury are in the avenue the area where group activity is physically most restricted.

ACKNOWLEDGEMENTS

I would like to thank Gavin MacGregor and Tony Pollard for offering constructive criticism on early drafts of the text and also Adrian Chandler who provided valuable information. Special thanks are due to Eilidh Campbell and Colin Richards who have both, not only offered comments on the text, but also, during several discussions, provided invaluable advice that helped develop its contents. Of course, that is not to say that they agree with all it contains!

REFERENCES

Atkinson, R. J. C. 1965. Wayland's Smithy. *Antiquity* 39, 126–33.

Bishop, C., Woolley, A., Kinnes, I. and Harrison, R. 1977. Jadeite axes in Europe and the British Isles: and interim study. *Archaeologia Atlantica* 2, 1–8.

Bloch, M. and Parry, J. (eds) 1982. *Death and the Regeneration of Life*. Cambridge and New York: Cambridge University Press.

Bradley, R. 1978. *The Prehistoric Settlement of Britain*. Harlow: Longman.

Bradley, R. and Edmonds, M. 1993. *Interpreting the Axe Trade: Production, and Exchange in Neolithic Britain*. Cambridge and New York: Cambridge University Press.

Britnell, W. J. and Savory, H. N. (eds) 1984. *Gwernvale and Penywyrlod: Two Neolithic Long Cairns in the Black Mountains of Brecknock*. Cambrian Archaeological Monographs no. 2. Cardiff: Cambrian Archaeological Association.

Burton, J. 1987. Exchange pathways at a stone axe factory in Papua New Guinea. In Sieveking, G. and Newcomer, M. (eds), *The Human Uses of Flint and Chert*. 183–91. Cambridge: Cambridge University Press.

Clough, T. and Cummins, W. 1988. *Stone Axe Studies*, vol. 2. London: Council for British Archaeology, Research Report 67.

Darbishire, R. D. 1872. Notes on discoveries in Ehenside Tarn, Cumberland. *Archaeologia* 44, 273–92.

Douglas, M. 1966. *Purity and Danger*. London: Routledge & Kegan Paul.

Edmonds, M. 1993a. Interpreting causewayed enclosures in the present and the past. In Tilley, C. (ed.), *Interpretative Archaeology*. London: Routledge.

Edmonds, M. 1993b. Towards a context for production and exchange: the polished axe in earlier Neolithic Britain. In Scarre, C. and Healy, F. (eds), *Trade and Exchange in Prehistoric Europe*. Oxford: Oxbow Books.

Edmonds, M. and Bellamy, P. 1991. The lithic assemblage from maiden castle. In Sharples, N. (ed.), *Maiden Castle: Excavations and Field Survey, 1985–86*. London: English Heritage, 214–29.

Gero, J. M. 1991. Genderlithics: women's roles in stone tool production. In Gero, J. M. and Conkey, M. W. (eds), *Engendering Archaeology*. Oxford: Blackwell, 163–93.

Hay, J. 1990. Stone axe, disc bead, flints. In *Discovery and Excavation in Scotland*, 39.

Hemp, W. J. 1936. The chambered cairn known as Bryn yr Hen Bobl near Plas Newydd, Anglesey. *Archaeologia* 85, 253–92.

Henshall, A. S. 1963 and 1972. *The Chambered Tombs of Scotland* (2 vols). Edinburgh: Edinburgh University Press.

Houlder, C. 1968. The henge monuments at Llandegai. *Antiquity* 52, 216–21.

Houlder, C. 1976. Stone axes and henge monuments. In Boon, G. and Lewis, J. (eds), *Welsh Antiquity*. Cardiff: National Museum of Wales, 55–62.

Lynch, F. 1969. The Megalithic tombs of North Wales. In Powell, T. G. E., Corcoran, J. X. W. P., Lynch, F. and Scott, J. G. (eds), *Megalithic Enquiries in the West of Britain: A Liverpool Symposium*, Liverpool: Liverpool University Press, 107–48.

Manby, T. G. 1965. The distribution of rough-cut 'Cumbrian' and related stone axes of Lake District origin in Northern England. *Trans. Cum. and West. Ant. and Arch. Soc.* LXV (n.s.), 1–37.

Meigs, A. S. 1984. *Food, Sex, Pollution: A New Guinea Religion.* New Brunswick: Rutgers University Press.

Mercer, R. 1981. Excavations at Carn Brea, Illogan, Cornwall – a Neolithic fortified complex of the third millenium BC. *Cornish Archaeology* 20, 1–204.

Neish, J. 1871. Notes of stone celts found in Glenshee, Forfarshire, 1870. *Proceedings of the Society of Antiquaries of Scotland* 9, 174–6.

O'Kelly, M. J. 1982. *Newgrange, Archaeology, Art and Legend.* London: Thames & Hudson.

Olausson, D. 1983. *Flint and Groundstone Axes in the Scandinavian Neolithic.* Scripta Minora 2. Lund.

Piggott, S. 1954. *The Neolithic Cultures of the British Isles.* Cambridge: Cambridge University Press.

Piggott, S. 1962. *The West Kennet Long Barrow: Excavations 1955–56.* London: HMSO.

Piggott, S. and Atkinson, R. J. C. 1986. The date of the West Kennet long barrow. *Antiquity* 60, 143–4.

Scott, L. G. and Calder, C. S. T. 1952. Notes on a chambered cairn, and a working Gallery, on the Beorgs of Uyea, Northmaven, Shetland. *Proceedings of the Society of Antiquaries of Scotland* 86, 171–7.

Sharp, L. 1952. Steel axes for Stone-Age Australians. *Human Organisation* 11, 17–22.

Shee Twohig, E. 1981. *The Megalithic Art of Western Europe.* Oxford: Clarendon Press.

Smith, I. 1965. *Windmill Hill and Avebury: Excavations by Alexander Keiller, 1925–1939.* Oxford: Clarendon Press.

Smith, I. 1979. The chronology of British stone implements. In Clough, T. and Cummins, W. (eds), *Stone Axe Studies.* London: Council for British Archaeology, Research Report 23, 13–22.

Thomas, J. and Tilley, C. 1993. The axe and the torso: symbolic structures in the Neolithic of Brittany. In Tilley, C. (ed.), *Interpretative Archaeology.* London: Routledge.

Turner, V. 1969. *The Ritual Process.* Chicago: Aldine.

Van Gennep, A. 1960. *The Rites of Passage.* London: Routledge & Kegan Paul.

Wickham-Jones, C. R. 1985. Stone. In Clarke, D. V., Cowie, T. G. and Foxon, A. (eds), *Symbols of Power at the time of Stonehenge.* Edinburgh: HMSO (for) Nat. Mus. Antiq. of Scot.

Williams, J. 1970. Neolithic axes in Dumfries and Galloway: a preliminary list of axes possibly available for thin section analysis. *Transactions of the Dumfries and Galloway Natural History and Antiquarian Society* 47, 111–22.

Wilson, G. 1881. Notes on a collection of implements and ornaments of stone, bronze, etc. from Glenluce, Wigtownshire. *Proceedings of the Society of Antiquaries of Scotland* 15, 262–72.

Woodburn, J. 1982. Social dimensions of death in four African hunting and gathering societies. In Bloch, M. and Parry, J. (eds), *Death and the Regeneration of Life.* Cambridge and New York: Cambridge University Press.

Woodman, P. C. 1978. *The Mesolithic in Ireland.* Oxford: BAR.

15

SELF AND SOCIAL IDENTITY

AN ANALYSIS OF THE MESOLITHIC BODY ADORNMENT FROM THE SCOTTISH WESTERN ISLES

BIDDY SIMPSON

INTRODUCTION

An attempt will be made in this paper to throw some light on a particular aspect of hunter-gatherer material culture, that of body adornment, and to suggest that the analysis of this can inform us about the expression of self and social identity.

Much attention has been paid in the past to hunter-gatherer 'arts and crafts' (i.e. cave art and portable art forms). Little attention, however, has been given to body adornment in any form. As White (1989a) has stated, if one is interested in the question of the expression of self and social identity, why would one not focus on the decorative objects worn by the individuals concerned? Due to the limited evidence of Mesolithic body adornment in Scotland the Western Isles will not be analysed in isolation, but within their wider British context. In general the British evidence, although also limited, reveals a degree of complexity. An analysis of this material may therefore aid our understanding of the earliest prehistoric periods in Britain in aspects such as, how these people presented their self and social identity, their social complexity, the distances covered to obtain specific raw materials, exchange and therefore alliance networks, differential belief systems and cultural identities. The approach adopted here will, I hope, reveal how important questions and observations can be, and have been, suppressed.

The term 'body adornment' encapsulates many elements, including ornaments, clothing, scarification, tattooing and body painting. This paper, however, will focus on the evidence of body ornaments. Ornaments being defined as artefacts which do not seem to serve any practical function other than as bodily decoration, for example rings, beads and pendants. There is obviously the possibility that some perforated objects were used for other purposes, e.g. more practical, as weights or as tools (for example, bone awls). However such artefacts are ignored here due to their size and obvious other practical uses.

RESEARCH PROBLEMS

First, if we acknowledge that archaeological remains can enter the archaeological record down various depositional pathways – either being lost, discarded or deliberately interred into the ground – it is *crucial* not only to try and understand which of the stages we are looking at but also to consider the post-depositional activities which effected the record thereafter.

Secondly, natural formation processes play a major part in the preservation of hunter-gatherer evidence. The only adornment evidence surviving in the Palaeolithic in Britain comes from cave sites, where the evidence has been partly preserved from the ravages of the last glaciation. In addition to the coastal erosion of Mesolithic sites, presumably many may lie under metres of peat further inland. It must be appreciated that we have only a partial picture of body adornment within the British Isles, the same being true of its associated and adjacent features, assemblages, etc.

Yet another factor which denies us a full picture of body adornment within Britain is our ability to find, recognise, recover, conserve or even bother recording personal ornaments. Basically, therefore, in Britain the direct evidence for adornment is rather limited. Finally, within hunter-gatherer archaeology, body adornment does not seem to have been regarded by archaeologists as an important source of evidence, unless it has been found within mortuary contexts. Within these contexts body adornment is continuously used as an indicator of status or position within a society. For example Harrold (1980: 205), when using grave goods to compare Middle and Upper Palaeolithic burials from Europe and Asia, concluded that: 'The strong tendency for males in the Middle Palaeolithic to be accorded richer and more complex burials than females allows a greater variety of social information, a more complex *persona*, to be expressed in male burials. By contrast, Upper Palaeolithic burials appear to allow at least some females (i.e. those who were buried) fuller participation in whatever status or rank systems existed'. However, within mortuary contexts ornaments are deliberately placed alongside the body, by others than the deceased. If we do not know in advance what *value* was given to these objects, how can these grave goods be truly representative or reflective of what ornaments may have meant on the *living* body? This paper, which is inspired by the work carried out on the continent by White (1989a, 1989b), concentrates on body adornment within its 'cultural' contexts and therefore the 'language' of body adornment and what it can tell us inside and outside of mortuary contexts.

THE EVIDENCE

The general consensus is that there was an 'explosion' of art and ornamentation at the beginning of the European Upper Palaeolithic (Gamble 1983, White 1989a and 1989b), and for Britain this statement appears at least partially true. However, an indication of earlier concerns with self expression is provided by a number of artificially-perforated fossil beads, which were found in a gravel pit

SITE	PERIOD	BURIALS	ORNAMENTS	ASSOC. WITH BODIES	TYPE	MATERIAL	DECORATED	REFERENCES
Bedford	Palaeolithic	No	Yes		Beads	Fossil	No	Worthington Smith 1894
Paviland Cave	E.U.P.	1 Elderly Male	Yes	Yes	8 Perf. teeth Pendant Bracelet	Wolf/Reindeer Ivory Ivory	No No No	Buckland 1823, Garrod 1926 and Campbell 1977.
Pin Hole Cave A	E.U.P.	No	Yes		Perf. shell bead	Winkle	No	Armstrong 1929, Campbell 1977
Pin Hole Cave B	L.U.P.	1 Juvenile 1 Adult	Yes	No	Pendant	Bone	No	Armstrong 1929, Jenkinson 1984
		1 Juvenile 1 Adult	Yes	Yes	Ornament?	Mother of pearl	No	
Church Hole	L.U.P.	No	Yes		Pendant	Horse bone	No	Campbell 1977
Kent's Cavern	L.U.P.	No	Yes		Perf. tooth	Badger	No	Garrod 1926
Kendrick's Cave	L.U.P.	4 Individuals	Yes	Unknown	c.107 Perf. teeth 2 Ornaments?	Bear/bovid/deer Horse mandibles	Yes Yes	Sieveking 1971, Smith 1992

Fig. 15.1. British Palaeolithic sites with body adornment.

in Bedford with 'possible' indications of the 'ligament' on which they were originally strung. These were assigned to the Middle Palaeolithic on account of the associated stone tools (Smith 1894).

Evidence of body ornaments from the Early Upper Palaeolithic and Later Upper Palaeolithic has been recovered from both domestic and burial sites, however it is at the latter that we have the highest concentrations (see Figs 15.1 and 15.2). During the Mesolithic there is even more evidence to indicate the different types of ornament-forms worn. Once again, they have been found within domestic and mortuary contexts (see Figs 15.2 and 15.3). As previously mentioned, body adornment has only been truly considered in relation to mortuary analysis, while also being utilised to argue for vertical social differentiation within hunter-gathererer groups (Harrold 1980, Clark and Neeley 1987, Mussi 1990, etc.). The general goal of this paper is to push the sole emphasis away from mortuary contexts and to give due consideration to those factors which may advance our understanding of the importance of body adornment within its wider cultural context. The following factors will be examined:

  a) how body ornaments were worn;
  b) the materials involved;
  c) long distance raw material procurement/exchange;
  d) the technology behind the making of ornaments;
  e) social identity.

HOW ORNAMENTS WERE WORN

Ethnographic research (for example Brain 1979, Faris 1972, Marshall 1976, O'Hanlon 1989, Sillitoe 1988, Strathern 1971 and 1979, etc.) has revealed that where body adornment is used it is crucial to the social *persona* of that group. Groups wear certain types of ornaments in different ways for many different reasons. Body adornment upon the living and dead body creates an 'unspoken' language which can communicate on an informal level between individuals or on a more formal level, to other social groups or even to ancestors. Basically, body adornment is culturally – and even group – specific and therefore the materials utilised for adornment are acquired or procured on ideological grounds and for the messages they convey. Therefore body adornment works functionally on a social level. If we consider how adornment was worn, the materials procured, and so on, it is possible to identify changes in beliefs throughout the Palaeolithic and Mesolithic and also to gain some understanding of how regional and local identities were expressed and maintained.

Throughout the ethnographic record specific types of ornaments have been found to hold different symbolic meanings for different people. For example, if ornaments are positioned on the body in a certain manner or are associated with other specific ornaments, an entire 'unspoken' language can be created which, as mentioned before, can communicate on an informal level, within and between

Mesolithic sites

1. Aveline's Hole
2. Gough's Cave
3. Star Carr
4. Nab Head
5. CulverWell
6. Portland Bill
7. New Windsor
8. Oronsay
9. Ulva Cave
10. Cardingmill Bay

Palaeolithic Sites

A. Bedford
B. Paviland Cave
C. Pin Hole Cave A
D. Pin Hole Cave B
E. Church Hole
F. Kent's Cavern
G. Kendrick's Cave

Fig. 15.2. Distribution of British Palaeolithic and Mesolithic sites with evidence of body adornment.

the ages and sexes or between social groups on an inter- group level. For example, in south-east Nuba (Faris 1972), boys wear a large stone bead around their necks whilst girls wear a nose-ring. Older men wear earrings, single chokers and a disc-ornament around the neck while older women wear earrings, a lip plug and necklaces (see Fig. 15.4). Not only may the wearing of specific jewellery types

SITE	PERIOD	BURIALS	ORNAMENTS	ASSOC. WITH BODIES	TYPE	MATERIAL	DECORATED	REFERENCES
Aveline's Hole	E.M.	c.50-70 Individuals	Yes	Unknown	Perf. shell beads	Winkle	No	Smith 1992, Wymer 1977 and 1991
		2 Individuals	Yes	Yes	c.60 Perf. shell beads	Winkle	No	
					3 Perf. teeth	Pig/deer	No	
					Ornament?	Horse incisor	Yes	
Gough's Cave	E.M.	1 Male Adult	No		2 Perf. teeth	Fox	No	Currant, Jacobi and Stringer 1989, Wymer 1991.
		2 Adults and 1 child	Yes	Yes	1 Perf. shell bead	Unknown	No	
Starcarr	E.M.	No	Yes		3 Pendants	Amber	No	Clark 1954
					33 Beads	Stone	No	
					Beads	Shale	No	
					1 Perf. tooth	Deer	No	
					1 Bead	Bird bone	No	
Nab Head	Mesolithic	No	Yes		Beads	Shale	No	Gordon-Williams 1926, Wymer 1991
Culver Well	L.M.	No	Yes		Beads	Various shells	No	Palmer 1971, 1976,1977, 1985, 1990.
					1 Bead	Pebble	No	
					Ornament?	Perf. scallop shell	No	
Portland Bill	Mesolithic	1 Individual	Yes	No	2 rings	Fossil ivory	No	Palmer 1969, 1970, 1977.
New Windsor	Mesolithic	No	Yes		Pendant	Flint	Yes	Wymer 1977
Cnoc Sligeach	L.M	Human remains	Yes	?	Beads	Cowries	No	Bishop 1914, Mellars 1987.
Cnoc Coig	L.M	Human remains	Yes	?	Beads	Cowries	No	"
Caisteal nan Gillean	L.M.	Human remains	Yes	?	Beads	Cowries	No	"
Ulva Cave	L.M.	No	Yes		Beads	Cowries	No	Bonsall pers comm.
Carding Mill Bay	L.M.	Human remains	Yes	?	Beads	Cowries	No	Connock et al. 1993
Risga	L.M.	No	Yes	No	Beads	Cowries	No	Lacaille 1954

Fig. 15.3. British Mesolithic sites with body adornment.

	BOYS	GIRLS	YOUNG MEN	YOUNG WOMEN	OLDER MEN	OLDER WOMEN
LARGE STONE BEAD	Yes					
NOSE RING/PLUG		Yes				
BRASS ANKLE BRACELET				Yes		
BRASS WRIST BRACELET				Yes		
BUCKLE AND STRAP BRACELET			Yes	Yes		
EARRINGS			Yes	Yes	Yes	Yes
LIP PLUGS						Yes
SINGLE CHOKERS					Yes	
NECKLASES					Yes	Yes
ALUMINIUM DECOR. DISC ORNAMENT					Yes	

Fig. 15.4. Ornaments associated with the South-east Nuba. Source: Faris 1972.

indicate age and sex, but the *position* of the ornament may have specific ideological meanings. In North Cameroon (Brain 1979), lip ornaments are worn by
the women. Young girls have their lips pierced during adolescence when they
are taught the 'things of women'. These 'things of women' are believed to have
been first taught in ancient times by the society's ancestress who, in turn, learnt
it from a frog. The teaching of the girls gains much from the association of the
ancestress-frog relationship with the lip ornaments, since they are said to make
the women look like frogs.

The choice of body parts to be decorated is never random. There are direct
symbolic links between ornaments and the parts of the body that are decorated.
In different societies certain parts of the body receive more attention and are
therefore more symbolically important than others. Other examples of this can
be found in Brain (1979), who describes how in certain societies eyes may be
decorated because they are associated with the soul, or 'seeing' in the sense of
'knowing'. Earrings are sometimes linked with the notion of 'hearing' and therefore behaving and obeying. The Dogon for example, associate the ear with female
sex organs yet other societies may protect the ear's orifice from evil intrusions.
Therefore, at an informal level body ornaments within a single society can be
ordered into a complex of signs which create a language understood only by its
members. These symbols can differentiate the ages and the sexes and demonstrate human physiological stages, which may be symbolic of specific events
or notions within their deeply rooted belief-system.

Unfortunately, the British burial record cannot give us much insight into how
ornaments were worn during the Palaeolithic and Mesolithic, therefore informal-
level statements cannot be seen. This gap in our understanding is largely due to
the limited amount of burials we have to date and compare, the fragmentary
nature of these burials and the disturbance of the associated ornaments. The
majority of British adornment evidence consists of pendants and beads. Presumably these ornaments were strung on some kind of chord or line and
suspended from the body, but from which part of the body? In addition, if they
are unassociated with a body it is impossible to tell how they were actually worn.
However, we must not forget that in death, differentiation of individuals on age
or gender grounds through the use of adornment may have been very different
from how it was portrayed in 'life'.

At a more formal level, personal adornment is used to communicate to a wider
audience, and in doing so can reflect distinct social groups and therefore group
identity. Ethnographic analysis (Strathern 1971, 1979) reveals that the more
formal the event (for example at exchanges, within death, warfare, etc.) the more
important it is that a strict cultural code is followed, thus allowing less room for
informal personal expression. There is therefore increasing homogeneity in what
is being worn and how it is worn, a uniformity which reflects their 'one' identity.
This is not only to reflect a group's identity and create statements of strength
and solidarity but confirm their own social values. In turn the daily recognition

of ancestors or mythological beliefs, as in the case of the 'frog-lips', within body adornment creates stability and social unity. It is unfortunate that the British burial data does not give us many clues as to how and exactly where on the body certain ornaments were worn. However, it is hoped that the foregoing discussion has suggested how adornment can serve to visually express identities, whether it be at a social-group level or an individual level, between ages and sexes.

THE MATERIALS USED IN BODY ADORNMENT

Ethnographic research has revealed that not only is the allocation of ornaments to certain body parts marked with importance but also what *materials* were used in manufacturing the ornaments. For example, the Hageners of Papua New Guinea used birds' feathers in their adornment because they wished to associate themselves with '… magically powerful things, such as birds …'. Instead of constructing masks, carvings or paintings of these birds they instead took parts of the birds – their feathers – and attached these to themselves (Strathern and Strathern 1971: 177). Specific meanings are attributed to specific ornaments and where they are placed. Although we cannot translate this symbolic 'unspoken language' in the archaeological record, certain factors can be noted. In general, throughout the Upper Palaeolithic in Britain we do not see a change in materials or styles in body adornment apart from the onset of engraved materials used for adornment towards the end of the Upper Palaeolithic (but this does not seem to follow through into the Mesolithic). Instead, we see a rigid use of animal materials such as teeth, bone and ivory (see Figs 15.1 and 15.3).

There are two distinct elements that separate body adornment in the Palaeolithic and the Mesolithic – materials and context. Even with the fragmentary nature of the British evidence, it is apparent that there is a change through time in the types of materials acquired for the production of body ornaments (see Figs 15.1 and 15.3). During the Palaeolithic, more accessible or 'easy-to-hand' materials were used for adornment, for example teeth, ivory, shells and bone, but during the Mesolithic we find a change. Ornaments made of such materials continued to be used after the last glaciation but we can also see the use of other materials such as shale and amber, which are marginally more difficult to acquire. We can also note that during the Palaeolithic ornaments always seem to be derived from faunal materials. Stone or pebble beads – which are very accessible – have not been found as yet in the Palaeolithic, but they have been at Mesolithic sites.

Although there is a trend during the Palaeolithic towards the use of predominantly faunal materials, different types of animals were used. For example, at Paviland Cave, wolf and reindeer teeth were found; at Church Hole, a horse pendant; whilst at Kendrick's Cave bear, bovid and deer teeth were found. Although there seems to be a common ideological value attributed to animals, could the evidence of different faunal types reflect regional and local preferences for certain types of ornaments based on more specific ideological values of specific animals? Can we therefore view the evidence of specific faunal materials being used in an emblematic way, not only to create an identity for themselves as a group, but to create an identity which would be recognised by others. This would in turn create regional and local identities. Unfortunately with the limited British evidence, these identities can only be 'glimpsed' if this is the case.

It is noteworthy that representational art depicting animals seems, during the onset of art and ornamentation, to be found within cave art and mobile art forms. Within Upper Palaeolithic body adornment, *material* elements of the animals themselves were used and perhaps chosen with a view to the perceived powers of these animals. As we move into the Mesolithic there is a decrease in the general homogeneity of materials used. Although faunal materials continue to be adapted into ornaments, other materials such as shale, amber and pebbles are increasingly used and fashioned into ornaments.

During the Mesolithic, body adornment seems to reflect a change in subsistence and an increasing emphasis on place rather than the animal. The continued use of faunal materials in some areas could perhaps indicate the continued ideological emphasis placed on specific animals and also reflect those hunter-gatherers who continued to derive much of their protein from hunting, in contrast to other social groups who drew from a diversity of food sources and presumably inhabited different environments throughout the annual cycle. Thus, use of non-faunal materials during the Mesolithic may reflect a change in beliefs since the Palaeolithic and/or groups merely expressing their cultural identity in different ways. Non-faunal ornaments may also be suggestive of perhaps mainly 'gatherer' groups, reflecting their somewhat different economies and the increasing diversity of food resources being exploited during the Mesolithic.

LONG–DISTANCE PROCUREMENT AND TECHNOLOGICAL CONSIDERATIONS

The long-distance procurement of materials for body ornaments is not greatly evident within the British hunter-gatherer record and therefore personal ornaments cannot be classed as deliberately fashioned from 'exotic' materials. However, when considering the techniques employed to fashion the ornaments previously mentioned it is evident that time was set aside not only to collect the material but to fashion that material into an ornament.

Within Britain there is evidence of at least six types of personal ornament:

-perforated animal teeth
-oval or round perforated stone beads
-perforated pendants of ivory, bone or amber
-carved rings of ivory
-perforated disc-like beads of shale and,
-perforated marine shells.

There are at least four production techniques represented here:

-perforation
-trimming of the material to produce a 'blank'

-secondary working for a desired shape and,
-the final smoothing and polishing stages.

All of these techniques were used throughout the Upper Palaeolithic and Mesolithic and therefore there is no evidence for major trends of ornament production becoming more labour-intensive. All of these stages would have been time consuming! This seems to contrast with the Neolithic in Britain, where there is evidence to suggest a tendency for more complex processes of material modification. For example, a number of beads made of bone, tooth, antler and shell were recovered from the chambered tomb at Isbister, Orkney (Hedges 1983). They no longer resembled their natural state but had all been cut, ground down and polished into similar forms. Apart from slight variations in colour, these beads were practically indistinguishable from each other. As Pollard (1994: 164) states: 'Though the final product may have been indistinguishable from other raw materials these differences would have been very obvious in the production stage with the different qualities of these materials requiring variations in manufacturing technique.' In conjunction with technological considerations and the time that was set aside to produce ornaments, the apparent lack of adornment evidence is interesting in itself. If body adornment is being used not only for aesthetic purposes but for social display, identity and ideological reasons, why (even if we take into consideration the problems outlined at the beginning of this paper) do we have no evidence of personal adornment at certain domestic and burial sites. For example no ornaments have been found at the Mesolithic site of Mount Sandel (Woodman 1985) or within the Later Upper Palaeolithic burial site of Robin Hood's cave in Creswell Crags, where five individuals were found (Jenkinson 1984). There are three possible reasons for this non-occurrence:

A. Body ornaments, including organic ornaments such as necklaces and bracelets of dried grasses, leather and/or seeds, simply did not survive.
B. There was not an emphasis with decorating the *body* with social groups in these areas.
C. If time is needed to, not only produce personal ornaments but create social distinctions and identities, were those groups inhabiting or using these sites, unable to find this time because of social and economic constraints?

THE SCOTTISH MESOLITHIC

In Scotland, the only body adornment evidence to date seems to be restricted to the West coast (see Fig. 15.5). Single and double perforated cowries have been found in the Oronsay middens (Mellars 1987), Carding Mill Bay (Connock et al. 1992), Ulva Cave (Bonsall, pers comm.) and possibly on Risga (Lacaille 1954), although Lacaille's source, Mann 1920, seems to be referring to the Oronsay cowries in his article on Risga. It should be mentioned at this point that these cowries, like other perforated ornaments, could have served as clothing

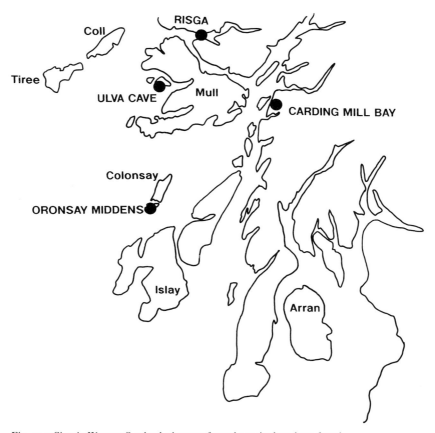

Fig. 15.5. Sites in Western Scotland where perforated cowries have been found.

attachments rather than strung on some kind of chord and hung around for example the neck, wrist, etc. As in all domestic contexts, it is very difficult to see how these ornaments were worn and used, however certain observations and questions can be raised.

1) The evidence suggests that some groups labelled 'Obanian' could be distinguished not only by their assemblages, but also by their body adornment;

2) If the group or groups who inhabited these sites had time and a need to adorn themselves why did they specifically procure and perforate cowries. No other types of ornaments have been found;

3) What was their significance? Were they portraying not only a functional dependency on the sea but a cosmological and mythological affinity with the sea, or were they used as a form of social identity with or without involving this belief?;

4) Why, if cowries are common to the Scottish Northern and Western mainland and islands, are perforated cowries restricted to these four sites? No cowries have been found on any of the adjacent islands;

5) Within the Oronsay middens the main human bone evidence consisted of toes and fingers which were '... recovered as isolated, relatively dispersed finds ...' (Meiklejohn and Denston 1987: 297), as were the perforated cowries. One interesting point to consider is, why are these cowries found within the middens and do they have anything to do with the fragmentary human remains?

Although definite answers to these questions cannot be provided at present, perhaps this shows how body adornment may help us look at self and social identity where other types of evidence within hunter-gatherer society, for example flint industries, dwelling structures, artistic representations, etc., have failed.

CONCLUSION

In conclusion, I realise that within adornment there must have been elements of personal expression, for example, the wearing of specific ornaments for purely decorative and aesthetic purposes. However, we must also remember that individual expression still pertains to some higher cultural code of conduct and therefore personal and individual adornment, to some degree, reflects to which social group you belong. Although our limited evidence obviously does not truly reflect how body adornment was fully exploited or why, the majority of early prehistorians tend to disregard the information that it can give us. The general literature considers body adornment only in relation to the definition of vertical social differentiation and socio-complexity. The ethnographic record informs us that where body adornment is used it is crucial to the self and social identity of a group. Whether this is rooted in cosmological or mythological belief will differ from group to group. However, it is also important to realise that group identities cannot be defined solely by body adornment but were created in conjunction with other factors – social, economic and environmental.

ACKNOWLEDGEMENTS

I wish to thank Alex Morrison, Tony Pollard and Alan Saville for helpful comments on earlier drafts.

REFERENCES

Armstrong, A. L. 1929. Pin hole cave excavations, Creswell crags, Derbyshire: discovery of an engraved drawing of a masked human figure. *Proc. Prehist. Soc. East. Anglia* VI, 27–9.

Bailey, G. (ed.), 1983. *Hunter-Gatherer Economy in Prehistory*. Cambridge: Cambridge University Press.

Bishop, H. 1914. An Oransay shell mound – a Scottish pre-Neolithic site. *Proc. Soc. Antiq. Scot.* 48, 52–108.

Bonsall, C. (ed.) 1985. *The Mesolithic in Europe: Papers Presented at the Third International Symposium*. Edinburgh: John Donald.

Brain, R. 1979. *The Decorated Body*. London.

Buckland, Revd W. 1823. *Reliquiae Diluvianae*. London.

Campbell, J. B. 1977. *The Upper Palaeolithic of Britain*, vol. I and II. Oxford:

Clark, G. A. and Neeley, M. 1987. Social differentiation in European Mesolithic burial data. In Rowley-Conwy et al. (eds), *Mesolithic Northwest Europe: Recent Trends*. Sheffield: Department of Archaeology and Prehistory, University of Sheffield, 121–7.

Clark, J. D. G. 1954. *The Excavations at Star Carr*. Cambridge: Cambridge University Press.

Connock, K. D., Finlayson, B. and Mills, C. M. 1992. Excavation of a Shell midden at Carding Mill Bay, near Oban, Scotland. *Glasgow Arch. Journal* 17, 25–39.

Currant, A. P., Jacobi, R. M. and Stringer, C. B. 1989. Excavations at Gough's Cave, Somerset, *Antiquity* 63, 131–6.

Faris, J. C. 1972. *Nuba Personal Art*. London: Duckworth.

Gamble, C. 1983. Culture and society in the Upper Palaeolithic of Europe. In Bailey, G. (ed.), *Hunter-Gatherer Economy in Prehistory*. Cambridge: Cambridge University Press, 201–11.

Garrod, D. A. E. 1926. *The Upper Palaeolithic in Britain*. Oxford: Clarendon Press.

Gordon-Williams, Revd J. P. 1926. The Nab Head chipping floor. *Archaeo. Cambren.* VI, 86–110.

Harrold, F. B. 1980. A comparative analysis of Eurasian Palaeolithic burials. *World Archaeo.* 12, 195–210.

Hedges, J. 1983. *Isbister: A Chambered Tomb in Orkney*. Oxford: BAR British series 115.

Jenkinson, R. D. S. 1984. *Creswell Crags*. Oxford: BAR British Series 122.

Lacaille, A. D. 1954. *The Stone Age in Scotland*. London: Oxford University Press.

Mann, L. M. L. 1920. Oransay period discoveries on Risga. *Glasgow Herald*, 21 Aug. 1920, 6.

Marshall, L. 1976. *The !Kung of Nyae Nyae*. Cambridge.

Meiklejohn, C. and Denston, B. 1987. The human skeletal material: inventory and initial interpretation. In Mellars, P. A., *Excavations on Oronsay*. Edinburgh: Edinburgh University Press, 290–300.

Mellars, P. A. 1987. *Excavations on Oronsay*. Edinburgh: Edinburgh University Press.

Mellars, P. and Stringer, C. (eds) 1989. *The Human Revolution: Behavioural and Biological Perspectives on the Origins of Modern Humans*. Edinburgh: Edinburgh University Press.

Mussi, M. 1990. Continuity and change in Italy at the last glacial maximum. In Soffer, O. and Gamble, C. (eds), *The World at 18 000 BP*, vol. 2: *High Latitudes*. London: Unwin Hyman, 126–47.

O'Hanlon, M. 1989. *Reading the Skin*. Bathurst: Crawford House Press.

Palmer, S. 1969. A Mesolithic site at Portland Bill. *Proc. Dors. Nat. Hist. Arch. Soc.* 90, 183–206.

Palmer, S. 1970. A fossil ivory pendant from Portland. *Proc. Dors. Nat. Hist. Arch. Soc.* 92, 172–3.

Palmer, S. 1971. Excavations at the Culverwell Mesolithic site Portland. *Proc. Dors. Nat. Hist. Arch. Soc.* 93, 132.

Palmer, S. 1976. The Mesolithic habitation site at Culverwell, Portland, Dorset. *Proc. Prehist. Soc.* 42, 324–7.

Palmer, S. 1977. *Mesolithic Cultures of Britain.* Poole: Dolphin Press.

Palmer, S. 1985. Mesolithic sites at Portland and their significance. In Bonsall, C. (ed.), *The Mesolithic in Europe.* Edinburgh: John Donald, 254–63.

Palmer, S. 1990. Culver Well – unique opportunities. In Vermeersch, P. M. and Van Peer, P. (eds), *Contributions to the Mesolithic in Europe.* Papers presented at the Fourth International Symposium. Leuven: Leuven University Press, 87–91.

Pollard, A. J. 1994. *A Study of Marine Exploitation in Prehistoric Scotland, with Special Reference to Marine Shells and Their Archaeological Contexts.* Ph.D. thesis, University of Glasgow.

Rowley-Conwy, P., Zvelebil, M. and Blankholm, H. P. 1987. *Mesolithic Northwest Europe: Recent Trends.* Sheffield: Department of Archaeology and Prehistory, University of Sheffield.

Sieveking, G. de G. 1971. The Kendrick's Cave mandible. *Brit. Mus. Quart.* 35, 230–50.

Sillitoe, P. 1988. From head-dresses to head-messages: the art of self decoration in the highlands of Papua New Guinea. *Man* (n.s.) 23, 298–318.

Smith, C. 1992. *Late Stone Age Hunters of the British Isles.* London: Routledge.

Smith, W. G. 1894. *Man the Primeval Savage: His Haunts and Relics from the Hilltops of Bedfordshire to Blackwall.* London: Stanford.

Soffer, O. and Gamble, C. (eds) 1990. *The World at 18 000 BP,* vol. 2: *High Latitudes.* London: Unwin Hyman, 126–47.

Strathern, A. and M. 1971. *Self Decoration in Mount Hagen.* London: Duckworth.

Strathern, M. 1979. The self in self decoration. *Oceania* 49, 241–57.

Trinkaus, E. (ed.) 1989. *The Emergence of Modern Humans.* Cambridge: Cambridge University Press.

Vermeersch, P. M. and Van Peer, P. (eds) 1990. *Contributions to the Mesolithic in Europe.* Papers presented at the Fourth International Symposium. Leuven: Leuven University Press.

White, R. 1989a. Towards a contextual understanding of the earliest body adornments. In Trinkaus, E. (ed.), *The Emergence of Modern Humans.* Cambridge: Cambridge University Press, 211–31.

White, R. 1989b. Production complexity and standardisation in Early Aurignacian bead and pendant manufacture: evolutionary implications. In Mellars, P. and Stringer, C. (eds), *The Human Revolution: Behavioural and Biological Perspectives on the Origins of Modern Humans.* Edinburgh: Edinburgh University Press, 366–86.

Woodman, P. C. 1985. *Excavations at Mount Sandel 1973–77.* Belfast: HMSO.

Wymer, J. 1977. *Gazetteer of British Mesolithic Sites.* Norwich: Geo Abstracts.

Wymer, J. 1991. *Mesolithic Britain.* Archaeology Series. Princes Risborough: Shire.

16

MESOLITHIC CHIPPED STONE ASSEMBLAGES

DESCRIPTIVE AND ANALYTICAL PROCEDURES USED BY THE SOUTHERN HEBRIDES MESOLITHIC PROJECT

BILL FINLAYSON, NYREE FINLAY AND STEVEN MITHEN

INTRODUCTION

Since 1988 the Southern Hebrides Mesolithic Project (SHMP) has been engaged in the excavation of series of Mesolithic sites on Islay and Colonsay. The most notable of these are Gleann Mor (Mithen 1990a) and Bolsay Farm on Islay (Mithen et al. 1992), and Staosnaig on Colonsay (Mithen 1990b, Mithen and Finlayson 1992). Chipped stone represents by far the largest class of artefacts acquired from these sites, with many hundreds of thousands of pieces currently being studied by the SHMP. In this paper we summarise the methodology adopted by the project for this daunting task embedding this within a general discussion of the analysis of lithic assemblages from stone age sites in Scotland.

THE ANALYSIS OF LITHIC ASSEMBLAGES: SHMP METHODOLOGY

The analysis of these lithic assemblages has benefited substantially from the publication of several recently (and not so recently) excavated sites. The Rhum project has provided the first properly detailed published Mesolithic assemblage for Scotland (Wickham-Jones 1990). Mercer's work on Jura has provided a large corpus of material, although not in such an easily digestible form (Mercer 1968–80, Mercer and Searight 1986). Newton on Islay provides directly comparable material to SHMP assemblages, both due to geographical proximity and to the fact that it has been catalogued in a similar manner (see Clarke in McCullagh 1991). Material from the late Tom Affleck's excavations at Auchareoch on Arran (Affleck et al. 1988) and the sites of Smittons and Starr in Dumfries and Galloway (Finlayson 1989) provide a wider Mesolithic context for interpretation of SHMP assemblages.

This situation is a dramatic reversal of the situation in Scotland only a few years ago when the only substantial corpus of work was Lacaille's *Stone Age in Scotland* (Lacaille 1954). This change in the available database will have a profound effect on Mesolithic studies in Scotland, although, at present, it exists largely as a series of unconnected site reports. The SHMP is the first project to explicitly attempt a regional synthesis of the new level of available data.

All chipped stone assemblages acquired by the SHMP, whether by field walking, test-pitting or excavation, undergo a general characterisation study involving the construction of a computer database. Tables extracted from these will provide the summaries within the final excavation report, while the databases will provide the quantitative data for inter- and intra-site comparisons. A sample of the assemblages undergo a more detailed study involving the technical and morphological analysis of cores, retouched pieces, and a sample of unmodified blades and flakes. The chosen assemblages for this second stage of study are generally those from excavations, such as Staosnaig, Gleann Mor and Bolsay Farm. The following provides a summary of this two stage approach.

STAGE 1: GENERAL ASSEMBLAGE CHARACTERISATION

The method of assemblage characterisation employed is similar to that used for the description of material from Kinloch Farm and the same general terminology, based on that used by Tixier (Tixier et al. 1980) is employed here (Wickham-Jones 1990: 58). Most of the characterisation work, except for the major season at Bolsay, has been done in the field, allowing the results of this work to be available during excavation. The following specific definitions are employed in the main computer catalogue:

Material

In the majority of assemblages the raw material employed consists of flint, quartz, quartzite and chalcedony. No attempt is made to subdivide the flint into beach pebble or other material. Chalcedony is the term used for all such materials as agate, which appear to have arrived as pebbles along with the flint.

Blank

This term is used in the computer catalogue to allow basic description of all pieces, and is not limited to blanks in the strict lithic analysis sense. The catalogue entry for each artefact is decribed as one or more of the following fields:

Bipolar Cores: These are pieces that have been used to detach as series of removals in a particular manner, known as the bipolar technique, in which a piece of raw material is placed on an anvil and struck vertically with a hammer (Hayden 1980). It was not clear at the commencement of this project whether they were being used as cores, or to create a modified piece, hence their separation from the remaining cores.

Blades: Removals that are twice as long as they are wide and have approximately parallel, straight sides which have acute edges. They are generally produced by a knapping strategy designed to deliberately produce such blanks.

Chunks: Pieces that have neither platforms nor ventral surfaces. They are generally an accidental knapping product, or the result of pieces shattering because of heat.

Cores: These are pieces of raw material that have been used to detach a series of removals. Cores are subsequently further subdivided.

Flakes: These are removals, other than blades and chunks.

Pebbles: These are whole beach pebbles, or pebbles that have had a small number of flakes removed from them.

Primary/Secondary/Inner

All flakes and blades are classified as to whether they are a primary removal, identified by having a dorsal surface completely covered by cortex, a secondary removal in which the dorsal surface is partly covered by cortex, or an inner removal in which no cortex is present.

Sub-blank

This is used to describe the regularity of flakes. Flakes with a minimum of 10 mm of edge that is straight in section and either straight or with a simple convexity/concavity and an edge-angle of less than 45° are described as Regular. Flakes without such an edge are described as Irregular. By definition, blades are always Regular and flakes less than 10 mm in length or width are Irregular.

Retouched

This field is used to describe whether any piece has been subjected to secondary modification. There are three categories: Retouched, Not Retouched and Edge Damaged. Categorisation as edge damaged does not imply that a tool has been used. Edge damage may be caused during knapping, as a result of curation, or as a result of post-depositional (including recovery) factors, such as trampling, burning or sieving, as well as by use.

Dimensions

All pieces with any dimension greater than 10 mm are recorded by length, width and thickness. Dimensions are recorded in millimetres. For removals the dimensions are defined as follows: Length is defined as the measurement at 90° to the platform of the plane. Width is taken at 90° to the length, in the same plane, at the widest part of the piece. Thickness is the maximum measurement at 90° to both length and width. For cores the dimensions are based on the length of the main working face of the core, with width measured at 90° to length across the face and thickness at 90° to both these measurements. Pebbles and chunks are measured based on their maximum dimension, which is described as their length, with other measurements at 90° as above.

Condition

The condition of a piece is described as Fresh, Patinated, Abraded, Burnt, or Rolled. These are broad categories, and do not attempt to divide the material by degree of patination. They are generally described preferentially by any evidence for the condition furthest along the list given. In other words, if a piece is burnt, but has some evidence for having been rolled, then it will be described as rolled; if a piece has been patinated, but also appears to have been burnt, it will be described as burnt. This arbitrary decision is based on the information gain represented by the category. It is considered most useful to know if any water-rolled artefacts have been brought onto the site, next most useful to know the distribution of burnt pieces, and so on.

Notes

The catalogue includes space for short notes, including preliminary categor-isation of retouched tools (e.g. as microlith, scraper, etc.) or of cores (platform, amorphous, etc.).

Number of Pieces

Where a number of pieces were catalogued identically from the same context (by definition pieces without spatial information, generally recovered from sieving), they were given a single identifier in the database and the number in the sample was recorded.

The locational information available for every piece is also recorded in the database at this stage. The level of detail available obviously varies, from indi-vidually plotted artefacts at Gleann Mor, through pieces recorded by 25 cm square, wet sieve samples, test pitting results, and field walking.

STAGE 2: TECHNICAL AND MORPHOLOGICAL ANALYSIS

In this second level of analysis certain classes of artefacts are subject to a more detailed technical and morphological study. It will be through these studies that the extent of inter-assemblage variability with regard to production methods and discard patterns can be established. The following summarises the manner in which each of the selected classes of material is studied.

Cores

Cores are a manufacturing waste product. The discarded core represents the final choices made in the reduction sequence, and do not necessarily represent the complete process. A simple classification of cores would normally describe the final state of a core on discard. While this description may give an indication of the reason for abandonment, it does not necessarily reflect dominant knap-ping methods. In this study, we have attempted to describe the core history in reverse sequence, as an active item, rather than at the moment of discard.

From each excavated assemblage undergoing detailed study a sample of 50 cores are examined in detail. The attributes described are given in Tables 16.1a and 16.1b. With any given core (or core fragment, as for this purpose fragments may be as informative as cores, and cores represent a fragmentary item), the first stage to be described will be the last stage of working before discard. Some of

Table 16.1a. Core attributes and codes.

Final Attributes

1. Probable reason for abandonment	0: Indeterminate[1]
	1: Size
	2: Flaws[2]
	3: Overshot
	4: Stepping/Hingeing
	5: Angle
	6: 4 & 5 combined
2. Cortex Type	0: None
	1: Smooth/Chalky
	2: Smooth/hard
	3: Pitted
	4: Semi-battered
	5: Heavily battered
3. Estimate of original pebble size[3]	0: Indeterminate
	1: Small
	2: Medium
	3: Large
4. Angularity/Sphericity	0: Indeterminate
	1: Angular (nodular)
	2: Sub-angular
	3: Sub-rounded (smooth lumpy)
	4: Rounded
5. Number of stages visible	0: Probably the only stage[4]
	1-n
6. % platform[5]	1: < or c 25%
	2: c 50%
	3: c 75%
	4: 100%

NOTES
1. In general, all of the indeterminate options given in the scoring system above are only used when no other choice is possible. '0' for abandonment does not only include indeterminate situations, but also where an improved knapping strategy has been adopted.
2. Flaws include all sorts of problems with the raw material, including fissures and inclusions. Overshot includes any kind of flaking that has prevented any further use of the core by removing an excess of material.
3. The pebble size is estimated against the known size of flint pebbles on Islay. Medium pebbles are approximately fist sized.
4. For number of stages, a '0' means specifically that a core has only had one stage. If it possible that a core has had more than one stage, but only the final stage is visible, then the number of stages is described as '1'. The stage number is described as '0' if the number of stages is '0'.
5. Percentage, as a final attribute, refers to the final platform.

the core attributes are constant, for example cortex type. Some attributes, such as weight only apply to the final stage. All of these types of attribute are fixed and are described as final attributes and are shown in Table 16.1a. One of the final attributes is the number of stages in the core's use, and each of these stages is then described by a number of stage attributes (Table 16.1b), as far as they are visible. Each stage represents a tactical decision, for example using a new platform, or changing the knapping strategy, for example changing from platform to bipolar knapping.

Table 16.1b. Core stage attributes and codes.

Stage Attributes	
1. Stage number	0: If the only stage
	1-n
2. Type	1: Bipolar
	2: Blade platform
	3: Flake platform
	4: Non-specific platform
	5: Amorphous[1]
3. Platform type	0: unprepared (always 0 for bipolar)
	1: simple preparation
	2: complex preparation
	3: lost
4. Average flake angle[2]	0: indeterminate
	n to nearest $5°$
5. Predominant removal	0: indeterminate
	1: Blade
	2: Flake
	3: Mixed
6. Negative bulbs	0: not present
	1: Marked
	2: Diffuse
7. Length of maximum f/b scar[3]	n (0 for indeterminate)
8. Width of 7	n (0 for indeterminate)
9. Abandonment, as above for each stage	

NOTES
1. Stages are only to be described as amorphous for very irregular knapping episodes. Occasional incidental random flaking is not considered to represent a stage.
2. Flake angles are based on the mean value of the last few removals visible, even if they have hinge or step terminations. Only if the flake has completely failed should they not be measured. All bipolar cores are assumed to be flat.
3. The longest removal is not necessarily the last removal, but the longest that can be measured.

Microliths

The entire essence of traditional microlithic typology is based upon the notion that Mesolithic assemblages can be examined in the same manner as the preceding Upper Palaeolithic. Here it is generally argued that, for a variety of reasons, typological differences become marked and are spatially and chrono-logically distinctive (for a good summary of many of the relevant arguments see Mellars 1989). There has been a general assumption that the Mesolithic in western Europe shares these traits. The two previous major studies of large microlith samples in Scotland have been by Mercer (Mercer 1968–80) on material from Jura, and by Wickham-Jones (Wickham-Jones 1990) on material from Rhum. The system used by Mercer is a very detailed typological system with numerous types and sub-types (Mercer 1968–80). While these provide a wide range of morphological pigeon holes for microliths, this implies a precise categorisation which it is impossible for lithic analysts to achieve in a uniform

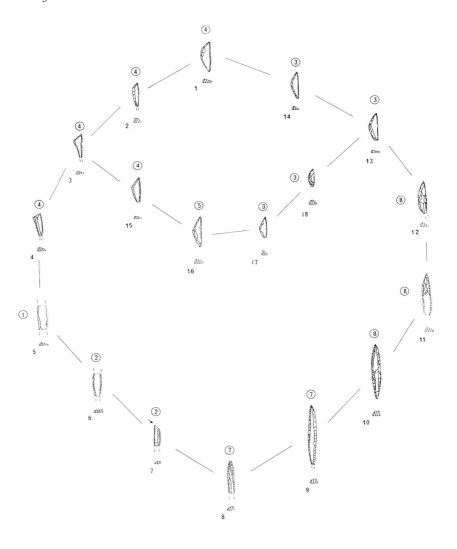

Fig. 16.1.

manner. They are based on morphological niceties which are unlikely to have been given equal weight by the manufacturers of the tools. Most importantly of all, such a normalisation of the data conceals that which the descriptive system attempts to meet; the morphological variablity of the microliths. Far from falling into discrete morphological types, the microliths tend to grade from one shape into another. For instance, as the backs of scalene triangles become increasingly curved, they grade into crescents, while as the apexes of crescents move towards the ends of the piece they become more like scalene triangles, and so on. Although it is clear that the basic types of triangle, cresent, backed blade, and so on, exist, close analysis does not break these divisions into sub-types, but blurs the boundaries between these higher order types. Figure 16.1 illustrates the morphological variability in microliths from Gleann Mor.

The system put forward by Wickham-Jones and McCartan (Wickham-Jones 1990) is very different from Mercer's, using only 11 types, including fragments and microburins. In this simplicity the system has much in common with that used here, indeed it has served as our starting point. However, it is felt that there is a need to investigate the finer detail more thoroughly. A glance at the illustrations of microliths from Rhum (ibid. 100, 101) will serve to show how much variability occurs within these classes. This system, like Mercer's is not designed to cope with continuous morphological variability.

The system proposed here has therefore attempted to reflect this variability. This has been done by assuming a general continuity between shapes. To document this it classes each microlith by assigning a value to six separate attributes, each taking a limited number of possible values (Table 16.2). A final attribute, with 9 possible values, summarises microlith type, excluding truncations, microburins and unidentifiable fragments, so enabling some comparison with Mercer and Wickham-Jones. (The truncations, microburins and related pieces are the subject of a similar exercise.) We fully recognise that the system is not objective and involves numerous biases, which we have tried to list in the accompanying notes, but we feel that it does provide an indication of the variation below the normalisation of typology.

We have extensively tested the system by using blind tests (different analysts classifying the same set of microliths independently and then comparing the results). Inevitably the first few attempts revealed problem areas in the definition of values, but the system has been gradually refined and definitions tightened. Blind test results scoring on all variables have been steadily improving, starting with 43 per cent, then 48, 53, 70, 77, 84, 71 per cent, the last on an exercise with a possible total of 602 points. In all the blind tests covered 136 microliths. Further refinement since the last test has now reduced the differences between analysts to only a few percentage points. Discrepancies between analysts still arise, but these derive principally from errors in processing rather than actual disagreements. This system controls these discrepancies to a greater extent than a normalised typological system, where artefacts are simply placed in different types by

Table 16.2. Microlith attributes and codes.

1. Curvature Dorsal[1]	0: Straight, as on backed blades or 'needle points'
	1: Irregular, mostly as on backed blades
	2: Shallow long curve, as on leaf points
	3: Curved, as on crescents
	4: Sub angular/rounded angles, as on off scalenes
	5: Angular, as on triangles
2. Curvature Ventral: as Curvature Dorsal	
3. Angle Position[2]	0: None (only for 0, 1, 2 curves)
	1: Bottom quarter
	2: Middle
	3: Top quarter
	4: Two (as on trapeze, not for retouched ends)
	5: Top eighth (i.e. between 3 and 7)
	6: Bottom eighth
	7: Flat top
4. Base	0: Bulb present (including on remnant spurs)
	1: Break snap, including post manufacture and indeterminate
	2: Burin snap
	3: Flat (90°) retouch
	4: Angled or curved retouch
5. Number of retouch edges[3]	1: 1
	2: 2
	3: 3
	4: 4
6. Point[4]	0: No point (crescents/triangles tend to 0)
	1: Clear spur (deliberate/functional, concave top quarter)
	2: Hollow tip, concave but no spur
	3: Single sided points
	4: Double sided points
7. Type[5]	1: Backed bladelet
	2: Double backed bladelet
	3: Crescent
	4: Scalene triangle
	5: Triangle
	6: Trapeze
	7: Needle point
	8: Leaf point
	9: Indeterminate

NOTES

General Notes: Specific notes have to made on: Whether broken, ignoring tiny chips, Presence of fine or inverse retouch, Presence of edge damage, Presence of staining, Burin terminations at top end.

1. If not clear, both faces to match best face. Ignore straight backing opposite a 'shaped' (i.e. 2–5) edge. It may appear unreasonable to describe dorsal and ventral faces as having different shapes, the description appears useful however, as some microliths do subjectively appear to have different shapes when viewed on opposite faces.

2. If orientation is unclear, tend to 3, also if position lies between 2 and 3, tend to 3.

3. Ignore minor breaks. Retouch has to be abrupt microlithic retouch. Other forms of retouch to be noted in notes. Assume a rectangular blank with four possible retouched sides. A crescent has 3 of those sides retouched (one side and two ends, possibly four if backed), a single sided point has two sides retouched (one side and one end). Triangles have generally at least three sides, although the system allows for two sided 'triangles', where an angled piece has parallel lateral margins.

4. Points are acute angles < 45°. The retouch must extend to the extreme tip, except for type 1.

5. Definitions as follows:
   1: Backed bladelet: backed bladelets have a single side backed by microlithic retouch to leave a straight backed edge. They are not distinguished from rods in this study.
   2: Double backed blades: These are backed bladelets with microlithic retouch down both sides to leave two, opposed, straight backed edges. They are not distinguished from rods in this study.
   3: Crescents: These are pieces that have been backed by microlithic retouch to form a convex backed edge.
   4: Scalene triangles: These are pieces with a minimum of two contiguous edges backed by microlithic retouch. The retouch forms a distinctive scalene form with one long retouched edge and a shorter oblique retouched edge.
   5: Triangles: These are pieces with a minimum of two contiguous edges backed by microlithic retouch. The two retouched edges form the two equal sides of an isoceles triangle.
   6: Trapezes: These are pieces with one side backed by microlithic retouch and both ends obliquely retouched by microlithic retouch to form a trapezoidal shape.
   7: Needle points: Needle points are microliths formed by having two sides backed by microlithic retouch to produce two straight sides converging to a point.

different analysts. At present all microliths classified are described by both analysts, a system which we believe rules out the remaining possibility of error.

Truncations

Truncations include such pieces as microburins, obliquely blunted blades/flakes and lamelles a cran (cf. Wickham-Jones 1990). The typological system as developed here maintains these broad categories for ease of comparability, but also involves an attempt to describe the pieces by a series of attributes, as is done with the other microlithic types. Both oblique truncations (*sensu strictu*) and obliquely truncated blades/flakes are treated together here, distinguished primarily by the presence/absence of bulbs.

Scrapers

With scrapers we are adopting a very simple morphological system. The system we are using is a cut down version of one used to examine scraper variability in the Neolithic of Orkney (Finlayson in prep.). It is cut down, because one immediate observation is that much of the scraper modification that has been made is determined more by blank form than by a deliberate attempt to reproduce standardised forms. This obviously has implications for the role of scrapers. Functional analysis work has so far concentrated on the microlithic component of the assemblage, but will be able to provide data on the variability of tasks and intensiveness of use of these morphologically defined scraper classes.

The classification used by the SHMP is strictly morphological and relatively simple to use. It involves placing scrapers into one of 17 categories (Table 16.3). A small number of pieces could fall into more than one category, in which a subjective decision is made as to its most appropriate category, rather than the creation of further categories.

Table 16.3. Scraper types

Short Convex (SC): A scraper with the scraper edge less than 10 mm thick, the scraper edge convex in profile.

Short Convex Flared (SC F): As above, but with marked narrowing of the piece away from the scraper edge. Sometimes this is achieved on a flake shaped in primary knapping, sometimes by secondary modification, usually on the ventral face.

Short Thick Convex (STC): As SC, but with the scraper edge being more than 10 mm thick.

Short Thick Convex Flared (STC F): As above, but flared.

Long Convex (LC): As SC, but more than twice as long as wide.

Long Convex Flared (LC F): As LC, but flared.

Long Thick Convex (LTC): As STC, but more than twice as long as wide.

Long Thick Convex Flared (LTC F): As STC F, but more than twice as long as wide.

Short Thick Disk (STD): Scraper retouch all round a flake greater than 10 mm thick.

Concave (CONCAV): A scraper edge that is definitely concave or hollow in profile.

Denticulate (DENT): A scraper edge that has a marked denticulation, or multiply notched appearance in profile.

Angled (AC): More than one scraper edge, meeting with sharp angled corners.

Sub Angled (SA): More than one scraper edge, meeting with rounded corners.

Straight (Strait): A scraper edge neither convex nor concave in profile.

Wide Convex (WC): A convex scraper edge on longest edge, longer than the other axis (i.e. tend to be side scrapers on long flakes).

Irregular (Irreg): A piece with retouch as in any other scraper class, but so irregular in shape or pattern as to make it impossible to fit into any of the above classes.

Fragment (Frag): A scraper fragment that cannot be identified as belonging to any of the above classes.

Other Retouched Pieces

There are a large number of pieces which either fall into very small groups, albeit recognisable classes such as denticulates or burins, and many other pieces with retouch that do not easily fall into any class. Such pieces tend to be lumped together into unclassified material, or 'other' retouched piece. This is not an adequate treatment for such material, but is simply a hangover from methodologies designed to establish cultural groups from regularities seen in the retouched tools. As part of the tool strategy they may form a significant element, at least numerically, which may conceivably be more useful in determining site function than such elements as microliths. While they may not carry any emblematic information, this may not be as an important element within the regional Mesolithic lithic repertoire as microlith studies elsewhere might suggest. At present a fairly basic classificatory system has been used to subdivide these pieces, it is intended to refine this further (Table 16.4).

Table 16.4. Other retouched pieces

Abruptly backed pieces: Pieces with abrupt retouch which (unlike with microliths) does not modify the form of the blank and is made on an acute flake edge.

Thick backed pieces: Pieces with backing on a thick edge opposed to a sharp (acute) edge.

Points: Pieces with slight retouch producing a sharp point.

Denticulates: Pieces with serrated acute edges formed by retouch.

Thick Denticulates: Pieces with thick serrated edges formed by retouch.

Burins: Pieces with burin removals that do not fall into any of the microlithic categories.

Debitage Analysis

By far the largest component of any of the SHMP excavated assemblages consists of debitage. For the second stage analysis two groups of this debitage is examined: the fine fraction debitage, which includes any piece less than 1 cm, and the blanks consisting of blades and flakes. To do this a sample of each are taken from selected contexts of a site, and each piece is described according to the attributes in Table 16.5 for the fine fraction debitage, and Table 16.6 for the blanks.

ADDITIONAL RESEARCH

The classification of the SHMP chipped stone assemblages in the fashion described above provides a framework for the other lithic analyses that are being conducted. These include spatial analysis, functional analysis, detailed studies of raw material availability, and experimental knapping. These various analyses are all entirely interdependent, with each providing information required to make sense of the lithic assemblage as a whole.

SUMMARY

The methods employed by SHMP are still being refined. However, in general the methods have now been employed successfully for several years. They attempt

Table 16.5. Attributes and Codes for fine fraction debitage.

1. Blank	1: Flake
	2: Chunk
2. Cortex	1: Primary
	2: Secondary
	3: Tertiary
3. Condition	1: Burnt
	2: Fresh
	3: Patinated
	4: Abraded
4. Fragmentation	1: Complete
	2: Fragment
	3: Indeterminate
5. Weight	1: Average weight per sample

Table 16.6. Attributes and Codes for the analysis of blanks (blades and flakes).

1. Condition/State	0: complete
	1: proximal missing
	2: distal missing
	3: prox frag
	4: dist frag
	5: med frag
	6: split/truncated width
	7: prox spalling
	8: dist spalling
2. Cortex	0: absent
	1: prox
	2: dist
	3: lateral – left
	4: lateral – right
	5: combination
3. Bulb type	0: absent
	1: pronounced
	2: diffuse
3a. Cones	0: absent
	1: present
3b. Fissures	0: absent
	1: present
3c. Ripples	0: absent
	1: present
3d. Lips	0: absent
	1: present
4. Platform type	0: absent
	1: cortical
	2: simple
	3: facetted (note if accidental)
	4: crushed
5. Preparation	0: absent/indeterminate
	1: simple
	2: shouldered
	3: isolated
6. Distal terminations	0: absent
	1: abrupt
	2: hinge
	3: plunging
	4: feathered
	5: jagged/irregular
7. Dorsal scar pattern	0: absent
	1: longitudinal
	2: opposed
	3: crossed, at 90° to removal axis
7a. Step/hinge	0: absent
	1: present
8. Miscellaneous	
8a. Presence of double bulbs	0: absent
	1: present

8b. Scrubbed preparation		0: absent
		1: present
8c. Hammer marks		0: absent
		1: present
9. Notes		

to address several of the problems facing archaeologists studying the Mesolithic in Scotland, including the need to maximise information retrieval from the chipped stones and not to simply pigeon-hole artefacts, and the need to be able to process enormous numbers of artefacts rapidly.

REFERENCES

Affleck, T. L., Edwards, K. and Clarke, A. 1988. Archaeological and Palynological studies at the mesolithic site of Auchareoch, Isle of Arran. PSAS 118, 37–59.

Finlayson, B. 1989. *A Pragmatic Approach to the Functional Analysis of Chipped Stone Tools.* Unpublished Ph.D. thesis, University of Edinburgh.

Lacaille, A. D. 1954. *The Stone Age in Scotland.* London: Oxford University Press.

McCullagh, R. 1991. Excavations at Newton, Islay. *Glasgow Archaeological Journal* 15, 23–51.

Mellars, P. 1989. Technological changes at the middle–upper Palaeolithic transition: economic social and cognitive perspectives. In Mellars, P. and Stringer, C. (eds), *The Human Revolution.* Edinburgh: EUP, 338–65.

Mercer, J. 1968. Stone tools from a washing-limit deposit of the highest post-glacial transgression, Lealt bay, Isle of Jura. *Proc. Soc. Antiq. Scot.* 100, 1–46.

Mercer, J. 1970. Flint tools from the present tidal zone, Lussa Bay, Isle of Jura, Argyll. *Proc. Soc. Antiq. Scot.* 102, 1–30.

Mercer, J. 1971. A regression-time stone workers camp 33 ft O.D. Lussa River, Isle of Jura. *Proc. Soc. Antiq. Scot.* 103, 1–32.

Mercer, J. 1972. Microlithic and Bronze-Age camps 75–26 ft O.D.N. Carn, Isle of Jura. *Proc. Soc. Antiq. Scot.* 104, 1–22.

Mercer, J. 1974. Glenbatrick Waterhole, a microlithic site on the Isle of Jura. *Proc. Soc. Antiq. Scot.* 105, 9–32.

Mercer, J. 1980. Lussa Wood 1: the late glacial and early post-glacial occupation of Jura. *Proc. Soc. Antiq. Scot.* 110, 1–31.

Mercer, J. and Searight, S. 1986. Glengarrisdale: confirmation of Jura's third microlithic phase. Proc. Soc. Antiq. Scot. 116, 41–55.

Mithen, S. 1990a. Gleann Mor: a Mesolithic site on Islay. *Current Archaeology* 119, 376–7.

Mithen, S. 1990b. New evidence for Mesolithic settlement on Colonsay. *Proc. Soc. Antiq. Scot.* 119, 33–41.

Mithen, S. and Finlayson, B. 1992. Red deer hunters on Colonsay? The implications of Staosnaig for the interpretation of the Oronsay middens. *Proceedings of the Prehistoric Society* 57, 1–8.

Mithen, S., Finlayson, B., Finlay, N. and Lake, M. Excavations at Bolsay Farm, a Mesolithic settlement on Islay. *Cambridge Archaeological Journal* 2, 242–53.

Tixier, J., Inizian, M. L. and Roche, H. 1980. *Préhistoire de la pierre taillée 1: terminologie et technologie.* Valbonne.

Wickham-Jones, C. 1990. *Rhum: Mesolithic and Later Sites at Kinloch, Excavations 1984–86*. Edinburgh: Society of Antiquaries of Scotland, Monograph Series no. 7.

Part 5
Social Change

17

THE TRANSITION TO AGRICULTURE

1 INTRODUCTION

IAN ARMIT AND BILL FINLAYSON

STRUCTURE

This section and the next two address the nature of the transition to agriculture in Scotland and more generally. The first sets out the perspective adopted in summary form, following ideas presented in more detail in a series of previous papers (Armit and Finlayson 1992, 1995; Armit forthcoming; Finlayson 1995). The second deals with perceptions of the Mesolithic and evaluates the mechanisms of culture change associated with the adoption of agriculture. The third deals more specifically with the application of these ideas to aspects of the Scottish Mesolithic and Neolithic.

PERCEPTIONS

In Europe there is a generally accepted division between Mesolithic and Neolithic, the first indigenous and the latter traditionally the product of outside people and ideas. While the start of the Mesolithic is defined by climatic change (the end of the last Ice Age), its end has been defined by economic and social changes – the adoption of a 'Neolithic package'. Such elements as pottery, formal burial monuments, long distance trade, social complexity and sedentism have all been considered to be bundled with agriculture. It has been widely assumed that the social practices of hunter-gatherers and farmers are different and incompatible, with opposed social and symbolic structures (cf. Hodder 1990) and that social transformations of some magnitude must occur to enable the adoption of farming and associated traits (Thomas 1991).

Paralleling this perceived disjunction between the Mesolithic and Neolithic there has been a long established division between the groups of scholars who study the two periods. Research on the Mesolithic has focused on the reconstruction of subsistence economy and human adaptations to environmental conditions, perhaps principally because of the paucity of survival of all but the most utilitarian material culture. The Neolithic, with its wealth of elaborated and durable material culture, has met with the full embrace of post-processualism, carrying on long traditions of concern with the meaning and nature of social and symbolic practice. Work on Neolithic subsistence has been of late a rather marginal aspect of the discipline and has seldom been framed in terms of its relationship to earlier, non-farming practices.

The fixed division of labour between Mesolithic and Neolithic specialists has encouraged the tacit belief that the Neolithic represents a new starting point for European prehistory and that later prehistorians need not concern themselves with the 'Mesolithic prelude'. Divergent research priorities have encouraged the acceptance of models in which society and economy are assumed to have changed in unison as part of a Neolithic 'package', whether that change is initiated by new people or by environmental pressures. Recent post-processual analyses have perpetuated this apparently clear-cut division. Thomas, for example, has suggested that the Neolithic was 'an integrated set of cultural media and practices which served to promote and reproduce a particular way of thinking about the world' (1991: 18).

UNWRAPPING THE PACKAGE

Re-examination of the adoption of the various traits associated with the transition to agriculture in different parts of Europe has shown up a wide range of variation (Armit and Finlayson 1992). Indigenous societies seem to have assimilated those media and practices that were not only available from contacts with neighbouring groups but which also had a perceived use within existing social strategies (Armit and Finlayson 1995). This suggests that the transition across Europe would have been highly fragmented and dependent on existing social practices in different areas.

We have therefore argued that there was no pan-European movement of a unitary cultural package. Rather than displacing indigenous practices, the cultural traits originally associated with agriculture or derived from agricultural practice provided new means of symbolic expression for Mesolithic groups. Because of the diversity of the European Mesolithic, the transition to agriculture varied markedly both in its nature and its rate.

In the traditional framework the spread of farming could be more or less equated with the spread of new peoples. Thus the study of this movement of economic ideas and practices became the central concern of scholars dealing with this period. Long after the eclipse of the wider diffusionist paradigm, the study of the Mesolithic/Neolithic transition in Europe has retained the spread of farming as its focus. We would argue that a more appropriate approach now is to focus on the transformations undergone by individual indigenous societies of which the adoption of agriculture was but one part.

REFERENCES

Armit, I. (forth.). Sedentism and the transition to agriculture in northern and western Europe. In Fletcher, R. (ed.), *Sedentism*. Papers presented at the 3rd World Archaeological Congress, New Delhi 1994.

Armit, I. and Finlayson, B. 1995. Social strategies and economic change: pottery in context. In Barnett, B. and Hoopes, J. (eds), *The Emergence of Pottery*. Washington: Smithsonian Institution Press.

Finlayson, B. 1995. Complexity in the Mesolithic of the western Scottish seaboard. In Fischer, A. (ed.), *Man, Sea and the Mesolithic*. Oxford: Oxbow Books, 261–4.

Hodder, I. 1990. *The Domestication of Europe*. Cambridge: Cambridge University Press.

Thomas, J. 1991. *Re-thinking the Neolithic*. Cambridge: Cambridge University Press.

Hodder, I. 1990. *The Domestication of Europe*. Cambridge: Cambridge University Press.

Thomas, J. 1991. *Re-thinking the Neolithic*. Cambridge: Cambridge University Press.

2 THE BASIS FOR CHANGE

BILL FINLAYSON

INTRODUCTION

Recent developments in European archaeology have increasingly suggested that the transition between a Mesolithic, hunter-gatherer, and a Neolithic, agricultural, economy may have been a more gradual transformation than was previously thought (Armit and Finlayson 1992, Zvelebil 1994). Most such considerations have focused on economic issues, or the possibility of a survival of developed or complex hunter-gatherer Mesolithic society (Rowley-Conwy 1986), while studies of social patterns have tended to concentrate on the differences between the two lifestyles rather than examine the way that change occurs. This paper examines the need to reconsider some preconceptions concerning both the Mesolithic and the Neolithic. It will go on to discuss some of the mechanisms and processes of change.

PRECONCEPTIONS: PACKAGE CULTURE

In our introduction we listed a number of the common perceptions of the Mesolithic–Neolithic divide. There is an historic background to the gulf between the two periods in western Europe. In the nineteenth century it was thought that humans did not occupy the area after the last ice age until the arrival of the first farmers and that there was a distinct hiatus in occupation (de Mortillet 1883). When that hiatus was filled, the term Mesolithic was invented to fill the gap between the Palaeolithic and the Neolithic in Europe (Piette 1895). It did not truly fit the stadial approach followed by first evolutionary models and then Marxist models which both required that the Mesolithic be part of a logical developmental progression (Clark 1980). The European Mesolithic was not seen to fill this role, as farming was clearly understood to originate in the east, as part of a revolutionary total socio-economic package that was brought to the west by colonists. Pre-farming, postglacial societies were therefore not perceived to be on the main trajectory of human development.

This late-nineteenth to early-twentieth century view has now dramatically changed. Today the Mesolithic period appears to be characterised by a dynamic adaptive approach to changing environmental conditions. However, that dynamism is still often perceived as internal to the Mesolithic, caused generally by environmental change as opposed to human innovation, and the period is still often studied in isolation, or as a final adjunct to the Palaeolithic, lacking even the grandeur of Upper Palaeolithic cave art.

In Europe there remains a generally accepted division between Mesolithic and Neolithic, a division between the close of a palaeolithic, hunter-gatherer way of life, and the introduction of farming. The Mesolithic is about hairy men hunting dangerous animals in the forest, while with the Neolithic we move to an open environment, with cleared fields, settlements and a role for women (the importance of gathering, or indeed women in general, has always tended to be underplayed in Europe). While the start of the Mesolithic is defined by climatic change (the end of the last Ice Age), the end has been defined by economic and social changes. Pottery, long distance trade, social stratification and sedentism are all bundled with agriculture to form the Neolithic package. Although the economic component of this change has been emphasised, it has been widely assumed that the social systems of hunter-gatherers and farmers are different and incompatible, with opposed social and symbolic structures (Hodder 1990) and that a social change has to be part of the process (Thomas 1991).

There remains also a division between scholars who study the Mesolithic and earlier periods, and those who study the Neolithic and later. Research in the Mesolithic has focused on reconstructing the subsistence economy and human adaptations to environmental pressures. This explains archaeological interests in anthropological studies of hunter-gatherer subsistence strategies. Research in the Neolithic has focused on human social behaviour. In effect scholars have been considering two separate models of human development. The distinct research priorities of the two fields have maintained the fault line between Mesolithic and Neolithic, which has encouraged an assumption that society and economy change in unison. In our introduction we quote Thomas who has recently suggested that the Neolithic was an integrated cultural and ideological package (Thomas 1991). That package comprised such elements as pottery, formal burial monuments, sedentism, domesticated animals and agriculture.

DESIGNER SOCIETY

We have proposed, in contrast to this view, that the set of media and practices which comprised the Neolithic formed an assemblage of traits, elements of which may have been adopted by Mesolithic populations in the context of their own changing cultures (Armit and Finlayson 1992). Rather than replacing indigenous cultures, material symbols associated with agriculture or derived from agricultural practice provided a new means of symbolic expression for Mesolithic groups, and because of the diversity of European Mesolithic communities, the transition to agriculture varied markedly. Indeed, as Zvelebil has observed, some elements of plant food procurement technology that have conventionally been regarded as Neolithic and agricultural, may long pre-date the Neolithic in western Europe (Zvelebil 1994). Such a phenomenon has become accepted in a Near Eastern context, but as part of the perceived gradual development of agriculture, not as practices within the normal range of hunter-gatherers.

Perhaps the best place to reconsider conventional stereotypes of the Mesolithic is with hunting. Since 1976, when Clarke published his well known paper on the Mesolithic in Europe, the point has been made that Mesolithic people did not subsist on meat alone (Clarke 1976). Given our latitude, meat will have been an important food source, but it was not the only one. This is an archaeological truism, but the microlith as a projectile element remains a powerful symbol for the period, indeed Rozoy argues that hunting with bows forms the common basis for the period (Rozoy 1989).

I have argued elsewhere, on the basis of use-wear traces for a wider range of functions for microliths, and this is crucial, as it changes our understanding of both their economic role and their emblematic status (Finlayson and Mithen 1995). This analysis is supported by other use-wear studies, such as that by Dumont (1988). The identification of a range of functions for microliths questions basic assumptions about who made and used what are traditionally seen as a masculine tool, as well as the attribution of site function on the basis of a single artefact category. It certainly affects the concept of the microlithic symbolising an epoch of bow hunters. Indeed, microliths represent a very small part of the real material culture of Mesolithic people. It is quite likely that it was the organic component that distinguished them as different tools, and which held emblematic significance. It is another archaeological truism that we have lost the bulk of material culture, but that we, continue to overstress the importance of microliths and stone tools because we have so little else.

CHANGE AND VARIABILITY

Crucial to archaeology is the study of change over time. Unfortunately, what we often seem to do best is to characterise static phenomena, with sharp breaks from one period to another. Within the Mesolithic, this is most apparent in attempts to identify regional resource exploitation patterns, amalgamating all the sites belonging to a few thousand years onto one map, to show the different uses to which different parts of the landscape might have been put – shell fish by the sea, salmon on rivers, and deer in the hills. This produces a static model of society and assumes an unchanging Mesolithic. It equally assumes a continent occupied by an endless repeated pattern of mixed resource exploitation.

This static model has been bolstered by the rather naive use of ethnographic studies, searching for close analogies with societies living in similar environmental niches. Again, this simply builds static models, the perfect hunter-gatherer society for each environment. Examples of this type of ethnographic study are not hard to find, and frequently lead to the development of generalised rules where, for example, hunter-gatherers at different latitudes may be expected to hunt more by building traps than by active hunting (Torrence 1989). This attempt to define ideal societies in the present and locate them in the past negates the value of conducting archaeological research, as it precludes change over time. We should not expect to find such static societies in the past, but rather a constantly changing pattern. This is not to say that all hunter-gatherer societies were somewhere on an evolutionary track to agriculture; far from it, change does not imply linear progress, but simply that society was not static.

There is a rather different source of comparative data, again mostly gathered by anthropologists, but collected with a rather different mission. There is considerable interest now in studying the adaptive processes amongst traditional societies, funded by the development agencies to assist them in 'improving' traditional economies. This provides information on change, rather than on how an ideal hunter-gatherer or early farmer society ought to behave.

Anthropological evidence suggests that neither the hunter-gatherer or early farming social organisations would have been stable, but may indeed have swung from one economy to the other and back again. Ellen has noted that some groups may practice agriculture only intermittently once it is available to them, and that hunter-gatherer/agriculturalist labels are exaggerated extremes (Ellen 1995). This pattern of variation from one economy to the other is perhaps best known in south-east Asia, but it was also recorded in north America, amongst such groups as the Illinois. The most frequent source of hunter-gatherer analogies in archaeological literature, the San of southern Africa, are another example of people who have practised agriculture in the recent past.

THE PROCESS OF CHANGE

There are a number of problems associated with most recent models of change from hunter-gatherer to farmer:

1. *Physical Environment:* There has been too great a stress on environmental factors causing change (Blankholm 1987). The adoption of agriculture has been interpreted as imposed by environmental forces, for example in southern Scandinavia, where the oyster population collapsed, following salinity changes in the Baltic (Rowley-Conwy 1983, 1985). This ignores the significance of society in the change and does not explain the adoption of agriculture away from the coast.

2. *Economy:* Hunting and gathering groups are only considered in terms of their economy. For example, maritime Mesolithic economies are seen as resistant to farming because of the wealth of natural resources available to them (Rowley-Conwy 1983), and because of their investment in economic specialisation (Zvelebil 1990). In this model, the adoption of agriculture is eventually imposed by economic stresses. This is a model

favoured by many Mesolithic researches, as it falls within the general focus on economic reconstruction. It has also been favoured by many Neolithic researchers, who have focused on the revolutionary impact of the economic farming package.

3. *Society and Ideology:* Where Mesolithic society is discussed, it is perceived as a force against agriculture, in opposition to Neolithic modes of thought (Hodder 1990). This model is most common amongst Neolithic researchers, as it falls within their focus on social issues.

The linking factor between these problems is that they are all based on a view that change in the Mesolithic is always directly caused by economic necessity, regardless of whether that economic necessity is originally caused by external factors such as the environment, the benefits of agriculture, or population stress. There is little room in these models for human decision making.

Indonesian anthroplogists have been studying the internal colonisation of their archipelago by widely different groups, with different social and economic backgrounds and examining which groups are successful in adapting to their new environments. They have observed that the sociocultural background of people is fundamental and that the economic strategies they adopt are not necessarily 'clear cut, mutually exclusive alternatives' (Oyhus 1995). While the physical environment presents restrictions, the economy is culturally mediated, and it is culture that determines success or failure in colonisation. Within each environmental constraint, there are options that can be selected. Some may not, in the long term, be as effective as others, and there may be a degree of normalisation over time and space, but societies are rarely faced with only one possible option. The natural environment does not determine, adaptation to it is determined by the existing culture. Environmental pressures cannot be translated into social and economic change without appropriate social mechanisms. The value of agricultural improvements may appear clear to an aid worker, for example, but their value has also to be perceived by the recipient group. Even when development is not only urgently required for survival, but is supported by massive infusions of outside money, it will not occur unless individual farmers decide it will. Economic rationality is rarely the sole or even the foremost consideration and subsistence practices become inextricably entwined with social practice and the wider culture of the community. No economic decision can be made without reference to its cultural context (Amerasinghe and Vithanadurage 1974). These observations have important implications for the way we view economic change in the Mesolithic.

A simple dichotomous model of hunter-gatherer and early farming societies is commonplace in archaeology. Mesolithic societies are characterised as egalitarian, mobile, non-territorial and passive, while Neolithic societies are considered as hierarchical, sedentary, territorial and active (Bender 1985). This is despite an overlap with the Neolithic in western Europe of at least several hundred years. Because of the presumed colonisation of Europe by farmers and its associated demise of Mesolithic populations, the interaction of final Mesolithic populations with the presumed incoming Neolithic populations has not been greatly considered until recent years. There has been an underlying assumption that economic behaviour is closely tied to social behaviour, that the social organisation of farmers is not only different to that of hunter-gatherers, but that it is opposite.

This linkage between subsistence economy and social organisation has recently become increasingly questioned (cf. Armit and Finlayson 1992). In the Ertebolle and the eastern Baltic sedentism, social stratification and pottery appear without associated agriculture. The east Baltic Neolithic is defined by pottery and polished stone tools, and clearly not by any change in subsistence strategy (Rimantiene 1992). In southern France it appears that exotic plants (lentils) and animals (caprids) (Erroux 1980, Lewthwaite 1986, Vaquer 1980), both elements of agriculture, were adopted without social change. Equally, the methods of agriculture, especially in plant husbandry, may have been independently developed and applied to indigenous resources in the Mesolithic (Zvelebil 1994). It therefore appears possible for either economic elements to be adopted without any associated social elements, or equally for social structures to be adopted without the economy. This accords with Ingold's observation that it is possible for two different systems to use similar technologies and similar work organisations while their respective social relations are diametrically opposed, and cannot therefore be deduced from the interaction between environment and technology (Ingold 1980).

Sedentism, another former hallmark of the Neolithic, has also been observed beyond conventional farming societies. Rowley-Conwy has discussed the potential for sedentism in the Ertebolle. But sedentism has more facets then simple residential permanence. Bender has separated this residential sedentism from ritual permanence, noting north American archaeological societies who have seasonal mobility, but also have large permanent ritual complexes (Bender 1985). A similar situation may have occurred in western Scotland during the Neolithic, where ritual monuments such as burial cairns suggests ritual permanence, while the settlement evidence does not indicate a fully sedentary lifestyle (Armit and Finlayson 1992, Armit forthcoming). The reasons for permanence of any kind must be considered; is it for convenience, the need to stay and guard crops, or is there perhaps a need to identify territories and resources for long-term access? In any event, sedentism does not necessarily imply the appearance of agricultural villages.

SOCIETY AND CHANGE

The context of decision making cannot be seen as purely economic. Traditional means of subsistence are a way of life rather than a business. Subsistence activities, whether hunting or farming, are part of family life, and as such are conditioned by that family life. Hagan, working for the Ministry of Agriculture in Nepal noted that 'Farmwork and some kinds of management decisions, [are] often are shared among husband, wife and other members of the family unit.' (Hagan 1971: 3). These characteristics of farming can be argued to be part of not just the farming way of life, but of subsistence economy societies generally, equally shared with most hunter-gatherers. No economic decision can be made without reference to its cultural context.

Even within hunter-gatherer societies, there will have been complex social relationships. Evidence from the 'Obanian' suggests that in western Scotland a stratified society may have been developing before contact with the Neolithic (Armit and Finlayson 1992, Finlayson 1995). The arrival of the farming societies in Europe will have provided further potential means of status differentiation. Ritual monuments and pottery could be adopted by hunter-gatherer groups. Even aspects of the agricultural economy, such as domesticated animals, could be adopted, as suggested for southern France. Rowley-Conwy's concept of complex hunters is a reminder that social organisations will have existed within hunter-gatherer groups, and that the primitive communism of the egalitarian band cannot be seen as a universal model for hunter-gatherer society.

The presence of social institutions, such as age groups, has an important function in change, as people who are members of organisations are more likely to be able to participate in decision making and differing local institutions are likely to have had a profound effect on patterns of change within their area.

It has been noted that change is most likely to occur where it can be absorbed with the minimum of effort, where change is not revolutionary, but fits not only the needs of a society and is compatible with the current situation. This compatibility is more important even than the economic importance of the innovation (Amerasinghe and Vithanadurage 1974). It means congruence with a culture understood as the total way of life of a people (Millar 1990).

The insights from work on developing societies supply useful information concerning the adoption of change. It is likely to occur initially on a very localised basis, dependent on the decisions of numerous individual family units, modified by wider group concerns. The elements of change that are adopted are likely to be compatible with existing, known, needs and to be congruent with the wider culture of the group. Mesolithic societies would not have selected individual elements consciously but simply absorbed elements that were congruent with their own local culture, and were compatible with previously identified needs. In such a situation, the apparent initial diversity in the early Neolithic in Scotland and the wider variation across Europe becomes explicable (Armit and Finlayson 1992).

RESISTANCE TO CHANGE

Part of our examination of change has to consider resistance to change. There is clear evidence that the rapid expansion of farming associated with the LBK culture slowed down in northern and western Europe. For centuries after the establishment of farming groups in inland areas, indigenous Mesolithic populations continued to thrive and develop. Various ideas have been put forward to explain the resistance of hunter-gatherers to farming. These range from the investment of hunter-gatherers in specialised economic practices (Zvelebil 1990) to the ideological opposition to agriculture proposed by Hodder (Hodder 1990).

In Hodder's view it was initially impossible for the Ertebolle to adopt farming because of its association with the alien ideology of farming groups: an ideology centred on the domestic sphere which Hodder has characterised as the domus (Hodder 1990). We have argued elsewhere that the development of distinctive forms and decoration in Ertebolle pottery clearly does not represent an ideological borrowing and that Ertebolle pottery became an integral part of the Ertebolle symbolic repertoire and was not seen as an alien or exotic product (Armit and Finlayson 1995). The adoption of pottery as an ideological package would have been revolutionary and therefore unlikely, but the adoption of pots as useful containers within the ideological expression of the Ertebolle, as evidenced by the indigenous form and decoration, fits within the model of congruency.

This malleability of cultural meanings has important implications for the adoption of other conventionally Neolithic traits elsewhere in Europe. It means that where aspects of the conventional Neolithic package can be borrowed as useful items and at the same time fit into the existing culture, they are likely to be adopted. This has a significant implication for our identification of so-called Neolithic traits within the Mesolithic. It explains why there is the apparent disassociation between material and economic culture and the complete Neolithic package. In other words, it is in fact more likely for a Mesolithic group to adopt exotic plants such as lentils, if it can do so without having to change its social structure at the same time. If, as Zvelebil has argued, aspects of plant husbandry were already practised in the Mesolithic, such an adoption would be relatively easy, would fill a perceived need (for a more productive plant), and would be congruent with what was already being undertaken.

CONCLUSIONS

Research on the European Mesolithic has shown it to be part of a wide phenomenon encompassing Europe and the Middle East. It is far from a blind alley, but a period when, in both Europe and the Middle East as a whole, society was changing rapidly and apparently producing a host of local adaptations. Some of these adaptations in the Middle East led directly to what we recognise as farming and the Neolithic. In Europe adaptations to the postglacial environment led to an intensive non-farming exploitation of the environment, notably on the western fringe of Europe, and most markedly of all in southern Scandinavia, where particularly good evidence survives. In the eastern Baltic, as well as in southern Scandinavia, Zvelebil has argued that an investment in a specialised intensive economy caused a resistance to the adoption of farming that lasted for a very long time (Zvelebil 1990).

Our perceptions of Mesolithic society have been changing dramatically in recent years from the notion of egalitarian hunter-gatherer societies to a far more complex and varied situation. It is now beginning to appear that the Mesolithic in Europe comprised a range of economic and social adaptations, none of them necessarily stable. Neither Mesolithic nor Neolithic represent monolithic entities, but internally varied and varying patterns of behaviour, with substantial overlaps between them.

REFERENCES

Amerasinghe, N. and Vithanadurage, N. 1974. Some socio-economic determinants of the adoption of improved management practices in paddy production. *Journal of the National Agricultural Society of Ceylon (Sri Lanka)* (12) 1–17.

Armit, I. and Finlayson, B. 1992. Hunter-gatherers transformed: the transition to agriculture in northern and western Europe. *Antiquity* 66, 664–76.

Bender, B. 1985. In Douglas Price, T. and Brown, J. A. (eds), *Prehistoric Hunter-Gatherers: The Emergence of Cultural Complexity*. Studies in Archaeology. Orlando: Academic Press.

Blankholm, H. P. 1987. Late Mesolithic hunter-gatherers and the transition to farming in southern Scandinavia. In Rowley-Conwy, P., Zvelebil, M. and Blankholm, H. P. (eds), *Mesolithic Northwest Europe: Recent Trends*. Sheffield University, 155–62.

Clark, J. G. D. 1980. *Mesolithic Prelude: The Palaeolithic-Neolithic Transition in Old World Prehistory*. Edinburgh: Edinburgh University Press.

Clarke, D. 1976. Mesolithic Europe, the economic basis. In Sieveking, G. de G. et al. (eds), *Problems in Social and Economic Archaeology*. London: Duckworth, 449–81.

Dumont, J. V. 1988. *A Microwear Analysis of Selected Artefact Types from the Mesolithic Sites of Star Carr and Mount Sandel*. Oxford: BAR, British Series 187(i).

Ellen, ?. 1995. *Models of Subsistence and Ethnobiological Knowledge: Between Extraction and Cultivation in Southeast Asia*, proceedings of the *Pithecanthropus Centennial 1893–1993*. Leiden.

Erroux, J. 1980. Les graines préhistoriques de la grotte de l'Abeurador. *Les Dossiers de l'Archéologie* 44, 20–1.

Finlayson, B. 1995. Complexity in the Mesolithic of the western Scottish seaboard. In Fischer, A. (ed.), *Man, Sea and the Mesolithic*.

Finlayson, B. and Mithen, S. 1995. Microliths as projectile points? A case study from western Scotland. In Knecht, H. (ed.), Anaheim: Society of American Archaeologists.

Hagan, A. R. 1971. Suggestions for farm management research in Nepal. *EAPD* Staff paper no. 7. Kathmandu: HMGN, Ministry of Food and Agriculture.

Hodder, I. 1990. *The Domestication of Europe*. Oxford: Basil Blackwell.

Ingold, T. 1980. *Hunters, Pastoralists and Ranchers: Reindeer Economies and Their Transformations*. Cambridge: CUP.

Lewthwaite, J. 1986. The transition to food production, a Mediterranean perspective. In Zvelebil, M. (ed.), *Hunters in Transition; Mesolithic Societies of Temperate Eurasia and Their Transition to Farming; New Directions in Archaeology*. Cambridge: Cambridge University Press, 53–66.

Miller, C. J. 1990. *Decision Making in Village Nepal.* Kathmandu: Sahayogi Press.

Oyhus, ?. 1995. Proceedings of the *Pithecanthropus Centennial 1893–1993.* Leiden:

Piette, E. 1895. Hiatus et lacune: vestiges de la période de transition dans la grotte du Mas D'Azil. *Bull. Soc. Anthrop. de Paris* 27–8.

Rimantiene, R. 1992. Neolithic hunter-gatherers at Sventoji in Lithuania. *Antiquity* 66, 367–76.

Rowley-Conwy, P. 1983. Sedentary hunters: the Ertebølle example. In Bailey, G. (ed.), *Hunter-Gatherer Economy.* Cambridge: Cambridge University Press, 111–26.

Rowley-Conwy, P. 1985. The origin of agriculture in Denmark: a review of some theories. *Journal of Danish Archaeology* 4, 188–95.

Rowley-Conwy, P. 1986. Between cave painters and crop planters: aspects of the temperate Europe forest Mesolithic. In Zvelebil, M. (ed.), *Hunters in Transition.* Cambridge: Cambridge University Press, 17–32.

Rozoy, J.-G. 1989. The revolution of the Bowmen in Europe. In Bonsall, C. (ed.), *The Mesolithic in Europe: Papers Presented at the Third International Symposium, Edinburgh 1985.* Edinburgh: John Donald, 13–28.

Thomas, J. 1991. *Rethinking the Neolithic.* Cambridge: Cambridge University Press.

Torrence, R. 1989. A cost-benefit study of functionally similar tools. In Torrence, R. (ed.), *Time, Energy and Stone Tools.* Cambridge: Cambridge University Press.

Vaquer, J. 1980. De la cueillette à l'agriculture: la grotte de l'Abeurador. *Les Dossiers de l'Archéologie* 44, 18–19.

Zvelebil, M. 1990. Economic intensification and postglacial hunter-gatherers in north temperate Europe. In Bonsall, C. (ed.), *The Mesolithic in Europe.* Edinburgh: John Donald, 80–8.

Zvelebil, M. 1994. Plant use in the Mesolithic and its role in the transition to farming. *Proceedings of the Prehistoric Society* 60, 35–74.

3 SCOTLAND

IAN ARMIT

The previous two sections have examined the nature of culture change in the period when farming came to be adopted in northern and western Europe. This contribution deals specifically with aspects of the Mesolithic–Neolithic transition in Scotland in the context of these wider perspectives. Specifically it examines the nature of the settlement evidence for this period and the role of pottery production as a case study in the adoption of novel cultural material by indigenous communities.

SETTLEMENT EVIDENCE

There remains a set of archaeological expectations concerning the nature of Mesolithic and Neolithic settlement remains. The former are perceived as transient camps, perhaps annually revisited but by no means central in themselves to the economic lives or to the ideologies of hunter-gatherer communities. By contrast, Neolithic communities are often perceived to have regarded the settlement as the central ideological metaphor for their world and to have concentrated much of their energies on consecrating and formalising their little patch of land. Hodder's concept of the domus provides a useful recent statement of this latter position (Hodder 1990). Despite a series of challenges to such assumptions in a northern and western European context (e.g. in southern England where Thomas has argued for more mobile Neolithic communities (1991) and in southern Scandinavia where interpretations of Mesolithic sedentism have emerged (e.g. Rowley-Conwy 1983, 1985)), such perceptions still underpin both the structuring of archaeological research and the interpretation of individual sites.

The reality of settlement remains in northern and western, if not central and southern, Europe is rather different and serves to blur rather than strengthen these perceptual divides. Much of the problem in Scotland has come from the concentration of Neolithic settlement research in Orkney where elaborate and often monumental settlements, such as Skara Brae and Barnhouse, provide a wealth of information on Neolithic social and spatial organisation. But Orkney cannot be said to be typical of the remainder of the Scottish Neolithic. Although sporadic instances of what appear to be substantial and monumental residences do occur, as at Balbridie (Ralston 1982), on the majority of Neolithic settlements substantial buildings are no less fugitive than on hunter-gatherer sites.

An example of this phenomenon is Kinloch in Rhum excavated by Caroline Wickham-Jones (1990). Aside from its wealth of Mesolithic settlement remains this site also produced evidence for Neolithic occupation. The features attributable to this latter phase were remarkably similar to those of the preceding Mesolithic; a mix of shallow pits and scoops with no identifiable structural form. Yet the conclusion was that while the Mesolithic remains were representative of the hunter-gatherer settlement, the Neolithic remains must be peripheral to a more substantial settlement outside the excavated areas (Wickham-Jones 1990). The assumption, in a Scottish context (derived ultimately from Orkney) that Neolithic settlements will be formal and permanent affairs with substantial, possibly monumental buildings, has determined specific site interpretations in numerous other instances where such structural evidence is not present – this has been a particular notable feature, for example, in the history of research on the Hebridean Neolithic (cf. Armit 1992).

THE HEBRIDEAN NEOLITHIC

The settlement sites of the Hebridean Neolithic exemplify a regional development quite distinct from that of Orkney and perhaps more akin to wider northern and western European patterns. The super-imposition of numerous Neolithic domestic buildings in the confined space of the islet of Eilean Domhnuill in Loch Olabhat, North Uist, demonstrated that the individually slight collections of stone alignments, areas of burning, pits and scoops found elsewhere in the

Hebrides – as at Eilean an Tighe (Scott 1950) and Northton (Simpson 1976) – should indeed be regarded as the remains of Neolithic houses (Armit 1992).

The recently published excavations at Carinish, also in North Uist, further showed what could be expected of such a settlement where spatial confines were less restrictive than on a small islet like Eilean Domhnuill (Crone 1993). The series of pits, isolated hearths and wall alignments associated with a profusion of Neolithic pottery at Carinish were reminiscent of the Neolithic phases from Kinloch, although, in the light of the evidence from Olabhat, there was no suggestion that this material related to a more substantial settlement off-site.

The nature of the evidence for Hebridean Neolithic settlement, particularly when the broadly contemporary monumentality of funerary architecture is considered, raises a whole range of questions regarding the degree of sedentism and the nature of the contemporary economy (cf. Armit 1992).

POTTERY

Since pottery is a conventionally Neolithic or later trait its mere presence in a British context is sufficient for an early prehistoric site to be described as Neolithic. Pottery thus provides a useful case study in the interpretation of the adoption and subsequent development of a classic piece of Neolithic material culture, part of the ideological package supposedly associated with farming.

SITE CONTINUITY OR RE-USE IN SCOTLAND

Many sites around Scotland contain both Mesolithic and Neolithic cultural material. Kinloch, for example, yielded around 300 sherds of Neolithic pottery as against around 100 000 lithic fragments (both Mesolithic and Neolithic), from contexts which, as we have seen, are otherwise largely indistinguishable from those of the Mesolithic occupation (Wickham-Jones 1990). Given our understanding of the nature of western Scottish Neolithic settlement there is no reason to believe that the Neolithic occupation of Kinloch was formalised or constituted in any way particularly distinct from the earlier occupation. As argued above, the nature of the deposits is reminiscent, given varying degrees of preservation, of sites like Carinish and ultimately Eilean Domhnuill.

There are a significant number of other sites yielding similar evidence either of continuity into the period of pottery use or of coincidental re-occupation of former sites. Ulva Cave for example has yielded sherds of Unstan Ware from the upper levels of a midden otherwise of Mesolithic character and with Mesolithic dates from its lower levels (Bonsall et al. 1989). Recent excavations at Spurryhillock near Stonehaven produced a pit containing a classic Unstan bowl in association with much earlier pits containing Mesolithic cultural material (Alexander 1993). Excavations at Bolsay Farm on Islay have produced Neolithic pottery as well as a Mesolithic lithic assemblage (Mithen et al. 1992). Numerous other juxtapositions of conventionally Neolithic and Mesolithic material from earlier excavations lie largely unacknowledged and uncollated in the pages of Scottish archaeological journals. The microlithic flint scatter at Lussa Wood 1 on Jura, for example, produced several non-microlithic finds including a chip from a polished axe of Antrim porcelainite and a leaf-shaped arrowhead (Mercer 1974: 77), while excavations at Lealt Bay, also on Jura, produced leaf-shaped arrowheads in association with microliths (Mercer 1968: 1). The significance of pottery in the Oronsay shell middens has also been little discussed.

In other cases conventionally Mesolithic cultural assemblages and activity areas extend well into what ought to be the Neolithic. At Carding Mill Bay, for example, a series of dates carries the occupation, with associated Obanian artefacts, later than 4 000 cal. BC, interleaving with Scottish Early Neolithic dates (Connock et al. 1992). The shell middens on the Forth, at Nether Kinneil, Inveravon and Polmonthill, again suggest continuity of economic activity, with the presence of domesticates at the former showing the adoption of farming traits (Sloan 1982, 1984).

Throughout Scotland, then, there is clear and recurring evidence for the appearance of pottery on sites already in use by hunter-gatherer communities. Ultimately in all such cases of juxtaposition we use the simple presence of pottery to bring down the whole weight of Neolithic ideology – farming, sedentism, monumentality and the rest – rather than address the nature of the evidence directly. Despite this, as we have seen, the evidence for slight, transient, Neolithic buildings at sites in the Hebrides, where a reasonable range have now been identified, shows that many Neolithic communities lived in settlements difficult to distinguish on a structural basis from those of the Mesolithic. The presence of Neolithic activity on otherwise Mesolithic sites may therefore be of much more significance than its conventional interpretation – casual re-use of earlier sites for activities peripheral to a stable farming economy – would suggest.

Does this evidence then mean that such sites were 'taken over' by Neolithic farmers? Or does it instead indicate that pottery production was adopted by indigenous Mesolithic communities? The consistent pattern of association of Mesolithic and Early Neolithic cultural material certainly merits closer study, particularly when it is appreciated that no such consistent re-use or continuity of settlement or activity sites is apparent between the Early and Later Neolithic. Grooved Ware, for example, is seldom found in association with earlier styles other than on prominent and long-lived ritual sites (cf. list of ceramic associations in Kinnes 1985: 49–50).

It has been argued elsewhere that the presence of conventionally Neolithic cultural traits cannot be equated necessarily with a radically new ideology or even with a distinct and quantifiable break from Mesolithic economic strategies (Armit and Finlayson 1992, 1995 and above). The possibility that Neolithic traits were adopted in a more staggered way, perhaps with pottery as a relatively early adoption, appears not to have been seriously entertained in a Scottish context.

POTTERY AND FOOD PRODUCTION

There is a great deal of evidence to suggest that there is no necessary connection between pottery and farming. Just as farmers need not have used pottery, as with the Pre-Pottery Neolithic of the Near East, so hunter-gatherers could and did adopt ceramics without any apparent commitment to other components of the Neolithic ideological 'package'. The case of the Ertebolle in southern Scandinavia is well known and is perhaps the most directly relevant to the situation in Scotland. Ertebolle groups adopted pottery manufacture when it became available through contact with farming groups. Yet the forms and decoration employed were distinct and owed little to outside influence. Clearly the use of pottery was considered congruent with existing social practices once mediated by the application of indigenous forms and motifs.

The same process can be seen elsewhere. In Africa, for example, pottery manufacture and use spread entirely independently of food production after its initial introduction (Close 1995). Similarly in northern and western Europe once the technology was understood, and this was presumably initiated through contacts with other groups, we might expect pottery to be widely disseminated and adopted. Ceramics appear to have represented a medium offering considerable potential for individual design and embellishment that was congruent within a wide range of communities and could easily lose its associations with alien economies and ideologies.

Seen in this wider context it is hard to understand why the occurrence of pottery on otherwise Mesolithic sites in Scotland, and indeed Britain as a whole, is taken to indicate the presence of food-producing Neolithic communities.

The answer may partly lie in deep-seated archaeological attitudes to the social complexity of hunter-gatherers in Britain. The study of the Neolithic tends to focus on symbolic behaviour, be it funerary, in the construction of tombs and other monuments, or in the symbolism of the home. The study of the Mesolithic tends to focus on issues of economy and technology and the likelihood of indigenous adoption of pottery within hunter-gatherer economies has been scarcely considered in a Scottish or British context.

Much of the problem is due to simple factors of survival. Pottery was not the first material available to indigenous populations in Scotland that was able to carry symbolic messages and references through its malleability of form and decoration. Recent studies have shown the likelihood that elaborate hide clothing, for example, was manufactured in Mesolithic Scotland (Finlayson 1995). However, in the continued absence of such preserved organic remains from Mesolithic sites in Scotland, pottery is the first such material that is available to archaeologists interested in the analysis of symbolic behaviour. Thus its appearance has been equated with the end of one period of archaeological study and the start of another. The nature of the transformations that led from one to the other have attracted little attention. But the appearance of pottery need not signal any sudden upsurge of symbolic behaviour; it simply makes the material residue of such behaviour available to archaeologists for the first time.

Early pottery in Scotland is characterised by several diverse regional styles with considerable stylistic variation and a wide variety of decorative motifs, albeit sharing a recurring series of basic forms. Such styles as Unstan Ware, Rothesay/Achnacree Ware, Hebridean Ware and Beacharra Ware are all quite distinct though apparently broadly contemporary, regionally-focussed variants (Fig. 17.1). Of course it is impossible to know how to equate archaeological typological distinctions with the original perceptions of the makers of these vessels but nonetheless, at a broad scale, pottery was highly diversified and well-suited to its role in the material construction of social identity.

Barnett, studying the early Neolithic pottery of the west Mediterranean (1990), has recognised similar regionally focused, diversified pottery types which he has termed 'delimiting' styles. These would have been closely identified with the expression of the ethnicity of their makers and users. In addition Barnett has identified another stratum of pottery production which he has termed 'unifying' styles, which were much more uniform and which were exchanged over wide distances and played a rather different social role. In Scotland it appears that the Early Neolithic witnesses the appearance of a set of delimiting styles which appear to exist in isolation with no widespread or unifying styles to represent other aspects of production and exchange. Indeed it does not appear that pottery in Scotland was traded or exchanged over significant distances as Barnett has suggested for the west Mediterranean unifying styles, but rather that it was a means of cultural expression for rather more inward-looking communities.

Such widespread variation of pottery in the Early Neolithic has always sat uneasily with the notion of rapid population movement introducing pottery along with the rest of the Neolithic lifestyle into Scotland (Armit and Finlayson 1995). Surely such a process would be expected to produce initial uniformity, perhaps with later divergence. Similarly, had a Neolithic ideology been imposed as an indivisible package such rapid diversification would seem even less likely. There is little room in such models for the creative input of the indigenous hunter-gatherers who appear instead to have quietly acquiesced to the new ideologies associated with food production. It is interesting in this context that the styles of Neolithic pottery in southern England appear to relate closely to 'style zones' of lithic production in the preceding Mesolithic (Bradley 1984: 12).

The diverse pottery styles of the Early Neolithic make more sense when considered as part of the piecemeal adoption of conventionally Neolithic traits within active and complex indigenous communities. The effects of increased economic intensification, and particularly incipient sedentism, on language have been

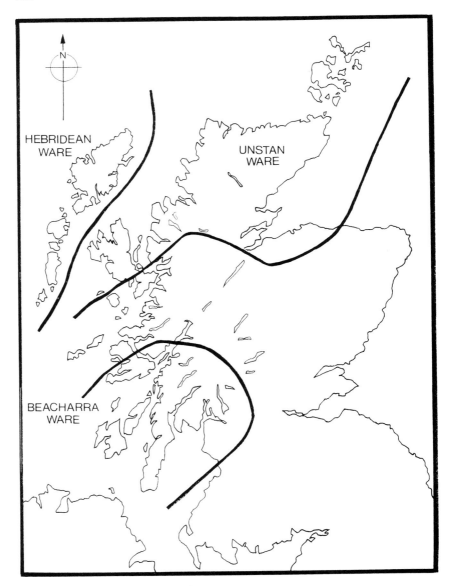

Fig. 17.1. Scottish Neolithic pottery styles, a.

discussed recently by Robb (1993). Following Robb's interpretation sedentism has a range of effects on society connected principally with the reduction of direct inter-group contacts and the need to forge and promote a greater sense of group identity. In linguistic terms these two trends would lead to a period of language formation with group identity and relations of inclusion and exclusion being expressed through forms and manners of speech (ibid.). This linguistic process has its material culture correlates. In essence Robb is seeing language as a form of material culture, used in the negotiation of social relationships, in much the same way as material culture in general is increasingly seen by archaeologists. The same processes of reduced inter-group contact and increased awareness of group identity would have led to a greater diversity of other aspects of material culture. Pottery, as a highly malleable and ubiquitous medium, prominent in social contacts involving food exchange and consumption would be exactly the sort of material in which such processes would find expression. Where complex indigenous hunter-gatherers were increasingly intensifying their economic practices and were involved in a range of complex social relationships we would expect that pottery, once the technology was available, would be adopted fairly readily, being congruent with the existing social context. In such a situation we would expect that the pottery thus produced would exhibit wide variation and that such variation would be regionally based.

Early pottery in Scotland is one of a range of material cultural forms that fits into this picture of indigenous intensification and social complexity. The diversity of funerary architecture is another. There have even been interpretations suggesting totemism among the chambered tomb users of Orkney that would suggest another, perhaps more explicit means of ethnic or tribal identification operating on a more local level than the more archaeologically visible items (Hedges 1985). Various forms of body decoration may represent a further dimension difficult to retrieve archaeologically (Simpson this volume). Following Robb's thesis, presumably language too would have diversified rapidly at this time.

The role of funerary architecture is particularly interesting for not only does it appear to be highly regionalised and diversified, perhaps paralleling the delimiting styles of contemporary pottery, but the monumentality of the architecture greatly overshadows the slight and transient settlements of the period. The possibility of a form of ritual as opposed to residential permanence developing in Scotland, following Bender's interpretation of the North American data has not been explicitly considered (Bender 1985). When social and economic change in the Late Mesolithic and Early Neolithic is seen as internally driven by indigenous communities this possibility gains considerably more credence and would repay more detailed study.

In the Later Neolithic pottery styles become increasingly 'national' in distribution with the spread of Grooved Ware (Fig. 17.2) and even 'international' with the adoption of beakers. Interestingly this convergence of aspects of material culture, which appears to be associated with the development of more outward-

Fig. 17.2. Scottish Neolithic pottery styles, b.

looking authorities, deriving much of their status from external contacts, parallels closely the linguistic convergence postulated by Robb for the Later Neolithic and Bronze Age in Europe (cf. Robb 1993, Armit and Finlayson 1995).

DISCUSSION

The purpose of this group of papers has been to stress the active role played in the Mesolithic–Neolithic transition in Scotland and elsewhere in northern and western Europe by indigenous hunter-gatherers. Both theoretical considerations and empirical data conspire to deny the existence of an indivisible Neolithic cultural and ideological package. Throughout northern and western Europe the Later Mesolithic seems to have been a period of economic intensification carried out at varying paces by a diverse range of hunter-gatherer communities. Once contact with food producers was established those items of material culture that were congruent within existing social strategies could spread rapidly and be absorbed and modified in new cultural contexts. Conventionally Neolithic traits such as pottery could thus be accommodated within, for example, the Mesolithic Ertebolle.

It has been suggested that social complexity was the rule rather than the exception in these communities and that the notion of the simple egalitarian hunter-gatherer band is, for Mesolithic Scotland and elsewhere, little more than an archaeological convenience that separates two fields of study with distinct agendas and concerns (Armit and Finlayson 1992).

Placing the emphasis on the active role of complex indigenous societies enables a rather different set of interpretations of the archaeological evidence for the Mesolithic-Neolithic transition in Scotland. This change in perception can begin to address the question of otherwise inexplicably common juxtapositions of Mesolithic and Early Neolithic cultural material on so many sites. It provides a conceptual framework in which the diversity of Early Neolithic pottery and the lack of early indications of substantial Neolithic houses in many areas and sedentism can be more easily understood. And it enables the development of sedentism and the eventual monumentalisation of the settlement in certain areas – the development of the ideology of the domus – to be seen within the context of social trends with their origins in the Mesolithic.

REFERENCES

Alexander, D. 1993. *Trunk Road, Aberdeen to Stonehaven: Realignment of Unclassified Road at Spurryhillock Junction, Stonehaven, Kincardine and Deeside District – Archaeological Assessment and Field Evaluation.* Centre for Field Archaeology, Report no. 142.

Armit, I. 1992. The Hebridean Neolithic. In Sharples, N. M. and Sheridan, A. (eds), *Vessels for the Ancestors.* Edinburgh: Edinburgh University Press, 307–21.

Armit, I. (in prep.). Sedentism and the transition to agriculture in northern and western Europe. In Fletcher, R. (ed.), *Sedentism*, papers presented at the 3rd World Archaeological Congress, New Delhi 1994.

Armit, I. and Finlayson, W. F. 1992. Hunter-gatherers transformed: the transition to agriculture in northern and western Europe. *Antiquity* 66, 664–76.

Armit, I. and Finlayson, W. F. 1995. Social strategies and economic change: pottery in context. In Barnett, B. and Hoopes, J. (eds), *The Emergence of Pottery.* Washington: Smithsonian Institution Press.

Barnett, W. K. 1990. Small-scale transport of early Neolithic pottery in the west Mediterranean. *Antiquity* 64, 859–65.

Bender, B. 1985. Prehistoric developments in the American midcontinent and in Brittany, northwest France. In Price, T. D. and Brown, J. A. (eds), *Prehistoric Hunter-Gatherers: The Emergence of Cultural Complexity.* Orlando: Academic Press.

Bonsall, J. C., Sutherland, D. G. et al. 1989. *Ulva Cave: Excavation Report Number 3.* Edinburgh: University of Edinburgh, Department of Archaeology.

Bradley, R. 1984. *The Social Foundations of British Prehistory.* London: Longman.

Close, A. E. 1995. Early ceramics in North Africa. In Barnett, B. and Hoopes, J. (eds), *The Emergence of Pottery.* Washington: Smithsonian Institution Press.

Connock, K. D., Finlayson, B. and Mills, C. M. 1992. Excavation of a shell midden site at Carding Mill Bay, near Oban, Scotland. *Glasgow Archaeological Journal* 17, 25–39.

Crone, A. 1993. Excavation and survey of sub-peat features of Neolithic, Bronze and Iron Age date at Bharpa Carinish, North Uist, Scotland. *Proc. Prehist. Soc.* 59, 361–82.

Finlayson, W. L. 1995. Complexity in the Mesolithic of the western Scottish seaboard. In Fischer, A. (ed.), *Man, Sea and the Mesolithic*. Oxford: Oxbow Books, 261–4.

Hedges, J. W. 1984. *Tomb of the Eagles*. London: Murray.

Hodder, I. 1990. *The Domestication of Europe*. Cambridge: Cambridge University Press.

Kinnes, I. 1985. Circumstance not context: the Neolithic of Scotland as seen from the outside. *Proc. Soc. Antiq. Scot.* 115, 15–57.

Mercer, J. 1968. Stone tools from a washing limit deposit of the highest post-glacial transgression, Lealt Bay, Isle of Jura. *Proc. Soc. Antiq. Scot.* 102, 1–30.

Mercer, J. 1974. Glenbatrick Waterhole, a microlithic site on the Isle of Jura. *Proc. Soc. Antiq. Scot.* 105, 9–32.

Mithen, S., Finlayson, B., Finlay, N. and Lake, M. 1992. Excavations at Bolsay Farm, a Mesolithic settlement on Islay. *Cambridge Archaeological Journal* 2, 242–53.

Ralston, I. B. M. 1982. A timber hall at Balbridie Farm. *Aberdeen University Review* 168, 238–49.

Robb, J. 1993. A social prehistory of European languages. *Antiquity* 67, 747–60.

Rowley-Conwy, P. 1983. Sedentary hunters: the Ertebolle example. In Bailey, G. (ed.), *Hunter-Gatherer Economy*. Cambridge: Cambridge University Press, 111–26.

Rowley-Conwy, P. 1985. The origin of agriculture in Denmark: a review of some theories. *Journal of Danish Archaeology* 4, 188–95.

Scott, L. 1950. Eilean an Tighe; a pottery workshop of the 2nd millennium BC. *Proc. Soc. Antiq. Scot.* 85, 1–37.

Simpson, D. D. A. 1976. The later Neolithic and Beaker settlement at Northton, Isle of Harris. In Burgess, C. and Miket, R. (eds), *Settlement and Economy in the Third and Second millennia BC*. Oxford: Brit. Arch. Reports 33, 209–20.

Sloan, D. 1982. Nether Kinneil. *Current Archaeology* 84, 13–15.

Sloan, D. 1984. Shell middens and chronology in Scotland. *Scottish Archaeological Review* 3, 73–9.

Thomas, J. 1991. *Re-thinking the Neolithic*. Cambridge: Cambridge University Press.

Wickham-Jones, C. 1990. *Rhum: Mesolithic and Later Sites at Kinloch, Excavations 1984–86*. Edinburgh: Society of Antiquaries of Scotland, Monograph Series 7.

18

FOOD FOR THOUGHT

MATERIAL CULTURE AND THE
TRANSFORMATION IN FOOD USE
FROM THE MESOLITHIC TO NEOLITHIC

ANDREW JONES

This chapter focuses on an area of research which is central to both the Mesolithic and Neolithic: food.

I will examine the way in which food procurement, processing and consumption engenders a particular understanding of the world. Both periods are largely discussed and defined in terms of their respective economies and form of procurement practices. However, for the Mesolithic these are usually discussed merely in terms of adaptation, with the environment determining lifestyle, whereas in the Neolithic, with a more sedentary form of lifestyle, the environment is percieved as controlled. Both sides of the Mesolithic/Neolithic interface are therefore perceived and studied using quite distinct strategies. This dichotomy is in part due to the differential quality of the data, but also results from normative perceptions of what it is to be a hunter-gatherer or agriculturist-pastoralist (Thomas 1988a). However, as recent studies have emphasised, these normative boundaries are beginning to blur and we must begin to reconceptualise our approaches (Barrett 1994).

Rather than seeing the various elements of environment, including landscape and its faunal and floral inhabitants, as passive and neutral phenomena simply categorised as 'nature' and acting to constrain human activity, we should recognise that the landscape is imbued with culturally specific meanings. Such meaning can be conceived as part of a complex cosmology; a holistic belief system which serves to provide a means for understanding the world. Thus, the environment is not passive, but is culturally and socially appropriated within systems of meaning, within which various elements of both plant and animal life metonymically signify and embody particular places. With the foregoing in mind we can begin to investigate the transition to agriculture by looking at the integration of domesticates in relation to changes in cosmology. Cosmologies represent not only a spatial ordering of the world but also a temporal ordering, allowing the individual to position themselves appropriately at particular times and places within the landscape.

Here I wish to suggest that the shift from hunter-gatherer to agriculturalist is one which involves a shift in a cosmology concerned with the spatialisation of the landscape to a cosmological concern with the temporalisation of the land-scape. The turn of the seasons and the biological cycles of plants and animals, are all ordered by time. However, the lifestyle of Mesolithic hunter-gatherers is one of movement and the occupation and experience of particular places in the landscape at particular times in the year, whereas the lifestyle of the sedentary agriculturalist is one which occupies a single fixed place in the landscape but ex-periences changes in that place. There is then a significant difference in the way that the landscape is experienced between the Mesolithic and the Neolithic.

A fuller understanding of this change may be achieved through a consider-ation of depositional strategies occurring in the late Mesolithic and early Neolithic, at a number of sites on the coastal fringes of Scotland. In order to understand how such strategies relate to the understanding and experience of the world we need to consider the notion of place as the temporal occupation of a particular space. Places may exist as natural features in the landscape or they may be created through the imposition of architectural forms in the landscape. We can see such a process occurring with the production and repeated occu-pation of particular coastal sites in the late Mesolithic through the creation of vast deposits of shell discard, with occurrences on Oronsay (Mellars 1987) and a series of deposits in caves around Oban (Pollard 1990).

For the north of Scotland we have a similar occupation pattern for the coastal zone with Mesolithic assemblages from Freswick, Reay, Skirza and Tofts Farm in Caithness with shell middens from Reay and Skirza, and flint scatters between Dornoch and Golspie in Sutherland (Morrison 1980: 164, authors data). In the Northern Isles a number of flint scatters exhibit Mesolithic elements (Rendall 1930: 22, Richards 1985: 8), these are however mostly concentrated on Main-land Orkney, though Wickham-Jones' work on Stronsay has identified a small microlithic industry (1994: 43).

Sites such as shell middens, while occupied seasonally, also become the focus of other activities. These may be evidenced by the creation of hearth settings in the mound structure, the location of activity areas next to the midden (Pollard et al. this volume) along with the deposition of terrestial species such as red deer and avians. Furthermore, these sites are also the focus of burial activities with the deposition of human *metatarsal* and *metacarpal* elements at sites such as Cnoc Coig, Caisteal nan Gillean and Priory Midden (Mellars 1987), as well as the skull and jaw elements found in the lower level at Carding Mill Bay and the Oban sites (Connock 1990, Pollard 1990).

If we conceptualise the occupation of such sites as part of the process of complex foraging (Rowley-Conwy 1983), with shell midden sites representing temporary camps, we begin to see the creation of places occupied seasonally with the massive imposition of human activity on the landscape through repeated deposition. Thus, such sites are utilised according to a form of temporality which emphasises the continued significance of a single place and the relation of that place to memory, the cycle of human existence and the past. The site itself becomes a focus into which a whole series of resources are brought, both marine and terrestial. Terrestial species are transported to the site from elsewhere and incorporated into deposits which signify a particular time and form of occupation of the landscape, this alters the perception of the landscape. These sites were now percieved as points at which other times, other places and other activities were signified.

It was the particular form of deposition which included animal species, other than those procured through marine exploitation, and other stages in human existence, i.e. the dead, which referenced other times and made it possible to live through forms of temporality which involved an ordering of time and place according to a notion of past, present and future. Such perceptions of temporality became embedded by the earlier Neolithic into a set of cosmological perceptions through which sedentism and the use of domesticates could be employed.

These issues can be understood further through reference to a single site: The Knap of Howar, an early Neolithic settlement on the island of Papa Westray, Orkney. The Knap of Howar has an occupational history which begins around 3 500 BC (cal.) with the formation of midden material which contained the remains of wild species such as red deer, seal and cetacean in small quantities, along with the more abundant remains of domesticates including cattle, pig and sheep, and grains of naked six-row barley (*Hordeum vulgare var. nudum*) with wheat (*Triticium*) pollen evident from the primary land surface.

The midden also contained sherds of plain bowls, decorated Unstan ware, an intact polished stone axe and a variety of flint implements, in the main consisting of scrapers, knives and *debitage* but also including a leaf-shaped arrowhead and a microlith. The paving of an earlier structure stratified beneath house 1 is related to this phase (Ritchie 1983: 46–56). The primary midden material was then levelled and a two-stage constructional process covered the remains of the first phase of settlement. This took the form of the construction of a bipartite house (house 1) which was aligned on the earlier paving. This was rapidly followed by a tripartite house (house 2), joined to house 1 by a passage. The inner wall core of both houses was then filled with midden material from the first phase of settlement. Further midden material from the second phase of occupation was deposited against the outer walls of the structures.

Analysis of faunal remains from the midden deposits, which consist largely of cattle and sheep bones, reveals two striking characteristics. First, in the case of both species around 50 per cent of the individuals are below the age of eight months. Secondly, the mature specimens of cattle are anatomically massive, certain characteristics overlapping with the wild species *Bos primegenius* (Noddle 1983). As the propensity of remains are of juveniles under 8 months old then this may indicate either the autumn slaughter of individuals (Watson 1931), or slaughter around midwinter, depending on the time of year in which the individual was born (Richards unpublished). The cull patterns for sheep are similar, also indicating autumn and winter slaughter. There appears to be no adequate explanation of these cull patterns, Noddle (1983: 97) discounts the autumn cull theory but offers no reasonable alternative. If we note that similarly high numbers of juvenile specimens of cattle, sheep and red deer appear in chambered tombs (Platt 1936) then it would appear that this practice has a symbolic dimension. Furthermore, it can be suggested that the carbonised cereal deposits are also the result of autumn activity, being harvested and dried then, after being sown in spring and ripening through the summer (Renfrew 1973).

Deposits of avian remains especially of coastal dwelling gulls, shearwaters and *Alcidae* species appear to be deposited in discrete layers. The recorded migratory behaviour of these species would suggest their association with summer hunting, while the remains of wildfowl appear to indicate winter hunting (Bramwell 1983: 102).

It would appear then that much of the midden consists of material derived from specific seasonal activities. Notably the remains of wild mammals such as red deer and seal occur only rarely in the midden material. Nevertheless, they are present in small numbers and therefore indicate that at particular times certain species are hunted further afield but not deposited in great numbers within the midden. The deposition of material within such midden contexts has traditionally been considered to be a product of expediency, however as discussed above it is notable that the deposits are structured. Certain events appear to be referenced in the deposition of specific components such as the bones of young animals and carbonised cereals. The presence and absence of certain species and age categories may therefore represent a classification of the landscape according to the species which inhabit it at particular times and the activities associated with their procurement at these times.

Ingold (1986) notes the differing relationship between the hunting of wild species and the slaughter of domesticated species, in the first instance hunting sets up a complex relationship between humans and the spirit world using the animal species as an intermediary, whereas the slaughter of domesticated stock enables a more direct link between humans and the spirit world, involving the substitution of a human life for that of an animal. The ritual slaughter of domesticated livestock is typically perceived as an offering to the gods, as a metaphorical substitution for the life of a human (de Heusch 1985, Evans-Pritchard 1956).

It would appear then that the midden deposits are drawing on the distinctions associated with these activities, hunted species appear to be largely absent while domesticated species especially those of young animals are emphasised. Indeed, the symbolic importance of domesticated livestock, especially cattle, in the earliest Neolithic is of note here. It would appear that in many cases in southern Britain cattle are indeed substituted for humans in chambered tomb deposits (Thomas 1988b: 549). Thus their significance in midden deposits as the product of particular propitious acts at specific social and natural junctures, such as the transformation from winter to summer at midwinter, seems reasonable. Since domesticated cattle are a recent component of the economy and being anatomically similar to the wild species, then it seems that the slaughter of domesticates is especially appropriate at autumn, where the products of animal husbandry and cereal cultivation are especially plentiful.

I would suggest then that the activities of the year are organised around the dual axes of spring and autumn; midwinter and midsummer. In spring the crops were sown, the livestock were driven to summer pasturage and young animals were born. Over summer hunting of coastal birds and possibly seals and red deer occured further afield, while in autumn the livestock were brought closer to the settlement and certain specimens selected for slaughter. Crops were harvested, dried and stored for winter. In winter small-scale hunting of migratory wildfowl occurred with the large scale consumption of young domesticates around the midwinter period.

In order to pursue this discussion further it is necessary to examine the social processes which relate to the preparation and consumption of food prior to the deposition of faunal and floral material within the midden. Each season will have been associated with a particular activity, and type of foodstuff. The months of late autumn and winter, culminating in the axial point of midwinter, appear to be an important natural juncture marking the transistion between the end of one summer and the beginning of another, this event is especially marked in Orkney, due to its northerly latitude (Richards 1991: 124).

The culling of livestock, at this point of the year, may have been percieved as socially necessary for the reproduction of life. The autumn and winter months and the activities associated with them therefore serve as one axis of the year, which simultaneously references the other axes of the year, spring, and to a lesser extent midsummer, through the use of young domesticates and cultigens.

Time is thus being removed from the domain of the natural and mediated through cultural processes which emphasise a rhythmic and repetitive notion of time. Such a notion of temporality involves a series of fluctuations between different points in a cycle, such as between spring and autumn, midsummer and midwinter, in which the life cycle of plants, animals and humans is drawn upon. This need not be seen as entirely seasonally determined, but may be symbolically perceived as punctuated by a series of events, surrounded by ritual activity, which serve to ensure the wellbeing of the community, thereby allowing a return to a socially prescribed point in time (Bourdieu 1977, 1990; Gell 1993).

The cultural and natural are not then mutually exclusive domains but, by the early Neolithic, are embedded in an understanding of temporal existence as punctuated by a series of pivotal events in the seasonal cycle of animal and crop husbandry which involved calfing, lambing, winter culling (Noddle 1983: 97), and sowing and harvesting. Such notions of temporality are articulated on a daily basis through the use of ceramics in the consumption and preparation of foodstuffs. The use of ceramics enables new ways of engaging with the natural environment and concomitantly new ways of thinking through cosmological and temporal relations with that environment.

Throughout the Mesolithic faunal and floral material was procured according to a system structured by seasonal and spatial concerns as the work of Mellars and Wilkinson (1981) demonstrates. Issues of storage and mobility are related to this (Ingold 1986, O'Shea and Halstead 1986) with the use of dried fish or seabirds and smoked meat, out of season (Fenton 1978, Clarke and Sharples 1985). At this time foodstuffs were consumed on a pragmatic basis with little secondary processing. The combination of foods eaten at a single point in the year would necessarily involve the consumption of specific forms of food at particular points in time and space over the annual cycle. While foods were ordered temporally on a seasonal basis, they were also spatially ordered according to place.

The use of ceramics facilitates the recombination of foodstuffs which would hitherto have been separated both seasonally and temporally: foods from two different seasons could now be combined. Meals, and the organisation of cuisine, need not have involved the consumption of one form of food before the other since with the use of a ceramic container they could be combined and consumed simultaneously. Food was then organised according to temporal rather than spatial principles of order. Along with the use of more complex modes of food consumption the actual process of preparation, as exhibited by the quern and rubber situated next to a shallow hearth in the end chamber of house 1, Knap of Howar and the grinding stones found close to the hearth in house 2, involved a number of stages in which the natural product was gradually broken down through the application of a number of methods, in particular crushing and cooking. It was this process which resulted in the transformation of raw materials to the domain of the cultural.

I wish to emphasise here the way in which ceramics and their use in the practical requirements of food preparation and consumption, involves the unconscious, habitual reproduction of a particular form of temporal existence. It is through the use of this material that cosmological beliefs are articulated. It is interesting to note that the mediation of this process which involved transforming food through crushing and cooking occured around the focus of the hearth, since the relation of female production to such a process is ethnographically well attested (Barley 1995, Hugh-Jones 1986, Hodder 1990). The female menstrual cycle itself embodies the notion of a rhythmic time and in particular the life cycle with the occurrence of birth. The hearth as focus for the energy of production and the process of ceramic production may therefore both be metaphorically linked to reproduction and birth respectively. The production of ceramics at times of year associated with transformation and the continued reproduction of society, for instance harvest, is strongly suggested by the high incidence of barley grain impressions on Unstan ware ceramics (Davidson and Henshall 1989). The occurrence of stray grains on site will only have occurred at this specific point in the agricultural year. Pots are then created at particular moments in time, and embody notions of memory through reference to previous existence (Gosden 1994, Rowlands 1993). Sherds of decorated Unstan ware were only found in the midden deposits associated with the products of autumnal activities, such as carbonised cereals and the bones of young domesticates. Furthermore, the relation of the decoration on Unstan ware ceramics to the outer face of chambered tombs (Callander and Grant 1934, Davidson and Henshall 1989), suggests that these ceramics were percieved as both essential to, and as an embodiment, of the life cycle with their inclusion in chambered tombs either overturned (J. Yorston pers. comm.) or smashed, neutralising this role on the death of an individual. It is those vessels which are likely to be used for the consumption of food, and essentially the reproduction of life which are deposited in this manner.

Ceramics may be perceived as essentially embodying the continuing process of biological and social reproduction through their use in food consumption, and as such may further enter other spheres of social differentiation, being used to mark social status and gender as well as being used to signifying appropriate times in the individual and communal life cycle. Material culture may therefore be seen as being contingent, enabling new ways of engaging with and understanding the world.

It was through specific strategies of procurement that shell middens came into existence, and it was through the repeated seasonal occupation of these sites and the association of the residue of this occupation with the past and the ancestors that new forms of temporal existence came into being. Such structures continued through to the Neolithic with the repeated occupation of settlement sites and the reincorporation of midden material into the walls of later settlement.

Similar forms of social practice were involved in the production of both later Mesolithic shell middens and earlier Neolithic midden deposits, in both cases resources were procured elsewhere and brought to the site, both involved repeated seasonal occupation and the referencing of the past through repeated occupation and the deposition of artefacts within the midden. The treatment of human bone, with the selective deposition of certain skeletal elements in both the Oban and Oronsay sites and the selective use of human remains within chambered tombs would also appear to be analogous (Pollard 1990).

It would seem then that we may understand the transistion to a more sedentary form of existence as being understood and negotiated through the use of metaphor. Social practices in the Mesolithic being a metaphor for similar practices in the Neolithic. In the first the landscape is occupied spatially according to seasonal cycles. In the Neolithic the same seasonal cycles are utilised but activity is undertaken according to a fixed temporal order. In both cases we see the occupation of a fixed place for a considerable period of time, in both cases hunting occurs according to specific seasonal regimes. It may be possible to understand the herding of domesticated livestock, particularly cattle, as metaphorical to the seasonal transhumance associated with the hunting of red deer. With one species metaphorically substituting for another. In other areas of Britain it has been suggested that the same paths used by hunter-gatherer groups in the Mesolithic were utilised for the seasonal herding of livestock (Tilley 1994: 207).

Zvelebil and Rowley-Conwy (1986) suggest that the transistion to sedentism occurs through a process or phase of substitution, in which the principle aspects of the Mesolithic are substituted for Neolithic cultigens, domesticated livestock and ceramics. In this model a distinction is made between an availability phase where the knowledge of the Neolithic economy was available, as opposed to the wholescale adoption of the economy. Zvelebil and Rowley-Conwy note that in the Atlantic fringes of Europe, especially in the coastal Danish Mesolithic, the period of time between these phases was considerable. However, if we consider practices associated with Mesolithic and Neolithic existence then it is notable that they are metaphorically related, thus the phase of substitution may have involved social processes which drew on notions of metaphor, thus allowing us to understand the 'transition' as a contingent process which involved the active use of material culture, as opposed to the passive adoption of agriculture according to external environmental necessity.

Ceramics enabled the continued day-to-day playing out of specific temporal structures through the processing and consumption of food, by drawing on notions of seasonality and the human life cycle, enabling further social differentiation through their use both spatially and temporally. It was through continued unconscious activity mediated by material culture, whether faunal remains or ceramics, which allowed an individual to experience and understand a particular form of social existence. The practical activities of food procurement and consumption allowed the transformation of temporal, spatial and social existence. Rather than creating a series of models specifying how the transistion to agriculture occurred I have instead attempted to emphasise the importance of considering the cosmological systems of societies in the transformation from one mode of existence to another. I do not suggest that such a transformation occurred rapidly but rather unfolded over a number of centuries neither as a causal factor or prime motivator for change. I would prefer to locate change through the habitual use of material culture and the relation this material culture had on perceptions of both the temporal and spatial. Thus, in the earlier Neolithic, the use of certain novel forms of material culture, such as ceramics, could be understood by reference to a specific temporal structure, but were also embedded in that temporal structure. Material culture and its knowledgeable employment in particular spatial and temporal structures therefore embodies certain perceptions about the world, but also enables the transformation of such perceptions. The use of metaphor in this process is one means by which a shift to sedentary agriculture may be understood.

REFERENCES

Barley, N. 1995. *Smashing Pots: Feats of Clay from Africa*. London: British Museum Press.

Barrett, J. C. 1994. *Fragments from Antiquity: An Archaeology of Social Life in Britain, 2 900–1 200 BC*. Oxford: Blackwell.

Bourdieu, P. 1977. *Outline of a Theory of Practice*. Cambridge: CUP.

Bourdieu, P. 1990. *The Logic of Practice*. Cambridge: Polity Press.

Branwell, D. 1983. Bird bones from Knap of Howar. In Ritchie, A. *Excavation of a Neolithic Farmstead at Knap of Howar, Papa Westray, Orkney. Proceedings of the Society of Antiquaries of Scotland* 40–121.

Callander, J. G. and Grant, W. G. 1934. A long stalled chambered cairn or mausoleum (Rousay type) near Midhowe, Rousay, Orkney. *Proceedings of the Society of Antiquaries of Scotland* 320–50.

Clarke, D. and Sharples, N. 1985. Settlements and subsistence in the third millenium BC. In Renfrew, C. (ed.), *The Prehistory of Orkney BC 4 000–1 000 AD*. Edinburgh: EUP.

Connock, D. 1990. A shell midden at Carding Mill Bay, Oban. *Scottish Archaeological Review* ?, 47–8.

Davidson, J. L. and Henshall, A. S. 1989. *The Chambered Cairns of Orkney*. Edinburgh: EUP.

De Heusch, L. 1985. *Sacrifice in Africa: A Structuralist Perspective*. Manchester: MUP.

Evans-Pritchard, E. E. 1956. *Nuer Religion*. Oxford: OUP.

Fenton, A. 1978. *Orkney and Shetland*. Edinburgh: EUP.

Gell, A. 1993. *The Anthropology of Time*. Cambridge, USA: Berg.

Gosden, C. 1994. *Social Being and Time*. Oxford: Blackwell.

Hodder, I. 1990. *The Domestication of Europe*. Oxford: Blackwell.

Hugh-Jones, C. 1986. *From the Milk River: Spatial and Temporal Processes in Northwest Amazonia*. Cambridge: CUP.

Ingold, T. 1986. *The Appropriation of Nature: Essays on Human Ecology and Social Relations*. Manchester: MUP.

Mellars, P. A. 1987. *Excavations on Oronsay*. Edinburgh: EUP.

Mellars, P. A. and Wilkinson, M. R. 1980. Fish otoliths as indicators of seasonality in prehistoric shell middens: the evidence from Oronsay (Inner Hebrides). *Proceedings of the Prehistoric Society* 46, 19–44.

Morrison, A. 1980. *Early Man in Britain and Ireland*. London: Croom Helm.

Noddle, B. 1983. The faunal remains. In Ritchie, A., *Excavation of a Neolithic Farmstead at Knap of Howar, Papa Westray, Orkney. Proceedings of the Society of Antiquaries of Scotland* 113, 40–121.

O'Shea, M. and Halstead, P. 1986. *Bad Year Economics*. Cambridge: CUP.

Platt, M. 1936. The animal bones. In Callander, J. G. and Grant, W. G. *A Stalled Chambered Cairn, the Knowe of Ramsay, at Hullion, Rousay, Orkney. Proceedings of the Society of Antiquaries of Scotland* 415–19.

Pollard, A. 1990. Down through the ages: a review of the Oban cave deposits. *Scottish Archaeological Review* 6, 58–73.

Rendall, R. 1930. Notes on a collection of flints from Wideford Hill. *Orkney Antiquaries Society* 4, 20–4.

Renfrew, J. 1973. *Paleoethnobotany*. London: Methuen.

Richards, C. C. 1985. *Orkney Survey Project: Interim Report 1984*. Glasgow: Unpublished Glasgow University.

Richards, C. C. 1991. The Neolithic House in Orkney. In Samson, R. (ed.), *The Social Archaeology of Houses*. Edinburgh: EUP.

Ritchie, A. 1983. Excavation of a Neolithic farmstead at Knap of Howar, Papa Westray, Orkney. *Proceedings of the Society of Antiquaries of Scotland* 113, 40–121.

Rowlands, M. 1993. The role of memory in the transmission of culture. *World Archaeology* 25, 141–51.

Rowley-Conwy, P. 1983. Sedentary hunters: the Ertbolle example. In Bailey, G. N. (ed.), *Hunter-Gatherer Economy in Prehistory*. Cambridge: CUP, 111–26.

Thomas, J. 1988a. Neolithic explanations revisited: the Mesolithic–Neolithic Transition in Britain and southern Scandinavia. *Proceedings of the Prehistoric Society* 54, 59–66.

Thomas, J. 1988b. The social significance of Cotswold–Severn burial practices. *Man* 23, 540–59.

Tilley, C. 1994. *A Phenomenology of Landscape: Places, Paths and Monuments*. Cambridge, USA: Berg.

Watson, M. S. 1931. The faunal remains. In Childe, V. G., *Skara Brae: A Pictish Village in Orkney*. London: Kegan Paul.

Wickham-Jones, C. 1994. *Scotland's First Settlers*. London: Batsford.

Zvelebil, M. and Rowley-Conwy, P. 1986. Foragers and farmers in Atlantic Europe. In Zvelebil, M. (ed.), *Hunters in Transition*. Cambridge: CUP, 67–93.

£27·00